The Geeks Shall Inherit the Earth

POPULARITY,
QUIRK THEORY,
AND WHY OUTSIDERS THRIVE
AFTER HIGH SCHOOL

The Geeks Shall

Inherit the Earth

Alexandra Robbins

HYPERION

New York

Some, but not all, of the names in this book have been changed. Occasionally, some identifying details have been modified. The perspectives portrayed in each of the characters' sections do not necessarily represent the author's views.

Library of Congress Cataloging-in-Publication Data has been applied for.

ISBN: 978-1-4013-0202-3

Hyperion books are available for special promotions and premiums. For details contact the HarperCollins Special Markets Department in the New York office at 212-207-7528, fax 212-207-7222, or e-mail spsales@harpercollins.com.

Design by Renato Stanisic

FIRST EDITION

10 9 8 7 6 5 4 3 2 1

SUSTAINABLE FORESTRY INITIATIVE
Certified Fiber Sourcing
www.sfiprogram.org

THIS LABEL APPLIES TO TEXT STOCK

We try to produce the most beautiful books possible, and we are also extremely concerned about the impact of our manufacturing process on the forests of the world and the environment as a whole. Accordingly, we've made sure that all of the paper we use has been certified as coming from forests that are managed, to ensure the protection of the people and wildlife dependent upon them.

To My Family,
Past and Present,
with Unconditional Love

Contents

SPRING: QUIRK THEORY'S ORIGINS: WHY THESE ISSUES ARE HARDEST IN SCHOOL

LATE SPRING TO EARLY SUMMER: POPULAR VS. OUTCAST

Prologue

Early 2011. Bullying in school has recently driven several teenagers to suicide. Exclusion and clique warfare are so rampant that the media declares bullying an epidemic and rallies for the public to view the tragedies as a national wake-up call.

Throngs of students who are not outright bullied are disheartened because it is getting increasingly more difficult to become an "insider," to fit into a group, to be accepted as "normal." Students feel trapped, despairing that in today's educational landscape, they either have to conform to the popular crowd's arbitrary standards—forcing them to hide their true selves—or face dismissive treatment that batters relentlessly at their souls.

Schools struggle to come up with solutions. Even the most beloved parents are met with disbelief when they insist, "This too shall pass." Adults tell students that it gets better, that the world changes after school, that being "different" will pay off sometime after graduation.

But no one explains to them why.

Enter quirk theory.

Chapter 1

MEET THE CAFETERIA FRINGE

DANIELLE, ILLINOIS | THE LONER

When the bell rang, Danielle slowly gathered her books as the rest of her class scrambled out of the room. She reluctantly made her way into the hall, slinging her green messenger bag—backpacks were too commonplace—over her shoulder.

The hallway was already beginning to empty as people disappeared into classrooms. Students didn't acknowledge Danielle and she didn't acknowledge them. She walked with her head down, slouching her five foot ten frame, her dark, shoulder-length hair shielding her face.

Stone Mill High, a large public school in a middle-class, racially diverse Chicago suburb, had a small cafeteria, which was why its two thousand–plus students were divided into four lunch periods. Usually juniors were allowed to leave the building during lunch, but not on the first day of school. Tomorrow, and probably during the rest of the year, Danielle would avoid the cafeteria altogether.

Danielle wandered the halls for as long as she could, stopping to take a long drink from the water fountain and to pick up a form in the main office. Then she tried to walk nonchalantly past the cafeteria's floor-to-ceiling glass wall, as if she just happened to be passing by. She could see students arranged predictably throughout the room. In front of the window sat the lucky students who had sprinted to the cafeteria to grab the small tables so they wouldn't have to sit at larger ones with students outside of their social circles. Behind them, underclassmen sat in rows of long tables. Goths, emos, and scene kids flanked the left side of the room, closest to the lunch detention area. Preppy popular students claimed the far corner of the cafeteria.

She scanned the room, searching ideally for any acquaintance at the end of a row whom she could join without intruding in the middle of a group. She couldn't find a single person she liked. On the bright side, she also didn't see Tabitha, the person she liked least at school, who would have been sitting among the preps.

The cafeteria had not been kind to Danielle in the past. She didn't think much anymore about the *flick flick* of projectile Skittles that a handful of "friends" pelted at her after they ousted her from their lunch table in sixth grade. She was still haunted by seventh grade, however. Until that year, Danielle had dressed like the tomboy she was. In seventh grade, she decided to start shopping at the stores other girls chattered about—Hollister, American Eagle—in order to fit in.

Her strategy didn't work. Classmates grew even more hostile toward her. Former friends started a note fight. One girl wrote a message so painful that when Danielle's mother came home from work that day, Danielle was uncharacteristically curled up in a fetal position on her bed. The school summoned the girls' mothers to meetings, and when administrators saw the notes that Danielle had written in retaliation, they penalized both girls by barring them from the middle school honor society.

Meanwhile, half of Danielle's class had joined the "I Hate Dominoes Club," which people discussed in front of her. In a last-ditch effort to conform to the crowd, Danielle let students in her gym class persuade her to join the club too. Only a few moments later, she discovered that "Dominoes" was a pseudonym (she never found out why). The club's real name was the "I Hate Danielle Club." Danielle had joined her own hate club. Her classmates thought this was hilarious. When Danielle underwent dermatological surgery later that semester, the club leader said she hoped Danielle would die from the anesthesia.

On the last day of school, Tabitha, Danielle's supposedly closest friend, passed her a note that said she didn't want to be friends anymore. Danielle told Tabitha it was dumb to end their friendship just because rejecting Danielle was the cool thing to do. That weekend, a group of girls called her from a party to which she hadn't been invited. They crowded around the speakerphone, telling her to stop "threatening" Tabitha. Danielle never forgave her.

Danielle hated reflecting on that year, but not because of the cruelty. She was most chagrined now because she had "joined the group, unaware that it was my own hate club, because I thought that since everyone else was joining, I should too. I wish I hadn't been so stupid in thinking that I needed other people's approval, even when I didn't even like most of them."

Because of that incident, Danielle withdrew, unwilling to trust anyone at school. She stopped talking to most people her age. Outside of school, for the next few years, she hung out only with four other girls: Mona, Paige, Camille, and Nikki, none of whom had many friends besides each other. Danielle liked these girls about 50 percent of the time; they could be funny and they usually got along. But they tended to neglect her such that Danielle often felt like an outcast even within her own tiny group. She stuck with them because they had been friends since kindergarten, even if the only thing they had in common was their past.

Danielle had other acquaintances, but they were "just school friends," because "I don't know how to ask them to hang out, and I suck at doing one-on-one things with people I've never hung out with before," she said.

Danielle turned away from the cafeteria window and meandered down another hallway, attempting to quash her anxiety. *If I don't find someone I know, I'm going to end up standing alone at the front of the cafeteria.* She hid in the bathroom for a few minutes, washing her hands to kill time, then waited by the sink until she decided to go to the library. On the way, Danielle bumped into Paige's freshman sister and followed her back to the lunchroom. They sat at the last of the underclassman tables at the far right side of the room.

That was how Danielle found herself spending the first lunch period of her junior year sitting silently among a bunch of freshmen she didn't know and, with the exception of her friend's sister, didn't especially like. She left early to spend the rest of the forty-minute lunch in the snaking line of people waiting to see the guidance counselors to change their schedules. It was going to be another long year.

———

INTRODUCTION

CAFETERIA FRINGE: People who are not part of or who are excluded from a school's or society's in crowd.

What could motivate kids to be so heart-crushingly cruel that they convince a girl to join her own hate club? In the decade I've spent examining various microcosms of life in U.S. schools—from the multitude of students pressured to succeed in school and sports to the twenty-something products of this educational Rube Goldberg machine—a disturbing pattern has emerged. Young people are trying frantically to force themselves into an unbending mold of expectations, convinced that they live in a two-tiered system in which they are either a resounding success or they have already failed. And the more they try to squeeze themselves into that shrinking, allegedly normative space, the faster the walls close in.

The students outside these walls are the kids who typically are not considered part of the in crowd, the ones who are excluded, blatantly or subtly, from the premier table in the lunchroom. I refer to them as "cafeteria fringe." Whether alone or in groups, these geeks, loners, punks, floaters, nerds, freaks, dorks, gamers, bandies, art kids, theater geeks, choir kids, Goths, weirdos, indies, scenes, emos, skaters, and various types of racial and other minorities are often relegated to subordinate social status simply because they are, or seem to be, even the slightest bit different.

Students alone did not create these boundaries. The No Child Left Behind law, a disproportionate emphasis on SATs, APs, and other standardized tests, and a suffocating homogenization of the U.S. education system have all contributed to a rabidly conformist atmosphere that stifles unique people, ideas, and expression. The methods that schools and government officials claimed would improve America's "progress" are the same methods that hold back the students who are most likely to further that progress.

In precisely the years that we should be embracing differences among students, urging them to pursue their divergent interests at full throttle, we're instead forcing them into a skyline of sameness, muffling their voices, grounding their dreams. The result? As a Midwestern senior told me for my book *The Overachievers*, high schoolers view life as "a conveyor belt," making monotonous scheduled stops at high school, college, graduate school, and a series of jobs until death. Middle schools in North America have been called "the Bermuda triangle of education." Only 22 percent of U.S. youth socialize with people of another race. U.S. students have some of the highest rates of emotional problems and the most negative views of peer culture among countries surveyed by the World Health Organization.

Too many students are losing hope because of exclusion or bullying that they believe they're doomed to experience for the rest of their lives. It is unacceptable that the system we rely on to develop children into well-adjusted, learned, cultured adults allows drones to dominate and increasingly devalues freethinkers. In 1957, theologian Paul Tillich told a graduating university class, "We hope for nonconformists among you, for your sake, for the sake of the nation, for the sake of humanity." More than half a century later, schools, students, and sometimes parents treat these nonconformists like second-class citizens, squelching that hope. There is too much pressure on children to conform to a narrowing in-crowd image, when we should be nurturing the outsiders who reject that image. In large part, those are the individuals who will turn out to be the kinds of interesting, admired, and inspiring adults who earn respect and attention for their impact on their community or the world.

Or even the celebrisphere. Author J. K. Rowling, who has described herself as "a squat, bespectacled child who lived mostly in books and daydreams," was bullied in school because she was different. Her heroic wizards and witches, who have entranced millions of readers worldwide, "are plainly outcasts and comfortable with being so," she has said. "Nothing is more unnerving to the truly conventional than the unashamed misfit!"

Musician Bruce Springsteen was so unpopular in high school that, "other people didn't even know I was there," he has said. He started a band because "I was on the outside looking in."

Television host Tim Gunn, who identified himself as "a classic nerd" in school, was "crazy about making things: I was addicted to my Lincoln Logs, Erector Set, and especially my Legos," he has said. "Between my stutter and my fetishizing of Lego textures, I was taunted and teased." Now Gunn is a fashion world icon precisely because of his eye toward "making things"—and his catchphrase, "Make it work," has become famous.

All of these people exemplify what I call **quirk theory.**

QUIRK THEORY: Many of the differences that cause a student to be excluded in school are the same traits or real-world skills that others will value, love, respect, or find compelling about that person in adulthood and outside of the school setting.

Quirk theory suggests that popularity in school is not a key to success and satisfaction in adulthood. Conventional notions of popularity are wrong. What if popularity is not the same thing as social success? What if students who are considered outsiders aren't really socially inadequate at all? Being an outsider doesn't necessarily indicate any sort of social failing. We do not view a tuba player as musically challenged if he cannot play the violin. He's just a different kind of musician. A sprinter is still considered an athlete even if she can't play basketball. She's a different kind of athlete. Rather than view the cafeteria fringe as less socially successful than the popular crowd, we could simply accept that they are a different kind of social.

To INVESTIGATE THE CAUSE and consequence of the gut-wrenching social landscape that characterizes too many schools, I followed seven "main characters"—real people—for a year and interviewed hundreds of other students, teachers, and counselors individually and in groups. I talked with students from public schools, private schools, technical schools, schools for the arts, boarding schools, college prep academies, inner city schools, small rural schools, and suburban schools. They have more in common than they know.

While for previous books, I acted merely as an observer, narrating stories as they happened, with this book I crossed a line. In the middle of the school year, I surprised my main characters by issuing them a challenge that dared them to step outside of their comfort zone. If successful, I hoped these experiments could bring them closer to the school experience they genuinely wanted.

To understand why the cafeteria fringe will be much better off after leaving the school setting, it helps to know how they become outcasts in the first place. Throughout the following chapters, I explain in what I hope is entertaining prose the psychology and science behind questions such as: "Why are popular people mean?", "Why is seventh grade the worst?", "Why are outsiders better off after school?", "Why do social labels stick?", "Why can't groups get along?", "Is popularity worth it?", and "How can we improve the school experience?" To explain these student group dynamics, I spoke to experts and reviewed hundreds of articles and books on psychology, sociology, anthropology, and other sciences. Much of what I learned was unexpected.

Slip with me a few tiers down below the in crowd—below the cliques that include people who say, as one popular girl told me, "I'm not friends with losers"—into a world of students who are overlooked, disparaged, or completely dismissed. Descend to the plane where beneath the gridded, rigid hallways of robotic social hierarchy runs a parallel labyrinth humming with a current of new ideas, alternative philosophies, and refreshing points of view. Here is where you'll find the people who are brave enough to be true to themselves, where you'll encounter the interesting and innovative minds that eventually will drive the engines of creativity and progress. Peer behind their labels. Immerse yourself in these forgotten corridors to meet the denizens known as the cafeteria fringe.

Mark Laurent (Blue), Hawaii | The Gamer

Mark, better known among students as Blue, was hanging out with his usual friends at the arcade, their typical after-school activity. Well, "hanging out with" wasn't exactly accurate. While the rest of the guys huddled around Street Fighter, Tekken, and Battle Gear (for which Blue held the machine record), Blue was absorbed in Tatsunoko vs. Capcom. The others made fun of Blue for playing Tatsunoko, calling it a "button masher" because it involved only four buttons and a joy-stick. Blue was one of the few people he knew who could "see the beauty in the game." The skill in Tatsunoko was to know when, where, and how to attack your opponent. Choosing combo breaks took preci-sion, rhythm, and imagination. Gaming was an art, really; at least some games were. It just didn't look that way from the outside.

That was one of the reasons why last year, as a junior, Blue founded Arwing, Kaloke High School's first gaming club. He wanted to change people's minds about gaming—and gamers. He wanted to demonstrate that gaming had integrity and valor, that it could be elegant. He had no idea that the results would be disastrous.

At first, Arwing thrived. One hundred seventy people signed up within weeks. Blue, as president, assigned his friends to the remaining officer slots and cajoled them to accompany him to a local senior citi-zens' home to play Wii Sports with the residents. Blue made posters to advertise the club. One read, GAMING IS MAINSTREAM. GAMERS ARE MAINSTREAM. IT'S THE PEOPLE WHO ARE SURPRISED BY THIS THAT HAVE SUSPECT SOCIAL LIVES.

Quickly Blue's friends grew apathetic toward the club, as they were toward most things. They said they would build the Web site and then didn't. They ruined an event because they didn't hand out the promotional fliers for fear of looking "stupid." One day at the mall, Blue was sitting with his friends when he put his head down on the table and fell asleep. When he woke up ten minutes later, they were gone. Thereafter, Blue's friends started ditching him for fun—at the mall, at school. From their posts on Facebook and Twitter, Blue could see when they went out together, intentionally excluding him. He was closest with Jackson, who attended a neighboring school, but even Jackson was less likely to socialize with Blue unless Ty and Stewart were there, if not Herman and his two followers.

Blue tried not to let this treatment faze him. He had become ac-customed to social setbacks in middle school after his closest friend, who had nicknamed him Blue after a Pokémon trainer, moved away. Uninterested in the superficial chatter that dominated classmates' typi-cal middle school conversations, Blue turned to technology and other solitary pursuits. He discovered outlets such as speedrunning video games: beating a game as quickly as possible, from beginning to end. (He could beat Portal, a game that took decent players at least two hours to win, in twenty minutes.)

Blue also expanded his offbeat interests. He listened to trance and shoegaze music and religiously watched Internet shows, machinima, and anime. He spent hours drawing, mostly Fox from Star Fox, as well as characters from other games. He liked Fox because, "When I see his image, I fill in the gaps: he's heroic, skilled, caring, and has a lot of close friends that amplify his power as a hero." Drawing led to photography. Blue loved the camera's precise machinery and that it could evoke a memory or emotion that meant more than the camera itself. Eventually Flickr featured Blue on the front page. When he was in eighth grade, companies began paying him for stock use of his photos. For years, he sold about six contracts per month.

Initially, Blue spent the money on computer parts and camera lenses. When he was fourteen, he bought a three thousand dollar car: a 1983 alpine white Audi Quattro. He couldn't believe his find. The car was in excellent condition: no body damage, a pristine engine, low mileage. Nevertheless, Blue decided to take it apart and rebuild it. Since then, he'd been doing so regularly, starting over about every six months, dismantling the car and replacing every miniscule part, exchanging rubber bits for urethane pieces, making it better in every way he could. He hardly ever drove it, however. (Even now, he didn't have a driver's license.)

The more Blue engaged in non-mainstream activities, the less he had in common with his classmates. He drifted among groups—jocks, skaters, punks—becoming friends with one person in a crowd and then assimilating into the rest of the group for a while. But he couldn't seem to achieve a level of total comfort with anyone. As a result, he spent a lot of time at home on the Internet becoming, in his words, "a geek/*otaku*."

During his sophomore year, Blue met his current group of friends at a video game store where they gathered most days after school. At the time, Blue assumed the others were gamers like him; he didn't discover until much later that they weren't serious about gaming. He knew now that those friends were not the friends he was looking for—

people who would understand Blue's inner elegance the same way he could see the beauty behind Tatsunoko. He was sure, however, that senior year was too late to establish a new social circle.

For months, Blue worked hard to organize a fundraising LAN (Local Area Network) party that would be Arwing's signature event. Inspired by a video of DreamHack, "the world's largest computer festival," Blue envisioned a party with rows of hundreds of PCs, neon lights, strobes, live dance music, and people of all ages and types playing individually, gaming together.

Blue labored tirelessly for months, lining up sponsors, locating equipment, and advertising and promoting the event. He gave a presentation to the PTA. He renamed his professional gaming tournament team after the club and won several competitions, racking up publicity and money. He worked hard to get the word out about the party. At least five hundred people were scheduled to attend.

In the spring of Blue's junior year, a Kaloke staffperson heard about Arwing. Concerned because she believed video games were a bad influence, she Googled Blue's name and found his personal blogs, game records, photos, tags, forum posts, and other information. She printed them out, circled everything she interpreted negatively, and distributed the pages to other school employees. She told the principal that Blue was a pedophile and that the club was corruptive. She and Blue had never met.

Mr. Pakaki, the Arwing advisor, showed Blue the pages the woman had submitted as evidence that Arwing could corrupt the school. These were some of the items the woman highlighted:

"Kill count," a gamer's term, and Blue's game statistics.

The age on Blue's MySpace page: 69. ("Hardy har har, I was like 13 when I made it," Blue said later.)

"Gamers at school," a title of a blog post by a student Blue didn't know who called the club "dorky."

A caption to one of Blue's Flickr photos about "a pedo." The line was an inside joke; Blue's friend wanted to date an underclassman.

A caption to a photo of the club: "woop woop." (Blue could assume only that the woman wrongly thought "woop woop," meant as a sarcastic cheer, was a sexual reference.)

"First period teacher," which was written on another student's blog about nothing that had to do with Blue. This item stymied him.

On the side of one of the printouts, the woman had written in large letters "BLUE IS MARK," as if she had solved some giant mystery.

At first, Blue didn't believe there was a problem. The woman's accusations were so ludicrous that he didn't expect them to amount to anything. Then the principal called Blue and Mr. Pakaki into his office. Blue brought along Angelique, the club secretary, because she was articulate. The principal explained that it would be easier to terminate the club than fight the woman's claims.

Blue felt as if he were on trial. He and Angelique made their rebuttals, which were somewhat dampened by Arwing's clueless advisor chiming in. Blue couldn't stand Pakaki, who sometimes called students "trash" and "stupid" to their faces. The principal, whom Blue liked, was understanding and sympathetic. He proposed that Arwing could continue as long as he approved all of its online activities. This was okay with Blue; it was what the advisor did next, he said, that "screwed it all up."

"We're going to be extra careful from now on," Pakaki said, then decided to illustrate obsequiously how extra careful he would be. "We won't play anything on PC anymore." Blue blanched. What was Pakaki doing? Forbidding PC use would take the serious gaming out of the gaming club.

Immediately, the advisor restricted Arwing's activities and yanked away Blue's responsibilities. Pakaki even took over Blue's LAN party. He disregarded Blue's work, halting all advertising and prohibiting PCs, the draw for the majority of attendees. He refused to let students bring their own consoles. He renamed the party a "video game tournament" and changed the events to three games that true gamers didn't play.

Blue's "epic LAN party," the event he had planned for months, degenerated into ten students at a table under the fluorescent lights of the unadorned high school gym. Blue left after setting up the equipment. He couldn't bear to watch. Many of the hundreds of people to whom Blue had advertised the party, unaware of the behind-the-scenes fiasco, blamed him for the failure.

In late spring, Arwing held its officer elections. Thirty students showed up to submit secret ballots. Blue began to worry when Herman's followers made their selections public. "Yeaahhh, Herman!" one yelled. "Herman gonna be president, awriiight!" the other echoed. Ty and Stewart abstained from voting.

After the vote, Pakaki pulled Blue aside, as if the rest of the students wouldn't hear their conversation from three feet away. "Mark, I want you to know that I voted for Herman because I think he needs it more than you." Pakaki's voice oozed faux compassion. "It's something to put on his résumé for college."

Pakaki was known for playing favorites; apparently he had chosen to anoint Herman as president no matter the vote. Blue watched as Pakaki flipped through the ballots without bothering to count them formally. As Pakaki announced the new officers, Blue went numb. Blue's club, the club that was supposed to start "a revolution in video gaming," the club for which he had sacrificed schoolwork all semester, was stripped of its gaming. Blue, out. Herman, in. Herman, who didn't even game in the first place.

When Blue's senior year began in August, he was more reserved than usual. Nobody asked what was wrong. His friends talked around him, tossing jabs at him now and then. So he wasn't surprised when they made fun of him at the arcade.

"Did you beat that guy on Tatsunoko yesterday?" Ty asked him.

Herman sneered. "Oh, you mean that game that takes no skill—just mash buttons all day?"

Herman's followers laughed maniacally and chorused, "Ooo."

At home late that night, Ty invited Blue to chat online with him, Herman, and two other classmates. Blue dipped in and out of the conversation as he built a Nirvash, a miniature mechanical model of a robot from an anime. After a while, Blue threw inhibition to the wind and said what he had wanted to say all summer. "It's ridiculous that the president of Arwing is somebody who doesn't play video games," Blue ranted, only half-joking. "He hasn't done [jack] with the club."

Herman responded, "I like how you're not even president material at all."

And Blue was done. Done with the conversation, done with

Arwing, and done with Herman and his followers. Blue worried that Herman both represented and perpetuated the way their classmates perceived Blue and his club. He logged off and resumed sanding the Nirvash.

Back in the spring, one of the posters that Blue had made to advertise Arwing displayed a group of gaming characters and announced, I'M NOT LONELY.

But he was.

WHITNEY, NEW YORK | THE POPULAR BITCH

Before leaving home for her last first day of high school, Whitney glanced at herself in all of her mirrors for the seventeenth time: the large mirror above her dresser, the small one by her TV for scrutinizing hair and makeup, and the full-length one behind her door. She had spent two hours getting ready this morning. Her white-blonde hair, highlighted from a summer of lifeguarding, cascaded to her shoulders in meticulously crafted, loose, bouncy curls behind a funky knit headband that she wore so she'd have an excuse to brag that members of a famous rock group had complimented her on it. Several bracelets dangled from her wrist, still tan from cheerleading camp the week before. Her makeup was flawless, accentuated by a smattering of glitter above her eyes; it looked good now, but she knew she would check her makeup again in the school bathroom three or four times that day, hunting for imperfections and correcting them with her Sephora-only arsenal.

People told Whitney all the time that she was pretty, as in beauty pageant pretty or talk show host pretty. Whitney thought this was because of her smile. In her opinion, her straight white teeth slightly made up for her body, which dissatisfied her when she compared it to her friends'. When they went to the local diner together, the girls did not eat; they only sat and watched the guys stuff their faces. If the girls were really hungry, the most they would order in front of the group was lemon water.

Whitney checked her makeup again in the kitchen mirror, forced herself to guzzle a Slim-Fast shake to jump-start her metabolism, grabbed her Coach purse, lacrosse bag, and book bag, and ran out the door, pausing briefly at the mirror in the foyer. She drove too quickly into the school parking lot, unapologetically cutting off people on her way, and parked her SUV crookedly, taking up two spots, but leaving it there anyway because she could. She met up with Giselle, her best friend until recently. Giselle, who had been the schoolwide Homecoming Queen as a sophomore, had become popular through cheerleading and by dating a popular senior—when she was in the eighth grade. "Well, this is it!" Giselle said, and they stepped into the building.

Riverland Academy, located in a small town in upstate New York, catered to a mostly white, Christian community. Its four hundred students crowded into the gym, standing in small groups or lining the bleachers. Amidst the chaos, the girls easily spotted their group, which other students called the "preps" or the "populars," in the center of the gym. Bianca, the queen bee, thin and tan, stood with Kendra, a senior; Peyton, a junior; and Madison, Bianca's best friend. Chelsea, the only brunette standing among the populars, had worked her way up from "being a loser," according to Whitney, by "sucking up to Bianca like crazy and giving her information about people." The preps tolerated Chelsea, but didn't include her as a stalwart member of the group. This meant they didn't allow her in their Homecoming limo, but they did invite her to take pictures with them.

A few of the prep boys orbited the girls: Chip and Spencer, hot high-society seniors; Bobby, a chubby, boisterous football star; and Seth, an overachieving junior. The preps were each on two or more sports teams, partied with college students, and in Whitney's words, "just own[ed] the school."

The girls appraised the surrounding students and whispered to each other, standing as they typically did, one hand on a hip, one knee bent, in what the cheerleading coach referred to as "the hooker's pose." Their long hair hung stick straight. They wore heels and dark skinny jeans. Whitney was the only one not dressed in what she called "country club urban prep," with which she had masked herself through the end of junior year. Whitney's group wore Guess and H&M when they weren't wearing designers, saving their splurges for shoes and makeup. They wore only certain cosmetics—MAC, Smashbox, Too

Faced, Nars—and designer perfume and accessories. Their clothes rarely ranged beyond cream, black, and a dark green that matched Bianca's eyes. They expected each other to dress the same way and to tan frequently at the local salon. Only Bianca was allowed to wear anklets.

Madison, Chelsea, and Kendra squealed and hugged Whitney and Giselle, as if they hadn't seen each other three days earlier at a small exclusive party Whitney threw for her group. Bianca air-kissed them on both cheeks, as was her custom. The preps skeptically eyed Whitney's outfit, which she had planned weeks ahead of time: a flowing seafoam empire-waist Anthropologie top and bell-bottom jeans. Rather than conform to the group this year, Whitney was determined to exert her independence by wearing her favorite styles.

"Dirty hippie!" Madison shouted.

"Wow, that's a bit much, don't you think?" Giselle told Whitney. *You didn't say that when we were alone, but now that you're in front of the group, you do,* Whitney thought. Giselle continued, "You look like a clown with too much makeup on!" Everyone laughed, including Whitney.

The group caught up briefly before resuming the assessment of the students swarming around them. "Oh my God. Who is that?!" Peyton sniffed, nodding her head toward a band girl.

"That's Shay," Chelsea answered.

"Dude, I didn't even recognize her," Peyton said. "Did she gain like fifteen pounds over the summer?! Why did her hair get so big and frizzy?" This led to a discussion about how there were too many skanks and trailer trash kids at Riverland.

The preps took stock of the new freshmen, as they did at the beginning of every year, to decide who was going to be cool and to whom they were going to be mean. They automatically deemed one girl cool because her older sister was dating a prep. The freshman cheerleaders were acceptable. If freshman girls didn't already have something going for them when they got to Riverland—an older boyfriend, a popular sibling, a varsity sport, money, or a parent with connections—they were out of luck. "If we don't know them already by some other affiliation," Whitney said, "they aren't worth getting to know"—and they were automatically labeled skanks.

The prep guys had an even clearer classification system. Only the ninth-grade football players who served as the seniors' "bitches" were granted cool status. These were the boys whom the senior preps could order to throw out their lunch trays or buy them chips in the snack line. "Basically," Whitney explained later, "those freshmen are, like, building up their popularity by sucking up to popular kids, so when they are our age, they're popular and can do this to other freshmen."

Students gathered together in the bleachers, group by group. The "badasses," allegedly bullies who liked to destroy property, were tossing basketballs in the air. The FFAs, or members of the Future Farmers of America club—the preps called them hicks and rednecks—sat at the end of the bleachers. The wannabes, dressed like their role models but discernible by their whiff of uncertainty, stood at a far corner of the room. Those were the kids who fed the preps' egos. Whitney would walk down the hall like royalty, while the wannabes would gush, "Whitney, you look so pretty today!" or "Whitney, you did such a good job cheering last night!" If a prep girl showed up at school with a shaved head, Whitney was sure the wannabes would visit the salon that night to do the same. It was the fact that they tried so hard that doomed them.

Whitney looked at the punks, who wore tight pants and band shirts. They could scream every word of the music they listened to. They were unafraid to strike up conversations with other groups, but they usually clashed with the preps. As Whitney saw it, the cliques were just too different. Whitney was certain that the punk girls thought the populars were loud and snobby. Besides, she mused, odds were that she and her friends probably had been mean to the punk girls before.

The popular guys referred to the punks as "weird" and "useless." They called Dirk, the punks' alpha male, a scumbag within his earshot. Whitney was as friendly with Dirk as her group allowed, which meant in hallways their communication was limited to awkward eye contact and brief exchanges. She was attracted to Dirk, a funny and talented drummer, but she didn't tell anyone, because a popular cheerleader dating a punk would cause "crazy scandalous controversy" and further escalate the tension between the groups. She was having enough trouble with the preps as it was.

After the welcome-back hug, the preps hardly acknowledged Whitney, though she stood next to them. The group brought up inside jokes and memories from the summer that didn't include her. Whitney recognized this weapon because she had used it before. The preps enjoyed purposely making someone feel bad for not being at an event. If you weren't at a party one weekend, the group wouldn't stop talking about it in front of you until the next party.

Whitney loved the power and perks of popularity. When the teachers began handing out senior schedules at the back of the gym, Whitney's group pushed to the front of the line en masse, as students parted without protest. The teachers didn't bat an eye at the line cut, instead complimenting the girls on their hair and their tans. *We haven't been in school for more than ten minutes and already our egos have grown,* Whitney thought. Her group got away with everything. For example, students who were late to class four times automatically received detention. Not Giselle. She regularly escaped detention because of cheerleading practice, and no one dared complain.

Some teachers fawned over the popular group. Whitney's mother was an administrator, and other preps' parents held powerful positions in town. Once, Whitney and her friends sauntered into a school entrance prohibited to students because it opened into a class in progress. The teacher stopped them and yelled that they couldn't go in that door. "Yeah, well, I'm going to my mom's office," Whitney shot back. The teacher asked who her mom was. When Whitney answered, the teacher's expression changed immediately. Not only did she let Whitney's group inside, but she also told Whitney to say hi to her mother. Whitney thought the staff's sycophancy was especially amusing because her mother was sweet and unintimidating. Whitney was close with both of her parents, who occasionally tried to encourage her to be more compassionate.

Schedules in hand, the preps left the gym before they were dismissed, and strutted toward "their" hallway. Other students walked by the Prep Hall quickly, so as not to attract attention in the area where the preps heckled the "weird kids." By the end of junior year, one such student was so fed up with the preps' rude comments that when they made fun of him for drawing a robot, he lashed out: "You're going to be sorry when I come to school with a gun and kill all of you." The preps didn't say another word to him.

"Ugh," Bianca shouted. "I hate when stupid freshmen don't know how to walk in the hall! You walk on the *right* side of the hallway! Goddamn!"

As the halls filled up, crowds parted for the preps. Some students said hello, but Whitney and her friends gave them the "what's-up-but-I-won't-really-acknowledge-you" head nod.

When Whitney walked into advertising class with Peyton, she spotted Dirk. "Hey, Whitney!" he yelled across the room.

"I'm not sitting with Dirk," Peyton whispered to Whitney. "I don't see why you like those people. They scare me."

Whitney shrugged and grinned at Dirk as she sat next to him anyway.

At lunch, the preps cut to the front of the line, as usual, and sat at "their" lunch table in the center of the cafeteria. Whitney hadn't waited in the lunch line since she was a freshman. In the past, when students told the preps to stop cutting, Whitney's group either ignored them or shot nasty glares. When the protestors walked off, the preps would follow them and make loud comments, such as, "Wow, fat-asses need their food quickly, don't they?! I mean, do you really think they *need* that much food? They look like they could do without lunch once in a while . . ." Nobody complained anymore. Because they favored the preps, the teachers in the room looked the other way.

Before cheer practice that afternoon, Whitney and Giselle claimed their gym lockers. It hardly mattered that they always took the lockers in the back corner of the last row. When the prep cheerleaders changed their clothes, the younger athletes waited until the preps were dressed and gone before going to their own lockers. Once, an underclassman tried to squeeze by and accidentally stepped on Whitney's Ugg boot. "Jesus Christ! Seriously?!" Whitney yelled. The girl looked mortified, blurted out a meek "I'm sorry!", and ran away.

As much as she loved being popular, Whitney wished other students understood that it wasn't so easy. Preps were stereotyped like everyone else, she said. "A prep talks like a Valley Girl, thinks she's better than everyone, is obsessed with looks, sleeps around, is usually a cheerleader, doesn't eat, parties all the time, and gets away with murder. Basically, emos want us dead."

Whitney insisted that the prep description didn't fit the "real" Whitney. "I'm not snobby," she said. "I have to be this way because it's what my friends do. If I wasn't like this, I wouldn't have any friends." She loathed the immediate judgments students made about her. She was a cheerleader; therefore she was a slut. She was a class officer; therefore she was stuck up. She wore expensive clothes; therefore she was spoiled. She said "like" too often; therefore she was flaky. She was a prep; therefore she was a bitch.

The funny thing was that if Whitney could have chosen any group at school to belong to, she wouldn't have chosen the clique that intimidated other students with cruelty. She would have chosen to be in what she considered the most nonjudgmental, down-to-earth crew at school: the punks. But it didn't matter. There was no changing groups. Once you were in a group, you were stuck there until graduation, no matter what. That was just the way high school was, Whitney was sure. So she didn't tell a soul.

REGAN DAVIS, GEORGIA | THE WEIRD GIRL

Here we go again, Regan thought, opening the yellow double doors of James Johnson High School. She loved her classes, but the social scene and high school bureaucracy dampened her enthusiasm. She had never walked through these doors on the first day of school without feeling a sense of impending doom.

Regan headed straight for the first-day-of-school assembly. She looked around at her peers, many nervously speculating about the principal's new rules. There had been rumors that the administration was going to enforce the dress code more stringently this year, partly to prevent students from exhibiting gang affiliations on school grounds. Regan usually wore innocuous sundresses and long necklaces, but she worried that the dress code would rein her in. Her long, often wild curly hair had been some permutation of every color in the rainbow since she was thirteen. She had removed her tongue piercing a few years ago, but had kept the orbital in her right ear. She would have to be extra careful this year not to expose her tattoos.

Regan merged into the crowd with some acquaintances, grateful to have her new, beautiful girlfriend, Crystal, at her side. Crystal had a calming effect on Regan. A hip-hop artist whose band seemed on the verge of hitting it big, Crystal had dropped out of school to pursue music. She was here this morning, only for the assembly, to give Regan moral support on her first day of school.

Crystal raised her hand as if to touch Regan's face, then quickly retracted it. "Oh . . . never mind," she said.

"What?" asked Regan.

"You . . . you have something on your face. I wanted to wipe it off for you, but I forgot we're at school."

Regan swiped her cheek and sighed. *Is this what I have to look forward to? A year of secrecy?,* she thought. Regan was in love with Crystal, but it was difficult to be gay in the Bible Belt. Her Georgia town was an urban mix of white conservatives and black families relocated from a rough neighborhood. Most Johnson students were black. So was Crystal; the town was more accepting of interracial dating than same-sex relationships.

Regan wasn't openly gay at school. Her friends knew, but at school she played the pronoun game, referring to her social plans using "we" instead of "she," or "significant other" instead of "girlfriend." She knew people wouldn't care enough to ask why she brought Crystal to the assembly.

Regan surreptitiously nudged Crystal's arm. "In the pink," Regan whispered and gestured with her eyes toward Mandy, the blonde queen bee, laughing ahead of them in line. "That's her."

Crystal looked her up and down. "Viola was right," Crystal whispered back. Regan squinted, trying to recall what her best friend at school had said. "About her ass," Crystal continued. "Yours *is* better." Crystal pointed with her chin. "And him? With the tattoos? That's him?" she asked, pointing to Wyatt.

Regan turned to look, her heart sinking. As little as she cared for him now, it still stung to see him with Mandy. "Yeah," she said. "That's Wyatt."

Two years before, when Regan had first arrived at Johnson, a lonely, anxious Vermont transplant, she was surprised to find that she immediately was attracted to Wyatt, who seemed her polar opposite. Where Regan was a mixture of dorky and punk, Wyatt was a popular, motorcycle-riding, often tactless jock. Regan thought now that his in-your-face machismo perhaps was why she had agreed to date him, after dating only girls and slight, artsy boys. Wyatt was her chance to be with someone undeniably manly so that she would know for sure whether she wanted to give up on males altogether.

Wyatt, who had swooped in on Regan that September, had his moments of tenderness, but even months into their relationship he insisted on keeping their connection a secret because "I don't want anyone to know I'm fucking the weird girl." This was especially hard for Regan, who was candid and outgoing. Wyatt made fun of her constantly for "being a dork." He told her that she was the first nerd he had ever been with. When she asked him why he was with her, he said, "I wanted to see what nerd love was like." Wyatt was fun to flirt with, though, which made school more interesting for Regan.

After nine months, Wyatt dumped Regan via text message. She learned then that he had been cheating on her with pretty, popular, cheerleader-types like Mandy. When they returned to school in the fall, Wyatt and Mandy were openly a couple. Mandy and her inseparable friend Francesca seemed intent on humiliating Regan. They gossiped about how Wyatt showed them PG-13-rated photos that Regan had taken for him (at his insistence). Francesca flat-out refused to be Regan's partner at a student fundraiser. Mandy spread lies, telling people that Regan was stalking Wyatt and trying to ruin Mandy's life. Regan had barely ever conversed with Mandy, but Mandy cut Regan off from some of the few friends she had made.

Regan was mostly on her own at school and feeling adrift in a state where people who worked at the grocery store didn't even know what falafel was. (When she asked someone to help her find falafel, the staffer said, "Tilapia?" Regan said, "No, falafel." He apparently thought she had a speech impediment. "Aw, don't worry. I understand what you mean," he said. Then he took her to the tilapia.)

Now, everyone took seats in the same places as they had before school had let out for the summer. The cliques were divided mostly by subject specialty: the math whizzes on one side of the room, the performing arts department on the other, etc. Separate groups of whites and blacks sat together. Regan thought the racial divide at Johnson was "vast and offensive." Most students hung out only with students of the same race. At lunch, even among teachers, whites grouped with whites, blacks with blacks, cliques with cliques. Regan ate lunch alone in an office. She tried to steer clear of social situations at school because they made her uncomfortable, as if she had to put on a show. "I don't want to 'choose' a group to hang out with," she rationalized. "I'd rather be an outcast."

The black peers with whom Regan had the most interaction formed a clique called "The Seven." Regan liked them, but they were exclusive. Once, she had walked in on them during a conversation and they immediately fell silent. When they realized it was her, one of them commented that Regan could be the marshmallow to their hot chocolate, and should therefore be included in their discussion, as if conversation could be racially segregated.

As the principal began speaking, Regan's attention wandered to the middle of the room where Mandy and Francesca were huddled over what Regan assumed was their infamous purple notebook. Mandy and Francesca called themselves "The Divas," referring to themselves as Diva 1 and Diva 2, even when they did the morning announcements. They had a list of Diva Rules, a Diva vocabulary, and Diva business cards. They even decorated their rooms with similar purple curtains. They brought the little purple notebook to assemblies and meetings, and wrote down the "sqs"—stupid questions—people asked, as well as the names of all late arrivals. They were the school gossips. Regan's friend Viola referred to Mandy as "the mouth of the South."

For a long time, their gossip had centered on Regan, who pretended not to know that people were talking about her behind her back. She explained later, "What people say about me isn't as important as what I know is true. If people want to talk about me, then that's their problem, not mine."

Wyatt sat near Mandy and Francesca, in the middle of the group known for being jocks, jokers, and chicks with reputations. They formed a tight clique, blathering over each other, holding exclusive cookouts once a month during lunch, laughing at inside jokes. During Regan's first year at Johnson, they even wore matching custom-made T-shirts. At assemblies, if one group member spoke up in front of the crowd, the rest of them made a scene, clapping and cheering raucously. Regan was both revolted by and jealous of them.

Regan hadn't intended to become an outcast at James Johnson. When she was dating Wyatt, she didn't talk much to people at school because Wyatt told her not to; he said their schoolmates didn't like her and, being new to Georgia, she believed him. Although Regan was generally strong and independent, she listened to Wyatt because, she said, "I was lost and scared. I was in a new place with new people, and I didn't really know what else to do."

Regan no longer cared that people at Johnson thought she was weird. She knew she was different. She was a self-described histrionic "artsy type" vegetarian who performed in community theater plays, went to museums, and often ate ethnic food. She was also a self-proclaimed nerd who liked documentaries, listened to spoken sonnets on her iTunes, adored English classes, and rarely watched television. She was obsessed with dinosaurs. She improvised strange skits starring her younger brother and posted the videos on Facebook. Back in Vermont, she and her best friend watched the three original *Star Wars* movies in a row and turned everything Luke said to Yoda in *The Empire Strikes Back* into an innuendo. She took Bengali lessons because she planned to spend next year's fall semester volunteering in Bangladesh.

Once, after reading *Cyrano de Bergerac*, Regan and her high school classmates had to write a paper about their metaphorical nose—the single insecurity that kept them from feeling comfortable around people. Regan wrote about her state of mind. She had a different way of looking at the world. She explained later, "I don't *want* to be like everyone else, so I just sort of do my own thing. Everything about my lifestyle is alternative. I'm extremely ambitious and antsy. I'm really silly. I don't try to conform to what people want from me. I'm outspoken and very energized. In school, people don't know how to handle me. So they're just like, 'Oh, she's awkward.'"

At Johnson, her peers teased her for not partying with them because she didn't drink. They laughed at her ADD and her clothes. People who didn't know her well joked about how she was "sunshine and rainbows," naïve and innocent, even as Wyatt and the Divas spread rumors that she was a slut. Regan took Middle Eastern dance classes as often as she could afford to. People at school suggested that Regan was too uncool for such a sensual activity.

Classmates had called Regan weird as far back as elementary school, when during recess she sat against the corner of a fence and daydreamed instead of playing kickball. (When people asked her what she was doing, she would answer, "Going to my imaginary world.") Her parents worried about how she usually had only one close friend at a time. But Regan felt that once she found someone who understood her, she would stick with that person forever. And she had; she'd made lifelong friends back in Vermont. Although she was gregarious, she inadvertently separated herself from people because she was so often inside her own head, focusing on her creativity. From an early age, she knew she was "different" sexually too, though for a while she dated boys, confused about what she wanted.

Once, in elementary school, she told her aunt that students made fun of her. "Always be yourself and don't change for anyone," her aunt said. "When you get older, you'll be glad that you did." So far, her aunt had been right. It was hard to be excluded, but gratifying to be herself. She explained, "I've had issues with being the odd one out my entire life, so it's nothing new to me for people to think I'm a little off. It's always been that way. God, I make myself sound like I'm socially awkward or something. I swear I'm not. I just . . . well, to put it in Johnson lingo, 'I do me.'"

The principal droned on. For no apparent reason, Mandy turned and glared at Regan.

NOAH GIANCOLI, PENNSYLVANIA | THE BAND GEEK

Noah stood at attention exactly three-quarters of a yard beyond the 46-yard line, scoreboard side, tingling with excitement. His crisp white uniform sparkled, the blue-and-gold sash sliced gallantly across his chest. He looked up at the stands, packed with hundreds of spectators, and scanned faces for family, friends, and teachers. He could see them shouting, their voices commingling into a chorus that swelled to a crescendo as the band took the field.

Few band experiences were as exciting as the moments just before the first performance of the year. Noah tensed and relaxed the muscles he used to grip his flag at a precise 45-degree angle. The ceremonial flag, which Noah would keep motionless in the air for the entire show, was heavy and he knew his arms would ache before the fifteen minutes were up. The drum majors raised their hands to ready the band, and the noise of the crowd drifted into silence as if the wind had swirled it away. The drum majors counted off the first four beats, and the band erupted.

Noah, a junior, was fiercely proud to be a member of the Redsen High School Marching Band. The group of two hundred students was so talented that it had been chosen to participate in the Macy's Thanksgiving Day Parade this year, in the band's first year of eligibility. Noah treasured the band because he'd met his closest friends there. In middle school, Noah joined the band as a saxophonist. He immediately fell in love with the camaraderie and the sense of belonging to something grand. In high school, however, Noah didn't have room in his schedule for band class. When he asked the director if he could play sax in the marching band without taking the class, the teacher turned him down.

Freshman year had been difficult. Without the band label to identify him, other students pigeonholed Noah with a more limiting label: Asian. Actually Noah was multiracial, although he had his mother's Chinese coloring. Both parents were raised in the United States. But as a smart, hardworking student—currently he was the class salutatorian—Noah fit the stereotype of the high-achieving Asian.

Classmates made fun of Noah's Chinese heritage. In the lunchroom, jocks and popular kids handed him scrawled caricatures of Chinese people. They greeted him with what he called the "ching-chong gesture," in which they pulled up the outer corners of their eyes and let loose a stream of nonsense words ending in -hong, -hing, or -wong. People "don't really like that others are different from what's 'normal' in our white, upper-class bubble of a town," Noah said. They also made fun of his hair, using it as an excuse to insult his masculinity. Noah kept his hair long, sometimes past his shoulders, for several reasons. He liked that his hair distinguished him from other guys at school, kept him warmer during the winter, and afforded him a versatile tool for self-expression. Best of all, by growing his hair long and then cutting it off in one fell swoop, he could donate it to an organization that created wigs for chemotherapy patients.

One senior in particular made a point of picking on Noah. Noah didn't know why Frederick, a popular partier in Noah's AP Calculus class, zeroed in on him. He had targeted Noah from the first day of school, jeering "Cut your hair!" at every chance. This week, he had loudly remarked, "Your frosted tips look horrible," and several classmates agreed. Today, he had thrown paper airplanes at Noah's head during a test. Noah supposed he had to get used to Frederick because they were swimming teammates who would see much more of each other come swim season.

Noah's hair didn't affect his swimming because it fit into a cap, but it bothered his teammates. At the end of Noah's sophomore season, he qualified for the district meet. A team tradition called for championship qualifiers to bleach their hair one night, which Noah did, and then shave their heads at the pre-competition team dinner. Noah refused.

"C'mon, it's just hair," chorused the other upperclassmen. "Quit being such a little girl!"

"You're not being a team player!" a senior yelled, kicking Noah out of the house. "Get out! If you're not willing to be a part of this team, we don't want you!"

Noah was wounded. He had hoped that some of his teammates would at least stand up for him. They averted their eyes and found other things with which to busy themselves. Several months later,

Noah still hadn't cut his hair. He kept the bleached ends because he thought they were "funky Asian."

Noah's busy schedule included swimming practices, tutoring, Chinese school, Chess Club practice, audio-video work and newsletter writing for his church, and several hours a week of voice lessons and rehearsals for various musical groups. He was the only member from his entire school district in the community's regional choir.

At the end of freshman year, the band had announced that it was accepting applications for the Honor Guard. Honor Guards carried banners and flags and were the band managers, in charge of setting up and moving props and equipment. Noah applied for the position and got it. He loved spending time with his friends every day throughout the football season. More important, he had convinced his girlfriend to be an Honor Guard too.

In Noah's opinion, Leigh, a senior, was smart, kind, funny, and mature. They had started going out in the spring of Noah's freshman year, when she asked him to a movie. Since then, Leigh had been his rock. Noah was stressed from pushing himself academically because both of his workaholic parents had been student overachievers. He was under the impression that "it was necessary to do well because I felt like if I could make them proud of me, I would know they loved me. My parents just don't show love as easily as I want," he said. Worst of all, Po's health was declining. Po and Gung (Cantonese for maternal grandmother and grandfather) had spent weeknights at Noah's house, helping to raise him and his younger brother when they lived in California. Po, especially, had been a major influence on Noah even after Noah's family had moved to Pennsylvania when he was nine.

After the move, Noah would come home from school and read or play video games, learning to be independent. Even now, Noah often took care of his brother, cooking dinner or picking him up from field trips and other afterschool activities. While Noah was able to remain close with his mother, he had a difficult time bridging the distance from his father.

When Po, who still lived in California, was recently hospitalized with kidney problems, Noah was distraught. He leaned on Leigh. Knowing that someone wanted to spend time with him raised his spirits.

As the second quarter wound down, Noah and the rest of the band descended from the bleachers again to prepare for their halftime show. Each member of the Honor Guard was in charge of assembling a specific set piece. Noah was assigned to the drum major podium, a six-foot-tall pedestal for the student director. He was also supposed to help another manager set up the bass guitar and its various accessories.

This year, the band director had promoted Noah to section leader. Now that he was an integral part of the band, however, students at school not only associated him with the band geeks but also ranked him lower in status than the musicians. Noah always defended the band when people said it was stupid. "What instrument do you play?" they inevitably asked, and then called him "the band's bitch."

The visiting team's band ran over its allotted time, but Noah didn't have a chance to dwell on the discourtesy. The moment the performance ended, Noah and the other Honor Guards stormed onto the field, lugging equipment while the Redsen band members took their places. As Noah set up the podium, he came across an item that he had never seen before: a podium skirt, folded in a box. Already the setup was taking too long; the managers had practiced, but never in real time, and they hadn't rehearsed taking the field together afterward. Noah yelled, "I need help!", gesturing to four other managers. When they finished assisting Noah, they rushed to the sideline.

The band was ready before Noah was. Noah frantically opened the bass guitar case on the sideline as the managers lined up to join the musicians. He was plugging the guitar into an amp while the other managers strode in step to their spot on the field, arms crossed, front and center of the band. As Noah turned on the battery, the introduction began over the loudspeakers. Panicking, Noah sprinted onto the field. He noticed that he had accidentally set up the podium five yards to the left of where it should have been, which could cause conducting problems. But the band was playing now and it was too late to do anything about it.

Despite Noah's concerns, the halftime show ended up running smoothly until a trumpet player fell down. The gaffe would not help the band's image at school. *Oh well,* Noah thought. *We still have nearly three months to get ready for Macy's.*

ELI, VIRGINIA | THE NERD

The girl who sat two seats northwest of Eli in government turned around as the teacher handed out quizzes. Eli thought she was looking at him. "I don't know the sixth amendment!" he whispered to her, attempting to commiserate about the quiz. The girl returned her gaze to the front of the room without noticing. Eli then realized that a) she wasn't looking at him and b) the people around him were smirking because they thought he was talking to himself.

After less than a week of school, senior year was just like any other year. Eli's awkward moments were already piling up. Upon meeting his new math teacher, he said, "Nice to meet you . . . I like math a lot." (A classmate told him later, "That was weird.") Or there was the time Eli was chatting in the hall with a few friends. When Chan, one of Eli's best friends (who sometimes played Dungeons and Dragons), came by, Chan said, "What is this, a gang?" Shortly thereafter, yet another friend approached. "What's going on, guys?" asked the newcomer. Attempting to continue the conversation, Eli joked, "We're having a Dungeons and Dragons gang meeting!" The others stared at him, confused. "Whaa? I don't get it," someone said. Welcome to Eli's world.

Most people didn't understand Eli's sense of humor. He was low-key and cheerful, but it was tough to stay positive at Strattville High, a large public school in Virginia. On the first day of the spring semester of his junior year, Eli approached a cafeteria table and asked the students—known as "black gangstas"—if he could sit with them. Without so much as a second's hesitation, they said no. He spent the rest of that semester eating lunch in the library.

Eli still remembered the day in seventh grade when a popular boy knocked a pile of books out of his arms and laughed. As other students joined in, no one helped Eli pick up the books, including a teacher standing four feet away. Eli hated middle school, but the teasing didn't stop then. Even in high school, sometimes when he walked by a group of jocks, one would follow him, "acting nerdy," as Eli phrased it, pushing up invisible glasses, mockingly walking in step with Eli, and muttering in a stereotypically nasal nerd voice, "According to my calculations . . ."

Eli had always felt different from his classmates. They didn't seem to know what they wanted for lunch, let alone what they wanted to do with their lives, whereas Eli knew he wanted to major in finance at Westcoast University and live in the Pacific Northwest after college. (As for lunch, Eli usually opted for pizza.) "I feel like a forty-year-old living the life of a teenager. I just don't have any connections with anyone at school," Eli explained. As cliques began to form in elementary school and middle school, his disconnectedness "evolved into nerdiness, just because that was the 'group' I best fit into."

Eli liked to think of high school groups as hierarchies of subspecies. The jocks, for example, could be tiered into football players, cheerleaders, gymnasts, soccer players, "random gym abusers," and baseball players. The nerds had their own hierarchy as well. This was how Eli described them in descending order of status: "The ADD nerds (who obnoxiously freak over everything, like they'll walk into class on the day of the test and go, 'Oh. My. God. Kill me! I didn't study at all! Aaah!' when it's so obvious they spent their whole lives preparing for this test and then they get an A+ on it . . .); the I-don't-really-care nerds (this is the rarest group. They do well, but they don't go out of their way to flaunt it.); the try-to-be-cool nerds (who are too oblivious to realize they don't belong with the popular kids and that the popular peeps make fun of them); the quiet nerds (who stay in the library during lunch and don't talk to anyone); and the geeky nerds (like, 'Oh jiminy crickets! Did you see that episode of *Battlestar Gallactica* last night?!' with the squeaky voices)." Eli classified himself as "ten percent quiet nerd, ten percent ADD nerd, and eighty percent I-don't-really-care nerd."

Eli had never fallen into the try-to-be-cool nerd category. Why bother attempting that masquerade? As he put it, "I'm not a cool cat." His school activities consisted of captaining his school's Academic Bowl team, which competed once a quarter, and participating in the Model UN Club, Spanish Club, and Future Business Leaders of America.

Eli loved Academic Bowl. He was good at Model UN. Other than in those two arenas, Eli felt "kinda out of place. I usually feel like an outsider and looked down upon." He didn't know anyone at school whose interests dovetailed with his own. He was a self-proclaimed "geography freak," often studying a map of the world that hung in his room. He practiced geography trivia, had a goal to visit all fifty states by the age of eighteen (he was missing only three), and in accounting class, while other students played games like Tetris, he was engrossed in the Traveler's IQ Challenge. His "life to-do list," which he had written this month, included 124 cities to visit (and 66 things to do). Eli loved the Spanish language and could often be found singing Spanish songs to himself. When he was bored in class, he hunted through his textbooks to find typos or grammatical and factual errors. When he was bored at home, he liked to make up silly conspiracy theories and try to connect the dots. His current favorite was that Scientologists ran the Taliban.

Eli almost never went out on weekends. Occasionally, he hung out with one or two friends and played cards or board games. Mostly he stayed home. He tried to make new friends and create social plans, but people insisted they were busy. Eli didn't wallow in self-pity. He knew plenty of people who had it worse. One of his closest friends, Dwight, was a mildly autistic student from another school. Dwight and Eli at first had bonded over their love of travel. As they got to know each other, their friendship deepened because they had a similar sense of humor and were both outcasts. Dwight also had been teased often in school. In eighth grade, when a science teacher joined in on the teasing, Dwight transferred to a private school. For Dwight it was worth waking up at 5 A.M. and taking a two-hour bus ride to and from school just to avoid the gibes.

Eli supposed that, like Dwight, he looked the part of the nerd, with short, straight reddish blond bangs, pale coloring, and a slouch that shortened his six-foot frame. Eli carried a gigantic backpack and wore wire-rimmed glasses. He used an expansive vocabulary and tended to fill awkward silences with jokes that inevitably made sense only to himself, though he wouldn't realize it at the time. Sometimes he tried repeating other people's jokes, like his math teacher's line: "Six over infinity equals zero. Kind of like my income over the federal debt." Eli's friends reacted with blank stares.

Eli was sure that his manner of speaking caused strangers to think he had Asperger's Syndrome. Eli would begin to say something, but the words in his mind weren't necessarily the ones that exited his mouth. He would think, "How are you today?", change his mind to say, "How are you doing?", and the jumbled result would be something along the lines of "How are doing?" When that happened, he would close his eyes for a second, take a deep breath, and try again, enunciating each word carefully. People would give him a half-understanding, half-wary look that made him feel even more self-conscious.

That was better than when they laughed at him, though. He guessed that classmates assumed he was vulnerable, so they took their aggression out on him without worrying about repercussions. Eli *was* vulnerable emotionally, but he typically didn't bother to fight back because, he explained, "It's just not that important to me. I figure I'll win the fight in twenty years or so anyways when I end up with a decent life and they're unemployed and living at home."

After classes ended, Eli and two friends walked together to a classroom to turn in homework early for extra credit. Josephine, an ADD nerd, approached the door, also with homework in hand. "Oooh!" she said to one of Eli's friends. "Let me check my answers with you!"

While they compared papers, Eli tried to jump in. "Did you get 'E' for this, too?" He held up his paper and pointed.

Josephine gave him a withering glance. "Um, excuse me!" she said. "I'm pretty sure I was talking to her, not you!"

"Oh, sorry," Eli muttered, and backed off. But he wasn't surprised. As he lamented later, "Awkwardness defines my life."

JOY, CALIFORNIA | THE NEW GIRL

On her first day of school, nearly a month later than everyone else's, Joy rolled listlessly in bed, unready to get up and move forward with her life. *Please let things be different here,* she pleaded silently. *Please let this school be different.*

Joy had worried about this day for months. Not only was she changing cultures, but she was also starting school late. Although she would be a freshman, these weren't first-time high school jitters—in Jamaica, high school began in grade seven. She had already been told that high school was the "first day of the rest of your life." But she wondered what she would do in this new country, whether she would make friends, and how long it would take her to stop missing home.

Joy cycled through fear, excitement, and sadness before her mother told her it was time to get up. A striking girl with large soulful eyes and full lips, Joy brushed her chin-length hair into a tight bun. She slipped into her most proper school attire—best to start afresh at a new school!—and ate a hearty breakfast of *fool* (an Arabic bean dish), Arabic bread, bacon, and eggs before leaving for the second first day of the rest of her life.

As she got lost on the way to the attendance office, Joy marveled at the differences she immediately noticed between her old Jamaica school and her new California one. This school was clean. There was no trash on the floor, which was carpeted, to her surprise. Here, decorations plastered the walls and classrooms had TVs and computers, whereas Joy's old school had only desks, chairs, boards, and plain walls unadorned save for spatterings of graffiti. In Jamaica, students usually remained in one classroom—except for outdoor classes in drama, music, PE, and agricultural science—and the various teachers came to them. In California, the students moved from classroom to classroom. Joy would have to learn how to open a locker by herself.

This was a lot to take in, coming from a developing country. She loved Jamaica, its vibes and its landscape, if not its poverty and its violence. She wondered if the American school experience would resemble the big party portrayed on the Disney Channel. If so, she wondered if she was ready for that.

Her heart racing, Joy sat down in her first-period health class as she had been taught in Jamaica: her bag in her lap, feet firmly on the ground, hands at her sides. She had never taken health before. When the teacher announced a test, Joy blinked back the moistness in her eyes—hadn't she had nightmares about being unprepared for a test? She stared at her paper, scrutinizing unfamiliar terms. Surely her classmates could see her pulse pounding hotly through her skin. They said nothing to her.

When the teacher told her he would not count her grade, Joy relaxed. She worked diligently until class ended. As soon as the bell rang, students sprang out of their seats. A few of them narrowed their eyes at Joy; she couldn't help but feel it was because she was the only black person in the room. More than half of the nearly three thousand students at Citygrove, a public high school in an urban valley north of Los Angeles, were Latino, about 30 percent were white, and 12 percent were Asian. Only 3 percent were black. Joy remained in her seat, following her Jamaican school's rules, until the teacher told her it was okay to leave.

During a break before PE, Joy pulled a box of apple juice out of her drawstring bag and called her mother.

"Hi, Mommy," she said.

"Hi, Joy, how you doing?"

"I'm fine." Joy wiped away a rolling tear. She noticed a tall student who sat across from her in second period. She hoped he would say hello, but instead he gazed through her at the wall.

"What are you doing?"

"I'm on break waiting for my next class to start." With her palm, she tried to catch the rest of the tears before they fell.

"Do you like the school? How's your day going so far?"

What could she say? Everyone here in California had already adjusted to the new school schedule and formed cliques with friends whom they had known for years. *Starting over is hard, whether or not you want to do it,* she thought. *It's still morning and I want to give up.* She promised herself that she would try her best to make this situation work.

Joy had moved from Jamaica so that her mother and stepfather, whom she loved dearly, could be together after two years of a long-distance relationship. She couldn't tell her mother that already she yearned to go home. She was exceptionally close to her mother, but Joy didn't want to tell her anything that would make her feel guilty about moving to the United States for her own happiness.

The bell rang. Joy wrapped up the conversation, glad that she didn't have to answer her mother's question.

In PE, a stout Asian honors student caught up to Joy and talked at her monotonously. Joy pretended to listen to Natalie while she observed how American students interacted. She was appalled at the differences. At Joy's Jamaican school the principal had instituted strict rules; for example, students couldn't embrace a member of the opposite sex for more than forty-five seconds. At Citygrove, students were sexually explicit. She also noticed a distinct difference in the amount of respect afforded to adults. In Jamaica, when a teacher walked into the room, the class stood up and said good morning. Joy could not do that here.

Joy ate lunch with Natalie at a table in the library, within eyesight of a group of Natalie's Asian friends, who shot Joy dirty looks. Joy immediately assumed they were angry because Natalie was eating with a black girl instead of with them. She supposed Natalie sat with her merely out of curiosity about the new girl.

Joy had never before felt like so much of an outsider. Everything about her was different from her classmates: her walk, her speech, her mannerisms, her looks, her clothes. She wasn't "highty-tighty," as they would say in Jamaica; she was "just a together person." It was going to be difficult to be herself here, she could already tell. She wondered if, one day, someone at school would see the whole of her.

———

EMOS, INDIES, SCENES, AND BROS: TODAY'S STUDENT LABELS

Imagine, for a moment, that like Joy, you are new to your high school and as yet unlabeled. You can manage your classes because they are structured and supervised, and you can survive the five minutes between them by focusing on getting from one place to another. Then you enter the overwhelming landscape of the cafeteria, where unspoken rules and assumptions overshadow what is, in terms of opportunities for social growth, the most important part of the day.

When the bell rings, you enter the cafeteria, lunch sack in hand. In some schools, preps and populars are virtually indistinguishable; an Alabama middle schooler described, "Preppy people [are] basically like the popular people, but you wear a lot of pink and you're really hyper and squeaky." A substantial percentage of the students I interviewed mentioned that the populars shop at prepster stores such as Hollister, Abercrombie & Fitch, and American Eagle when they're not focused on more high-end designers. (Among students at one Texas high school, a new trend is to keep the price tags on their clothes so classmates can see that they paid full price at a non-discount store.) When a Midwestern eighth grader transferred from private to public school, she felt so pressured to fit in that she not only revamped her wardrobe, but also changed her email address to "hollisterlover."

You scan the tables for an empty seat. A few Goths are engaged in conversation in a corner. They might favor boots, spikes, piercings, or dog collars, and dye their hair black or bleach it blond. They're often perceived as artistic or creative writers. A Texas teacher observed, "We get a lot of Goths in the art department and they are generally very pleasant and quirky children. They are almost always very well-mannered."

Nearby, the reclusive emos brood; they are clad in black and therefore commonly but wrongly lumped together with Goths. Emos don't bother erecting the prep façade of perpetual chipperness. "Emo" is short for emotional; one running joke is, "I wish my lawn were emo so that it would cut itself." A Maryland freshman observed, "Goths wear all black and talk like they're depressed and suicidal but they're really not. Emos wear all black and actually *are* depressed and cut themselves."

In some schools, emo boys might wear tight pants and the girls might wear thick eyeliner. Their hair might be dyed or partially shaved. An emo in Florida said that emos are misunderstood. "People constantly criticize kids for being emo, like we're trying to keep up an act, but really, the kids who are more normal-looking are the ones who have the most problems," she said.

Students can confuse emos with scenes because of the eyeliner, tight pants, and attention to music. Scene is a relatively new label, typically used to describe people who prefer alternative or obscure bands. Scene kids say they are more musically inclined than hipsters. They might be identifiable by a bandana adorning a choppy haircut or poking out of a pocket, piercings, funky eye makeup, sparkles, perhaps a vintage look, or long bangs swooping over one eye (which a non-scene described as causing them to "have to do a hotshit head toss every five seconds"). Scenes' hair might be bleached blonde on the surface and dark underneath, or multiple bright tones. Their T-shirts might advertise screamo or techno, hardcore or ska. Scenes, said a Virginia eighth grader, are "the kind of people who recognize every song in the Apple commercials."

Scenes are neither punks nor rockers, although some observers might mistake them for either label. Rockers, said an immigrant in Massachusetts who gratefully found a high school identity in the rocker label, "usually have long hair, wear skater shoes (DCs, Etnies, Vans), and listen to rock, alternative, or screamo."

In some schools, students use the Japanese word *otaku* to describe anime connoisseurs. This is a limited version of the true Japanese definition, in which *otaku* refers to an obsession with any sphere, whether anime, trains, or celebrities. Anime devotees say that *otakus* are more knowledgeable than the average "anime kid." Blue, whose gamer label relates to another supposed obsession, compared the difference between *otaku* and anime kid to the distinction between geek and dork.

Geeks and nerds also can find roots in perceived obsessions, nerds with academia and geeks with technological gear. Many students describe nerds as the kids with giant backpacks who, as a Hawaii band geek put it, "even if they aren't tardy, they run while everyone else is walking." These types of nerds may overlap with AP or IB kids, but fall below "nerdy jocks" and overachievers on the social totem pole. Various debates have tried to pin down the differences between nerds and geeks. Blue once sent me the following unsolicited table representing his distinctions among "normal" students, geeks, nerds, and dorks. (Note: Blue's table is biased because, as he said, "People call me a geek. A lot.")

LABEL	TECHNICAL SKILLS	SOCIAL SKILLS
Normie	No	Yes
Geek	Yes	Yes
Nerd	Yes	No
Dork	No	No

I generally subscribe to the idea that although both groups are known for smarts and social marginalization, nerds might be inclined toward unusual intellectual pursuits, and geeks toward unusual recreational ones.

As you traverse the cafeteria, you notice that many students are absent from the room. Just as some overachievers might opt instead to dine in the newspaper office, for example, the band geeks, or "bandies," might eat in the band practice room. Band geeks are not to be confused with the reportedly quieter orch dorks, also known as "orchadorks."

On one side of the cafeteria you see the area that some students refer to as Africa, with Mexico not far away and Asia in another corner. Of these, Asia has the most subdivisions. A West Coast Filipino junior broke the categories down into "smart Asian nerds, normal Asians, whitewashed Asians, FOBs ('Fresh off the Boat: They don't speak English fluently and wear Asian-style clothes'), Koreans, Cool Asians, and Filipinos."

The religious students also subdivide. When students consider classmates to be more spiritual than average, they might stamp them with one of a number of labels, like Jew Crew, Superjews, church girls, or Young Life addicts, after the Christian ministry.

Today's students are so label-conscious that there is even a label for students who consider themselves independent of labels. Students described a range of indie characteristics, from "they wear alternative clothes and are obsessed with global warming or they play guitar and draw weird pictures" (Maine), to "the kind of people who are weird on purpose, but aren't looked at as losers; they're looked at as 'individuals'" (Hawaii). Indies gravitate toward "underground concepts," as opposed to "shallow modern culture," an indie explained to me, which sometimes gets them mistaken for scene kids. Indies may view themselves as descended from beatniks; many cite Jack Kerouac and Allen Ginsberg as influences.

A California junior said she is proud to be indie. "It makes me more sure about myself. I think, 'Wow, this is what people call me when I'm *real* with myself,'" she said. She described the label as a mix of geek and fashionable artist that manifests in clothes, music, hair, and concise MySpace About Me's. "Indie kids are into the abstract things in life. You have to be really in the know about things. Being indie means being artistic and finding your own eccentric identity. The name of the game for being an indie kid is to never admit you are one. If you do, it goes against all your beliefs against labeling, thus making you a hypocrite."

On the way out of the cafeteria, you pass the gangsters (or "gangstas"), who are often characterized by baggy pants for the guys, tight clothes and hoop earrings for the girls, and nice sneakers for both genders. Gangsters sometimes overlap with ghetto kids, who supposedly listen to rap and hip-hop and act up in class. At some schools, gangsters are synonymous with fighters. A Florida gangster told me that he participated in a fighting ring in middle school that was supervised by adult gang members. Now a high school junior who wishes he had more social connections, it took until this year for classmates to gradually "become aware that I'm not going to eat them or jump them in a dark alley."

Described by some students as a mix of gangster, scene, and skater, "bros" comprise another new student label. Often wearing caps with the brim flipped, these devil-may-care partiers might wear polos and khakis in the South or skater clothing in the Southwest. Bro-hos, their female counterpart, might mix skater attire with Abercrombie.

You go outside. Following the brick wall past a group of skaters, you see the skanky girls, who are rumored to sleep around and dress the part. Out of the shadow of the school building, you spot the tanorexics, the girls who are overly tan and not in the cafeteria, for obvious reasons. In the distance, the druggies, also known as chronics, fade into the woods.

And then there are the floaters, friendly with a variety of groups but wholly embraced by none. They could squeeze in at the edge of a lunch table without being rebuffed, but there will be inside jokes they don't get and rehashing of weekend activities they weren't in on because each group assumed the floaters were hanging out with another.

By the time the bell rings, you realize you've spent the entire period traveling, searching, torn between your appreciation of the freedom from label stereotypes and your inability to shake the feeling that perhaps you wouldn't so much mind a label, even an outcast label, if only it accompanied a group that made you feel as if you had a place to belong.

TO BE SURE, ALL of these characterizations are broad, blanket composites (contributed by combinations of students in various areas of the country). That's what each label supposedly represents. We take mental shortcuts by clustering people together, making assumptions, and forming stereotypes to shrink our social world into a grid that's easier to process. But why is the perimeter of this grid expanding, with escalating numbers of labels relegated to cafeteria fringe?

The evolution of these labels may be illuminating. Between emo and indie, labeling is shifting from targeting what a student does—studies hard, dresses darkly, plays a band instrument—to what a student *feels*. The shifting of labels into personality compartmentalization illustrates the increasing marginalization of students who don't conform. Suddenly, there are not only acceptable and unacceptable standards of dress, but also standards of being. All of this points to the reason that student bullying is up, self-esteem is down, and social warfare is fierce: The concept of "normal" has narrowed.

Late Summer to Early Fall

The Popularity Myth

Chapter 2

QUIRK THEORY AND THE SECRET OF POPULARITY

Throughout years of meeting thousands of students during my interviews and lectures at schools across the country, I noticed that the people who I was most drawn to—whether because of their personalities or because they had genuinely interesting things to say—were rarely part of the in crowd. Whether excluded by their peers or marginalized by their schools, many of them believed that they were socially inadequate. But there was something special about them that made me both want to get to know them better and believe that they would accomplish interesting, creative, and perhaps great things as adults.

This got me thinking. Many of the successful and appreciated adults I know were not part of the mainstream popular crowd at school: the onetime multi-pierced, combat-boot-wearing artsy girl who inspires hundreds of people with her quirky magnetism; the Goth theater geek who turned into a dynamo in the publishing industry; the green-haired high school "freak" who is now a publicist-to-the-stars. Indeed all of these people are thriving *because* of at least one of the attributes for which they were excluded as teens. The artsy girl is now a beloved art teacher who has made additional money and a wide circle of friends with her creative freelance ventures. The Goth, whom Midwestern classmates picked on because her intense curiosity diverted her interests from parties and sports to museums, classical music, and books, now prospers in Manhattan, where friends and colleagues can relate. The freak, rejected partly for her willingness to be confrontational, used her place on the margins to become a shrewd people observer. "I've been able to use that to my advantage in my life and especially in my career," she said. "I'm good at dealing with a lot of different personalities, so, for that, I'm thankful that I was a friendless freak. Also, I think it all trained me to be a bit of a bulldog, and I like that about me."

Meeting current and former student outsiders like these inspired me to develop the concept of quirk theory. Quirk theory is intended to validate students' inability or refusal to follow the crowd. It serves as a way to explain that, once they leave the school setting, their lives can improve.

Students are excluded for many reasons that depend, of course, on their environment, their peers, and their school. Each of the main characters in this book was snubbed for assorted combinations of attributes. Danielle, the Loner, was cynical and droll with a disdain for superficiality; she was the ultimate outsider, whose seventh-grade rejection made her want to reject her classmates in return. Noah, the Band Geek (also labeled the Asian), whose discipline and dogged sense of responsibility gave students the impression that he was too serious, was at the same time emotionally expressive, occasionally to the point of melodrama. Joy, the New Girl (also labeled the Foreign Girl and the Black Girl), refused to temper her strong cultural pride or her feistiness. She battled to maintain her precocious focus on the positive even through shockingly trying times.

Eli, the Nerd, indulged in eclectic tastes and was devoted to expanding his knowledge base, whether of academic subjects, global issues, or trivia, even when they did not relate to his schoolwork. He didn't believe in the concept of normality and, therefore, made no attempt to change his stereotypically awkward image. Regan, whose peers identified her as the Weird Girl because of her alternative style and hobbies (she was also labeled the Artsy Girl and the Lesbian), was viewed as another kind of nerd; her youthful exuberance and unabashedness were often mistaken for naïveté. But while inside school peers excluded her, outside of school people adored her.

Something about Whitney, the Popular Bitch, made me think that she was not meant to be in the popular crowd; I designed her challenge accordingly. And Blue, the heartbreaking underachiever who was known at school as the Gamer, was excluded because he was unafraid to explore unpopular viewpoints and because of the intensity with which he pursued his passions. When he cared about something, he injected all of his energy into it, "loving it up to the very last five percent," even if other matters he cared or knew less about consequently fell by the wayside.

Like most outcasts in school—including many of the thousand-plus people I contacted for this book—these "characters" were excluded because they were different, because they didn't or wouldn't blend in. But to me, the qualities that set them apart from their classmates were intertwined with the qualities that made them stand out from the crowd in positive ways. I saw in each of these embattled individuals sparks that convinced me that they would thrive once they left the school setting, characteristics they unveil, amidst their trials and tribulations, throughout this book.

As part of my argument that cafeteria fringe should be highly valued, I wanted to help the main characters learn to see the value in themselves. So I took an unorthodox approach by offering each of these individuals a challenge in the middle of the school year. In my twist on traditional makeovers, I wanted to know whether they could alter people's perceptions of them without directly changing who they truly were. And whether that tweak in perception would in reality create an opportunity for them to improve their high school lives.

Every member of the cafeteria fringe has something to offer. One only has to care deeply enough or look hard enough to find out what that is. I decided to write a book about quirk theory because too many students are neglected or disparaged due to qualities, interests, or skills that we should instead nurture and embrace. I issued the challenges to discover what happens when we do.

Blue, Hawaii | The Gamer

Blue had planned to go home after school, but he lingered after his last class, hoping to spot Jimmy. A pudgy fellow half-Korean, Jimmy was considerably taller than Blue, who was five foot five and muscled.

Since the IM conversation in which Herman had offended him, Blue had withdrawn from his friends. Although he still liked Jackson, Ty, and Stewart, who sometimes joined him at the arcade, Blue took such pains to avoid Herman and his followers that he avoided the cafeteria altogether. This new distance was relaxing. "Sometimes," Blue explained later, "you just have to log out, you know?"

Instead, he spent lunch, recess, and before and after school killing time in the AP Government classroom. Sometimes he biked to school ninety minutes early to unwind there. The tiny classes (Blue's class had nine students) left the large room always at least half-empty. The teacher, Ms. Collins, had created a welcoming lounge area with beanbag chairs. Blue was supposed to be her teaching assistant, but he had been wrangled into TA-ing autotech instead because of his expertise in the subject. He helped Ms. Collins with her computers anyway, fixing and improving them whenever he could.

From a distance, Blue saw Jimmy enter the classroom, where a handful of students had congregated. Blue followed him, planning his strategy on the way. Kaloke's "hallways" were sidewalks ringed with hibiscus, bird of paradise, and other tropical flowers whose scent drifted with the trade winds through tall open-air shutters into classrooms overlooking lush mountains. From some classrooms, students could see the horizon of the Pacific Ocean.

Blue stood at his usual spot by the teacher's desk for a few moments, fiddling with his iPhone. Then he called out, "Hey, Jimmy, I'm gonna sit with you."

"Okay!" Jimmy said, smiling.

Blue grabbed a laptop from the classroom's computer cart and slid into the chair next to Jimmy, where he pretended to do homework.

A few desks away, four girls discussed AP classes and colleges. Blue stole glances at Jimmy, who gradually set his homework aside as he tuned in to the conversation. "Hopefully I can get into MIT," he told Blue.

"Why, what do you want to do?" Blue asked.

"I want to work for NASA one day, or Boeing. But I want to work on the planes, not fly them."

Blue was intrigued. It was unusual for his friends to want to attend a prestigious mainland school. He had his heart set on Berkeley. "What's it take to get into MIT?" Blue asked.

"Good grades and all that stuff," Jimmy said. "I might not have a chance, so I can just apply for fun, you know? And if I get in, I get in."

Blue told Jimmy he wanted to major in entrepreneurial studies at Berkeley.

"I'm trying to get into Berkeley," said a girl who had scored straight 5s on her AP exams.

Another girl asked what her GPA was. "4.3," she said. "What's yours, Jimmy?"

"4.0," he said.

The girl looked at Blue, who was finding this conversation more eye-opening than he'd expected. "I have a 2.6," he said. Everyone in the room stared at him in amazement.

"*What?!*" exclaimed one of the girls.

"What?" Blue said. He knew what. He knew they assumed that smart geeks got good grades. And he had. He used to have a 3.9.

"Nothing," the girl stammered. "I just assumed . . . you were really . . . I don't know."

"Let's just say, some things happened," Blue said casually. Meanwhile, his mind frantically compared GPAs, whizzing through statistics that hadn't seemed meaningful until now. *Jimmy is going to live out my dreams*, he thought. The bubble of denial in which Blue had been placidly residing slumped suddenly as if to suffocate him.

Blue was not going to get into Berkeley. He hadn't realized until now that it was too late to restore his once-stellar GPA, which had tumbled precipitously last spring because of a host of issues that erupted at once. He had skipped AP Language, the traditional junior year AP English course, to take AP Literature because he was excited to analyze books. As the only junior in a class of seniors, he did well at first. But as the months went on, Blue realized that the analysis he expected wasn't going to occur. The class had more nightly homework than any other class he'd taken. By second semester, unless Blue thought that an assignment would either teach him something valuable or challenge him, he didn't do the work. Other than French and autotech, easy classes with few homework assignments, and Ms. Collins' AP U.S. History class, which he aced, Blue barely managed Cs. He failed AP Lit.

It might not have been coincidental that Blue's grades dropped when he was pouring most of his energies into Arwing and practicing Call of Duty for gaming tournaments that would bring money and publicity to the club. But at the same time, Blue's relationship with his mother had deteriorated. Blue had had family issues for as long as he could remember. On three separate occasions in elementary school, child services nearly put him in foster care because he had been left home alone so often. After his parents divorced when Blue was a toddler, his father moved to France, where Blue's older brother now lived. Usually, Blue talked to his father only when his mother made him ask for money.

Blue's mother refused to pay for college, although she could afford to. Student loans were not an option, she said. If Blue could not find a way to attend college for free, then she would make him join the military. When she pressured him to buckle down academically, he gave up, unwilling to allow his mother to take credit for motivating him when he couldn't motivate himself. "So I always get off-track because it feels like I'd do things for nothing," he said.

Recently, while driving to the mall, Blue had told his mother that he wanted to go to Berkeley. She began another version of her usual lecture. "You have to start getting serious about school! Don't expect a fucking dime out of me. I've been raising you eighteen years and I'm done with it already. I'm emailing your teachers every day asking for your work and grades and future assignments. And you have *got* to apply for every scholarship. And you need to consider the military. You like money, don't you? These officers, they buy new BMWs in cash their first year!"

Blue's guidance counselor had inquired about his falling grades, and some of his teachers allowed him to make up work. While they were vaguely aware of his situation at home, Blue didn't want to admit "I'm not doing my work to be rebellious. It seems immature. [I have] too much pride."

Nobody told him that he was ruining his chances of getting into Berkeley. Now, among some teachers, Blue had the reputation of a student who was going nowhere.

Blue's mom "had it all backwards," Blue said, in assuming he didn't care about the future. He thought about college constantly. And now he sat heavyhearted in the Government classroom, envisioning Jimmy leaving for MIT, achieving *Blue's* goals. Throughout junior year, Blue had been convinced that he could "bounce back at any moment." Now he knew his dreams were dashed.

As Jimmy and the girls discussed scholarships, Blue noticed that periodically Jimmy looked at him and their eyes locked for longer than a typical glance. When conversation waned, Jimmy packed up to leave. Blue gazed after Jimmy until he disappeared from the doorway.

WHITNEY, NEW YORK | THE POPULAR BITCH

The preps started taking advantage of their seniority immediately. Knowing that teachers wouldn't punish populars, they skipped classes and wandered the halls, parked in the school lot wherever (and however) they wanted to, walked upstairs before the security guards allowed students to do so, and sat on the heaters in some classrooms instead of at their desks.

Before school one morning, a teacher asked Whitney to show two new girls to their first period class and help them adjust. Initially Whitney was annoyed, because new kids were usually outcasts. But as she chatted with the girls, she found them to be surprisingly cool. They were stylish, they seemed friendly, and they were twins, which scored them extra points. Whitney's friends immediately allowed the twins at their lunch table because they "dressed cute" and carried Kate Spade purses.

During the second week of school, Riverland held its senior class elections. As usual, the populars ran the meeting. They had monopolized the student council since seventh grade: Chip had always been the president, Giselle the vice president, Bianca the secretary, and Whitney the treasurer. Most of the other seniors, including the punks, didn't bother to show up for elections anymore. The band kids, the wannabes, the FFAs, and a few "weirdos" were the only groups represented.

The advisor called the meeting to order. "Do I have nominations for president?"

"I nominate Chip," said Bobby. The populars cheered and the teacher wrote Chip's name on the board.

A band kid nominated a fellow bandie, who laughed because he knew the nomination was a joke.

"Okay," the teacher continued, "next are nominations for vice president."

"I nominate Giselle," Bianca said. The teacher wrote Giselle's name on the board. When she asked if there were any other nominations, no one spoke.

"Now, nominations for secretary," the teacher said.

"I nominate Shay," a band kid said. Shay was the girl who had supposedly gained weight and frizz over the summer. The teacher wrote her name on the board.

"I nominate Bianca," said Giselle.

Shay's face fell. "Can I drop out?" she asked.

"No, it's too late," the teacher replied.

"Ugh," Shay groaned.

"Next, nominations for treasurer," the teacher said.

"I nominate Whitney," Giselle said.

Whitney laughed. "Haha, for the sixth year in a row!" she said. No one ever opposed her.

Someone from the back of the room muttered, "Wow, hilarious," under her breath. The teacher wrote Whitney's name on the board.

Then Jessica, an FFA, spoke up from the back of the room. "I nominate myself," she said. The room hushed. Whitney's jaw dropped as the teacher wrote Jessica's name on the board. Someone was running against her? An *FFA girl* actually thought she had a chance?! The preps shot "How dare you" looks at Jessica until they left the room.

Whitney was glad that her friends had her back. She was on shaky ground with Bianca these days because of Luke, her new best friend.

Whitney had met Luke through mutual acquaintances after he gradu-ated in June from another school. Whitney and Luke sensed a connection that they had never experienced with anyone else. Luke's background fascinated Whitney; he had been a hard drug user until his little brother was born, which inspired him to quit. Luke made Whitney feel safe. He had street smarts and interesting stories. He also happened to be punk.

That was all the preps needed to know. They told Whitney that Luke was a loser and a stoner. Actually Luke had been clean for four years while every one of Whitney's popular friends smoked pot. Whit-ney had relatives who had been in rehab, so, after trying once and re-gretting it, she had promised herself she wouldn't smoke. When the preps pressured her, she explained later, "since saying 'no' isn't enough, I have to fake excuses like I have asthma, or I got arrested for it a while ago."

The populars were rude to Luke when Whitney brought him to their parties. At one gathering, a popular guy shouted, "Who brought the weirdo?" Besides his blue hair, Luke didn't look that different; he was relatively short, with ripped abs and a baby-cute face. But the prep girls told Whitney bluntly not to bring Luke to future parties because "he wouldn't be welcome."

Eventually, Whitney decided that if the preps didn't allow Luke at their summer parties, then she wouldn't go to them either. While her clique bonded without her, Whitney thought nothing of the tempo-rary abandonment of her friends. All she wanted was to be with Luke, with whom she didn't have to act fake. He encouraged her to be more of an individual and less judgmental. She accepted his plea not to do drugs, ever. Happier and starry-eyed, Whitney decided she was a new person. She wore bohemian clothes to reflect this change. She wanted to be different from everybody else.

By the end of the summer, Whitney and Luke were spending most of their days together. When Whitney threw her end-of-summer party, she invited her new best friend, somehow expecting her group to un-derstand. But the preps didn't talk to him, glowered at him, and whis-pered to each other in front of him. They told Whitney they were angry she had spent the summer with him. Luke waited out the party inside, playing Rock Band with Whitney's younger sisters. Whitney felt bad, but what could she do? Telling off her friends would only start the year with drama. Now that the summer was over, Whitney had to face reality. The populars would be at school with her. Luke would not.

WHEN THE CANDIDATES DELIVERED their speeches, Chip and Giselle gave respectable talks. Bianca's speech made no sense, which didn't matter because Shay's speech was, "I don't want to be secretary. Vote for Bianca."

Whitney stood up. "So I've been your treasurer basically forever," she said. "I know the ropes and all. Why break tradition?" She ad-libbed a few quick items and sat down.

Then Jessica rose. Whitney had heard that Jessica had told class-mates she was tired of the same students winning every year. Jessica apparently had rounded up other non-popular groups in an attempt to overthrow Whitney. She gave a long, detailed, polished speech that outlined her plans for the senior trip, graduation, and community service. Even Whitney had to admit that this FFA girl deserved to be a class officer.

Whitney found out at the end of second period that she had won for the sixth consecutive year. She acted blasé but secretly breathed a sigh of relief. She vowed to glare at Jessica whenever she spoke for the rest of the year.

————

THE SECRET OF POPULARITY

Some readers might wonder why, in a book about cafeteria fringe, I chose to follow someone who had a prime seat at the center table. Let me be clear: There are plenty of popular students who are friendly and gracious, just as there are outcasts who are not. Even the best-intentioned kids might make social blunders because they are still growing up. In Whitney's case, as much as she espoused the benefits of popularity, she was conflicted. "I've never felt one hundred percent part of my group," she admitted. She dealt with a double-edged sword. Because she some-times acted like the bitch that the populars wanted her to be, she wasn't fully embraced by other students. Because she sometimes revealed what she considered her true self, she wasn't fully accepted by the rest of the popular clique.

What does it mean to be popular? Sociologists report the common finding that students' involvement in extracurricular activities can affect their popularity. For boys, participation on certain sports teams—basketball at some schools, football at others, etc.—automatically can make them popular. While this link also can be true for girls, there is an even more direct and exclusive route to popularity at many schools: cheerleading. Why? Although cheerleaders' focus on appearance and membership in an elite group surely could contribute to their social status, the single most important factor that brings cheerleaders prestige is the same factor that lends some athletes popularity: They perform in front of large student audiences. Whether they are cheering at a game, bookending a pep rally, or wearing their uniforms in the halls, cheerleaders are easily identifiable. You can't miss them. This feature forms a key part of popularity. Studies have shown that, at least among students, popularity equates with visibility.

If to be popular means to be seen, it follows that the students who happen to be labeled nerds or geeks might not be popular because they spend so much time studying or engaging in other solitary pursuits. They don't have the time, or perhaps the interest, to make themselves visible. The same could be said for students who are passionate about writing poetry or stories, creating artwork, staying abreast of the music scene, working on cars, or reading. Their talents might not thrust them in front of the student body.

Another major criterion for popularity is being recognizable. (This is one reason that dating someone popular can enhance popularity.) Many studies have found that the students whom classmates deem popular tend to be the ones with whom they try to have the most frequent interaction. As Sacred Heart University psychology chair Kathryn LaFontana observed, "It is interesting that children focus on the quantity rather than the quality of interaction to determine popularity. From a social networks perspective, it seems that children see those peers who have a large number of peer contacts and are more central to the social network as popular."

Other research reveals that to be popular means to be influential. People usually prefer the things they see most often, which could partly explain why many students often mimic the populars. Popularity means having an impact on others, and not necessarily a positive one. Bianca, for example, was popular not because she was sweet as pie to her classmates, but because she had power. She gained that power through manipulation. Studies show that the students classified as popular are often able to actively maneuver their position in the social hierarchy. They are savvy about the Machiavellian methods useful to climb into and then cling to the popular label—and they don't hesitate to use them. These same studies find that the students who are unpopular are also viewed as lacking the skills to vault to the top of the hierarchy. I would submit, however, that in some cases these "unpopular" individuals know the manipulative behavior necessary to be popular; they simply choose not to use it.

While scientific studies have reported that girls are more likely to associate popularity with social domination, many boys described similar situations. A popular coed clique in Arkansas called itself The Exclusives and wore T-shirts that said, "We are what you wish you could be." Members adhered to a list of rules they called The Code, which one boy listed for me:

"No more than one ponytail a week for girls.

No hair below the collar for boys.

Jeans have to be designer.

No dating 'normals' but one can have sex with them.

All sex is to be admitted to the group and scored 1–5.

All shirts are collared except for Friday for boys.

Girls can wear dresses but only collared shirts.

Girls wear heels every day and guys wear either dress shoes or cool flip-flops.

All weight gain is reported to the group.

Boyfriends/girlfriends must be approved.

Weed is a must, but no hard drugs.

Eating disorders are okay, but they have to be secret."

The Exclusives gathered at someone's house every Friday night. Populars who missed that event without a valid excuse were not allowed to sit with the group at lunch for a week. Any member who broke the rules was similarly banned from the cafeteria table and could not sit with the group at the next football game.

It's not uncommon for popular cliques to use these types of rules to keep their members in line. A Canadian junior said that at her all-girls school, the populars hold each other to strict standards. "Hair color has to be blonde or brown and God forbid it's curly," she said. "My best friends won't go out on weekends if their hair isn't straight. We all strive to look anorexic, which is awful, but it's reality. We are not friends with fat people. If your eyebrows are not perfect, you will be judged. You have to make fun of everything. You obviously have to drink, not throw up, smoke cigarettes and weed. A popular girl needs to be pretty, skinny, dress nice, party hard on weekends, not be a virgin, [and] be funny, daring, and rebellious."

Many adults know that membership in the popular clique does not necessarily indicate the dictionary definition of popularity. A more accurate definition in the high school context could be "a shared recognition among peers that a particular youth has achieved prestige, visibility, or high social status." It took a long time, however, for developmental psychology literature to catch up to this definition. For decades, when researchers conducted surveys and experiments on popularity, they measured it in terms of sociometrics, which means that psychologists asked students to rate their classmates by how much they liked them or wanted to spend time with them. The researchers would simply tally up the results and consider those with the most votes to be the most popular.

More recently, however, a funny thing happened. Psychologists started noticing that when they asked students directly to rank how *popular* they thought classmates were—separately from how much they wished to spend time with them—the two lists were strikingly different. To address this discrepancy, psychologists created a new term: perceived popularity. Perceived popularity refers to how students rank a classmate's reputation rather than their personal opinion about her.

Other studies examined the traits that students attributed to perceived popular students versus sociometrically popular students. Students viewed classmates who were sociometrically popular as kind and trustworthy. They viewed classmates who were perceived popular as dominant, aggressive, and conceited. Students reported that those who were perceived popular and sociometrically popular—some students are both—exhibited all of the aforementioned traits. (Anecdotally, many students with no knowledge of these terms call popular subgroups "mean popular" and "nice popular.")

Whitney often wondered how she could be popular and yet have so few real friends at school. Eventually, she realized that social standing does not necessarily translate to social acceptance. This is a crucial concept that so many teens—those who are trying to achieve popularity and those who are disappointed that they can't—tend to miss: To be popular does not mean to be liked.[1]

NOAH, PENNSYLVANIA | THE BAND GEEK

Band practice moved along tediously as the director broke down the show, practicing segments four measures at a time with each instrument, then bringing all of the sections together for a fifteen-second blast of music. Noah and the rest of the Honor Guard raced around, moving props and setting up instruments and microphones.

Afterward, when Noah waited with Leigh for her father to drive them home, Leigh asked him to come over. "I can't tonight," Noah replied. "I really need to study for my physics test. It's important." Noah wanted to do well in all of his classes, but he especially wanted to prove himself as the only junior in AP Physics.

Leigh quieted. Noah knew he had upset her, but wasn't sure why. On the ride home, she barely spoke to him. Noah, in the backseat behind her, felt guilty.

Every night, Noah lay in bed, pulled up his Winnie the Pooh comforter, closed his eyes, and listed his joys and concerns, always ending with a joy to hold on to as he went to sleep, a practice instilled by his church. Tonight his concerns centered on Leigh. So did his joy. *Let tomorrow allow me to have a better experience,* he prayed.

The next morning, Noah got to school early, anxious about the

---

[1] *For the sake of simplicity, in future chapters, "popular" refers to perceived popularity.*

physics test. At his locker, Leigh approached him, looking uncomfortable. "Can we talk?" she asked.

Noah's stomach plummeted. "I'd like to, but I have to get to physics," he said. She agreed to wait until lunch.

Noah was breezing through the test when, about midway through the period, he got nauseous. His stomach twinged in painful waves that would have doubled him over were he standing. Two classes later, he was so anxious he could hardly focus.

When the lunch bell rang, Noah stored his books in his locker and reluctantly walked to Leigh's, where she waited with a piece of paper folded in half. "Can we talk now?" she asked. They sat on the floor, backs against a row of lockers.

"So," Leigh said, her fingers fiddling with her lunchbox strap. She looked away from Noah, down the empty hall. "I don't think our relationship is working out anymore."

Noah's eyes watered. He stared down at his palms, which reflexively curled. *All the joy in my life is gone.* "Is this something we can talk about?" Noah asked, wiping his face with his sleeve.

"No, we can't," she said. For twenty minutes, she explained why they had to break up. They had different outlooks on life, she said. He liked to argue (he preferred the term "analyze"); she didn't. He was too immature, and yet he was also too serious. She loved him, she said. He was sweet, she said. It wasn't going to work, she said.

Noah bent over his knees. His hair fell into his face and dampened. Leigh told him how hard it was to break up with him. She repeatedly urged Noah to read the letter she held. Grudgingly, he skimmed it through tears: thirteen bulleted points of heartache. The letter listed reasons why their relationship was failing. Leigh reached an arm toward Noah to comfort him. He flinched away.

The lunch bell rang. Noah stood up. "Can we be friends?" Leigh asked, her blue eyes sincere.

"We'll have to see," Noah replied. He couldn't say yes. He thought he would throw up if he did. He needed to compose himself for school. As he walked away, he glanced back once to see a circle of supportive friends closing in on Leigh. No one looked twice at Noah.

At home that night, the hurt washed over him. He wrote a song for Leigh that she would never hear. He shuffled through a deck of *Star Wars* cards, seeking the kind of comfort he could find in doing something he considered geeky. Padmé Amidala, the Jack of Spades, surfaced. The quote on her card read, "I will not let you give up your future for me." This reminded Noah of his sixth-period conversation with his guidance counselor, whom he had told that he wanted to help his ailing grandmother in California.

"That's selfless, but you need to ask yourself what she would want you to do," the counselor told him.

Noah stared at the card. His grandmother wouldn't want him to sacrifice his schoolwork, but he would do anything to keep her around. He momentarily forgot about Leigh as he focused on Po. Noah finished going through the deck, unsoothed. It had been eleven hours since his "life came crashing down," and he wasn't in any less pain than he had been that morning. *I have no idea what I've become. Nothing will be the same.* This was one of the worst days of Noah's life. He fervently prayed that he would find some way to cope. *I want to be loved,* Noah wrote in his journal that night. *I want to be loved, I don't care what it takes.*

Because of the breakup, Noah had to switch cafeteria tables. Since freshman year, he had eaten lunch with Leigh and her friends, although her friends had never really become his friends. Over the next few weeks, Noah sat alone at a table full of Asian students who spent the period doing homework without conversing.

Noah's seating issues repeated themselves on the band bus to football games. Noah typically was the last student to get on the bus because he wanted to ensure that the equipment and instruments were loaded properly before the band left school. He didn't know why he was the only bandie who felt responsible for this duty. Other bandies mocked his work ethic when he loaded supplies on the box truck or practiced marching formation. "Quit working so hard, man. You're a band *manager*," one senior said to him. "It's not like working harder is going to get you to be drum major," another bandie said. Noah knew that people thought band managers were a joke, but he wanted to prove that he deserved to be there. He liked that people considered him responsible. The adult volunteers, parents and staff, always thanked Noah effusively, as if he were going beyond the call of duty.

Seats on a band bus—Redsen's band filled five buses, a forty-foot trailer, and a truck—were supposed to hold a few dozen students, volunteers, and a pile of uniforms. Usually by the time Noah got onto the bus, only a couple of seats would be left: inevitably one with the adults and one next to a stack of uniforms. Other kids saved blocks of seats for friends, but since Noah and Leigh's breakup, the Honor Guards hadn't been saving Noah a seat.

Noah knew he was different from "most high school kids who are crazy, outgoing, and fun," he said. Recently, his Spanish teacher led an exercise in which she asked who in the class best exhibited certain traits. "Who's nice?" she asked in Spanish. "Who's tall?" For most traits the students offered various names, but when she asked, "*¿Quién es serio?*", the class answered in unison, "Noah!" Noah laughed because it was true.

He liked his serious side, though he sometimes worried about how it set him apart from his peers. He was in touch with his emotions, rather than airbrushing them with fake happiness. But he was okay with that. And he had thought Leigh would have been okay with that too, after seventeen months.

Noah had always been in tune with his emotions and unafraid to express them. These characteristics were partly why classmates called him an emo throughout eighth and ninth grades, when he wore all black to reflect his mood. It didn't mean much to him to be emo, but he identified with the label because he believed he was more emotional than his classmates. He had also briefly considered cutting on several occasions. Once, a student had reported to the school guidance office that Noah was suicidal. He wasn't, though he had considered suicide in middle school. But classmates were thrown by his attempts to have discussions "on a higher plane" about feelings and deep, hard-hitting issues. They didn't realize that he tried to help other people with their problems so he wouldn't have to think about his own.

THE BREAKUP HAD DESTABILIZED Noah, who was crashing more than usual lately. Crashing was Noah's term for anxiety attacks that made him at once confused, angry, and morose. Instead of crashing once a month, he was crashing every few days. He got two to three hours of sleep a night.

But Noah and Leigh set aside their conflict for an important meeting. Before the breakup, they had spearheaded Redsen High School's first recycling program, for which they received permission from the administration to put recycling bins in eight classrooms. Once a week, Noah and Leigh collected the recycled paper and drove it to a designated bin outside Noah's church. A recycling company picked up the paper and gave money to the church. At the meeting, Noah and Leigh delivered an impassioned presentation to persuade the church board to give a portion of the revenue to their school for student scholarships. The board listened patiently, then agreed to give Redsen 100 percent of the profits.

That night, when Noah, distraught over the breakup, was crashing again, his father came into the room. He hugged Noah, who cried in his father's arms, surprised at the embrace. "There are a lot of good people, but not everyone is compatible," he told Noah. "Forget about her and enjoy your life."

Noah realized that he had been wallowing in the downsides of the breakup rather than enjoying positive aspects of his life, such as looking forward to the Macy's Parade and other events. He reflected on the dozens of songs he had written about how much he wished his father would show him that he loved him. *My dad was there to comfort me,* he thought. *I wonder if the breakup was "supposed" to happen. I was supposed to find love from my dad because of Leigh.*

Back at school, Noah tried to shift his attention to the upcoming student government elections. Noah had run for class president twice and had lost decisively both times to Kent, a popular jock who'd barely campaigned. Last year, all four students on Noah's slate had lost to populars. Nevertheless, Noah decided to try again.

He had wanted to be involved in student government since middle school, where the general student council was selected by teachers who in three years didn't choose a single boy. In ninth grade, Noah decided to appeal to his classmates. By the day of the deadline, he was the only student who had submitted a form for class president. He assumed that because the school had set a firm deadline, he would win by default. Instead the adviser extended the deadline, leading two other students to announce their candidacies. Noah graciously accepted his resulting defeat to Kent because he agreed that it was important for students to have options. In tenth grade, a dark horse ran; he was known for shaving his head and reading medieval fiction. He Nadered some of the non-popular kids' votes from Noah, ensuring that Noah couldn't collect enough votes to win.

This year, Noah's hopes were riding on one of two possibilities: that in addition to Kent, another popular student would run, thus splitting the popular vote, or that no third-party student would run, and somehow Noah would manage to make an impact through his message. Noah liked Kent, but after last year's loss he had vowed to run every year, "because even if I lose, I'll be able to use the experience to grow."

At the first official election meeting, Noah fervently hoped that the new class advisor would disclose that, somehow, this year's officers would be selected by the quality of their speeches, their agendas, or, really, any factor other than the student popular vote. No such luck.

The teacher wrote the name of each office on the board and asked the students to sign up. Noah waited until the room emptied before adding his name under President. As he left the room, he looked back over his shoulder and smiled. This year's election would be between Kent and Noah alone. Popular versus Unpopular.

REGAN, GEORGIA | THE WEIRD GIRL

Regan opened the door to the community theater, rushing to get out of the rain, which hovered thickly in the air, typical of a Georgian September sky. She pulled Crystal into the building behind her, careful outdoors not to clasp Crystal's hand in any way that could imply a relationship.

In Vermont, people had suggested that Regan try acting because of what they called her "grandiose personality." She auditioned for a high school musical, scored a role in the company, and immediately was hooked.

Theater allowed Regan to be artistic and creative in an acceptable outlet. Most of all, it was a relief to inhabit someone else's life for a while, to shed her personal issues for a brief respite. In a play, she knew exactly how all of her character's problems would be resolved. No matter how the cast performed, the end turned out the same. No questions, no worries, no unknowns.

"Theater people" had always treated her differently than people at school did. They appreciated her openness, ebullience, goofiness, and offbeat interests. Theater people genuinely liked her, while schoolmates patronized her, calling her ridiculous and silly. Regan explained, "You know how when you talk to a little kid who's rambunctious and talking a mile a minute, you're kind of like, 'Uhhh, ookayyy' and make a face to adults like, 'What is wrong with this child?' That's how people react to me. They say things like, '*Okay, Regan,*' talking down to me. Wyatt always said I'm like a little kid. I think I just am not cynical. I'm a realist, but I'm still happy that life exists and that I'm a part of it. Personally, I think that's a strength." Sometimes she compared herself to Ally Sheedy's *Breakfast Club* character, who was quiet in the beginning of the movie; once she started talking, the students "thought she was odd, like they understood her less once she started sharing herself. That's sort of how I am at school."

When Regan moved to Georgia, she couldn't be involved with James Johnson's drama program because she wasn't part of the performing arts department. So she had auditioned for a role in a community theater play.

"Regan's here!" yelled Naomi, the thirtysomething female lead, as Regan and Crystal slipped into the theater. Naomi smiled at Regan's rehearsal clothes: a T-shirt, cutoff sweats, and a bandana tying back her newly dyed pink hair. When Regan had shown up at school with pink hair, her peers scoffed. (The administration didn't penalize her, she assumed, because many of Johnson's mostly black students—and even some teachers—added color when they got their hair done.) The theater cast, by contrast, was unfazed.

Only a few people were at rehearsal today. "This is my Crystal," Regan announced. Lately she had taken to introducing Crystal that way to people who didn't necessarily know she was gay.

"Ohh myy Gaahhd," squealed the middle-aged woman who was playing Regan's mother in the show. She seemed to be taking to the role in real life as well. She cupped Crystal's face in her hands. "I have been waiting to meet this gorgeous woman. She . . . is . . . beautiful."

"Thank you," Crystal said, smiling.

"Thank you," Regan repeated.

As the woman returned to her seat, she continued to beam at Regan and Crystal. Regan breathed a small sigh of relief. In a world in which so many places were unsafe for Regan and her relationship, the theater was a sanctuary.

The director handed Regan a script. "Will you stay on-book for me?" she asked. Regan was so busy reading her lines and those of the absent cast members that she didn't have time to think for the rest of rehearsal.

Afterward, the group met for dinner at a diner down the street. "You did a good job today!" Naomi said, elbowing Regan when she sat down.

"Yeah, no kidding," said the male lead. "Thank God you were there to read for everyone. I didn't know you could play everyone in the show."

"You're really good, you know," said Naomi. "I hope you continue to act."

Regan glanced up from the menu. "Oh, hey, I appreciate it, but I need a little break. This show took up my entire life."

"Isn't that always the way?"

Regan pressed Crystal to choose a dish she really wanted, knowing that she would choose something cheap, as usual. Regan always paid. Crystal was embarrassed that she didn't have the money, but Regan didn't mind treating her girlfriend. Neither of them had much pocket change. When they went out on weekends, they usually looked for free activities: Johnson plays, public festivals, fairs, and concerts.

As her castmates smiled at their coupleness, Regan thought, *What a comfortable place to be.* She never felt this way at school.

Mandy seemed to be making an extra effort to glare at Regan lately. Her blatant hostility mystified Regan. They had conversed only twice. The first time Regan saw Mandy after Wyatt had dumped her, Regan had wanted her to know that she didn't hold anything against her. So on the first day of school that year, when Mandy came through the main doors, Regan nervously approached her. "Mandy!" Regan exclaimed, and hugged her. They made brief small talk about their summers and parted.

A few minutes later, as Regan walked upstairs, she overhead Mandy and Wyatt making fun of her in the hallway. "And she hugged me and everything, like how fake is that?" Mandy said, laughing.

The second time they had talked was the previous year. Regan was walking out of the bathroom when Mandy happened to be coming in. Regan stopped, turned around, and said, "Mandy."

Mandy also turned. "Yes. I'm glad we're about to have this conversation."

"I just want you to know that the things you heard about me aren't true," Regan said.

"I'm starting to figure that out."

"I really don't have a problem with you, and I think it's stupid that we're supposed to hate each other. It's just not worth it to feel awkward," Regan said.

"Yeah, and to think it's all over a stupid boy," Mandy said. "Really, we should be on the same side." But Mandy had been rude to Regan ever since.

Luckily, Mandy's gossip about Regan had been overtaken by an incident near the end of the school year. A drama had exploded when two people were caught having oral sex in the parking lot; they were discovered because they were skipping class. One of the two, who was black, left the school permanently. She told students that white people were getting her kicked out and asked a group of boys to gang up on Wyatt, who had gossiped about the incident, including to the head of the English department. They did. They found him in a classroom, took their shirts off, and threw them on the ground, ready to fight him. He was able to summon administrators, who broke up the mob and suspended the boys. For the rest of the day, the school police escorted Wyatt to his classes. At least, that was what Wyatt said. Sometimes Regan believed that Wyatt was James Johnson's gossip mill.

A few days after play practice, Wyatt approached Regan in the hallway. For once, he didn't tease her. "So what's new?" he asked.

"Not much. My life is pretty standard."

"That's good." He paused expectantly.

Regan took the hint. "So, uh, what's new with you?"

"A lot."

"Is everything okay?" Regan asked.

"I think it's going to be. I got rid of a lot of things, and I think it'll make things better."

"Like what things? Objects or people?"

"Both. We broke up."

The next day, Mandy passed out during class. She left school in an ambulance and didn't return for a week, later citing "exhaustion."

Danielle, Illinois | The Loner

Danielle was in a local store helping her friends hunt for Homecoming formalwear when she saw the dress. Strapless, satin, and short, the fuchsia number nicely complemented her relatively dark hair and eyes. Along with her "annoying, big, Hispanic eyebrows," those were the only features she had inherited from her Costa Rican father, who lived in Florida. The dress came to mid-thigh and showed off her long, slender legs. The top of the skirt puffed out, disguising hips that Danielle was self-conscious about. It was nothing like any of her other clothes. She liked the idea of wearing something that no one expected her to wear.

She called her mother. "I found a dress I like. Can I get it?" she asked.

"I thought you weren't going to Homecoming," her mother said. "You don't need a new dress unless you're going."

Danielle hated school dances and had broadcasted that she had no intention of going to Homecoming. Why would she want to spend any more time with her classmates than was required? On weekends, Danielle usually stayed home and read, watched movies, or researched Internet topics that interested her. But she loved this dress. "Well, I guess I'm going now," she said.

Danielle knew her mother would get her the dress because her mother understood her. Danielle was a lot like her mother, tough and independent, and she appreciated their relationship. "Since we're the same, personality-wise, I can tell her pretty much whatever. And she has a good sense of humor, and is up for doing some funny things," Danielle said. "I admire that she doesn't take crap from people, although sometimes I wish she wasn't so in-your-face about it; it's really embarrassing at restaurants when she gets pissed off. And I like that she doesn't need constant interaction with people. And the past couple of years she's seemed to give me more trust. For the most part, it's a pretty chill, understated relationship."

As soon as Danielle's group walked into the decorated gym for Homecoming, Danielle already regretted going. Her friends mingled, darting about so quickly that Danielle lost track of them in the crowd. Danielle grew lightheaded, as she usually did in the middle of large social gatherings. Why was she here? She didn't like dancing—at least, not the grinding that surrounded her. She preferred "old-people dancing," the elegant waltzes she saw in the classic movies she loved, and wanted to learn the flamenco, the tango, the salsa. For now, she tried to ignore her discomfort.

When her friends dragged her onto the dance floor, Danielle swayed awkwardly and tried to think of an excuse to do something else. She surveyed the other students, who were laughing and frolicking in the crowd. It hit Danielle then just how different she was from her classmates.

It wasn't her looks. She could blend in, and outside of school, people insisted she was pretty. No, she figured it was everything else about her that made her stand out. She didn't listen to the same music her classmates did; she preferred to listen to her mother's favorite bands: Deep Forest, Marillion, or James. For extracurriculars, she took tae kwon do classes with her younger brother and played varsity tennis only reluctantly. Even her conversation topics meandered from the mainstream; she liked to raise random questions, like "How are sweatshirt drawstrings made?!" She couldn't relate to other students' provincial, high school–oriented goals. They talked about partying at the local university and staying together in town for the rest of their lives, while Danielle dreamed of someday doing something "really great," like joining Doctors Without Borders or discovering ancient ruins. She preferred not to act phony, so she refused to pretend that shallow topics were interesting or that unintelligent comments were witty. Better to say nothing than to be fake.

Danielle didn't *feel* like she assumed other people her age did, either. Classmates never seemed to understand why she hated talking on the phone and texting. She didn't date, shop, or watch much TV. Also, Danielle enjoyed her own company. Danielle's mother, who was a childhood outcast too, had taught her not to care what other people thought. "If I believed in fate," Danielle said, "then I would say that I was destined to be an outsider, based on my genetics. The entire maternal side of the family is extremely antisocial, and I definitely got those genes."

Sometimes Danielle considered being an outcast pretty cool, actually. Because she didn't feel the need to follow trends like other students did, they didn't scrutinize her; or if they did, she wasn't aware of it. She didn't feel strange doing things that other students wouldn't do, like reading in odd places. Danielle read incessantly; she thought perhaps it was because reading made her feel smart and she liked the quietness of it. She liked watching movies, too, but not as much, because with movies "you miss the really cool sentences."

More than three hundred books were divided among three bookshelves in Danielle's room. One was the Young Adult section, with Harry Potter, the series that first inspired her to read, and the Gossip Girl Series, which she read during the year of the hate club to try to learn how to be popular. She hadn't read the YA books since middle school, but she couldn't bring herself to get rid of them. The other large bookshelf was her literary shelf: Tolstoy, Orwell, Rand, Dickens, Hardy, Lessing, Faulkner, Proust, Shakespeare, Austen, Saramago, García Márquez, both Brontës. She kept her favorite books on a shelf attached to her headboard. There she could find *Gone with the Wind*, *A Farewell to Arms*, *For Whom the Bell Tolls*, *Out of Africa*, and *Into the Wild*.

Danielle treated her books like museum treasures, cringing if a book cover so much as creased. When a classmate borrowed her *Les Misérables* paperback and told her the cover fell off, she gave him the book permanently and bought herself a new, unblemished hardback.

Books were so sacred to Danielle that she wouldn't check them out from the library. She wasn't "some creepy book worshipper," as she phrased it; she just didn't like the idea of touching things with unknown histories. Also, one time a friend had opened a library book and found a piece of salami.

Besides, there was something gratifying about owning books. She didn't have to read them within a predetermined time limit. She took good care of them because she figured that in twenty years, she wouldn't want a torn-up, dog-eared copy of *Snow Falling on Cedars*. She'd want a clean read.

Danielle read in classes because she was bored, and aced the tests anyway. Her classmates made fun of her for it, but their opinions didn't outweigh her love of reading. She could relate better to the worlds in her books than she could to the teens at her school.

Recently, two physics classmates near Danielle had discussed phoning significant others just to talk. "I don't know if I should call her or not," the boy said.

"[My boyfriend] calls me every night. Sometimes when he doesn't call, I get mad," the girl said.

Danielle looked up from her book. She wouldn't want a guy to call her. Not that she had to worry. Danielle had never had a boyfriend, and didn't want one. She figured that was yet another thing distinguishing her from other teenagers. She couldn't identify with the girls she saw fluttering over their latest boy dramas. A relationship seemed like a waste of time and effort if you weren't going to marry. "What do people even talk about when they call each other?" Danielle asked. "'Oh, hi honey, how was your day? . . .' It seems boring."

"What?! You are so weird, Danielle," the boy had said.

There were downfalls to being an outsider, even for a loner. When Danielle did want company, her few friends were usually busy. Beyond her tiny group, Danielle had not once hung out with anyone else outside of school. Just because she liked being alone didn't mean she always preferred to be. "You know how in *The Sisterhood of the Traveling Pants,* they're all such good friends and they can tell each other anything and they always give each other hugs and stuff?" she said. "I've always wanted to have friends like that. I'm kind of averse to hugging, and I'm obviously not very good at sharing things about myself, but those are the kind of friends I wish I had."

It was difficult, too, when everyone else in the room seemed to be having fun, while Danielle couldn't fathom how she could possibly relate. Like now. Danielle spotted a familiar color. One of the preps was wearing the same Homecoming dress as her. *Ugh,* Danielle thought. *I knew I shouldn't have gotten a dress from the mall.*

Danielle lasted maybe half an hour on the dance floor before she began hunting for open doors through which she could sneak out of the building. Stone Mill kept doors locked until 10 P.M. in an effort to keep students from drinking and driving. When she finally found one near the art hallway, her friends weren't ready to leave. By the time Paige agreed to join her, chaperones were allowing students outdoors. Danielle and Paige spent the rest of Homecoming at a local Wendy's, waiting for Mona and Camille to get tired of the dance so they could spend the night in a backyard tent like they had planned.

Joy, California | The New Girl

Joy sat with Natalie in the library, talking over lunch as they had every day in the two weeks since Joy had arrived. Natalie peered at her Asian friends at a corner table, briefly at Joy, then at the clock. Joy knew what was coming.

Natalie cleared her throat. "Hey, Joy, um, tomorrow I'm gonna eat lunch with my friends, okay?"

"No problem. That's cool," Joy said. She had seen the looks Natalie's friends gave her. She understood why Natalie didn't invite Joy to sit with the group. Races stuck together. Joy was not the type of person to hold grudges, but even she wasn't immune to the sting of rejection. She didn't know anybody else at school.

The first weeks at Citygrove were some of the loneliest of Joy's life. In English, Joy's favorite subject, the teacher asked for an interpretation of a vignette and clapped at Joy's response. The other students frowned at her. The only other black person in the class was

Latrice, a cheerleader, whom Joy spoke to sporadically. Joy had tried to socialize with other black students, but they didn't welcome her. She didn't "talk gangsta," hang out with boys who wore baggy jeans, or "stick to her own race"; therefore, in their eyes, she didn't have "flava" and, she believed, they viewed her as a white girl.

In Joy's Jamaican schools, students had targeted her because she wasn't 100 percent black. They teased her about her mixed-race Ukrainian mother, whom they called brown, and they made fun of Joy's skin, a medium-brown shade of chocolate. Once, Joy had asked a friend to ask another girl why she didn't like her. The girl said that Joy's nose was too straight and her eyes were too large, "white features" that reminded the girl of slave owners.

Students had found other reasons to pick on Joy in Jamaica. Because Joy's mother was lighter skinned than most Jamaicans, people believed that Joy was wealthy. She was not. They teased her because in school she spoke standard British English rather than the more mainstream Jamaican dialect, even though she peppered her Facebook profile with local colloquialisms. They seemed puzzled by Joy because she was proper, yet spoke her mind loudly when provoked. They mocked her because she was an actress on a local academic television show. They were unimpressed that she had won a national award as one of the best theatrical actresses on the island. Eventually she had adjusted to her classmates' mannerisms and learned "how things operated" socially. By the time she left Jamaica, she had finally figured out that environment. And now she had to master a new one.

Joy expected that making friends would take time, particularly because she didn't believe in cliques and didn't want to be a part of one. "People will always exclude me; it's up to me to do things on my own terms and become the person I want to be," she explained. "I don't believe that everyone should like me. That's nonrealistic. If you don't wanna be my friend, I ain't gonna cry over you, doll." Instead she hoped to try to talk to individuals from various groups to find a friend.

The day after Natalie abandoned her, Joy decided to skip the cafeteria and eat in her next period class—biology—where she could spend time on quiet introspection.

In October, Joy's parents and teachers switched her to AP English.

In order to make the change, Joy had to switch PE classes, too, which weighed on her because another class shift meant being the new girl all over again. She was dismayed to learn that she was the only black person in a class of fifty students, most of them Mexican.

While she kept up a brave front at school, at home Joy had cried at least three times a day since she first landed at Citygrove. She cried in the shower, while walking to and from school, when she talked to her Jamaican friends, and before she went to sleep. She felt stuck. To her peers, she was neither white enough nor black enough. She didn't even fit into her classes; she was too advanced for "regular" classes, but refused to succumb to the hyper-competitive undercurrent of her AP classes. She couldn't see herself belonging to either group socially. She found the "regular" students to be unambitious and pessimistic about their future, and the AP kids to be "lifeless people who are willing to step on others to get ahead."

Joy tried to forget her troubles as her new PE class ran the mile for the first time. She maintained a brisk pace despite the heat, ahead of all of her classmates. On her fourth of six laps, Joy was the only student still running. Behind her, classmates either walked or jogged, fanning themselves in the stagnant air.

"Jamaica!" a boy bellowed. "Usain Bolt! Asafa Powell!" Joy turned around—and suddenly felt a ripping sensation near her pelvis. *I can't stop now,* she thought. At the next lap, she mentioned the pain to her teacher, who told her to walk. She slowed down and the pain knifed her in the groin. "Joy!" the teacher said. "Go sit on the bleachers."

Joy hobbled to the bleachers and tried to stretch her leg. As her classmates finished their laps, they left her alone in the sun. After a while, an Indian girl with glasses, braces, and a thick, sloppy ponytail sat down beside her.

"Hey, are you done with the mile? Wow, you're fast. I was watching you. You're a really good runner!"

Joy smiled. "I'm not that good. Thanks, though! I hurt my groin, so I had to stop."

"Don't worry, it'll get better. Hey, where are you from? You have a different accent."

"I'm from Jamaica. I'm Joy, what's your name?"

"Oh, you probably won't remember it. It's Nishantha, but call me Anisha."

"That's an interesting name! Don't worry, I'll try to remember."

"Yeah, well, at least I won't get mixed up with anyone else," Anisha said.

The girls laughed. When the bell rang, Anisha helped Joy walk to the locker room.

Joy was relieved that finally someone genuine had reached out to her. Within a week, Anisha and Joy were practically inseparable at school.

Chapter **3**

WHY ARE POPULAR PEOPLE MEAN?

WHITNEY, NEW YORK | THE POPULAR BITCH

Whitney had ignored a cold for about a week, hoping it would go away before Saturday. A guy she had dated from another school invited her to a party he was throwing with a friend and told her to bring other girls. Whitney loved the power trip of being the only popular who knew the guys. She looked forward to this party for days.

At lacrosse practice on Saturday, Whitney trailed behind her teammates, wheezing uncharacteristically as they ran wind sprints around the field. When the team was halfway done with the last lap, Whitney's breath whistled and her throat closed. She fell to the ground, on the brink of a blackout. The other girls screamed for the coach. Whitney put her hands over her head and tried to take deep breaths, thinking, *I wish Luke were here.* Although she had treated him like dirt lately, she knew that if she called him, he'd come running. That was power too. But no one other than Luke would have guessed that she was engaged in a miserable inner struggle between the person she was and the person she wanted to be.

Whitney supposed she had started acting like a mean girl during the sixth grade, when she was the queen bee. She was cruel to her classmates, shooting them wicked looks, creating drama, acting phony, and feeding off of their adulation. She knew that students disliked her, but she didn't care. She thought she was better than everyone else. She was on top of the world.

Then things changed. During one assembly, Whitney's clique sat on the top row of the bleachers behind two "loser girls." One of the girls said with a thick lisp to a popular girl, "I like your earringthss." Whitney's friends burst out laughing. They turned to each other and exclaimed, "I like your earringthss!" with obnoxiously exaggerated lisps. The girl wept. The preps looked at Whitney strangely for not joining in, but she just couldn't. She wanted to give the girl a hug.

When Whitney realized how vicious she had become, she tried to be nicer to people and yelled at her friends when they were mean. The clique didn't like this new behavior and cast Whitney out of the group. Depressed for the last two months of seventh grade, Whitney tried to cope with having no friends. Eventually she decided to conform to avoid ending up alone.

Once again, she strutted around school, acting superior, manipulating her peers. In short order, students became afraid to upset her. Common knowledge warned that if you angered Whitney, she would exert all of her energy to try to ruin your life. She would spread nasty false rumors about you, steal your boyfriend, and then turn all of your friends against you. Whitney continued to do these things until partway through freshman year.

"I hated how I wasted energy like that. I hate who I am. I hate that I feel I can't trust my friends," Whitney said now, as a senior. "I suck up to the queen bee so I'm on her good side. No one understands I do it out of fear. I'm a bitch because I, like, have to be tough so people are afraid to kick me out and hurt me again. I would rather have people be a little intimidated by me than take advantage of me. But I always end up being meaner than I want. I just want to be able to be nice and not lose all my friends again because at lunch I'd have no one to sit with, on weekends I would have no one to hang out with. I would be completely alone with seriously no friends. I'd be a loser, and I'm deathly afraid of that. Basically, I'm friends with my friends due to lack of options. I'm forced to be."

Terrified of being left out again, Whitney had recently resumed dressing like the populars, digging in the back of her closet to find urban prepwear that looked like her friends'. Now it was all H&M, all the time—vests, cardigans, zip-ups—with Hollister jeans and Uggs. Whitney desperately hoped that at least on the most superficial level, wearing the same clothes would reforge her connection with the group. She also repressed her faith. Catholicism was important to Whitney, but Bianca was an atheist who always blabbered about "how stupid religion is." So Whitney kept her beliefs under wraps and bit her lip when Bianca assailed religion. Popularity required those kinds of sacrifices.

She pandered to Bianca more often, inviting her out and showering her with compliments. That's the way it was with Bianca: If you wanted what she considered to be the enormous favor of her friendship, you'd best have something to offer in return. Whitney tried bringing up memories of good times they'd had as a group. She was mean to the people whom the populars wanted her to be mean to. In the library one afternoon, she found an online photo of an overweight, sweaty classmate. Whitney felt bad for her, but still summoned the populars to the computer to make fun of the girl.

Whitney's most difficult compromise was allowing her friends to persuade her to push Luke away. "He's so ugly," Giselle said. "You can do so much better than a loser like him. You need a guy more fit like you."

"I don't know why you hang out with him," Madison said. "When he texts you, just be really short and put a period after everything you say."

As soon as Whitney returned from the hospital after lacrosse practice, she IMed Bianca. Her doctor had sent her to the hospital for X-rays of her lungs and diagnosed a combination of bronchitis and severe walking pneumonia.

Whitney: *Yo, I don't think I'm going to go out tonight.*
Bianca: *Dudeeeeee. Why?* (Bianca knew full well that Whitney was sick.)
Whitney: *Son, I have pneumonia lol. I'm like dying.*
Bianca: *Whitney, it's your senior year, you HAVE to go. I'm not going to let you miss out on ONE SINGLE PARTY your senior year. You have to go out.*

Whitney hesitated. For the populars, everything revolved around their party schedule. If there was going to be a day off from school, the populars absolutely had to socialize the night before. Partying was more than just a way to kick back. It was a way to manage and monitor the preps' pecking order. Who was in control? Bianca. How did she exert her power? With the party car. Whitney's group would pile into one car to go to any party thrown by someone outside of the clique. Only five people could fit into a car, but there were, at any given time, eight or nine populars. Bianca automatically got a place in the car. On Friday and Saturday afternoons, the preps raced to talk to Bianca to battle for one of the four remaining spots, each not caring who was excluded as long as she got to the party. Once, Whitney was left out of the car only because she had spent the day with her parents and didn't have a chance to catch Bianca. It was that clear-cut. If you didn't get a place in the car, you couldn't go to the party. (As Whitney sarcastically remarked, "God *forbid* we take two cars, ever . . .") Whitney frequently offered to be the designated driver just to claim a spot in the car.

Whitney wavered when Bianca pushed her to attend the party, even if going would compromise her health, because she would automatically get a seat in the party car. *One party won't make me any sicker, right?* she thought. She texted Luke for advice. He told her she was an idiot for contemplating going out, but that she should decide based only on how sick she felt and not on her friends' opinions. "Think for yourself," he texted.

> **Whitney:** *Dude I just got back from the hospital and got X-rays. There is no way I can go anywhere tonight.*
> **Bianca:** *You'll be fine. It's your senior year. You don't have to drink.*
> **Whitney:** *You met the guys a couple times. It will be fine if you go.*
> **Bianca:** *Oh, I'm totally not worried about you not going because you're the only one that knows them . . . I know them too.*

Whitney rolled her eyes. Bianca didn't know them; she was trying to make Whitney feel less important. Whitney decided that she was too tired to go. "Exactly, you'll be fine," she said. "Go and have fun."

The following week, Whitney found Bianca and Giselle in the middle of a conversation about the party. They mentioned Chelsea.

"Oh, Chelsea went?" Whitney asked casually.

"Yeah, we love Chelsea!" Bianca replied.

Since when?! Whitney thought. She said later, "You *love* drama within cliques as long as it doesn't involve you, because, like, everyone runs to you. But it's dangerous when people start getting close because you never know if you'll be replaced and left out." Just as Whitney feared, someone had taken her spot in the party car. Unnerved, she said nothing.

In the cafeteria, Whitney was sitting with the populars, as usual, when Chelsea said, "Oh my God, turn around, turn around." The entire group turned to stare. "That really fat girl's crack is hanging out! That's so disgusting."

One of the guys said, "Damn, I'd like to tap that." Another said, "Big girls need lovin' too!"

The girl pivoted, obviously having heard the populars talk about her. Like the rest, Whitney's efforts to muffle her laughter were merely halfhearted.

———

UNDERSTANDING THE POPULAR BITCH

Many of the descriptions of populars that students nationwide reported to me sounded like this: Populars, said a Maryland public school senior, are "the girls who could model in their free time, have the best clothes, shiniest hair, coolest parties, and seem totally together. The guys who have that 'sweet at life' confidence, a lazy arrogance you can't help but admire because they look the way they do. These people play sports, are very rich, have had their cliques formed since middle school, and you look at them and wonder, 'What exactly did you do in a past life to deserve all this?'" Popular students seem to have it all, and what they don't have, classmates often attribute to them anyway. Then why are so many popular kids so mean?

Meanness can be divided into two categories: overt aggression and alternative aggressions, which include social aggression (such as excluding) and relational aggression. Relational aggression, also known as relational bullying, covers ignoring, spreading rumors, shunning, eye rolling, glaring, snickering, and sneering. It is intended to harm by damaging or manipulating others' self-esteem, social status, or friendships.

For at least half a century, experts considered students who engaged in aggressive behavior to be socially incompetent. This was because researchers measured a child's rates of aggression alongside rankings of sociometric popularity, or how much other students liked him. Naturally, students didn't much like those who verbally or physically beat the crap out of them. But when researchers began measuring aggression alongside *perceived* popularity, they found an undeniably strong link. Recent studies conclude that aggressive behaviors are now often associated with high social status. Psychologists no longer view aggression as a last-resort tactic of social misfits. Now they see aggression as a means toward social success. (This does not, however, mean it is admired. As author Daniel Goleman wrote in *Social Intelligence*, "being manipulative—valuing only what works for one person at the expense of the other—should not be seen as socially intelligent.")

Some researchers describe a "popularity cycle": Initially, a girl rises through the ranks to popularity. She might stay popular for a while, but at some point, she could be perceived as too popular. Maybe she's getting too many perks, drawing too much attention from too many boys, or distancing herself too far from old friends. At that point, students either in the popular clique or outside of it might turn on her out of resentment, causing her status to plunge.

A girl can also provoke such resentment by appearing to think she's "all that." At some schools, experts say, a quick path to losing popularity is to act as if you perceive yourself to be popular. In an anthropological study, Ball State University professor Don Merten observed, "Loss of popularity in this manner was especially disconcerting in that being labeled stuck-up used the 'force' (to use a judo metaphor) of a girl's popularity against her to invert her status. Therefore it was precisely when a girl enjoyed popularity that she was most vulnerable to being labeled stuck-up. . . . Any action that suggested that a girl considered herself popular, however, could be taken as an indication that she thought she was superior and hence was stuck-up. Yet to be popular and be unable to express it, and thereby not enjoy it, was less than satisfying. Thus, these girls faced a cultural dilemma that is common for women: They were being implicitly asked to encompass both aspects of a cultural dichotomy—to seek popularity, but when they were successful, to pretend they were not popular." This attempt to be popular without admitting it is similar to the way students battle for top grades without wanting to confess that they're competing hard. Or how young women might be expected to appear virginal but, at the same time, put out.

How can girls demonstrate their popularity while still managing to keep it? Merten studied this exact problem. His answer: Be mean. Some girls, of course, can be both popular and nice. But niceness involves treating other students as equals, while the goal of perceived popularity is to climb recognizably to the top of the social hierarchy, an aim that contradicts the idea that others are equal. Many popular girls aren't nice to lower-status students because they are concerned about undermining their own popularity. Treating other cliques as inferior creates a social distance that allows popular girls to feel exalted and invulnerable. Meanwhile the cruelty, ignoring, gossip, and exclusion are expressions of power and dominance.

Merten argued that students would rather be viewed as mean than stuck-up because stuck-up girls could lose their popularity, while mean girls generally didn't. I asked Merten why a girl with a reputation for being mean could avoid the reputation of being stuck-up. He explained that as a cultural anthropologist, he peered through a lens that focused more on cultural basis than on psychology. "Whereas being stuck-up seems to have nothing positive about it, being mean does. In athletics, having a 'bit of a mean streak' is often taken as a compliment," Merten said. "In the context of middle school, being mean also involves mobilizing peers to support one's efforts, [which is] also an enactment of one's popularity. Moreover, it has the effect of intimidating girls who may be inclined to try to undercut one's popularity. Finally, the girls I write about are not mean to everyone. Often they can be nice to people who don't threaten them."

Whitney's experience, however, shows that perceived popular girls can be both mean and stuck-up without losing their status. The preps practically flaunted their snobbishness. So what changed in the decade since Merten conducted his study? Or, if Merten's insightful anthropological observations still hold true, what could be an alternative explanation for the change?

It became cool to be a bitch.

Whitney chose the identifier "The Popular Bitch" herself. Late in the year, I asked her if she had been proud to be a bitch. She said, "Yeah, I was proud. I would feel like I had power when I could get what I want and people feared me. Bianca especially loved it. She would always be like, 'I love being a bitch.'"

Why has contempt become a tolerable quality? I am not the type to blame video games for violence or music lyrics for attitudes. Yet popular girls agreed that shows like *Gossip Girl, 90210,* and the *Real Housewives* series make bitchiness seem glamorous. The rush of reality shows that have become an inescapable part of regular programming highlight the notion that to stand out, even as a villain, could make you famous. Fame equals celebrity. Celebrity equals perceived popularity. Bitchiness is viewed as an acceptable strategy if it gets you what you want.

Even the word "bitch" has gained increasing acceptance in the public sphere. Broadcast TV networks can air it without repercussion; the word has even hit the *Today* show. Books with "bitch" in their titles surface on best-seller lists. Celebrities like Paris Hilton openly call their friends bitches. Hollywood diva tales are ubiquitous, and what is a diva if not a euphemism for a bitch? We have come to accept diva behavior among celebrities as not only expected but, sometimes, deserved. This attitude has trickled down quickly to the student world. When I asked a popular sophomore in Maine what characteristics made someone popular, she answered, "Shopping at only designer stores and Hollister, dating older boys, being known for rumors and sex—and being a bitch to other people."

During the first month I followed Whitney, I asked her about the influence of media like *Gossip Girl* and *Mean Girls*. She answered, "Those *definitely* make it desirable to be the mean girl. Even though those girls get what's coming to them, it still isn't enough to make them seem bad. I have been three-way-call attacked, I have been kicked out of my lunch table for stupid things, and I have had friends go after guys I said I liked. That scene when they are all walking down the hall like they rule the world is definitely true. They are all pretty, skinny, worshipped, get all the guys, get away with anything, and *seemingly* have no cares in the world."

Whitney unwittingly broached another reason why popular people can be mean: Often, they get away with it. Unpopular kids might be too intimidated to retaliate, wannabes might tolerate and support the cruelty, and even teachers and administrators might be less likely to punish a girl for meanness if she's popular. (Also, relational aggression can be difficult to punish because the meanness is indirect or the identity of the perpetrator isn't obvious.) Some studies even report that students reward populars who engage in relational aggression, because mean kids can become more popular over time.

This behavior isn't limited to girls. Several popular boys told me about utilizing relational aggression. A Missouri eighth grader who said he was popular because "I throw a lot of parties, and I'm fashionable, and a gossiper," added that his group "usually knows things before most people, and we usually write them on our Facebook statuses to humiliate our enemies."

When I asked a popular boy from Arkansas how people at his high school treated students who were different from others, he said, "We crushed their dreams. We had a kid who wanted to be cool but he wore eyeliner, so we invited him to a party and got him drunk and pushed him into a fire and then some guys peed on him when he passed out. He moved the next week. [Supposedly due to technicalities, charges against the aggressors were dropped.] We cut off a Pentecostal girl's hair and hid her skirt in gym class, just because we were all Baptist and thought Pentecostals were weird. We felt like it was our right to do whatever we pleased. Part of being cool was uniformity and anything that isn't part of our hive mind needs to be mocked."

Granted, populars are certainly not the only students who are mean. Many teens told me about members of various other groups dumping kids in trash cans *Glee*-style, shouting insulting racist or weight-related comments, and cyber-bullying. Violence and burning books have not disappeared from American high schools, despite anti-bullying campaigns. Female athletes described teammates who gang up on newcomers they don't like, "accidentally" causing black eyes, sprained ankles, nosebleeds, or concussions at practice until the target quits the team.

Whereas being likeable involves simple gestures of friendliness, the fight to get and keep perceived popularity is a competition. Contenders must strategize, wheeling and dealing their way to the top, all the while watching their backs. Their maneuvering may involve realigning relationships, finding followers, or casting out less loyal members to shift their support base. From the populars' perspective, meanness can be an effective way to execute these tactics. Meanness is a language that allows a girl to enjoy her popularity, protect her status, wield her influence, display her seemingly invincible power, and force peers to recognize her dominance. It is a technique that some students believe is necessary to manipulate the confusing social world in school. I don't aim to defend meanness, but rather to explain it from a less common view. From the populars' perspective, the question might not be "Why are we mean?" but rather, "How can we afford not to be?"

BLUE, HAWAII | THE GAMER

In leadership class, which Blue took only because the student council had appointed him the school Webmaster, the substitute teacher was talking to two class officers. Other students crowded around the teacher's desk.

"Nobody could ever possibly take over Google," the substitute said.

Blue looked up from his iPhone. From his seat in the back of the room he called out, "Hey, you know, Facebook has the potential to take over Google."

"Shut up," the senior class president said. "You're stupid."

Wow, you're not a critical thinker at all, are you, Blue thought. He persisted, wanting to share a provocative concept. "No, just listen. Facebook is the only place on the Internet where people use their real names. And Facebook is gathering more new users a day than any other site right now. And what they have that Google needs is personal info on each of those people," Blue explained. "Google only has what you type into the search box. If Facebook were to start something like Ad-Words, it would be more effective at selling you things, thus generating much more money than Google, and therefore being worth more in the future, ruling the Internet, Facebook being the hub."

The substitute looked down her nose. "I was on the Internet before you were even born," she said. "You can Google anybody's name and find all their info."

The students laughed at Blue. "How could Facebook possibly take over Google?!" they said.

The sub continued, "Sorry, I just don't see the point of chatting with people you don't know."

"That's not even what I'm talking about," Blue protested. "That's such a small portion of the Internet. You're thinking too closed-minded."

One of the students butted in again. "Okay, sorry, Mark, we're not talking about whatever it is you do on the Internet. We're talking about *normal* people."

Blue should have been used to this sort of treatment by now, but it still angered him. Although he was generally reticent, he was not shy about vocalizing his opinions in class, no matter how unpopular they might be. As he put it, "I'm different from everybody else in almost every respect and I'm not afraid to talk about it." Blue was that student who played devil's advocate, who enjoyed defending viewpoints that dissented from the majority. Often, he could appreciate both sides equally, and therefore found it interesting to argue whichever one was underrepresented. In some classes, like AP Government, his classmates and teacher liked to engage him in debates. In other classes, students told him to shut up.

A few nights later, Blue, Stewart, Ty, and Jackson were stargazing at a local playground. The 2 A.M. sky was so clear they could see the faint cloud across the area that Blue called the edge of the galaxy. They lay on top of the jungle gym and talked about girls and the usual intro-spective subjects they discussed when they were sleepy but not ready to go home.

While the others conversed, Blue thought, *I wish I had a close friend.* Blue couldn't even trust Jackson completely. Initially, gaming together had cemented their friendship. When Jackson and Blue, who had won a few thousand dollars in gaming tournaments, teamed up junior year for their first tournament together, they not only lost, but, worse, they lost to noobs (inexperienced newcomers). Jackson refused to speak to Blue for three months.

From the top of the jungle gym, Stewart lazily turned to Blue. "Would you rather have stayed in the closet?" Actually, most people didn't know Blue was gay. Sometimes students didn't even believe him, because, as they insisted, he wasn't effeminate and didn't appear stereotypically gay. He came across as tough, having been in several fights (always to defend people he cared about).

Blue was still working up the courage to converse with Jimmy, whose sexuality was unclear. If Blue had a puppy crush on Jimmy, however, he was thoroughly infatuated with Nate, a senior at Jackson's school. The best gamer on Blue's tournament team, Nate had quick reaction times, superb aim, and a rough style of play. Blue believed there was a chance that Nate was gay because Nate knew Blue liked him yet was still nice to him. On a recent, rare group outing to the movies, Blue happened to sit next to him. Halfway through the movie, Nate's arm brushed Blue's on the armrest they shared. Blue could feel his body heat.

"No," Blue answered Stewart, "I don't have any regrets, because otherwise I would have never been satisfied with myself or with my relationships with other people."

"It's not like you talk about girls or anything, anyway," said Stewart, teasing him. "It wouldn't have made any difference."

But to Blue, it *did*. While Blue knew that his credibility among his friends had dropped along with Arwing's demise as a gaming club, Jackson had told him point-blank that he took Blue even less seriously because of his sexuality. This admission hurt Blue more than he let on. Now Ty and Stewart ganged up on him more frequently, mocking his alternative perspectives, advanced technological gear, hyperorganized bedroom, and aspirations to compete in a Modern Warfare tournament in Sweden next summer.

As Blue lay on top of the jungle gym, staring toward the edge of the galaxy, he realized now that they probably weren't targeting him because he was gay, specifically. They targeted him because he was *different*.

ELI, VIRGINIA | THE NERD

The summer before Eli's senior year, he was one of sixty students selected to attend a three-week intensive academy known informally as Spanish camp. The campers attended classes, gave presentations, did homework and projects, and were forbidden to speak English. Eli had viewed Spanish camp as "a second chance at starting school again." He said, "In my high school, everyone already knows who I am, so it's hard to branch out. So I figured these people don't know anything about me and I could be who I wanted, outgoing and friendly with everyone."

The first three days of the academy were exceedingly awkward, even by Eli's standards, as the campers tried to get to know each other while speaking only Spanish. But by the fourth day, Eli felt as if he'd known the campers for years. By the end of the session, Eli said he had made "the best friends of my life. I know them better and they know me better than my high school friends. I'll even call some of them family. It was refreshing to meet people who actually cared. I've never met people like that before." The campers gave him the Nicest Guy superlative award. Eli called those three weeks the "number one best experience of my life." On the last day of camp, Debra, the only other attendee from Eli's school, asked, "So are you going to talk more in school now? This is completely different from the Eli I know!"

Once he returned home, for much of August, Eli IMed with camp friends until two in the morning. He met up with a few fellow campers a couple of times. When school started, the contact dwindled, chats tapered off, and enthusiasm waned.

In the fall, Eli and four other campers convened for a mini-reunion, sprawling out on couches at a local mall. Eli had been excited to see them, but now that they were together, he felt a familiar sinking feeling of being excluded. Whenever he began to speak, someone would cut him off after approximately five words. They talked about Spanish class. "Oh, yeah! In my Sp—" Eli began, then was cut off. They talked about their high school football teams. Eli asked, "Do you know if th—" and was cut off. They talked about Virginia. Eli started to say, "Have you ever noticed how—" and, again, was cut off. Eventually he gave up. Half-listening to the conversation, he stared ahead with the same fixed face he adopted when he was bored while driving.

Eli left with Raj, his closest friend from camp. "You are so awkward," Raj said when they were out of the others' earshot.

"What do you mean?" Eli asked. He hadn't expected a camp friend to say so.

"We were all sitting there talking and you didn't say a word! You were just sitting with your legs crossed. You were even in the center!"

"Yeah, well, every time I tried to say something, I got cut off, so—"

"Whatever," Raj interrupted. "You need to talk more. Like what do you do at parties?"

"I've never been to a party," Eli answered. No one had ever invited him.

"We need to change your social life. Lesson one: Talk more. You are going to have a party."

"Hahaha, no I'm not."

"Well, you need to start going to parties."

Eli gave an exasperated sigh. "What am I going to do? Invite myself?"

"Start by talking to people more in school," Raj suggested.

"Okay, I've been going to school with these people for years and their opinion of me isn't going to change if I try to start talking to them again."

"Just talk about something. Do you watch any sports?"

"No."

"What about movies?"

"My taste in movies is different." Eli preferred thrillers and Hitchcock-era black-and-white films.

"Music?" Raj tried again.

"Okay, so I'm just supposed to walk up to someone and go, 'Hey, what do you think of so-and-so?'"

"Yeah, why not?"

"You're ridiculous."

"Just *talk* to people."

"Okay, you have no idea, do you?" Frustrated, Eli was on the verge of tears. This felt like one of those conversations instructing him on how to be "normal." Eli got enough of that at home. "I try. Like I say, 'Hey, what's up' to people in the halls and stuff, but—"

"It's not the same. You need people you can depend on."

"I depend on myself. It's high school. I'll be fine," Eli said as he pulled up to Raj's house.

Eli thought about the conversation for the rest of the night. He explained later, "The fact that he was telling me that my social life was a failure wasn't necessarily true, but the fact that it holds such importance to him bothers me. I don't think being on the social scene is really that important."

Everyone else seemed to think so. Even Eli's mother had been jubilant that he was leaving the house to meet with camp friends. Eli was convinced his mother thought he was "nerdy," he said, "because she always says, 'Honey, why don't you ever go out on a Friday night? No normal teenager sits at home with his mother.'"

Eli's mother had played the 'normal' card for years, even when he was small. "Honey!" she said, "normal guys don't study maps, do they?!" "Normal guys don't spend that much time coloring!" "Normal guys don't study on weekends." "Normal guys don't watch cooking shows."

Sometimes Eli believed his mother was embarrassed by him. "I swear, my mom thinks if I do one thing differently than the average person, I'm weird," Eli said later. "It's like she thinks I'm a freak or something. No matter what I do, it's not 'normal' enough for her."

Eli loved Academic Bowl more than anything else at school: the anticipation of the questions, the slap of the buzzer, the pride when he answered correctly and swiftly. Sure, sometimes teammates told him to take it easy and stop "freaking out on the buzzer," but that was because he occasionally was so eager that he slammed the button frenetically.

Radiating excitement, Eli sat at the ready, nearly bouncing with anticipation for his first Academic Bowl practice of the year. Because they had only eight buzzers, most students shared with a partner. Eli got his own buzzer because he used it the most.

About halfway through the practice, the first geography question came up. The teacher began, "The Galapag—"

Eli buzzed in. "Ecuador!" he shouted. He couldn't contain his wide, childlike grin.

The teacher declared, game-show-host style, "Yes!" He then turned to the rest of the room. "Pay attention to what happens here with the geography questions." For every one, Eli buzzed two or three words into the question and answered correctly. The rest of the team marveled at his speed. "How do you even know this stuff?!" they asked. To their astonishment, Eli nailed five answers in a row.

At Academic Bowl practices, Eli was in his element. (He liked competitions, too, but he became so nervous that he would get the shakes.) When he watched game shows like *Jeopardy* and *Cash Cab* at home, he answered most questions accurately, but no one saw him do it. Showcasing his talent in front of people validated that the seemingly obscure trivia he picked up was a way to "actually make myself useful," he said. At practice, he was an object of wonder, not derision.

For the first time in recent memory, Eli's school was an Academic Bowl contender. Strattville won a fall match against four other schools, one of which was a perennially dominant team. Eli's team advanced to the tournament's final round, which would take place in April.

In classes, Eli tried to avoid appearing like a know-it-all, but sometimes his teachers made it difficult for him to do so. With a few exceptions, either they seemed to look down on him because he was so clearly unpopular, or they treated him as if he were superior because he was a straight-A student.

Sometimes classmates came to their own conclusions. Recently, Eli had decided to read a Spanish novel for fun. Several students—and two teachers—wondered aloud why he was reading in Spanish when he didn't have to. He was poring over it in physics one day when an Academic Bowl teammate said, "Wait, is that book in Spanish?"

"Yeah."

"Do you have to read it or something?"

"No, it's just for fun."

"Nerd!"

In Chinese, the teacher passed out grade reports. Immediately, students asked Eli how he did. "I'm not going to tell you," he said, shoving the paper into his binder without looking at it. A few students tried to pry the paper out, but Eli stuffed the binder into his backpack.

"Come on, what'd you get?" someone prodded.

"I bet it was a ninety-nine," someone else chimed in.

Eli didn't respond.

"A hundred?"

Eli busied himself with math homework. On the one hand, he was mildly amused that he had this power over his classmates; he had something they wanted. That didn't happen very often. On the other hand, he wished they would leave him alone. Except with close friends, Eli mostly preferred "brief, impersonal conversation."

"Come on, just tell us."

"C," Eli said.

"You're lying."

"D," Eli answered. "F."

"Come on!"

"B-, B, B+, A-, A."

"Okay, now I believe you."

"A+, C+, D+, E."

"Why don't you just tell us?"

"It's not relevant," Eli said.

He was sure nothing good could come out of answering truthfully. Increasingly, students were also bugging Eli about where he planned to apply to college. He wasn't offended that they asked, but he was wary about sharing that information. If he named some of his choices, he knew people would ask him why he wasn't applying to, say, Harvard. If he named the more prestigious schools on his list, he was afraid they would think he was a snob. Usually, Eli answered honestly: "I want to go as far away from here as possible."

Students looked at him strangely when he said that. "Why?!" they asked.

"Because I hate it here," Eli would answer, and left it at that. He never told anyone the schools on his list besides Westcoast University— Berkeley, UNC-Chapel Hill, William and Mary, and Wake Forest among them.

Eli hoped classmates didn't interpret his answer to mean that he didn't like them. "That's not necessarily true," he later explained. "I know everyone always talks about how senior year is 'the greatest year of your life,' but I just want to get through it as quickly as possible."

After school, Eli looked at his Chinese grade report. He had earned a 101.

REGAN, GEORGIA | THE WEIRD GIRL

In first period, Regan heard a guy say, "Man, you such a faggot."

Regan was so incensed that her hands quavered. She hated that word. It didn't matter that no one in the room knew she was gay. "What did you just call him?!"

The student repeated himself.

"Pick a different word," Regan said. He did.

"What's wrong with that word?" another student asked.

Regan was fed up with the ignorance of people at Johnson. She had heard them use that word—and "That's gay" as an insult—too often. "Let me tell you a little story. Back in the day, they used to burn witches. You know that, right? Have you also heard that 'faggot' really means 'a bundle of sticks'? See, when women were being burned at the stake for witchcraft, sometimes law officials and townspeople would round up the gay men and women and use them as *faggots* to light the stake. So when you call someone a faggot, you're saying that person deserves to be burned alive. So stop."

Her explanation caused an uproar. "The Bible says it's wrong, so it's wrong," a guy said. Another student stood up and gave him a high five.

"The Bible also says not to eat shrimp, so I hope you don't like seafood," Regan retorted, still trembling with anger.

"If someone a faggot, he a faggot," the high-fiver said. "S'okay to call someone out on what they is."

"That means I can call you the N-word then, right?" Regan asked.

"Well, you could, but then me and you is gonna have a problem."

"But that's just calling you out on what you are, isn't it?" she pressed. Regan was glad she stood up for herself, but as class began, the discussion ebbed without resolution.

Regan felt better during second period, when her class finished reading *Oedipus the King*, one of her favorites. Even though she knew the end lines by heart, she still got what she called "literary chills" when, once Oedipus finally sees the truth, he is blind.

But the homophobic slur stuck with her throughout the day. Outside of school, Regan's friends, family, and theater castmates were wholly supportive of her and her sexuality. Inside school, where she spent most of her waking hours, she hated having to hide her gayness. Regan regularly volunteered at a local LGBT youth center, which was a bright spot in her life. The stories of the kids at the center sometimes broke her heart.

When Regan vented to Crystal, who had come out only recently, how much it crushed her that gay people didn't have the same rights as heteros, Crystal asked, "Is there anyone fighting for those rights?"

"Well, yeah, of course there are people fighting," Regan replied. "The Human Rights Campaign, for instance. I donate to them. And gay people have marches, petitions, sit-ins, and things like that. They say gay is the new black. And it is. It's the new civil rights movement."

Regan later explained, "Being gay sucks because you're forced into silence. People assume that straight people fall in love and gay people have sex. Even my mother says, 'I don't understand why gay people have to come out. It's none of anyone's business what you do in bed,' as if being gay is a fetish or something and only pertains to the bedroom. It's hard to be gay at school mostly because I don't want to lie." She tried never to lie.

Regan didn't have the energy to constantly battle homophobia. One day she was dawdling in a classroom while her friend Josiah discussed video games with an assistant principal. Regan sighed dramatically a few times, bored because the topic precluded her from participating in the conversation.

Finally the administrator said facetiously, "Well, let's talk about something that Davis can talk about. Let's see, what kind of muffins

do you like? You seem like the kind of girl who would like muffins."
He smirked at her. He knew about Crystal. Regan laughed awkwardly.

The administrator turned to Josiah and said, "What, what? Is 'muffin' a code word for something that I'm unaware of? Am I going to lose my job?"

"Noo, nope, noo," Josiah replied sarcastically.

After the administrator left the room, Regan said to Josiah, "I was tempted to say, 'Chocolate.'"

A few weeks later, the boy who had uttered the word "faggot" approached Regan. He told her that he was gaming online and someone typed, "You're a fag." The boy grinned. "Man, I was about to type it back and everything, but then I remembered you told me not to say that word, so I didn't. I called him a bastard instead."

Regan smiled to herself. The victory was small, but it was a victory nonetheless.

WHEN THE FIRST FACEBOOK message came in, Regan laughed it off. "Oh my God," she said. Crystal, who was hanging out in the kitchen, looked up.

"You won't believe this," Regan said. "You know my friend Theodore at school? He sent me a message: 'Funny story . . . well, maybe not! I totally called your archenemy Mandy your name! She was PISSED.'"

As soon as Regan got to school the next morning, she found Theodore in the art room. "So . . . *what?*" she asked.

"It was ridiculous," Theodore said.

Tess, a mutual acquaintance, walked into the room. "Oh, are you telling her about Mandy?" she asked, looking thrilled to be part of the gossip. Her eyes widened. "It was unbelievable. I walked in after the whole thing happened, and she was still yelling and ranting, her hands flying all over the place. I was like, 'What the hell happened?' When I heard it, I couldn't even believe it."

"Okay, what happened?" Regan asked.

"First of all," Theodore started, "I didn't even know about the Wyatt thing. I wasn't even aware that she—"

Tess broke in: "When he told me he called her your name, I was like, 'Do you know what you just did?' I had to explain the whole thing to him." Apparently Mandy had acted as if Theodore obviously should have known about the Mandy-Wyatt-Regan triangle.

"I saw her sitting in the auditorium," Theodore said. "And all I saw was blonde, curly hair." Regan had recently dyed her hair blonde.

"Oh!" Regan said. "She was sitting? Thank God. I thought she was standing up, and I was like, 'Oh no, you did *not* mistake her ass for mine.'"

"No, no," Theodore laughed. "So I went up to her, and I was like, 'Hey buddy, haven't seen you in a minute.' She turned around and gave me the look of death. I was like, 'Oh, sorry, I thought you were Davis.' And then white girl got ghetto. I mean *ghetto*. She was putting her neck into it and everything, snapping and all. She was like, 'Don't ever make that mistake again! I am *not* that bitch. I am *not* that lesbian. I am *not* annoying.' She went on and on!"

"She called me *annoying*? And a *bitch*? What have I ever done to her?"

Theodore went on. "Then she just started going off. Screaming. Yelling. Francesca was trying to get Mandy to calm down, but she was flipping out. She was so loud that people in other rows were turning around. I was like, 'I don't even know you,' you know?"

Regan fumed. "That is the most unprofessional thing I have ever heard in my life. And why did she call me out on being gay? That has nothing to do with her, and it has even less to do with why she hates me!"

"She's just pissed because she got your sloppy seconds," Tess said.

"Yeah," said Theodore. "Clearly she's just jealous."

"But she shouldn't be!" Regan yelled. "If anyone should hate anyone, *I* should hate *her*. She's the one who stole my boyfriend! But I don't hate her! I mean, I don't *like* her. But I certainly don't hate her or talk trash about her. I can't believe it. Part of me wants to say something to her." She rolled her eyes. "I've gotta get to class," she said, glancing at the clock. "But thanks for the story."

Regan was more frustrated than deeply offended. "I'm completely blown away," she said later. "I'm aggravated that someone would be that rude and inconsiderate. Not to mention, I thought we were over that. So that puts me on edge because that means there's someone in close proximity to me who considers me an enemy. And I think it's unfair that I should have to feel uncomfortable at my job. It amazes me to no end how immature and ridiculous people act—especially *grown* people. You would think that someone in her thirties would have a little more sense than a typical teenager."

Mandy wasn't a typical teenager. Neither was Regan. Or Wyatt, Theodore, or Tess. All of them were James Johnson teachers. At twenty-four, Regan, an English teacher, might have been the youngest of the bunch, but she was experienced enough to realize that the same school setting that stifled unique students could make teachers feel badly about being cafeteria fringe too.

TEACHER CLIQUES

All of the James Johnson characters in Regan's story—Wyatt, an English teacher; Mandy and Francesca, history teachers; even the couple that hooked up in the parking lot—are teachers or administrators, unless I specifically identified them as students.

In too many ways, the Johnson staff adopted the same behaviors that schools often disapprove of in their students. Teachers were cliquey, and divided by department and race, a practice the administration did not discourage. In fact, at the staff assembly on the first day of school, the principal told the teachers to sit with their department and to come up with a name for their group. (Before Regan and her colleagues even pulled their chairs together to discuss it, the African-American English teachers had already decided on the name of a black celebrity.)

Teachers gossiped about each other on a daily basis—and, worse, they gossiped about students. One teacher asked Regan whether she taught a particular student; when Regan said she did, the teacher sniped, "She's a cunt." Regan said to me, "Being a high school teacher is the same as being a high school student. Teachers act just as badly as the students do."

As a reporter, I was surprised to learn that some of the adults who are supposed to be role models, mentors, and above all, educators openly form exclusive cliques themselves. With *names.*

Several teachers hailing from an Illinois junior high school, for example, told me about the ruling clique there. The group called itself the PIGS, for People In Good Standing. They invited certain teachers—young, good-looking, fun, outgoing, "usually the cheerleader or good-old-boy types"—to a social event or two, and would let them know if they had "PIGS potential." If they didn't make the cut, the PIGS no longer invited them to happy hours, weekend outings, or school-event after-parties that they discussed in front of uninvited teachers.

When the PIGS got together outside of school, they apparently spent much of their time making fun of other teachers and playing drinking games. In school, they were worse. They ostracized non-PIGS, sometimes calling them derogatory names or turning other colleagues against them. When an older teacher's beloved dog died, they stole a photo of the dog and built a mock shrine to it, pretending to mourn. They persuaded the principal to place a teacher on remediation, a probationary process for low-quality teachers, during her last year before retirement because they claimed she wasn't working collaboratively with some of the PIGS members. The devastated teacher, who had worked for the district for thirty-five years, had won several awards for her teaching. A non-PIGS teacher explained how the PIGS made her feel. "I remember thinking that this is how I felt in high school. It was so strange to get those feelings again, self-conscious, unsure of myself, flawed," she said. "Then I was angry. I should not be feeling this way. I'm an adult, a professional, someone who teaches children to not feel this way."

Barb, one of the teachers whom the PIGS often berated, left the school because the PIGS' behavior affected the services the school was supposed to provide to students. As the "at risk" teacher, Barb worked with all of the teachers to help struggling students. She relied on the other teachers' lesson plans and materials to teach study strategies to the students. When the PIGS took over the eighth-grade team, the team stopped providing Barb with copies of tests and quizzes. She confronted the teachers during a meeting to ask why they had suddenly stopped furnishing these essential materials. The team didn't respond.

After the meeting, sixth- and seventh-grade teachers who were PIGS also stopped providing materials to Barb. The principal, who was chummy with the PIGS, refused to intervene. "It was the most disturbing thing I ever saw professionally," Barb said. "If you were not a part of their clique, they didn't help you, which meant you might struggle with a student who was at risk of failing. Some of the cliquey teachers would go as far as to exaggerate stories about you so that you felt isolated by the remainder of your peers, causing some teachers to quit education altogether or retreat into their classrooms where they eventually burnt out."

High school, middle school, and elementary school staff around the country described the ways colleagues' behavior mirrored that of the popular students. Evan, a teacher who founded the first Gay-Straight Alliance in Texas, annually organizes a Day of Silence at his magnet school, during which participating students do not speak in "recognition of the silence many LGBT suffer in keeping their sexual orientation hidden." Even though the Day of Silence is a school-wide event approved by the principal, other administrators and teachers openly have called it "Stupid Gay Day" and have emailed Evan protests expressing disgust about "your gay group."

Teachers in various states described cliques divided by religion, race, and/or seniority. A Minnesota teacher said, "The labels are the 'veterans' and the 'young staff,' and the veterans really let you know that you're not a veteran teacher and that as a young teacher you should know your place until you put in your years."

Because of these divisions, teachers can come to dread the faculty lounge—which one teacher called "the lion's den"—just as much as students might dread the cafeteria. Eliza, who quit teaching partly because of teacher clique behavior, said that some teacher cliques at her Virginia school didn't allow certain people to sit with them at lunch. "There were the 'haves' and the 'have nots.' If the table went silent when you sat down, they didn't like you, and made it clear you were not welcome. I felt like I was on a season of *Survivor*. I didn't know who I could trust," Eliza said. Disheartened, she and other young teachers would "hole up in our classrooms and eat by ourselves. We would get frustrated with the older bunch because they had lost sight of why we were all teachers in the first place. It was kind of ridiculous. Aren't we all adults who should be setting good examples for our students? And the faculty meetings were hilarious. The members of the departments would be clamoring to sit together and save seats. Situations like this made me want to run away as far as I could from teaching."

Even in some schools in which administrators have funded programs to try to combat bullying or hostilities among student cliques, educators are engaging in those same social behaviors. Teachers told me about secretaries who gossip about other teachers' private appointments with the principal, departmental stereotypes (such as "wacky" fine arts teachers), and coaches of certain sports who get away with more than other staff members do. They said that other teachers make fun of their online photos or simply give, as one California teacher put it, "the distinct impression that I'm simply not cool or smart or cultured enough." They talked about coworkers picking on them in order to impress other, cooler teachers.

A counselor in Virginia described an intimidating drama teacher who wielded power by controlling access to the auditorium. A Tennessee special education teacher said she is frequently excluded by other teachers, "as if I am special ed. also." Teachers even discussed, in their words, "mean-girlish" teachers and "teacher bullies."

Often teachers are pitted against each other in direct competition for teacher bonuses, giving further support to Eliza's *Survivor* comparison. In some states, schools allocate various bonus amounts based on performance, but because each school has a limited pool of bonus money, one teacher's gain is another's loss. This system, like grade curving, does nothing to help foster a cooperative working environment. A Southwestern teacher told me, "I have seen teachers try to get students transferred into another teacher's classroom or even call or email a teacher with a 'pressing matter' during that teacher's evaluation. No one becomes a teacher because they plan to get rich, but a couple hundred dollars can make a teacher forget the reason they became a teacher in the first place."

Just as student cliques can affect a student's academic life, teacher cliques can impact an educator's professional life. Teachers told me about cliques palming off extra lunch assignments, bus duties, and chaperone responsibilities onto younger coworkers eager to please. "I have seen cliques destroy some teachers. But the worst part about cliques among teachers isn't about teachers at all," said Phoebe, who taught in Arizona and Kansas, and blames teacher cliques for driving her to take a break from teaching. "Cliques can create a hostile environment that changes the entire climate of the school and directly impacts student learning. If teachers are uncomfortable in their own school, they will pass on their uncertainties or negative attitude to students. That is simply unacceptable. The students are the ones who suffer. Teachers are supposed to play for the same team. Educating students should always be the number one goal. Unfortunately cliques change the priorities for some teachers."

Students know this. Several students told me about hostilities among teachers without my asking them. They overhear teachers talking about each other; one senior, for example, told me about the "teacher gossip frenzy" at his school. Some teens justify their own behavior by saying that teachers sometimes act even younger than students do. The kids aren't wrong.

To students who worry that people never outgrow cliquish behavior, it's important to point out that many—perhaps most—people do. Adult cliques are more likely to surface among teachers than among non-school professionals because it may be harder to grow out of school-child habits when one works in a school. Outside of school, adults—like Regan—are appreciated much more for their individuality. The school setting, specifically, can have this distressing effect on people.

Teachers who are members of cliques rationalize them by saying they need a select group of coworkers to complain to, that they are not exclusive, or that they are left out of other colleagues' cliques. Tiffani, an Arkansas teacher, is a member of a teacher clique that calls itself a "secret sorority" and goes by the name TADA: Teachers Against Dumbasses. TADA meets occasionally after school to "get together over margaritas and vent about the administration, discipline, and anything else we deem necessary. We've even taken weekend trips, like to Memphis, where we hit all the bars on Beale Street!" Tiffani said. TADA claims to be inclusive because members put up signs in the copy room (TADA TO-NIGHT! 4:30 AT [THE BAR]!), but Tiffani admitted, "Most of us have been personally invited. A core group of us really stay together." And wear pink TADA T-shirts. "When the students ask about our T-shirts," Tiffani said, "we all say, 'Oh, it's just a teacher sorority!'"

Fall

Why Quirk Theory Works

Chapter 4

IN THE SHADOW OF THE FREAK TREE

W hen I asked students at one high school to describe their classmates' labels, their attitudes toward those groups varied considerably— except in one instance. No matter the label of the person responding, the descriptions of the students who hung out by the "freak tree" were similar. "Eccentric, over-the-top, and pretty perverted," said a "newsie" devoted to the student paper. "The sci-fi convention; the weird ones interested in anime, magic cards, and anything most middle and elementary students are also interested in," said a student government officer. "The *otaku*/odd person group is bizarre," said a senior girl. "Socially awkward and totally irritating," said a geek. "They're completely different. Average people are weirded out by the tree people," said a loner.

So I decided to talk to one of them. On most weekdays, Amy, a senior, spends time before school, during lunch, and sometimes after school with the tree people. She says that they are a mix of "freaky kids, drama kids, white kids, and slightly emo kids. And almost all of them are not afraid to speak their minds and be loud, proud, and wacky about it." For fun, the tree people like to go to the park to "DRAT," their term for massive team battles in which they shoot each other with nerf guns or engage in close combat with plastic swords or PVC pipes. To others, DRAT may look like chaos, but the skirmishes are regulated by a set of predetermined rules and can be framed by more well-known games like Capture the Flag or King of the Hill. "If you look at this game, it seems immature," Amy says, "but it's really fun and a great stress reliever. Everyone finishes the game relatively happy, even if they lost."

Amy says she fits in with the tree people because she is a self-proclaimed "anime freak" who founded her school's anime club and reads a lot of manga. Some classmates call her a weirdo because she doesn't follow trends, whether they involve clothes, behavior, or interests. Others call her a freak because her jokes can be "out there" and because she feels more comfortable using words she made up to replace curses and other phrases.

As a member of a school sports team and the band, Amy could hang out with other groups. Sometimes she does; she'll have a sleepover with her AP friends or go out to eat with teammates. But she always comes back to the freak tree. Her rationale reminds me of her description of DRAT: It looks juvenile from the outside, but in reality it serves as a haven of comfort, acceptance, and stress relief. "The tree guys are more fun. When I'm with the tree guys, I'm never bored, whether there's a wacky conversation about a TV show, an anime, or what would happen if the school was taken over by zombies, or maybe someone's doing a mock fight or reenacting a movie scene," she says. "When I'm with these guys, I don't have to think about school or anything else that stresses me out. I can just relax, have fun, and act like a kid for once."

When I ask Amy how the tree people feel about students calling their gathering place "the freak tree," she says they usually laugh about it. "We know we're weirdos, but we pretty much don't care. Even if all the other kids are staring at us and thinking we're freaks, it doesn't matter. We're having fun, all of us, together. At the tree, it doesn't feel like you have to restrain yourself from what you say or do. One of my friends dresses up in clothes that look like something out of an anime," she says. "In fact, if you do something that's just the right crazy, the others might join in. One time some people started this thing where they clapped in front of themselves and then in back constantly, and we had a line of about ten people doing it in time with each other. It looked crazy, but it was funny. Yeah, it can be a little off-putting being known as the freak tree, but at least we aren't afraid to have fun."

When Amy goes to college, in her free time she hopes to join a Masters Water Polo team and continue practicing kendo and aikido. She plans to keep writing fiction. Someday, she says, "I can see myself as a CEO of a local company that helps my state's economy by helping small businesses. I want to help out my community. That job appeals to my interests in business, marketing, advertising, and management, and I may be able to help my friends from all groups find jobs."

It's hard not to wonder what Amy's classmates—the same ones who dismissed her group as bizarre, perverted, irritating, and "completely different"—would think of her if they got to know her. If they let go of some of their image concerns, some of those students would probably benefit from tree people pastimes that let them blow off steam by recapturing their childhood. Some of them would probably appreciate "just the right crazy." It's hard not to wonder whether, if those classmates took the time to get to know the tree people, they might not think they were so bizarre after all.

IN THE MINDS OF their peers, too often students become caricatures of themselves. They are reduced to stick figures, save a "weird" feature that others blow up into mythic proportions and then use as an excuse to dismiss them; they gather by the freak tree, for example, dye their hair pink, or unself-consciously display their emotions. Throughout the course of reporting *The Geeks Shall Inherit the Earth,* I encountered many fantastic kids considered weird. To me, they seemed to be the type of students whom classmates were too quick to judge, students who have so much more to offer than is evident during a forty-minute class or a quick lunchtime glimpse. To me, they seemed to be the type of students whom others should be proud to befriend.

Suzanne, one of those students, is not popular. A senior at a Georgia private school, she wears band T-shirts and grungy jeans that kids make fun of. Classmates tease her for spending a disproportionate amount of time in the art room. They don't necessarily dislike Suzanne, but they don't invite her out on weekends. In seventh grade, classmates posted nasty messages online about her. "Whore," they called her. "Slut." "The ugliest girl." Suzanne was bewildered. She was thirteen. She had never kissed a boy.

Today, some students refer to Suzanne as the artsy girl because it seems like she's always off doing art projects. Some call her an indie kid because she doesn't listen to the same music they do. They continue to exclude her. She just doesn't seem to think like everybody else.

Laney, an eighth grader in Indiana, is not popular. She's the kind of girl who dances randomly in public, occasionally gives human names to inanimate objects, and once tried licking her cat just to see how it tasted. (She concluded, "It tastes like cat!") Her friends tell her that some people don't talk to her because they're too embarrassed to be seen interacting with someone that far down the social chain.

Students have called Laney creepy because she wears dark clothing and has "a death glare." Many have asked her if she is emo, but she says she's "too weird to be emo." She just doesn't seem to behave like everybody else.

Allie, a sophomore in northern California, is not popular. Students have picked on her since elementary school. Most recently they jeered at her in the cafeteria line because she unabashedly wore a black felt bunny hat with long floppy ears that grazed her shoulder blades. Allie watches anime frequently and plays Warhammer 40K, a miniature tabletop war game set in a fantasy world.

Classmates give her the same label they give other students who differ from the in crowd: They call her a freak. She just doesn't seem to interact like everybody else.

Flor, a junior in Oklahoma, is not popular. She never plays sports or runs around with other kids. Students call her a slacker because she turns in assignments at the last minute and she dropped out of school for a while. They make fun of her ethnicity. At school, a white boy asked her recently why she didn't "act more Mexican."

"How are Mexicans supposed to act?" Flor asked.

"You're supposed to wear a lot of makeup and have a boyfriend, wear lots of jewelry, and speak Spanish all the time." This upset Flor, who is proud of her heritage. It didn't upset her nearly as much, however, as when people told her "go back to where you came from." Flor was born in the United States. She just doesn't seem to assimilate like everybody else.

Suzanne, The Artsy Indie

There's a reason that Suzanne wears plain, grungy clothes to school. She spends as much time as she can in the art room, where she paints. Most of Suzanne's impressive senior portfolio consists of watercolor, a difficult medium. "I love watercolor because it's not very precise," she says. "Your lines may not be exactly straight, your colors a little strange, but it still looks really cool."

She favors indie music because she identifies with it. "It's really good music that was disregarded by the mainstream. I guess I kind of relate to the bands, feeling left out by my peers," she says. "What's fantastic about the indie or DIY subculture is that people are doing it without the help of major record companies or a traditional art school education. These people have different ideas that have the power to change art, music, and fashion forever."

When I check in with Suzanne again after high school graduation, I learn that her artwork led to a pre-college summer job as a wardrobe assistant on an independent film. When the wardrobe head quit, Suzanne replaced her—at age eighteen.

Laney, The Creepy Girl

When someone calls Laney weird, she is thankful for the validation "that I'm not a copy of the popular people," she says. She doesn't mean to walk around the hallways with a death glare; she's usually just deep in thought as she observes her surroundings.

Laney not only enjoys doing the things for which other kids call her creepy; she also revels in the originality. She high-fives strangers, talks to her hamster in funny accents, runs barefoot in the snow, drinks her milk with food coloring, and reads the dictionary. A teacher who has taught Laney for two years describes her as someone who "stands out in a good way because she breaks the typical eighth-grade girl mold." She is a spirited eccentric who is happy, smart, and comfortable with herself, with no qualms about daring to be different.

Allie, The Freak

It's exhilarating for Allie to do her own thing; she is content to befriend the people who like her for herself and to ignore the ones who don't. She guesses that the reason people call her a freak is that they can't categorize her accurately. She says, "Do you remember how little kids put a circle inside a circle shape and the box inside the box shape? It's like that. [I'm not the circle or the box.] I'm a platypus."

Allie's clothes reflect this carefree attitude. She decorated her purse with pins from a Fanime convention. She likes picking out items to wear from her dad's closet—ties, buttoned shirts, suit jackets, a Nirvana shirt—because "they smell like him and are interesting," she says. She can't raid her mother's wardrobe. She died when Allie was three.

Allie likes being different. She enjoys Warhammer 40K because it's fascinating and collaborative. Undaunted by the jeers, she continues to wear the bunny hat about twice a month. And she has no concerns about trying to sort out her identity as she maneuvers through high school, because she already knows who she is.

Flor, The Mexican Slacker

The students who call Flor a slacker don't know what they're talking about. Flor turns in assignments at the last minute because her family can't afford a computer. She does her best to finish her work on time, often giving up lunch hours to complete and print out papers at school. She's trying hard to get a scholarship so that she will be able to attend college. She wants to study math and neurology.

Flor dropped out of school as a freshman to take care of her little brother while her parents were two thousand miles away for two months. She never plays sports because she has a congenital heart defect that requires a pacemaker. Yet she remains strong and positive. "I enjoy being unique at school. At the end of the day, I have the few people who were able to step out of their comfort zones to realize that I'm not crazy, or an airhead, or a slacker, or a stereotype Mexican. I'm just me."

BLUE, HAWAII | THE GAMER

At a teacher conference requested by Blue's mother, the teachers tried to explain to her that the Fs on Blue's progress report were not formal grades, but merely indicators that he hadn't caught up on his homework. Most of his grades were As and Bs. He did not attempt to cheat as did other students. He excelled at in-class work. "He just needs some space," they told his mother. "He's really trying."

When Blue's mother offered him a ride after the conference, Blue didn't want to go home. He biked to the arcade to play DrumMania. An hour later, when he arrived home, his mother was in the car, about to pull out of the driveway to look for him. She was furious. As he stored his bike in the garage, she yelled at him. "What the *fuck?!* You're really starting to Piss. Me. Off." She told him to go straight to the kitchen and sit down. He thought he knew what was coming. He was wrong. "How fucked up are you?! What the fuck are you doing?" she shouted.

Blue didn't know how to respond.

"Answer me, goddammit, before I beat the shit out of you." Blue paused before answering. He knew her threat was not idle.

At his silence, she cocked her head and asked suddenly, "How would you draw a lion?"

"What?!"

She repeated the question. Blue looked at her quizzically. She ran out of patience, walked to the cutting block, and picked up a knife. "You better start answering me before I hit you with this," she said. "Don't be like your father. I *hate* that about your father."

Blue had no idea what she meant. As she waved the knife a foot away from his face, he came to the conclusion that his mother was crazy. This was a relief. He couldn't take her demands seriously anymore.

"Uh, you'd draw . . . a lion?"

"Don't fucking play with me!" his mother said, still brandishing the knife. "Be more specific!"

"Uhh . . . catlike features? A tail?"

"But *how* would you draw it so if I looked at it I would know it's a lion?" she asked.

Baffled, Blue evaded her questions until she left him alone. The issue went against values he strongly believed in. He couldn't explain art, even if he tried to, because he didn't think it should be explained. He felt the same way about English class. How could you *teach* students to write creatively? Art was passion, to Blue. He tried to infuse his activities with feeling, tucking emotion into skating, gaming, drawing, debating. He couldn't explain to his mother the process of animating art with a little piece of his soul without sounding like he was crazy himself.

Later that night, Blue's mother told him, "Here's the deal. If you don't get full scholarships and straight As, you're going straight to Air Force. I don't give a shit. From now on, if you aren't home thirty minutes after school, I'm taking away everything. Everything."

When his mother told him that if he failed a class this quarter he wouldn't have enough credits to graduate, he froze in fear. "I don't care how late you have to stay up tonight. You're finishing all of this. You are never going out with your friends or having friends over again! Until you graduate with straight As. Bring your computer here. Right now! You're not getting it back until you graduate. Actually, you're selling it. Post it! But not tonight. Do your homework. I'll compare it to your reports to make sure you did everything. Go!"

Blue went to his room. His mother was still yelling, but her words were just noise to him now. He thought about running away. *But I don't have any friends who care enough. Where would I sleep? What am I going to do?* His resentment chilled him. *I hate it here. I don't have my own life anymore.*

Blue's room was lit only by the glow of the twenty-four-inch monitor he had stared at for eighteen months. *I have poured so many emotions into that window,* Blue thought.

"You have one minute until I unplug you!" his mother shouted.

He closed the browser. *That was filled with the tabs of my life,* he thought.

Blue reached around the back of the computer case and dejectedly disconnected the wires. This computer had taken him ages to build perfectly. He rested his hands for a moment on the chassis. The steel was cold—there was not a trace of heat from the hum that he had just silenced, precisely the way he had designed it. He put the computer next to his mother's desk.

When he returned to his room, he assembled an old iMac with various spare parts so that he could do his homework. His mother came in to show him his progress report. She had circled his Fs, even though some were from last quarter. She didn't understand the grading system.

"Okay," he said, exhausted by the evening's strange events. "I'm going to bed." It was late.

"Are you done with your homework?"

"Yes."

"No you're not. You're lying."

I actually did what I'm supposed to do and she doesn't believe me, Blue thought. "Mom, I can show it to you."

"Then go do it again. I know you didn't do a good job. You never do."

"But I want to go to sleep."

"Go do it all over again," she said.

A week later, Blue was lying in bed, late at night and sleepless, when the sobs came. He hadn't cried in five years. Even after he was able to stop the tears, he shook and spluttered for at least an hour.

Blue considered himself an unapologetic romantic, indulging in giddy crushes on people and things, generally in a good mood with great hopes for each day. When he talked to students and Ms. Collins about his troubles at home, they were surprised that he seemed so unflustered by the tatters of his life. "Don't worry!" he would tell them. "I'm used to it by now!"

Recently, however, when he was alone, waves of depression caught him unaware. *This has never happened to me before,* he thought, his chest tightening as dark frantic images crowded out any chance he had of getting to sleep. He was afraid he was falling back into "the cycle of failure" at school, whereby he would establish an impressive momentum, and then his mother would "come in and destroy it with something" so he would have to start over, again and again. *I will never be good enough for my mother.*

Blue had started to do his homework at Starbucks with a laptop Ms. Collins had loaned him. Away from home, he explained, "My concentration is freaking sublime. But now that my mom has actually ordered me to do [homework], the plan is tainted. She's constantly hovering over me in my head, taking all the credit."

With only thirty minutes to work outside of home, Blue couldn't complete his assignments. After his mother went to bed, he stayed up late to work on Ms. Collins' laptop, which his mother didn't know he had. Then he would oversleep and get to school late. Arriving an hour late to school became a regular occurrence. His grades plunged. His teachers recommended he emancipate himself, but he thought that doing so would create a new list of uncertainties that he wasn't prepared to handle.

Sometimes Blue wondered if his efforts mattered. His backup plan was to go to the University of Hawaii, minor in business, and major in future studies, a new field that fused foresight, philosophy, science, and art to postulate worldviews. But when he looked online, he saw that UH required Algebra 2, which Blue hadn't taken. Blue worried that he wouldn't be able to go to college at all.

Because Blue wasn't allowed to game at home anymore, he snuck out to the arcade more often. To Blue, gaming was "one of the only times where you only have to focus on one thing." But, even more than that, "It's like an anchor. As long as I know it's there, it's a part of me. It's some form of continuity that in my life I desperately need."

In bed, alone and scared, Blue thought about his social life. *I have never had and will never have that friend I'm looking for.* He thought about Jimmy. Blue had discovered that they read the same tech blogs, like Engadget and Gizmodo. But Jimmy wasn't taking Blue's hints. Their conversations led nowhere. Blue still didn't know if Jimmy was gay.

Blue remembered a recent discussion with Jackson about what would happen if they suddenly woke up and were still in kindergarten. He thought about how much he would like that. He thought about killing himself. He mulled over how he would compose a suicide note. It would have to be short. Direct. Something that left no questions as to why he did it. *The suicide note is an act of kindness, really. Why would he do it? Because my life is so undeniably hopeless. I can't even do things for myself anymore. I'm lonely and am sure the rest of my life will be similar. I would do it because I give up and am tired of trying.*

He thought about his fear of change. He thought about how scared he was of his mother's threat to ship him to the military. It wasn't the military itself, or combat, that frightened him. He was terrified that he wouldn't come out the same person. He knew some people needed the kind of change that the military offered, but Blue liked himself the way he was.

He believed he was struggling to simply survive. *I want what other kids have. I'm tired of being different,* he thought. *Still, the only person I want to be is me. I can't let her win.* He realized why his immediate response to his mother was one of increasing rebelliousness. He didn't want to live his life doing things to please other people. *I'm gonna push her out,* he resolved, *so I can feel more of my own self-satisfaction.*

Not long afterward, Blue's mother informed him that she had signed him up for ROTC, informed ROTC of the colleges to which he would apply, selected his intended majors of Japanese and engineering, and lined up Air Force and National Guard recruiters. Blue, she said, was going into the military.

NOAH, PENNSYLVANIA | THE BAND GEEK

On Leigh's birthday, Noah could hear her friends singing to her four tables away from the "Asian table" where he miserably stared at a textbook. Noah was trying to move on, but lunch was the hardest period of the day. The cafeteria made him feel like an observer of rather than a participant in the high school experience. "I'm just not using the cafeteria to have fun," he explained later. "All around me, kids are laughing, joking. I feel like I'm not a part of it. I don't feel like a high school kid; I feel closer to the teachers monitoring it, working on their grades, glancing to make sure there isn't any trouble."

Even with elections looming, Noah didn't campaign in the cafeteria. He assumed that even other outcasts didn't want to be approached during lunch. Outside of the cafeteria, however, he boldly delivered his spiel to classmates: "Hey, what's up? . . . So, I'm running for class president, and"—here he'd give a quick rundown of his agenda. "Would you be willing to vote for me?" Sometimes people said no, but many students at least listened to what he had to say. Mostly, Noah stuck to campaigning among mainstream students. Some kids he was too afraid to approach, like the drinkers, stoners, Goths, and "prostitots," Redsen's term for underclassman girls who appeared to be promiscuous.

After gym, Noah noticed semi-popular students looking at campaign fliers on the wall. "Hey, guys," he said. "You know, I'm running for president this year."

They turned to him. "Again?" asked one. "Didn't you run last year? Kent beat you, right?"

Noah nodded. "Yeah, well, I've looked at a lot of cool stuff we can do, and I think I can help make this an awesome year."

"Yeah, right," snorted another student. "Haha, I'm just gonna vote for Kent. You're way too serious."

In study hall, he approached a group of classmates and told them how he could improve class trips and other student privileges. The students nodded. "I hate how the popular kids win," one said. "They don't care about anyone else. They just sit there and do nothing."

Noah's opponent was not campaigning, content to sit back and "ride the popularity train," as Noah put it. Noah had about fifty posters. Kent had zero. Noah set up a Facebook group and spent hours sending messages to classmates. Kent had done none of that. Noah believed he had a decent chance to win the election, much better odds than he had the last two years. Maybe this was the year he could "finally overthrow the popular regime."

It didn't matter to Noah that students didn't understand some of his posters, such as the one that displayed Noah and two friends dressed as ninjas. SUPPORTED BY THE NINJA APPRECIATION CLUB, the poster read in large letters. Small print at the bottom of the poster read, "If you don't know about the Ninja Appreciation Club, that's because it's made up of ninjas. Duh."

On speech day, Noah walked into AP Physics boomeranging between excitement and nervousness. As he navigated to his seat, his classmates called out to him from their perches on top of their desks. "Hey, man, are you ready?" one asked. Another playfully rubbed Noah's shoulders and tried to get him to jump around like a boxer warming up in the ring.

As class time wore on, the seniors' silliness grew infectious. "Hey, can we pregame the speech?" a boy asked the teacher. "Yeah, can we tailgate?" another asked, laughing.

"No," replied the teacher, with no hint of emotion.

One senior suggested body paint. Another found a set of speakers, hooked them to his iPod, and blasted dance music. Finally, the teacher handed Noah his ballot. The seniors crowded around him, teasingly bad-mouthing some of the candidates and cheering for others. "You know, it'd be a shame if Kent met with an 'accident,'" a student joked in a Mafia voice. "Is he going to be around any windows later today?"

The digital whiteboard blinked on. Kent's speech aired first. Noah listened attentively as Kent coolly emphasized his experience, having been class president for two years. Then it was Noah's turn. When Noah had taped the speech the prior week, he was confident; he enjoyed public speaking. Watching himself on-screen now, however, he was bothered by his crooked posture and his messy hair. He picked his speech apart as it aired.

He wondered what Leigh would have thought of his talk. Presently, Noah and Leigh were no more than cordial acquaintances. He found that the best way to get over Leigh was to be angry at her. Now that he believed reconciliation was impossible, at least the pain of losing her was buried deep.

On election announcement day, a number of students approached Noah in the halls and during classes. "I voted for you!" many of them said. "Good luck today!" One boy said he had persuaded his entire first-period class to vote for Noah. Their words of encouragement buoyed him. They made him believe he could win.

At the end of last period, a student appeared on the whiteboard to announce the results. Noah tensed. "Junior class president: Kent—" Noah's heart slowed to a dull thud as his classmates continued their business, unaffected. Nobody so much as looked at Noah. He had lost again.

MOST BANDS IN THE Macy's Thanksgiving Day Parade either marched or stood still. Redsen was going to do the equivalent of a choreographed halftime performance. The director had given Noah the most important job of the Honor Guards: He had to maneuver a modified golf cart decorated like a taxi through the two hundred marching students to transport a performer to the other side of the moving band.

Noah sat in the golf cart on the side of the parking lot, spacing out as the band rehearsed the song, measure by measure. Noah wouldn't have to do anything until the band played through the entire song. At the appropriate cue, he was supposed to drive the taxi through a tight gap in the crowd with less than a foot of space on either side; if he was too early or too late, the choreography was such that he wouldn't be able to make it. Sometimes, when he knew he wasn't going to fit the car into the gap in time, he bailed, stopping or turning to avoid hitting someone. He wouldn't be able to bail at Macy's.

Rather than pay attention to the rehearsal, Noah thought about Leigh, who stood out of sight behind dozens of bandmates. He had recently had a revelation. One of the reasons he had been so devastated by the breakup was because Leigh once told him he was her best friend. Now that he was trying to move on, he couldn't imagine life without her in any role. They had never been friends; they had gone straight from acquaintanceship to romance. *What if the person I'm supposed to be is her best friend?* he wondered, swallowing his anger.

Noah thought he could use another friend; classmates were picking on him again. In AP Calculus, Frederick had reminded him that varsity swimming season began in a week. "I can't wait to cut your hair," he added, smirking. He turned to the teacher. "Hey, can we cut his hair in here?"

"No, Frederick," the teacher replied. "He's like Samson. If you cut his hair, he'll lose his powers of math." Noah laughed with the class.

Noah had avoided Frederick in the halls and at lunch. In class, Frederick's comments were largely innocuous, because the teacher was in the room. The presence of adults didn't deter other kids from making rude comments, however. A senior in Noah's computer class constantly made fun of Noah's ethnicity. This week he had said, "Are you sure you can read that board? Your eyes are pretty squinted." The senior pulled up the corners of his eyes with his fingers.

"When I look in the mirror, my eyes don't look like that," Noah retorted, copying the gesture. "Maybe you should stop before people start making comments to you."

Now that swimming was about to resume, Noah wondered what the season had in store for him. His top swimming goal was to qualify for the district championships. Noah liked swimming, if not all of his teammates, but the beginning of swim season inevitably meant the end of band, his favorite school activity.

Many of the bandies were ready for football season to end. They wanted their Friday nights back. During the most recent football game, which Redsen won by multiple touchdowns, some band members cheered when the opposing team scored. Word spread to the football players, who angrily blamed the entire band and berated the bandies' disloyalty.

A few periods after calculus, Noah's gym classmates had chatted with a handful of football players about the upcoming game. One player said, "This Friday is going to be close. Maybe if *the band*"—here he shoved Noah, who stumbled a few feet—"didn't cheer for the other team, it'd be easier." The populars in the room cackled. This happened several more times. Noah didn't bother explaining that he wanted the football players to keep winning so that he could cling to band season for as long as possible. The football team lost the next game.

Fortunately, Noah had other good things going on in his life. In mid-autumn, Redsen had hosted its annual speech competition. Noah spoke about the advantages of certain expensive swimsuits that, using increased compression technology, could reduce swimmers' times by an average of 3 to 5 percent. Noah's speech had won first place.

Noah jolted back into the present. The band seemed to be playing through. He saw the gap twenty feet ahead of him. Noah panicked. His head spun as he weighed his choices: drive now, and fast, into the spot that the band already expected him to be in, or wait, risking the director's wrath because he wasn't in position.

In the split second he had to make his choice, Noah scrutinized the rapidly closing gap and thought he could squeeze into it. He shot forward, more quickly than usual. Belatedly, he realized that the mallet player who was supposed to be on Noah's left by now was one step too far forward, followed by the rest of his line. The hole wasn't big enough. As Noah hurtled toward it, marchers closed in behind him, blocking his reverse. "Stop! Stop, stop! Don't march!" Noah yelled. No one heard him over the music.

The line to Noah's right completed its maneuver and began moving toward Noah. He knew a collision was inevitable unless he continued to attempt to squeeze into the gap. He slammed on the accelerator, trying to scream through the din of the instruments for the drum majors to cut, as he careened toward the space that was shrinking by the beat. He almost made it. "Look out!" someone hollered.

Half of the band, unseeing, continued to advance toward Noah, while the other half marched in place, staring with horror as the front bumper hit a trombonist's leg below the knee, knocking him over. "Oh my God!" someone yelled. "What the hell are you doing?" another bandie screamed. From behind, Noah heard other shouts. "What's going on?!" "Is he okay?"

Noah stared in shock, terrified. He had just hit one of his best friends *with a golf cart*. The director cut off the band, made sure the trombonist was okay, then came over to talk to Noah. When the director ascertained that nothing had been damaged save Noah's ego, he resumed the rehearsal. They only had an hour to practice before the school needed the parking lot available.

On the next band bus ride, Noah saw Leigh sitting near the back of the bus. He recalled something his father had said: "Push yourself into conversations and become more involved." He plopped down next to Leigh and cheerily talked about every subject that came to mind, made her laugh with jokes and songs, and otherwise tried to show her he cared. He tried to be her friend.

Over the next several days, Noah and Leigh talked on the phone for hours. They went out for a friendly dinner. After a recycling presentation, Noah and Leigh had breakfast together before school. At the end of the week, Leigh asked him to get back together. Elated, Noah agreed.

DANIELLE, ILLINOIS | THE LONER

At the first National Honor Society meeting of the year, an officer told the club about two girls with disabilities who spent their days at Stone Mill and looked forward to having student visitors. "Not very many people are able to do it," the officer said. "It can be kind of weird for some people." Danielle liked the idea that most students couldn't work with the girls. She was up for the challenge.

When Danielle walked into Emily and Viv's classroom for the first time, she was nervous. The sisters were both in wheelchairs. Emily, a short, round-faced girl in pajamas, perched on a platform where a machine massaged her back. Viv, taller and skinnier than her sister, wore a dressy scarf around her neck. One other student sat in the room, a prep whom Danielle knew from sophomore year English. Danielle sat next to her. They exchanged uncomfortable looks.

The sisters' aide reviewed a long list of guidelines about how to act around the girls. Neither girl could see or talk, and both of them had hypersensitive hearing. Visitors had to enter and exit the classroom quickly so the closed door blocked out the sounds of students in the hallway.

Danielle returned the following week. When she made spin art with Viv, she had to hold the girl's hand on the button to rotate the device. Viv's hand was limp, and Danielle, who had never been around people with handicaps, was apprehensive about touching her. She imagined that Viv's hand felt like a dead person's hand. Danielle didn't like touching people to begin with, which made it that much more awkward to touch a stranger, let alone an unpredictable stranger. Viv's hand kept falling off of the button—Danielle assumed because she wasn't enthusiastic about spin art—so Danielle held the button down herself.

Despite her discomfort, Danielle realized it was a relief to spend time with the sisters and their aide. She didn't have to force herself to make inane small talk; she could talk about whatever interested her, and the aide told stories about the girls. Also, the hush was nice. The sisters' classroom was a refreshing oasis amid the superficial pandemonium of high school halls.

It seemed as if every year Danielle grew quieter; and the less she talked, the more she withdrew from people. She wasn't sure why this year she was having a particularly difficult time connecting with classmates. Sometimes Danielle's mother suggested she had a superiority complex. She did sometimes feel superior to other students, because they didn't have any meaningful aspirations. At other times, Danielle's mother said she had an inferiority complex. Danielle agreed with both assessments. Physically, surrounded by bone-thin girls at school, Danielle, who fluctuated between sizes six and eight, felt fat, and mentally, she felt unintelligent because she hardly bothered talking in class. Ever since the seventh-grade hate club, Danielle had adopted an Abraham Lincoln quote as a mantra: "Better to keep your mouth closed and be thought a fool than to open it and remove all doubt." She found another kindred spirit in Xenocrates, whose quote hung in her creative writing teacher's room: "I have often regretted my speech, never my silence."

When she was comfortable, Danielle wasn't reserved at all. She could be loud, outgoing, and daring. She had a sarcastic wit and was immensely creative and generous. She donated her own money to charities, volunteered at animal shelters, and regularly saved abandoned animals. She spent her free time learning about the environment and foreign cultures. Yes, Danielle had high standards that set her apart from many of her peers. But she held herself to those standards too.

JOY, CALIFORNIA | THE NEW GIRL

In biology, Joy had noticed an odd, silent junior who sat against the wall and usually drew pictures in class. She was so white Joy could practically see right through her.

Then one day the biology teacher chatted with Joy just before class. "Hey, Joy!" he said. "You know, you don't have to be so quiet in class. Look over there; that's Cleo. She's a nice girl to talk to."

Joy glanced at Cleo, who was hunched beneath her backpack as if the weight of the world were strapped to her shoulders.

When Cleo saw Joy, her face changed. Joy noticed that her eyes shone bright blue. Cleo gave a bashful wave.

"Okay, class," the teacher announced, pointing to a stack of papers on his desk. "We're going to be doing an experiment on cohesion and adhesion today. Find partners!"

Joy looked at Cleo. "Hey, Cleo, I'm Joy. Do you want to be my partner?"

"Yeah, okay."

Joy and Cleo laughed as they conducted the experiment, which was more silly than difficult. They talked about the class and, eventually, themselves. Cleo was artistic, could sing, and enjoyed discussing philosophy, all of which Joy felt they had in common. Joy was surprised to find that Cleo was hilarious. She learned that Cleo was quiet in class because she was shy and focused on learning the material.

Before long, Cleo joined Joy for lunch in the biology classroom every day. Over the next few weeks, Joy grew almost as close to Cleo as she was to Anisha.

But friends were still few and far between. Too many classmates displayed a level of prejudice that astounded Joy. In between classes, Joy and Xavier, a blond, bespectacled boy in her English class, walked down an outdoor hallway. "I want to be a teacher," Xavier said. "I think it would be cool."

They passed by the English department. "If I were a teacher, I'd be an English teacher," Joy said. "I love English. Or a drama teacher."

"What? I've never heard of a black person being an English teacher before," Xavier said.

Joy made herself pause before responding. She looked down at the water pooling on the sidewalk. She breathed in the air, crisp from fresh rain. "What's that supposed to mean?" she asked. "The last time I checked, I was an articulate person and could present myself well."

"All I'm saying is that it would be like a Mexican working with computers," he said, laughing. "I'm not trying to sound racist. I'm just saying."

Joy's eyes bulged. "Wow, you're not sounding racist at all," she said, her voice thick with sarcasm. "What a way to show your ignorance! I've had impeccable black English teachers, even better than the one we currently have."

As they continued to walk in silence, a look of recognition crossed Xavier's face, as if he had just realized what he had said and to whom. "Don't get upset," he pleaded.

"I'm not getting upset," she said calmly. "I'm just telling you: You need to learn what and what not to say. I'm a diplomatic person. I'm not looking for conflict." As the bell rang, she squeezed in, "Just watch out; some people would punch your lights out."

Joy had to deal with racism every day at school. Some Asian students wouldn't even speak to her when they were assigned to work with her on group projects. In PE, Mexican students referred to her as "black *puta*" and "black bitch." During the class's salsa unit, the boys stood in a stationary line while the girls' line rotated in front of them so that each person danced with a partner for a few minutes, then moved on to the next. Joy was the best dancer in the class, but the Mexican boys refused to dance with her. Each would stand in front of her with his arms crossed, refusing to move. "It's okay if you don't want to dance with me," Joy would say as her partner glowered. "Just keep moving."

One Mexican student used to spit on the floor in front of Joy, to classmates' laughter, whenever the teacher took attendance. When he had done this for a few days in a row, despite Joy's requests that he stop, Joy said, "Why don't you just fuck off?!" The boy tried to stare her down. "I'm not afraid of a coward like you," Joy said to him. He didn't spit at her again.

Joy only spoke to one Mexican in school because, she said, "She's the only one who isn't ignorant and small-minded. I'm not friends with the cholos and Asians because they don't converse with blacks. I will say hi to Natalie, but I can see her discomfort." Joy had one black acquaintance, Latrice, the cheerleader from her first English class. Latrice had been begging Joy to tutor her in biology, but the rest of the African-Americans at school still looked at her "weird." As Joy put it, "Here they say, 'You either white or ghetto.' I'm not either, so I don't see why I should be subjecting myself to any classifications."

In the following weeks, Joy continued to talk to Xavier, who made sure to point out, "I dated a black and a Mexican girl, so how could I possibly be racist?"

JOY WOKE UP ONE Monday morning and knew she had hit rock bottom. Her depression had begun as stress and homesickness, but now, more than two months later, it was picking at her, biting away until she felt like she barely existed. She couldn't bear the thought of getting up and going to school. She had been through so much worse than anything Citygrove could throw at her, and yet she was at her breaking point and didn't know why.

Joy believed that some of her classmates were "green-eyed"—and unnecessarily so. She guessed that people perceived her as someone who was "pretty, smart, and has an excellent life, when in truth they don't know the half of it." Indeed there were things that Joy kept bottled up, things she had told no one in Citygrove and few people in Jamaica.

Joy's parents had split up when she was two years old. Her Ukrainian mother—who had moved to Jamaica with Joy's father without knowing a word of English—retained custody, but Jamaican courts forced Joy to visit her father every other weekend. On many occasions, he beat her.

Sometimes he beat her because he claimed she lied. Sometimes it was because she pronounced a word wrong. Sometimes it was because she cried too much. He would tell Joy or her younger half brother, "Go get the belt," sending them to his bedroom, where he hung his belts from a hook on the wall. He would take them to the living room and force each sibling to watch while he beat the other. When it was Joy's turn, her father would grab her by the arm and she'd try to run, but she could only pinwheel around him as he slapped her or hit her with the belt buckle. She could still remember her shrieks when she begged him to stop hurting her. "Daddy, please, I'm sorry!" she'd weep. "I won't do it again. Oh God, oh God." He never yelled when he beat her. When he was through, he'd smile and leave her crumpled and bruised on the floor. Her mother, distraught but powerless, once had to take her to a doctor to treat the open wounds that striped her back.

Usually, the next time he saw her, he would smugly say, "What happened to you? Who did this to you?"—mocking her pain. Then he hugged and kissed her as if nothing had happened. That was the scariest part.

The abuse wasn't always physical. He verbally made her feel worthless, or taunted her by insulting her mother. Nearly every night, Joy had nightmares about him coming after her. She cried in her sleep. Joy endured the beatings because her father wasn't always a monster. She kept going back because she hoped that eventually her father would change, that he would make her feel loved, or at least worthy of his time.

When Joy was nine, her father invited her to spend Christmas Eve at his mother's house while Joy's mother worked at the local hospital. He lured her with promises of presents under the tree and games with her younger half siblings, whom she didn't know well. Despite her nightmares, Joy was thrilled. *He couldn't possibly beat me at Grandma's house,* she thought.

Joy's father picked her up at the hospital. Her mother didn't speak to him; she only hugged her daughter and told her to be safe. She had not wanted Joy to go, but Joy convinced her to let her spend Christmas with family while she worked. Joy had no other family in Jamaica.

Joy was supposed to spend the night at her father's house before their trip to her grandmother's the next day. When they arrived, her father instructed her to look inside his house for her Christmas presents. She eagerly searched everywhere—no presents. Outside, she found him leaning on his car, in deep discussion with his cousin. They stopped talking when Joy appeared. Her father grabbed her hand, threw it down, and demanded she remove her nail polish.

Joy's father and his new wife took her to a plaza to shop for gifts for his mother. After a couple of hours, he received a phone call and escorted Joy and his wife to the parking lot. He strode toward a white car. "Can I go with you, Daddy?" Joy asked. He told her to stay with his wife. Joy saw her father open the trunk of the car. The driver gave him a baseball bat, which he put in the trunk.

Back at her father's house, Joy tried calling her mother to check in, but she didn't answer the phone. At about 1 A.M., while waiting for

Joy's dad to return, his wife was braiding Joy's hair into cornrows when they heard sirens. A cousin went downstairs.

Joy ran to her room, frightened without knowing why. She stuck a pack of gum under her pillow for safekeeping. She went outside to join her cousin and stepmother by the large gate that divided the open-air house from the driveway. A police officer shouted for her father.

Joy peered through the gate. Her mother's friend rushed out of a police car. "That's Joy! That's her daughter. She told us to take her."

Joy's stepmother looked at her nervously. Joy's hair was only half done.

"Come Joy, we're leaving," said her mother's friend.

Joy was confused. "But why? Where's Daddy? Why do the police want Daddy?"

"Just come, Joy. I'll tell you later. We have to go. Get your things."

As the police interrogated her stepmother, Joy removed one piece of gum from the package, which she placed under her pillow for next time. She put on a pair of slippers and went downstairs.

In the back of the police car, Joy's mother's friend held her. "What's wrong?" Joy asked. "Where are we going?"

"To the hospital," the officer said. "Your mom has been hurt."

At the hospital, Joy's mother was bleeding and her arm was in a sling. She had stitches in her forehead, a broken hand, and her skull had nearly cracked. She told Joy what happened. While Joy sat contentedly in her father's house, his new wife combing her hair, Joy's mother was driving home. There was a white car parked on the hill on the way to Joy's apartment. When Joy's mother passed it, the car followed her. She drove to the gate, stepped out of her car, then heard the other car pull up and screech to a halt alongside her. One of the four men in the car, his face covered, came running at her with a baseball bat. She tried to get back into her car, but he blocked her way. She recognized him. It was Joy's father. She called out his name. He hit her on the head and the hand with the bat. Joy's mother fought for her life, screaming and struggling until her ex-husband stole her car and sped away.

The police arrested Joy's father that night, but because of his political position, his employer was able to bail him out and secure for him nothing more than a one-year probation. Eventually Joy and her mother moved to another town.

It had taken a long time, but Joy wasn't angry anymore. She refused to let her experiences turn her into a victim. Instead, she drew strength from her past. Determined to find a silver lining, Joy believed that because of her pain, she was better at listening to people, doling out advice to the Jamaican friends who constantly called her for counsel, and helping them to "value themselves and pursue their goals." She was so grateful that she and her mother were alive that she was able to brush off life's twists and turns by telling herself that things could be worse. They could be dead. She had learned that it was easier to cope when she looked at things positively; if she had faith in herself and hope for her future, her life would continue to improve. And it had. So why, years later, couldn't she lift herself from her current funk?

She missed communicating daily with friends who understood her culture, her background, and her morals. No matter how kind her U.S. friends were, they couldn't relate to her. She missed island life and Caribbean vibes: the sunsets, the breezy air, the verdant mountains, the trees swaying in the wind, and especially the people. She missed playing badminton in the evenings at her apartment complex, dealing cards on the stoop, and riding bicycles with her friends—even just washing cars on the weekends. She said later, "Jamaicans are a rough and loud people, but I love it about them. Even when they cuss, it's the sweetest thing you'll hear. I love the music and the food, the dance, the lifestyles. I love the Rastas, superstitions . . . Here it's like I'm lost. I hate having to pretend to be a certain way, dumb down myself, act less Jamaican."

When Joy trudged into the bio room, her classmates kept coming by to ask if she was okay, which made her even sadder. A girl who had just transferred to Citygrove gave her a card, which Joy put into her bag unopened.

The biology teacher came over to Joy. "Hey, kiddo, what's up? How ya doing?" he asked.

"I'm fine. Just . . . here." Joy tried hard to hold back tears.

The teacher looked sympathetic. "Joy, you know you have people here who care about you," he said, referring to the crew that ate lunch in his classroom every day. "Try to relax. You'll visit Jamaica soon."

Joy nodded and kept to herself for half of the period. During this time of introspection, she needed to *make* herself be who she wanted to be. It wasn't going to happen passively. If she was stressing too much over work and social adjustments, then she just had to stop. She decided to accept that she, and only she, could control whether worries consumed her or slid off her back.

Joy dug into her bag. She found the card from the transfer student. "Hey Joy, I know you've been stressed a lot lately. I hope you feel better." Joy smiled. *Not everyone at Citygrove cares only about themselves,* she thought. *Maybe being depressed has been a way to teach me that.*

Later, she emailed a Jamaican friend. "i made a promise 2myself which i am leaving here . . . to be happy and satisfied with everything i have. And starting now I'm gonna go have fun. And stop worrying over this crap." She was fed up with being sad.

Whitney, New York | The Popular Bitch

One day, Madison approached Whitney in the hallway. "Hey, I'm having a party Saturday night. I invited the twins in gym today."

Finally, Whitney thought, she could show up at a party with non-phony people, and also snatch a spot in the party car. "Okay!" she said. "I can drive them since they're on the way."

Students treated the twins differently than other new kids. The twins partied and dressed to fit in, and they did. Meanwhile, Fern, another new student, sat in the corner of classes and hardly ever spoke. Word had gotten out that Fern, who was overweight, with acne and greasy hair, was so poor that she lived in a ghetto. Immediately branded a loser, Fern appeared not to have any friends at Riverland. Whitney's only interaction with her was on Fern's first day of school. When a fabric bow on Fern's shirt unraveled, Whitney reached over and tied it for her.

Whitney picked up the twins at a house littered with beer boxes. The twins confided that they had moved to town to start over after a troubled stint in their old school district. At Riverland, the twins had merged into the popular group, but some cracks were beginning to show. They fought with each other often and reeked of smoke, neither of which typically would have been acceptable to the populars, but the girls were cute cheerleaders who dressed well. For now, the preps overlooked their shortcomings.

At Madison's, Whitney was getting drunk when Luke, already intoxicated, stumbled into the house. Whitney and Luke grew increasingly cuddly, putting their arms around each other, caressing each other's legs as they chatted. Whitney knew that Luke got horny when drunk. He was the only person to whom she wanted to lose her virginity. Her wheels turned. "Come with me to get something from my car," she told him.

She took his hand and walked him outside. She leaned against the side of her car. The chilly October air made her shiver through her filmy shirt. Luke took off his zip-up and put it around her. He zipped her in slowly, and when he got to the top, their eyes met. Her heart pounded. He hugged her to him tightly. She stopped shivering.

He whispered in her ear. "What do you want right now?"

"I'm not sure," she whispered back.

"I don't want to ruin our friendship."

"Me either, but I totally think it's going to happen."

"Yeah. Me too."

Neither of them moved for at least five minutes, seemingly wrestling over what they were going to do. *Please let us hook up tonight*, she thought as they hugged. *Please, please.*

Then he said, "We need to swear that nothing will be weird with us and that it won't change our friendship."

Whitney reached her hand above her head, pinky extended. He did the same. "I promise," Whitney said.

Luke broke the embrace, looked into her eyes, and kissed her. It was better than she could have imagined. If she hadn't been leaning on the car, she was sure she would have fainted from happiness. Her fingers curled around the back of his neck. He ran a hand through her hair. It wasn't cold at all anymore.

They heard voices and sprang apart. Two drunk guys from the

party were rounding the corner. "Oh, hey, Whitney! People are look-ing for you," one of them slurred as they walked by.

As soon as the guys left, Luke and Whitney resumed making out. His hands moved down her stomach and began unbuttoning her jeans. She had no doubts that she wanted this to happen. She couldn't stop smiling. Her hands slid down his body. They went into her car.

When they were through, Whitney reveled in her afterglow, ec-static that she had lost her virginity to someone she loved. As they dressed, they decided they weren't going to tell anyone what they had done. When they walked back into the house, however, the partygoers stopped what they were doing and eyed her "crazy sex hair," dishev-eled clothes, and flushed cheeks. Whitney knew they knew. She slith-ered through the crowd to get her coat. Giselle came dashing over.

Whitney later found out that the two guys had told Giselle that Whitney was throwing up by her car because that was what their in-toxicated minds assumed. Giselle had gone outside looking for her, peered into the car, caromed back into the house, and screamed to the entire party, "WHITNEY AND LUKE ARE HAVING SEX!"

"Whitney, oh my God, are you okay?" Giselle said, large, drunken tears streaming down her face.

"Uh, yeah?" Whitney said, perplexed. "Why are you crying?"

"Because you just had sex."

"But, like, you just had sex five minutes ago."

"But you expect *me* to have sex," Giselle said.

The next day, Whitney and Luke discussed their relationship. They decided to hook up only with each other, but without the boyfriend-girlfriend label. Whitney accepted these terms because she was overjoyed that their relationship had moved beyond platonic friendship.

Irene, a short, loud junior, had been trying to manipulate her way into the popular group ever since she had moved into town a few years before. This year, as a cheerleader, she managed to get onto

Giselle's good side. She regularly invited the populars to her large house and offered to steal liquor from her mother.

Irene's status changed at a party at Giselle's, where she hooked up with one of the popular guys. For the next few weeks, because she was dating a prep, Irene officially became one. Whitney was suspicious; she didn't think Bobby was attractive, and Irene had never expressed an interest in him. Before long, Irene was taking Whitney's spot in the party car more often than not.

As Irene's popular stock rose, the twins' plummeted. They argued during lunch and skipped classes. Rumors spread that they slept around for coke.

One day, Bianca announced to the populars, "Yeah, so who is starting to get annoyed with the twins?" Everyone but Whitney firmly raised a hand. *Aw crap,* Whitney thought, and reluctantly added hers.

"They stand there like they're out of it," Chelsea said. "And they talk like they're on serious drugs."

"Oh my God, I've never hated someone more than I hate those two girls," Irene declared. Whitney noticed that Irene now dressed exactly like the preps.

And so it was resolved, without Bianca having to say another word. The group gradually froze out the twins. They stopped inviting them to parties and ignored them in person. They edged them out of the lunch table and spent entire lunch periods talking about them behind their backs. Irene in particular went out of her way to be mean to the twins, calling them names and starting cruel rumors, especially when Bianca was within earshot. Consequently, the twins looked elsewhere for companionship, allegedly finding questionable people in unsavory places. Their new acquaintances further tarnished their image among the preps.

Except for Whitney. Whitney thought the twins were well-meaning girls who were stuck in an inescapable social cycle. She said, "They hung out with bad people because they had no one else to hang out with, and they had no one else to hang out with because they hung out with bad people." The populars issued a decree that no one could talk to the twins. Whitney texted and talked to them in secret anyway.

In public, when the preps disparaged the twins, Whitney reluctantly joined in so as not to call attention to herself. On the nights that Whitney was left out of the party car, she hung out with the twins. When they asked her why everyone suddenly was ignoring them, she said she didn't know.

Within weeks, Irene broke up with Bobby. The next time Whitney saw Irene, at the local diner, she struck up a conversation about it, curious what Irene would say.

"So, you and Bobby, huh," Whitney prompted.

"Yeah, I wanted to end things before it got bad, you know?" Irene said.

"Yeah, I guess. You two did work at Giselle's, I heard . . ."

"No, we just made out," Irene replied. "We didn't have sex."

"That's not what the rumors are."

"Ugh, great. Honestly," she said, sounding relieved to confide this, "I didn't really want to be making out with him. I felt my body doing it, but in my head I was thinking, *Ew, this is so weird.*"

Whitney wondered if any of the other populars realized that Irene had used Bobby to get into their group.

Not long afterward, Whitney was at a school library computer when one of the twins sat down next to her. "I'm going to punch Irene in the face if she says one more thing to me," she told Whitney.

Whitney looked up from the computer. "What happened this time?"

"My sister was wearing a shirt with a beer can on it, so she was given a sweatshirt from guidance to wear. Irene comes storming over, accusing her of stealing the sweatshirt from the school."

"Eww," Whitney said. "What is her deal?!"

"I don't know. But it's turning everyone against us. Preps, like, hate us now for some reason. We can't even sit with them anymore. We just sit by ourselves."

"That's so weird," Whitney said, acting clueless. She didn't have the same lunch period as the twins.

"Yeah. I hate coming to school because I have to put up with all of this. We skip school all the time now because we hate coming here so much. You're our only friend, because Giselle and Bianca and them made everyone hate us."

A week and a half later, the twins moved to another district. Whitney was disappointed; she believed they had moved to town to try to be better people, but left the way they had arrived, all because of the populars' rejection.

———

WHY IT MAY BE BETTER NOT TO BE IN A GROUP

The preps' treatment of the twins may be rooted in a phenomenon called group polarization, a tendency for groups to form judgments that are more extreme than individuals' personal opinions. Experts have theorized that polarization occurs for three reasons: individual members (1) are exposed to the group's rationale during discussions, (2) may feel pressure to conform to the group's opinion, and (3) may take even more extreme positions than the group average in an attempt to get the rest of the group to like them better. Irene was meaner to the twins than the rest of the preps because she probably was desperate for the preps' approval.

Group polarization occurs among adults as well. For example, juries whose individual members sway toward guilt as a group are more likely to recommend a harsher sentence than would each member alone. Even federal judges can succumb to group polarization. A study of civil liberties decisions in U.S. district courts in the 1960s revealed that in more than 1,500 cases in which a person claimed a violation of constitutional rights, the single judge sided with the plaintiff only 30 percent of the time. In cases in which three-judge panels presided, however, the percentage jumped to 65 percent.

In an experiment on group polarization in France, researchers asked individual high school students about their feelings toward the United States and toward General Charles de Gaulle. Then the students participated in a group discussion on those topics. The researchers again surveyed the students individually. After the discussion, they felt more positive toward de Gaulle and more negative toward the U.S. than before the discussion. Other studies have found that group polarization can make students feel more negatively about their school, push students' evaluations of faculty to either extreme, and lead already prejudiced high school students to adopt even more racist attitudes.

Polarization is just one of many ways group membership can change an individual. Perhaps the most striking effect of group membership is that it can modify individuals' perceptions of themselves. Unable to separate their personal introspection from the ways they believe other people perceive them, teenagers may have what psychologists call an "imaginary audience," meaning they believe that other people are just as attuned to their appearance and behavior as they are (cue any pimple cream commercial). These perceptions can affect various aspects of their lives. For example, psychologists found that when Asian girls were subtly reminded about their Asian identity, they performed better on math tests. When they were subtly reminded about their gender, however, they performed worse.

Students can come to see themselves as they believe their groupmates see them. It's one thing for parents and teachers to influence children's self-views, but when a child sees herself through the prism of her peer group, the resulting self-image can be distorted. She might suddenly believe that she's too heavy (Danielle and Whitney), too serious (Noah), too foreign (Joy), or too eccentric (Eli). It may be no coincidence that when Blue's friends told him that they couldn't take him seriously, he stopped taking himself seriously as well; his descent into hopelessness could not be blamed solely on his relationship with his mother. Eli didn't feel badly about not going to parties until Raj called him strange for not wanting to. Students usually don't refer to themselves as nerds until someone else accuses them of being one.

Many students think that to be accepted, they have to fulfill the role their group has imposed on them. A California sophomore accustomed to being excluded was pleased when upperclassmen on her Model UN team took her under their wing. But their fellowship came with a price. "My older friends called me the 'happy freshman' and I felt obligated to keep sad feelings to myself," she said. "Now I'm with a different crowd and I feel immensely relieved. I changed myself to be more socially acceptable, but now I embrace who I am."

This pressure can add not only emotional strain, but also academic stress. A number of students told me that because classmates viewed them as nerds or smart kids, they felt extra pressure to pull straight As. An eighth grader in Indiana told me he didn't mind being labeled a nerd—"it's a lot better than being a nobody"—but he was tired of feeling like he had to continue to get perfect grades to be socially accepted. "That's what defines my group, and if I don't live up to their expectations, I would be letting them down."

When so much of students' brainpower is concentrated on their peers, it can be challenging to distinguish their social identity from their personal identity. Granted, this struggle is a natural part of growing up. But the process of group polarization is not so different from groupthink (defined by Merriam Webster as "a pattern of thought characterized by self-deception, forced manufacture of consent, and conformity to group values and ethics"). In both cases, individuals feel less personal responsibility for the consequences of the group's decisions. They can take a more risky stance, because if the group is unsuccessful the responsibility is shared. Groups threaten to de-individualize people in a process that primatologist Richard Wrangham called "the mindless sinking of personal identity into the group of Us."

This mindlessness can occur both in small groups and large crowds. Some psychologists have espoused the controversial theory that in the midst of a crowd, an individual's layers of restraint peel away, revealing potentially barbaric instincts and a susceptibility to "crowd contagion." This theory could help to explain why kids in the bleachers at a pep rally or a football game can get so out of hand so quickly, or, as a Pennsylvania high school teacher told me, "Usually one person starts making fun of a weird kid or nerd to his face and everyone else in the class joins in."

More subtly, groups can trigger the brain's inclination to take shortcuts. "The human brain takes in information from other people and incorporates it with the information coming from its own senses," neuroscientist Gregory Berns has written. "Many times, the group's opinion trumps the individual's before he even becomes aware of it."

This tug-of-war between the group and the individual has been a matter of deliberation for centuries. Does one act in his own interest or that of the group? Follow the urge to be unique or give in to the yearning to belong? Psychologists say these needs are in opposition, that "the satisfaction of one tends to come at the expense of the other." As Concordia University psychologist William Bukowski described, "Insofar as groups require consensus, homogeneity, and cohesion, they eschew individuality, diversity, and independence. As homogeneity and conformity within a group increase, diversity and individuality decrease."

These elements can characterize groups of any age. But students in middle and high schools might have neither the cognitive development to be able to extricate themselves easily from the influence of a group nor the awareness that they are mentally programmed to be so vulnerable to its whims. For them, the struggle between individuality and inclusion both adds to the confusion of adolescence and counters likely the strongest lure toward groups that they will ever experience in their lives. Which makes it all the more remarkable when a student is bold enough to swim against the tide.

Chapter 5

IT'S GOOD TO BE THE CAFETERIA FRINGE

Noah, Pennsylvania | The Band Geek

The hotel wake-up call rang ten minutes before midnight, less than three hours after Noah had fallen asleep. The boy nearest the phone missed the receiver in the darkness, accidentally knocking someone's glasses to the floor. Noah and his roommates groggily put on their uniforms and wished each other luck.

At about 3 A.M., Noah steered the golf cart taxi into Herald Square for the single on-site rehearsal. Afterward he drove his friend Jiang through the New York City streets to the Hard Rock Cafe, where the band was to eat breakfast. For kicks, Noah stopped six inches away from a parked BMW, laughing about the juxtaposition of a luxury vehicle with a foam-covered golf cart.

At dawn, the band unpacked the instruments. When Noah maneuvered the taxi around the floats toward the Mary's Thanksgiving Day Parade loading zone, students in other bands cheered. *I am not going to let Redsen down*, Noah thought. *I want this to be the best day of my life.* Two police officers jokingly asked Noah for his license and registration.

Finally, the parade began. As Noah drove through the streets in the middle of the band, he smiled and waved at people lining the sidewalks. Someone threw a ball of confetti at Noah, who swatted it to bystanders' applause. A band parent walking behind the taxi warned him to keep his eyes on the road. For more than an hour, Noah drove on. He heard a parent ask another where Jiang was marching. Noah turned to answer, "With percussion."

"NOAH!" several parents shouted. His taxi bumped a flutist, who stumbled. Noah heard what to him sounded like a sickening crunch as the parade spectators gasped. The flutist righted herself and kept marching, but Noah felt nauseous. *I just ruined the entire Macy's Parade,* he thought.

"Can you look at the damage?" Noah croaked to the band manager who walked beside the taxi.

"No, Noah. Just keep moving on."

Noah kept driving. Finally they reached the "Quiet Zone," adjacent to the telecast area. Noah inspected the taxi, saw no obvious damage that would show on TV, and exhaled in relief. He heard the tapping of the drums, pulled into position, tipped his cap to 45 million television viewers, and sped off, grinning widely. Noah dropped off the performer at her designated spot. He drove to the front of the band alongside the Honor Guards and looped around them.

As he proudly watched his band, he almost forgot to drive into his final position. He raced into the center of the formation to squeeze into the same rapidly narrowing space that had caused him to crash in practice. He could feel the foam of the taxi brush against a saxophonist's uniformed leg. Noah ignored the friction and drove toward the gap, where trumpeters and saxophonists were marching toward each other. Hundreds of days of counting down, months of afterschool and weekend practices, rehearsals at band camp, run-throughs at football games, run-ins with athletes . . . all came down to this flash of time, in which Noah zipped into his spot just before the marchers met and colorful streamers exploded around him in a revelry that echoed the exhilaration in his heart.

BLUE, HAWAII | THE GAMER

At the top of the street not far behind his home, Blue longboarded in the moonlight, which was bright at two in the morning. Back and forth, he carved across the pavement. He preferred longboarding to skateboarding. While skateboarding was raw and harsh, longboarding had more of a graceful flow, an emphasis on balance and poise. Back and forth, back and forth. He was getting better at skating, and he was teaching himself a new artistic freestyle. It was like a dance, or an ice-skating routine, a sinuous glide that combined drifting, bombing, pumping, and technicals. It was beautiful. The steep hill was about a mile long, but Blue could make one run last an entire hour. Besides a touch of bravery, carving down this hill took little thought. He could empty his mind of matter, letting the repetitious sound of the board calm him. He had been longboarding regularly since he was nine.

This semester, he visited the hill late at night when he felt depressed, which was about twice a month. Nothing seemed to be going right. Blue had few people he could talk to about his feelings. He was still friends with Ty, Stewart, and Jackson, but he questioned the strength of their friendship, especially because they still participated in Arwing.

After school, Blue had gone to the teacher's lounge to microwave a snack. Mr. Pakaki happened to be there.

"Hey, are you coming camping with us?" he asked Blue. Blue hadn't done anything with Arwing since the group had edged him out.

"Yeahhh, no," Blue said.

"You drive me crazy sometimes," Pakaki said. "I know me and you never agreed on anything and your views are different, but without you the club is different. Herman doesn't really do anything. He's not like you."

No kidding, Blue thought. "Really, now," he said, leaning casually against the door frame.

Pakaki looked sheepish. "You know, we're planning this event against other schools. It's a lot like what you wanted to do. We could really use your help."

Blue had heard about this event, an interschool Madden tournament that wasn't remotely like the LAN party Blue had planned. "I'll think about it," he said.

"Wait—" Pakaki called out before Blue could leave. "Are you mad at me or something? You seem different."

"No, I'm fine. Seriously. See you," said Blue, who walked out of the room feeling as if he'd had a conversation with a junior high ex. He wasn't going camping.

With one week left to go in the quarter, Blue still hadn't begun his makeup work. He tried, but couldn't bring himself to do it. He had learned that his mother couldn't force him into the military without his consent. But he was now paralyzed by her constant reminders that he wouldn't graduate if he didn't pass every class.

He had IMed Jackson to ask for motivation. Jackson hadn't been nice to him lately, going so far as to tell Blue that he was naïve about Nate, that Nate was a jerk, even though Blue was still infatuated with him. Instead of motivating Blue, Jackson forgot to meet him when he said he would, laughed when Arwing members broke Blue's drumset, and generally drifted into Blue's life only when he needed something. Often this involved gaming. Blue's gaming team expected him to play in Modern Warfare 2 tournaments every day over Christmas weekend. He barely ever saw his friends in person anymore and he learned that they criticized his gaming skills behind his back.

Blue's days grew monotonous. After school he went to the mall alone, where he played one game of DrumMania before going home. Gaming was one of the few things that made him feel better about his life. He relished having control over a world, even if it wasn't his own. "I lack determination towards school because I've been feeling hopeless," he explained. "So instead I turn to things like video games, like 'Let's see if we can do *this* right.' And then I do and I feel better."

On days when he did manage to finish his homework, Blue felt he had accomplished a noteworthy feat. The next day, he would come home ready to complete his new assignments straightaway, but then his mother would yell at him for something or other, crushing his eagerness to be on task. So tonight, like many recent nights, with his homework unfinished and his motivation shot, instead of staying up late to work, he went skating. Back and forth, back and forth. His mind cleared, glazing over his troubles to languidly ponder more positive things. Gaming. Manga. Cars. By the time he reached the bottom of the hill, he would be able to go to sleep.

After school the next day, Blue walked into his guidance counselor's office, bracing himself for news that he might not graduate. The AP

Language class structure confused him. The teacher assigned a few practice AP essays each week, and gave one test at the end of the quarter. She had told the students she expected them to take notes on her lectures, which Blue hadn't done because he hadn't seen his classmates taking notes. He got As on most of the essays, then learned they didn't count toward his grade. He was shocked when one day the teacher asked to see the students' notebooks, and everyone else produced pages apparently written at home.

"What's up?" the counselor said.

"Uh, I think I failed AP Lang."

"What do you want me to do?" she asked.

"Well, I asked to be transferred into normal lang last quarter." He told her why he didn't like the AP class.

"Okay . . ."

"So what happens if I fail this quarter?" Blue asked.

"Well, you're just going to have to bust your ass next quarter then," Ms. Pierce answered.

Blue paused. Something wasn't adding up. "Wait . . . what? Wouldn't I be missing a half credit?"

"No, you get the credits at the end of the year. We average your two semester grades."

Blue's mind was blown. The panic that had swirled his thoughts, immobilizing him for weeks, was based on a fallacy. As he digested the counselor's words, he breathed, "I thought my whole life would be determined by this one stupid quarter. My mom's been telling me that this entire time."

"You thought that the whole time?!" Ms. Pierce asked, astounded.

That night, Blue decided to buy himself a blank keyboard. He could use a clean slate, a fresh motivation for productivity. A blank keyboard would force him to improve his typing because even if he looked down, the keys would be empty. As Ms. Collins told him so often, he could be disciplined when he wanted to be.

ONE AFTERNOON, BLUE DROVE Ty and Stewart to the beach. Midday it was too crowded, hot, and overrun with tourists, but by late afternoon, the beach emptied and the air cooled. Ty and Stewart grumbled as Blue led them on a half-mile walk to his favorite spot, a stretch of ocean that was mostly sandbar and shallow for dozens of yards in. The boys floated on their backs in the water, listening to a local band playing on shore.

When the sun began to set, Blue tapped Ty on the shoulder. "Look out to the horizon."

"Wha? Why?"

"Shut up and look."

Exasperated, Ty turned and looked. "Holyyy wowww."

"That's why we walked out this far," Blue said. The sky faded into blended bands of orange and purple. The water, stilled as if it were watching too, reflected a warm amaranth red. Swimmers in the distance turned to shadow.

"Blue, I think I'm going to stop making fun of you," Ty said.

On the way back to town, as Stewart plodded behind them, complaining about the walk, out of nowhere Ty called out, "So what do we do now, best friend?"

Did he really just say that? Blue thought, beaming. *Nobody's ever called me that before.* He said later, "For so long nobody knew I existed. I felt relieved, like maybe I don't need to keep thinking of excuses for being subpar anymore."

The following week, Ty broke up with a girlfriend who had caused too much drama. He told Blue he wanted to start his life over, beginning with the purchase of an Xbox.

Blue scanned Ty's room. It was disgusting. Whenever Blue made a major purchase, he liked to clean his already pristine room so that he could display his new gear in a suitably reverent setting. As Blue surveyed the piles of garbage on the floor and the moldy plates hanging out of desk drawers, he thought he could help his new best friend start with a clean slate, too.

He turned to Ty. "Can I clean your room?"

"What? Seriously?"

"Yeah. I mean, when was the last time you slept in your bed?" Mounds of trash, including petrified food, hid whatever linens lay beneath.

"Three years ago."

"WHAT?!"

Ty explained that he slept on the living room floor.

Blue began with cable management, using cable ties to neaten the wires around the computer that he had built for Ty last year. Ty watched Blue, reminiscing about the items that Blue pulled off the desk. After six hours and three giant trash bags, Blue wiped down the desk and shelves with tile cleaner, the only solvent he could find in the house. *Now that I've finally found someone willing to listen, I can't wait to teach him stuff,* Blue thought. Really, he had already begun. Earlier that week, he had taught Ty how to speedboard—bombing hills and making turns as quickly as possible on a low longboard. Speedboarding was difficult; it involved careful footwork and weight shifting. Ty hoped that accomplishing something scary would boost his confidence with girls.

Blue rearranged the remaining items on Ty's desk and set up the Xbox. When he returned the next day to tackle the rest of the room, Ty was inspired to help. Blue swept the carpet, filled six more trash bags with piles from the bed and the floor, changed the linens, and took Ty to a store where he could sell his books and manga. When Blue was finally finished, he vacuumed the room, then flopped on Ty's bed.

"Oh my God, Mom, come look what Blue did!" Ty called out.

When Ty's mother came in, she gasped. The room looked like a new college dorm, clean and organized. She turned to Blue in amazement. "You did this? For Ty?"

Blue gave a small smile. Ty left the room.

"Oh my. I can't believe this," she continued. "He's been stuck in a hard part of his life for a while. This all sort of built up. I'm really happy he has a friend like you."

"Don't worry. I like cleaning," Blue said. He went to his car to get a controller he had customized for Ty. When he returned, he overheard Ty's mother say, "He's an amazing influence on you, you know that?"

"I know," Ty said.

Over the next couple of weeks, Blue taught Ty how to drive stick shift and surf. He showed him his favorite parts of the island, taking him to a new beach every day. Ty leaned on Blue, who was glad to be there for him. Yet something was still missing. It was nice to have a friend to share interests with, but Blue still didn't feel the connection he craved.

Regan, Georgia | The Weird Girl

Rumors started to swirl among students about Regan's sexuality. Last year it had been easier to lie to her classes by omission because she didn't have a steady girlfriend. She worried now that if she came out, students' blatant homophobia would turn her from an outcast to a victim.

Regan didn't care what her colleagues thought of her, which was why she had brought Crystal to the first-day-of-school faculty assembly. But her students were another story. "My relationship with my kids is so wildly important to me; I'd be crushed if anything ruined that rapport," she said. "A lot of them love and trust me on a level that is very special and beyond the average teacher-student bond. I'm afraid it will be shattered. Then I would be shattered."

Regan made a point of not lying, and yet she had been concealing the truth from some of the people she cared about most. "What kind of role model am I if I perpetuate a culture of shame?" she said. When she asked a former administrator if she could be open about her sexuality, the administrator told her not to "flaunt" her private life. "If you were married, it would be different," the administrator said.

In the Bible Belt? Not likely. As Regan told Crystal, "I could be fired, or not hired, for being gay. Do you know how hard that makes what I do for a living? I'm so close to so many of these kids, but I can't tell them or anyone else at school that I'm gay because I could lose my job, the one thing that I've worked so hard to get and love above all else. That could be taken away from me in a second because I'm gay. And I feel like I'm the only one, and I have no one to talk to." By late fall, Regan decided that if anyone at school—teacher or student—asked her about her sexuality, she would tell the truth.

Her opportunity came quickly. In first period, when Regan was again explaining why the word "faggot" was offensive, a freshman said, "Damn, you always defending gay people. Are *you* gay?"

Startled by the bluntness of the question, Regan nodded. The rest of the class followed intently.

He looked incredulous. "Are you bisexual?" he asked, as if that would make more sense.

Regan shook her head.

"You're really gay?"

She nodded again. The students were silent for a moment before erupting. "Duh, why didn't we figure it out before?!" Various students cited instances in which Regan's gayness should have been obvious to them. The class was unfazed by her coming out. They were offended only because she had hidden such an important part of her life from them.

Soon afterward, Regan helped freshmen organize a student performance of spoken word poetry to an audience of four English classes. Regan arranged with the school for Crystal's band to play a set. The event went fairly well, Regan thought. In third period, however, a student said to Regan, "I just want to let you know that some of your friends are two-faced."

"What do you mean?" Regan asked.

"I heard people talking bad about you at your event." The girl said that most of the students had enjoyed it, but she overheard two teachers complaining that the event was out of control and that Regan was to blame. They were upset that one of the student poems discussed two boys falling in love and another used "the n-word." They dragged their classes out of the event before it ended.

At lunch, an administrator who had not attended the event sternly told Regan that it had been a disaster. She said Regan would not be permitted to organize another similar event at school. Regan was taken aback. She had never been in trouble at school before and didn't think either poem was explicit or inappropriate. By the end of the day, a rumor ricocheted around the hallways that Regan might be fired.

The next morning, Regan's second period students—who had known for weeks that Regan was dating a musician—asked which member of the band was her "S.O."

One student whispered to another, "I think it's the girl."

"Is it the girl?" the other asked Regan. "She thinks it's the girl."

Regan paused. The room was quiet. All faces turned toward Regan expectantly. "Yes," Regan said. "It's Crystal."

The class was placated. "It's okay, Davis, we still love you," someone said.

"It's okay," a girl repeated, "I have a girlfriend too."

A boy stood up. "Well, since we're all coming out of the closet, I too have a girlfriend." The class laughed.

It felt so much better to be open with people, which was Regan's nature to begin with. Over the next several days, students freely asked her about Crystal. Regan loved being out at school.

DANIELLE, ILLINOIS | THE LONER

Danielle was excited to hear that the snow team season was under way. The snow team was a club that organized trips to a Wisconsin resort every week or two from November to March. The bus left after school on Fridays and brought the students back later that night. Eager to try out her new snowboard, Danielle asked, in succession, Paige, Camille, and Nikki to go on the first trip with her, but none of them agreed. She didn't bother asking Mona, who wasn't athletic. Danielle went anyway.

She didn't mind that she was the only student who had come by herself. On the hills, she spent much of the time falling on her knees and her backside, to the point where she almost cried out from the soreness. Frustrated, she kept getting back up to try again, determined to improve. She loved speed, snow, and extreme sports. (Despite her mother's protests, Danielle planned to skydive on her eighteenth birthday.) Once her psychology class had taken a test that measured students' penchant for thrill-seeking. Danielle scored 12 out of 14 points, the highest score in the class.

After three hours of boarding, Danielle took a break. Inside the lodge, students gossiped loudly. Danielle sat down to eat at an empty table by the window. Everyone else was hanging out with a group, and Danielle didn't want to infringe on people's space. She tuned out the noise and watched snowboarders and skiers gliding down the black diamonds. When she finished dinner, she went upstairs to explore. In a lounge area with a large window overlooking the slopes, she saw a couple of girls from Stone Mill sitting with guys from another school. Shelby, the snow team president, spotted her. "Danielle, come sit with us!" Hesitantly, Danielle sat at the edge of the table next to the other girl, a sophomore whom she recognized from meetings for the school literary magazine.

"Hey," said the girl, smiling at Danielle.

"Hey. Does Shelby actually know these people?!" Danielle asked in a low voice, gesturing to the guys.

"No, she just met them and decided to sit with them."

"Oh."

"How long have you been snowboarding?" the girl asked.

"I took lessons last year, but this is my third time. You?"

"Three years."

"Oh." Danielle tried hard to think of something else to say. *I suck at small talk with people my own age,* she thought.

Shelby looked over and mentioned an art class that she had TA'd when Danielle was a sophomore. "You were always so quiet in that class! I hated that about you!"

Danielle shrugged. "Oh, yeah . . . I didn't really know anyone in the class, so . . ." She didn't see why her reticence mattered. Danielle wandered outside again and spent the remaining hours of the trip by herself.

At school, Danielle had shifted to visiting Emily and Viv during lunch instead of during her free period. That way she didn't have to deal with finding lunch companions. The aide would sit Danielle and two other student visitors in a semicircle to answer questions about themselves. In response to their answers, Viv, who could understand speech, would nod or raise her eyebrows.

As Danielle returned to the sisters' classroom week after week, she realized she enjoyed visiting them. She liked making crafts with the girls, and helping with the goofy stuff they did, like the "Armadillo Race," which they looked forward to every year. Each visitor planted an amaryllis; the student whose amaryllis bloomed first won a prize. Because the sisters couldn't see the plants, the students wrote their names on note cards in puffy glitter ink and glued on a symbol so the sisters, who judged the race, could tell the plants apart. Danielle's symbol was a bead in the shape of a conch shell.

When Danielle had picked up her amaryllis plant from Viv and Emily's classroom, she walked through the halls, head down as usual, half-hidden by a large white flower with flashes of pink. Other students made snide remarks. "What is she *carrying?!*" various students said, giggling.

Danielle nearly snapped at one guy that he must be "a complete idiot" if he couldn't tell that she was carrying a plant, but she held back. *It's not worth it,* she told herself. *They're stupid. They don't have any idea that the flower is a big deal to Viv and Emily.* She told herself not to get angry, but it wasn't easy. *Those people can see and do pretty much whatever they want, while Viv and Emily can't really do anything. Yet they make fun of the things that Viv and Emily like. Kids at this school are such asses.*

Danielle relished the challenge of working with people who had mental and physical handicaps. It wasn't easy to abide by new rules, steel herself from freaking out, and get used to seeing someone drool. Danielle was pleased that with the sisters, she was able to be patient without getting frustrated; patience was not Danielle's strong suit. Best of all, she liked talking to them. They seemed sincerely interested in Danielle's opinions and answers to the aide's random questions. They didn't judge her or pressure her to be someone she wasn't. Because the sisters couldn't talk, Danielle liked guessing their reactions by their facial expressions. Danielle slowly came to the realization that the girls' mutual appreciation of each other's company meant that Emily and Viv were her friends.

———

THE COURAGE OF NONCONFORMISTS

If there is one trait that most cafeteria fringe share, it is courage. No matter how awkward, timid, or insecure he or she might seem, any teenager who resists blending in with the crowd is brave.

A closer look at this age group's psychology reveals that the deck is stacked against singularity from early on. Studies have shown that children are psychologically drawn to peers who are similar and more likely to end friendships with kids who are different. From the age of five, students increasingly exclude peers who don't conform to group norms. Children learn this lesson quickly. A popular Indiana eighth grader told me, "I have to be the same as everybody else, or people won't like me anymore."

Numerous studies show that students in the same social circle tend to have similar levels of academics, leadership, aggression, and cooperation. The most influential kids are also typically the same ones who insist most stridently on conformity; researchers have found that even in late adolescence, popular cliques are more conformist than other groups. Given that many children often try to copy populars' behavior, it makes sense that conformity trickles down the social hierarchy.

But conformity is not an admirable trait. Conformity is a cop-out. It threatens self-awareness. It can lead groups to enforce rigid and arbitrary rules. Adolescent groups with high levels of conformity experience more negative behavior—with group members and outsiders—than do groups with lower levels of conformity. Conformity can become dangerous, leading to unhealthy behaviors, and it goes against a teenager's innate desire to form a unique identity. Why, then, is conformity so common?

In the mid-twentieth century, psychologists discovered that when asked to judge an ambiguous test, such as an optical illusion, individuals usually parroted the opinions of the other people in the room. In the 1950s, social psychologist Solomon Asch decided to gauge levels of conformity when the test answers were absolutely clear. Asch assumed that people wouldn't bother to conform to an incorrect group opinion when the answer was obvious.

Asch was wrong—and his results stunned academia. For the experiment, he brought college students, one by one, into a room with six to eight other participants. He showed the room a picture of one line and a separate picture containing three lines labeled 1, 2, and 3. One of the three lines was the same length as the line in the first picture, while the other two differed by as much as several inches. Asch then had each volunteer call out the number of the line he believed to be the same length as the first. Unbeknownst to the college student, who was the last to be called on, the other participants were in on the experiment. Asch had instructed them to call out the wrong number on twelve out of eighteen trials. At least once, even when the answer was plain to see, nearly three-quarters of the students repeated the group's wrong answer.

Sixty years later, scientists are discovering that there are deeper factors at work than even Asch could have imagined. New research using brain imaging studies suggests that there is a biological explanation for the variation in people's ability to resist the temptation to conform. Neuroscientists monitoring brain images during conformity experiments similar to Asch's have found that participants are not necessarily imitating the majority merely to fit in. Instead, participants' visual perception seems to change to align with the answers of the rest of the group.

To understand how this change could take place, it's helpful to know that the brain is an efficient organ that likes to cheat. In order to conserve energy, it takes shortcuts whenever possible, such as the reliance on labels explained earlier. Another shortcut is a concept known as the Law of Large Numbers, a probability theorem according to which, "the more measurements you make of something, the more accurate the average of these measurements becomes." When the students in Asch's experiment conformed to group opinion, their brains were taking the Law of Large Numbers shortcut, assuming that the opinion of the group was more statistically accurate than any individual's. In 2005, neuroscientist Gregory Berns conducted a similar experiment, this time using MRIs to measure participants' brain activity. Berns observed that deferring to the group took some of the pressure off the decision-making part of the brain.

Berns also noticed something else, as he wrote in his intriguing book *Iconoclast*: "We observed the fear system kicking in, almost like a fail-safe when the individual went against the group. These are powerful biological mechanisms that make it extremely difficult to think like an iconoclast."

Berns saw increased activity in the amygdala when his test subjects did not conform to group opinion. Amygdala activity can lead to a rise in blood pressure and heart rate, sweating, and rapid breathing. "Its activation during nonconformity underscored the unpleasant nature of standing alone—even when the individual had no recollection of it," Berns wrote. "In many people, the brain would rather avoid activating the fear system and just change perception to conform with the social norm."

Researchers in the Netherlands discovered an even stronger link between nonconformity and fear. In 2009, they published their finding that when a person learns that his opinion differs from group norms, his brain emits an error signal. The signal is produced by the same area of the brain engaged when someone faces financial loss or social exclusion. That signal, the researchers said, triggers a process that can impel the person to conform to the group, changing his opinion even when the group opinion is wrong (as in the Asch experiment).

These scientists took MRIs of volunteers' brains as they evaluated the attractiveness of a series of faces. After the volunteers rated a face, they were told the "group" rating, a fictional number manipulated by the scientists. Thirty minutes after the experiment, the researchers unexpectedly asked the participants to rate the faces again. The participants who conformed the most to the group were those whose brains had emitted the strongest error signals when they learned the ratings. The researchers concluded that a person's tendency to conform is partly based on his brain's response to social conflict; the strength of the error signal determines the threshold that triggers conformity. "Deviation from the group opinion is regarded by the brain as a punishment," Vasily Klucharev, the study's lead author, said, which "explains why we often automatically adjust our opinion in line with the majority opinion."

Nonconformists, therefore, aren't just going against the grain; they're going against the *brain*. Either their brains aren't taking the easy way out to begin with, or in standing apart from their peers, these students are standing up to their biology. In their struggle to stay true to themselves, the featured characters in this book ultimately were not deterred by the emotions or physical sensations caused by the brain's error signals. Blue expressed unconventional theories, Regan came out, Danielle went alone on a school-sponsored trip. Simply by being cafeteria fringe, these defiant outsiders were braver than they knew.

WHITNEY, NEW YORK | THE POPULAR BITCH

At a winter break party thrown by a Riverland alum, Luke and Whitney got drunk. Whitney tried to convince Luke to have sex with her in her car, but he didn't want to be rude to the partygoers. Whitney tore out of her car, slammed the door, and went back into the house, drunk-crying and smiling at the same time.

"Yeah, Whitney!" said Spencer, and slapped her palm.

When Luke walked in after her, the prep guys feigned enthusiasm. "Yeahhh, woooh!" they shouted. "Yeah, Luke!" Spencer yelled obnoxiously, and tried to give Luke a high five.

Luke, still angry, walked by Spencer, muttering, "Nah, man, it's not like that."

Whitney kept drinking. She was in the kitchen with some of the popular guys and an older girl when Spencer said, "You know, Whitney, my brother's been talking about you all night."

"Really?"

"Yeah," the girl agreed. "He's been really lonely since [his girlfriend] broke up with him."

"Really?" Whitney tried to pay attention through her drunken haze.

"I heard he has a huge dick," the girl said.

"REALLY?"

"Yup. I've seen it."

"I can't because of Luke," Whitney said.

"Whitney, girls would kill to be in your position," Spencer said. "He's so much better than Luke. Luke's just stoner trash." He badgered her about Luke being "weird and different."

Whitney's head was foggy. Were her friends sincere or attempting to sabotage her relationship with Luke? "I don't know." She turned to the girl. "You make the decision for me. You're like my big sister."

Whitney was fighting desperately to keep her status in the clique.

Earlier that week, Whitney had IMed Bianca to ask if anything was going on. Bianca said that several people were going out for lunch. *Thanks for inviting me*, Whitney thought, and met Bianca, Giselle, Madison, and Bobby at the pizzeria. When Seth (who was now Giselle's boyfriend) and another popular guy showed up and asked if anyone wanted to go to the school's basketball game that night, the group quickly arranged a car, leaving Whitney out. No one seemed to notice.

Whitney made the two-hour drive to the game anyway; because the event wasn't a party, it was acceptable to take a second car. In the parking lot afterward, Seth mentioned to Whitney that the group was going out to dinner. Whitney turned to Bianca and Madison. "Would you guys mind riding with me so I don't have to drive alone? We could be one car and Bobby, Seth, and Giselle could go in Seth's car."

Bianca and Madison exchanged a look. "Uh," said Madison, "well, Seth is bringing me home after dinner."

"I could drive you," Whitney said.

"Uh, maybe!" Madison said.

Whitney watched in disbelief as Bianca and Madison speed-walked across the parking lot and jumped into Seth's car. Whitney got into her own car and, crying, followed the populars' car to the restaurant. She sat at their table, quietly sipping lemon water and pretending she wasn't upset.

Now, her inhibitions drowned in seven shots of vodka, Whitney threw herself at other guys in front of Luke until he got fed up and left the party. Meanwhile, Whitney's friends told Spencer's brother that she wanted to sleep with him. He texted Whitney from the living room. "I want to see your underwear on the outside. Let's go to my truck."

Whitney flashbacked to junior year prom, when she had been so intoxicated that she had almost been date-raped. Luke was the only person she'd told about that. Whitney found Spencer in the dining room and told him she didn't want to sleep with his brother. She and Luke were exclusive.

Spencer got angry. "Luke's a fucking loser, Whitney. He looks like a girl and is this tall!" Spencer held his hand up to his nose. "You're

better than that. You're stupid if you don't fuck [my brother] tonight."
She didn't do it. Whitney spent the rest of the night passed out and
vomiting.

The next day, still hungover, Whitney volunteered to be the
designated driver for that night's New Year's Eve party. Irene asked
for a ride. Whitney checked with Bianca online. "Tell her 'No,'"
Bianca said. "Tell her there isn't any room," though there was.

Without a spot in the party car, Irene spent New Year's Eve at home.

ELI, VIRGINIA | THE NERD

Eli desperately tried to organize an outing for his Spanish camp friends.
He invited eleven of them to a large local mall. He had reservations
about inviting Debra—he was sure she had laughed at him behind his
back since middle school—but he asked her anyway.

"Hey, Debra," Eli called out from his seat as she entered their Spanish classroom, "Me, Raj, and Ashley are going to [the mall] this weekend. Would you wanna go?"

Debra, who was semi-popular, looked around the room, seemingly
embarrassed. "Uh, I have to ask my mom first," she said, her voice cold
and dismissive. She leaned over to whisper to a friend, who stared directly at Eli.

Am I really that awkward? he thought.

That night, Debra IMed Eli:

Debra: *Why'd you ask me to go with you guys this weekend?*[2]
Eli: *I thought you'd want to go . . .*
Debra: *okay. It's just, I mean . . . I've been kind of a jerk to you. And I
don't know why*
Eli: *Hahaha don't feel bad about it.*
Debra: *but I do. I have so much fun when I hang out with you and everyone
but then I get to school and I'm like a witch-with-a-b and idk why*
Eli: *I blame the school environment in general for people's bitterness.*

---

[2] *IMs and texts have been edited for punctuation.*

Seriously. I don't hold anything against you. (He sincerely believed that. Later, he explained, "People feel a need to act in conformity to what everyone else wants them to do. I know that half the people aren't really like how they act in school.")

Debra: *because I know that I am/was a jerk. And I just wanted you to know that I do feel really bad*

Eli: *Thanks, that actually really means a lot. To be honest, I didn't think you were mean. I just thought you didn't like me as a person.*

Debra: *no I do. But at school I get negative feelings towards you FOR ABSOLUTELY NO REASON*

Debra: *and I do like you so I'm like wtf brain. Stop it.*

Eli: *I really appreciate that you said all that, but you didn't have to.*

Debra: *okayy. But if it is okay, i'd like to go with y'all this weekend*

Eli: *YES!!!*

Debra asked Eli for a ride and logged off.

That Saturday, Eli picked up Raj and Debra, who immediately unplugged Eli's iPod and replaced it with hers. They met Ashley at the mall. Eli had been discouraged that only three of eleven of his supposedly closest friends had shown up, but what was worse, the three were unenthusiastic. When Eli attempted to keep the conversation flowing, someone inevitably talked over him.

Eli found himself walking behind the others, who traipsed through the crowded walkways side by side. Whenever Eli tried to step into their line, Raj shifted so that Eli couldn't squeeze in. On one such attempt, Raj said, "He's so socially awkward!" to the others in a voice he knew Eli could hear. *I was nice enough to give you a ride, and that's how you treat me?* Eli thought.

After Debra and Ashley veered off to check out a girls' store, Eli followed Raj into The North Face. Eli was at the mall for the company; he hadn't planned to shop. He trailed Raj around the store, expecting to chat. As Raj thumbed a jacket, he turned to Eli and said, "Why don't you just go look around yourself?" When Eli obliged, Raj meandered toward another store, leaving Eli feeling awkward because they had told the girls they would be in The North Face and Eli thought it would be "tacky" to make them search the mall.

Eventually the group rendezvoused at Barnes & Noble so Eli could buy a new biography. Undeterred by his friends' arguments that fiction was a much better genre, he picked up a biography that interested him. "What is *that*?!" Debra asked.

"A Grace Kelly book." Eli liked Grace Kelly because she had been in Hitchcock films.

"You are such a movie junkie. 'Oh, I won't watch anything after 1970.'"

"I just think most of the good movies were made before 1970," Eli said. He asked Debra, "Have you seen any Hitchcock movies?" She hadn't. "Okay, you haven't seen a movie until you've seen a Hitchcock movie." Eli mentioned a few specific Hitchcock films he loved.

"We get it," she said. "You like Hitchcock. I don't understand why you don't like any recent movies. They're so good!"

Later that weekend, Eli pondered his disenchantment over what should have been his big social outing. The mall trip had reaffirmed his desire to get as far from home as possible, as quickly as he could. "I've been wondering," he mused, "am I really cynical toward society? Is there even a place for me? What is it even like to have friends? I feel really isolated because there isn't anyone who identifies with me. I have a few strong ideals and interests: adventurous travel, old movies, conservatism, Agatha Christie books, British music. But there isn't a single person who seems to relate with me on any level, especially when taking those interests into account. I guess part of the reason I want to get out of Virginia is to leave everything behind."

Soon afterward, Eli was rummaging through the mail on his father's kitchen table when an envelope caught his eye. The return address label read "Westcoast University Admissions." Eli held his breath. *Uh-oh,* he thought, *the envelope is super-thin.* He skipped to the end of the letter to determine whether he wanted to read the beginning. He saw a line about sending him more information in the mail at a later date. He began to get excited. Finally he forced himself to read the first line of the letter. "Congratulations!" *Wow, this is it!* he thought. *It's all over. I never have to live in Virginia again.* He couldn't wait to make the move.

———

THE OUTCAST SUCCESS STORY

In 2010, press headlines crowed about Lady Gaga's sudden meteoric rise to iconic stardom. Known as much for her unique apparel and outrageous performances as for her music, the singer and shock artist debuted at number four on *Forbes* Celebrity 100: The World's Most Powerful Celebrities. *Time* also included her on its 2010 list, prompting Cyndi Lauper to observe, "When I see somebody like Gaga, I sit back in admiration. . . . I did an interview with her once, and she showed up with a sculpture on her head. I thought, 'How awesome.' Being around her, I felt like the dust was shaken off of me. I find it very comforting to sit next to somebody and not have to worry that I look like the freak. She isn't a pop act, she is a performance artist. She herself is the art. She is the sculpture."

Lady Gaga's outfits are not just a fashion statement. They are a life-style statement intended to encourage fellow cafeteria fringe to be themselves. "I didn't fit in in high school and I felt like a freak," she told Ellen DeGeneres. "So I like to create this atmosphere for my fans where they feel like they have a freak in me to hang out with and they don't feel alone."

At her all-girls private school in New York City, Lady Gaga was a self-proclaimed "nerdball in theater and chorus" whom classmates teased for her eccentric style. Meanwhile she played open mic nights at clubs as early as age fourteen; by age twenty, she was signed to a label. "This is really who I am, and it took a long time to be okay with that," she said. "Maybe in high school you . . . feel discriminated against. Like you don't fit in and you want to be like everyone else, but not really. . . . Sometimes in life you don't always feel like a winner, but that doesn't mean you're not a winner; you want to be like yourself. I want my fans to know it's okay. . . . It's all about letting people who don't fit in know that someone out there is fine with who they are—and that other people have gone through the same thing."

Like Lady Gaga, quirk theory assures marginalized young people that someday they will be welcomed for the same reasons that classmates relegate them to what one former outcast called "the land of misfit toys." Whereas the popular crowd in school might reward conformity, aggression, and a silent acceptance of the status quo, people outside of the school setting tend to admire entirely different qualities.

In a comprehensive review of literature about success, happiness, and influence, the same core qualities repeatedly appear as the characteristics that cause people to be respected, honored, and appreciated outside of school. They are applicable in both personal and professional lives, and to artistic endeavors, corporate undertakings, and the vast range of pursuits in between. And all of these qualities are found in the cafeteria fringe in droves.

CREATIVITY, ORIGINALITY

No matter how trite the observation, there can be little doubt that creativity and originality, earmarks of the cafeteria fringe, are valued exponentially more outside of middle school and high school walls. Companies scramble to come up with The Next Big Thing. The "life of the party" is the adult who has the most interesting stories or the most novel ideas. The celebrity sphere revolves mostly around actors, musicians, and fashionistas, all of whose public works involve artistic expression.

Many companies that have distinguished themselves in the twenty-first century have done so by prioritizing creativity and originality. HBO, which holds the record for Emmy nominations in a single year, is successful because of its originality. When deciding the fate of a show, HBO executives ask themselves, "Is it different? Is it distinctive? Is it good?" Southwest Airlines, which focuses on an unusual low-cost, direct point-to-point route system and ebullient customer service, is the only airline that has thrived in recent years; in 2010 Southwest celebrated its thirty-seventh consecutive year of profitability. Even training for the most senior government executives in the Senior Executive Service emphasizes unique thought processes. The six-week intensive training course makes a number of suggestions to jump-start that thinking, including commuting different routes to start the day by thinking differently. As William Taylor, the founding editor of *Fast Company* magazine, has written, "The work that matters most [is] the work of originality, creativity, and experimentation."

Yet so many of the students who demonstrate these qualities in school are branded as weird. Take Steven Spielberg. The legendary director has said that classmates saw him as "a real nerd—the skinny, acne-faced wimp who gets picked on by big football jocks."

In one high school, Spielberg was beaten up because he was Jewish. "I got smacked and kicked to the ground during PE, in the locker room, in the showers," he said. "Pennies were thrown at me in the study hall in a very quiet room of one hundred students. People coughed the word 'Jew' in their hand as they passed me in the hallway."

In another high school, students mocked him because they thought he was "weird" and "independent-minded," said a classmate who played in the school band with Spielberg. At that time in his life, Spielberg was already preoccupied with filming, constantly snapping photographs with the camera he carried around school. His mother recalled, "He always saw things differently than anybody else." Described by classmates as shy, introverted, and ostracized, he "formed his own tight little social circle in response to his exclusion from the jockocracy of Arcadia High School," according to biographer Joseph McBride. "Steve's friends were mostly creative oddballs like him, and the things they were doing were not mainstream interests at Arcadia. When he became part of the drama group, it was the first time he 'realized there were options besides being a jock or a wimp.' But he still could not help regarding that group as 'my leper colony.'"

Outside of school, Spielberg concentrated on filmmaking, creating impressive special effects and shooting movies in his backyard. For one of those movies, he cast his most intimidating bully as a fighter squadron leader. "He was my nemesis; I dreamed about him," Spielberg said. "Even when he was in one of my movies, I was afraid of him. But I was able to bring him over to a place where I felt safer: in front of my camera. I didn't use words. I used a camera, and I discovered what a tool and a weapon, what an instrument of self-inspection and self-expression it is. . . . I had learned that film was power." The film won first place in a statewide amateur film competition. Spielberg was fourteen. He would go on to become what the *New York Times* called "the most bankable director in the business," and to win countless awards, among them Best Director and Best Picture Oscars for *Schindler's List*, the first major Hollywood film to portray the Holocaust.

FREETHINKING, VISION

"Big ideas come from big thinkers: the eccentric genius, the inspired founder, the visionary CEO," *Fast Company*'s William Taylor wrote. "Business history is filled with heroic tales of breakthroughs fueled by unique imagination and individual determination. Alexander Graham Bell and the telephone. Henry Ford and the assembly line. Edward Land and instant photography." Innovation of thought is just as important as creativity of expression. We wouldn't have progress—cures for diseases, ways to harness new energy sources—without the foresight of people who devise or are willing to operate under different philosophies and points of view.

In 1896, French naturalist Jean-Henri Fabre developed an interest in processionary caterpillars, which move in long, head-to-tail lines. Fabre observed the caterpillars circling the rim of a flowerpot in a continuous loop. He placed the caterpillars' favorite food "not a hands' breadth away." For seven days, the caterpillars instinctively followed each other around the rim until they died of hunger and exhaustion. They were so focused on the trail in front of them that they could not see that a simple six-inch deviation from the line would save their lives.

As opposed to the habitual human equivalents of these followers, freethinkers are people who are able and willing to look beyond the rim of the flowerpot. *Fortune* magazine's Manager of the Century, Jack Welch, who, during his tenure as CEO of General Electric turned it into the world's most valuable corporation, addressed the importance of this trait in his book *Winning*. He sought in a senior-level leader "the ability to see around corners. Every leader has to have a vision and the ability to predict the future, but good leaders must have a special capacity to anticipate the radically unexpected."

The cafeteria fringe are well-suited to seeing around corners; they are not so mired in the mainstream that they cannot step back and view multiple angles. Blue demonstrated such freethinking when he opined that Facebook could take over Google. (Incidentally, I ran Blue's argument by *The Google Story* coauthor Mark Malseed, who said, "Overall his point is valid and shows a deeper understanding of how these services and businesses truly work.")

Living life on a tangent to the prevailing norms places the cafeteria fringe uniquely at the threshold of new movements and new directions. As National Book Award winner Don DeLillo observed in the *Hungry Mind Review,* "The Writer . . . is situated now, if anywhere, on the margins of culture. But isn't this where he belongs? How could it be any other way? And in my personal view this is a perfect place to observe what's happening at the dead center of things. . . . The more marginal, perhaps ultimately the more trenchant and observant and finally necessary he'll become."

Experts say that this kind of vision is why Albert Einstein was able to understand physics' biggest puzzles. Considered a rebel and a loner as a child, Einstein, said a colleague, "was inclined to separate himself from children his own age and to engage in daydreaming and meditative musing." He often preferred to tackle mathematical proofs than to socialize. "Play and playmates were forgotten. For days on end he sat alone, immersed in the search for a solution, not giving up until he found it," his sister told biographer Walter Isaacson.

As a child, Einstein was slow to speak. "When I ask myself how it happened that I in particular discovered the relativity theory," he said, "it seemed to lie in the following circumstance. The ordinary adult never bothers his head about the problems of space and time. But I developed so slowly that I began to wonder about space and time only when I was already grown up. Consequently I probed more deeply into the problem than an ordinary child would have."

At school, Einstein wrote, being bullied gave him "a lively sense of being an outsider." Although he earned good grades, he was so uncomfortable with the "mechanical," militaristic teaching style, which was devoid of creativity, that his obvious aversion to it led teachers to push him out of school before graduation.

Being an outsider helped Einstein immensely; because he wasn't accepted into the physics establishment, he had nothing to lose by challenging the status quo. "He comes in entirely as an outsider. He lets his mind wander. He's not endangering his academic position because he doesn't have one, and he can take those risks," Einstein scholar Gerald Holton told the *Boston Globe*. While other scientists metaphorically climbed the north face of Mount Everest, Holton said, Einstein thought "it's the wrong mountain and it's the wrong face, and you ought to really be hovering above it all."

Einstein developed the theory of relativity precisely because of his different way of thinking. "Other scientists had come close to his insight, but they were too confined by the dogmas of the day. Einstein alone was impertinent enough to discard the notion of absolute time, one of the sacred tenets of classical physics since Newton," Isaacson wrote in a *Wired* article. "What made Einstein special was his impertinence, his nonconformity, and his distaste for dogma. Einstein's genius reminds us that a society's competitive advantage comes not from teaching the multiplication or periodic tables but from nurturing rebels. Grinds have their place, but unruly geeks change the world."

RESILIENCE

Activist Marian Wright Edelman is the founder of the Children's Defense Fund, the nation's foremost child advocacy organization; she was also the first African-American admitted to the Mississippi Bar. When asked for her secret to success, she identified two characteristics that happen to be applicable to people who have been on the margins. She said, "Give me the man or woman who sees the big picture, who grabs the larger view. Show me the child who has heart and purpose and stands firm amid ridicule and defeat. It is the homestretch that builds the individual."

Resilience is a globally admired quality. The character-building and fortitude gained from missteps can lead to endurance, patience, passion, growth, knowledge, and a host of other key qualities. Bestselling business author Jim Collins called this feature "the hardiness factor," in praise of people who have used a negative experience "as a defining event that made them stronger."

Television and film actor Freddie Prinze Jr., a onetime teen idol, is an example of this type of resilience. He was too young to know his famous comedian father, who, under the influence of drugs, killed himself when Prinze was a baby. But he had to cope with the resulting feeling of abandonment, combined with constant reminders of the void in his life; reporters grilled him about his dad even as he stepped onto his school bus. He dealt with these issues by creating a fantasy world in which to escape.

An avid comic book collector, Prinze found comfort in Stan Lee's characters because, he said, "somehow they embraced who they were and they became great heroes. They made me feel that everything could be okay." He especially related to the X-Men, outcasts who used their superpowers for good even as society rejected them only because they were different. "I would always pretend that I was this new member of the X-Men, this kid, this young boy, who really didn't fit in with society because he couldn't control his power," Prinze has said. "I named him Prism because he would absorb emotion from other people. Like, if they were mean to him . . . it would be released in all these different directions, and he wouldn't be able to focus his energy."

He spent afternoons on his high school athletic fields pretending to be Prism, battling villains like Magneto, "running and diving and trying to dodge magnetic blasts." Students called him freak and weirdo and isolated him. Bullies threw rocks at him. "Kids thought that was really strange. And it is, okay? I know that I'm weird and I'm the first to admit it. But that's what I loved to do," Prinze said. "Instead of getting pissed off, I tried to hone my skills, so eventually one day people would understand what I was doing."

Now they understand the actor, who had a recurring role on the final season of *24*. As the *Los Angeles Times* observed, "The quirks that made him a misfit at school bring him fame and fortune in Hollywood." In school, people thought Prinze was odd because he was quiet and sensitive, and they made fun of him for creating plays for girls in his class. As an actor, Prinze exhibits what one journalist called a "vulnerable humanity." Director Darren Stein dubbed him "a male Julia Roberts, the kind of actor that projects the inner self and makes a character glow." *She's All That* costar Rachel Leigh Cook said, "He's just an incredibly natural actor, and by far the nicest guy in the business. That's said about a lot of people, but it's actually true about Freddie."

"Back then I was considered weird and a freak, and now I'm considered artistic and an actor, and I do the exact same thing that I was doing back then. . . . People think I'm cool now for the reasons they thought I was strange when I was a kid. I am absolutely committed to my imagination," Prinze has said. "I look at it like this: I sit back and watch. My whole life, I've always been on the outside looking in, I've never fit in, and I love it like that."

AUTHENTICITY, SELF-AWARENESS

Former United Nations Secretary General Dag Hammarskjöld once said, "The more faithfully you listen to the voice within you, the better you will hear what is sounding outside. And only those who listen can speak." Self-awareness is an authenticity of being. It is a commitment to the values and philosophies that you have already figured out are important to your individual identity. It is an understanding of what will make you happy, successful, respected, or valued. In school, cafeteria fringe may not yet know precisely who they are, but at least they are more true to themselves than the students who conform to the in crowd. Self-awareness, wrote Stephen Covey in the best-selling *The 7 Habits of Highly Effective People*, "enables us to stand apart and examine even the way we 'see' ourselves. . . . It affects not only our attitudes and behaviors but also how we see other people. It becomes our map of the basic nature of mankind."

In the business world, people who live their lives according to their core values tend to have strong brands with devoted followings. Craigslist, which is worth more than $5 billion, succeeds because of its down-to-earth "nerd values," wrote founder Craig Newmark, who "grew up wearing a plastic pocket protector and thick, black glasses, taped together, the full nerd cliché." Ben and Jerry, of the eponymous ice-cream brand, have said that they became successful because, although they didn't always know what they were doing, they knew why they were doing it. They view the company as a values-led business that promotes "social progress for the common good: advocating for the many people in our society whose needs are not served by the status quo; giving a voice to the people who normally aren't heard." (Ben and Jerry, who met in school as shy boys and the two slowest students in gym class, are also known for their creative marketing and business policies.)

Certainly one need not be a leader to be successful, admired, or respected in adulthood, but it's worth mentioning that self-awareness is extolled by many management experts. In *The 108 Skills of Natural Born Leaders*, University of Houston management professor Warren Blank listed self-awareness as number one. "Self-awareness is fundamental to leadership growth," Blank wrote. Self-aware people "know their strengths, weaknesses, and assumptions. They understand their motives and recognize what deserves attention. . . . Master leaders also know how to demonstrate strong emotions."

Fall Out Boy, the multiplatinum, Grammy-nominated punk-pop band that has been called "the kings of emo," is famous for expressing emotions authentically. As one magazine observed, "an entire generation hears its own experiences described in the genre's diaristic lyrics about tortured romances and crippling self-doubt, and it prizes these scars like priceless jewels. Emo bands don't merely wear their heart on their sleeve—they lift up their sleeve to show the bloody wounds underneath." Frontman Pete Wentz, the bassist and lyricist famous as much for his guyliner (male eyeliner) as for his outspokenness, has called his music "a giant pop-culture idea, but it's still weird and different."

Wentz, who once dyed his hair blue, can relate. In high school, although he was a talented soccer player, he was also an emo, "a solitary guy. I was definitely into invisible friends and making up stories," he has said. "I was pretty outcast, but a lot of it was by choice. I was kind of a geek. . . . I looked weird." He has been open about his depression and stints in therapy.

Today, Fall Out Boy, as one reviewer put it, is known for "Wentz's deeply personal, introspective lyrics about self-doubt and self-loathing." (It is also known for its long song titles, such as "Our Lawyer Made Us Change the Name of This Song So We Wouldn't Get Sued" and "I Slept with Someone in Fall Out Boy and All I Got Was This Stupid Song Written about Me.") The band is "equal parts protector and patron saint of misfit underdogs," said another reviewer. By listening to the voice within him and sharing it unabashedly, Wentz has led Fall Out Boy to become not just a band, but, as Jay-Z called it, a movement. "People don't realize it's okay to feel down and sad sometimes. It is part of the cycle of feeling okay," Wentz has said. "There is an honesty in our music and I think people appreciate it. . . . We have always written what we are really feeling."

Wentz has created many outlets for what has been called his "confessional bravado." He wrote a comic book series based on Fall Out Boy's music, developed a clothing line, hosted a radio show, exhibited his own mixed-media art, and founded a record label for which he discovered bands like Gym Class Heroes and Panic! At the Disco, whose first record went platinum. VH1 named Wentz, a dedicated activist who was UNICEF's 2010 Tap Project national spokesperson, one of its "Top 20 Celebs Gone Good."

"I'm happy to be part of a culture where the guys who were made fun of in high school are now the ones the jocks go to see onstage," Wentz said. "I like the idea that everyone can get depressed and that there is a way to get through it."

INTEGRITY, CANDOR

If self-awareness and authenticity refer to being true to oneself, then integrity and candor refer to being honest in the ways one lives and interacts with others. Individuals with integrity earn people's trust because they consistently adhere to a code of ethical values, making good on promises and fulfilling expectations. Integrity is not the province of someone who engages in gossip or other relational aggressions, or who attempts to influence people by manipulating them. "Integrity also means avoiding any communication that is deceptive, full of guile, or beneath the dignity of people," according to *The 7 Habits of Highly Effective People.* "One of the most important ways to manifest integrity is to be loyal to those who are not present. In doing so, we build the trust of those who are present."

Candor expresses in language what integrity embodies in spirit. Honest interaction is valued not only in personal relationships—it's also good for business. "Lack of candor basically blocks smart ideas, fast action, and good people contributing all the stuff they've got," Jack Welch wrote. "Candor gets more people in the conversation and when you get more people in the conversation, to state the obvious, you get idea rich. By that I mean many more ideas get surfaced, discussed, pulled apart, and improved. Instead of everyone shutting down, everyone opens up and learns. . . . That approach—surface, debate, improve, decide—isn't just an advantage, it's a necessity in a global marketplace."

Grammy-winning country/pop superstar Taylor Swift is known for her candor. She writes her own material that describes real people, often by name. When the Jonas Brothers' Joe Jonas broke up with her in a twenty-seven-second phone call, for example, she wrote a song about it. She is beloved because, as one reviewer observed, "She listens to her heart, and it beats to the tune of teen angst, love lost and found, hurt feelings, and life being wonderful and unfair at the same time. . . . Her lyrics connect with the young and young at heart who understand those feelings. That gives her street cred, makes her believable far beyond most other older tunesmiths trying to write for teens."

Often her message is about how, while it's easier to conform to the crowd, being different makes people extraordinary. "The farther away you get from middle school, junior high, the more you realize that," Swift has said. "In the real world, if you have something about yourself that's different, you're lucky. It's not a curse."

Swift speaks from experience. In school, she was an outsider who "became a people-watcher when I lost all my friends." When she sat down at a lunch table, girls would get up and move to a different table. Why? "The kids at school thought it was weird that I liked country [music]. They'd make fun of me," she told *Teen Vogue*. Her clique cast her out because "in middle school there really doesn't have to be that much reason for people to not like you. Maybe it's because your hair is frizzy . . . or maybe it's because instead of getting drunk and going to parties on the weekends when you're thirteen, you write songs and play at coffeehouses."

Besides the obvious way in which being excluded because of her devotion to music exemplifies quirk theory, Swift has also attributed her success to the experience of being alienated by classmates. "It was so healthy for me to go through that rejection. Because I wouldn't be able to look at people and read a situation if I hadn't developed that skill when I was twelve," she said. "Looking back . . . I wouldn't have changed anything. If I had been popular, I would have been perfectly content with staying where I was."

In ninth grade, Swift moved to Nashville, earned a record deal, and at fourteen, became the youngest person that Sony/ATV Publishing had ever signed as a professional staff songwriter. When, a year into her career, she returned to her hometown, the girls who had shunned her "showed up, wearing my T-shirts and asking me to sign their CDs. It was bittersweet, because it made me realize that they didn't remember being mean to me and that I needed to forget about it too," Swift said. "Really, if I hadn't come home from school miserable every day, maybe I wouldn't have been so motivated to write songs. I should probably thank them!"

In 2008 and 2009, Taylor Swift sold more albums than any other musician or band in the world. In 2010 she became the top-selling digital artist in music history. As she told an audience at a concert in Nebraska, "What does it matter if you didn't have any friends in high school when you've got 15,000 of your closest friends coming to see you in Omaha?"

CURIOSITY, LOVE OF LEARNING, PASSION

When Yahoo! executives evaluate job candidates, they look for what the company calls the Y-Gene, described as a quality of people who "marvel at life and milk it for all it's worth. They're curious and energetic. They value openness and want to live unbridled and unrestricted. They appreciate that life is huge. They don't settle for the status quo—they want to grow."

Such qualities represent a zest for learning, for continually expanding the boundaries of one's knowledge and abilities. This ardor can manifest as unbridled emotion (as Noah felt toward the band) or as quiet devotion (as Eli felt about geography), as a curiosity that borders on skepticism (Danielle), or as a youthful enthusiasm (Regan). In a book about bridging the old economy with the new, London Business

School professor Gary Hamel, whom the *Wall Street Journal* ranked as the number one most influential business thinker in the world, wrote, "You must marry a thorough understanding of business concept innovation with the wide-eyed curiosity of a precocious five-year-old. Phrases such as 'disciplined imagination,' 'routine creativity,' and 'informed intuition' capture the challenge. . . . Imagination, creativity, and intuition [have] been bred out of you—first by school, then by work. Yet you can, and must, regain your lost curiosity. You must learn to see again with eyes undimmed by precedent."

When you do, both work and life can be informed by an outlook born from mastering something you love. When Yvon Chouinard, the founder of Patagonia, was in school, he was a loner and a "misfit" who subsequently looked to the outdoors for entertainment. To band eagles and falcons for the U.S. Fish & Wildlife Service, he learned how to rappel down cliffs, which sparked a lifetime love of rock climbing; he has since climbed mountains on every continent and has been called "the godfather of ice climbing in this country." A craftsman at heart, Chouinard developed his own climbing equipment and, eventually, the outdoor clothing and gear company Patagonia.

Patagonia's most widely acclaimed policies stem directly from Chouinard's passion for the environment. One of the first green companies, Patagonia annually gives 1 percent of its sales to environmental causes and makes all products from recycled or recyclable fibers. The company has worked with larger companies like Walmart, Nike, and Gap to help them become more eco-friendly. Every year, forty employees take paid two-month internships with environmental groups. Solar panels power one company building, and a recent extension was built using 95 percent recyclable materials. The employees with the most fuel-efficient cars are given the best parking spots. The company was one of the first to offer on-site child care and now hosts lunchtime yoga and Pilates sessions and occasional fly-fishing classes. Employees work flexible hours, often taking two-hour surfing jaunts or bike rides in the middle of the workday. Patagonia covers 100 percent of health premiums for all employees, including part-time workers. In his autobiography, Chouinard wrote, "Only those businesses operating with a sense of urgency . . . constantly evolving, open to diversity and new ways of doing things, are going to be here 100 years from now."

In 2007, *Fortune* ran a cover photo of Chouinard and called his company "the coolest company on the planet."

COURAGE

It is well-documented that courage is one of the most admired characteristics across the world. For their book *Character Strengths and Virtues*, psychologists Christopher Peterson and Martin Seligman studied various religions and attitudes in more than seventy countries, in order to develop a shortlist of "those abiding moral traits that everyone values" and the practice of which could bring about personal happiness or "the good life." Courage emerged as such a universally cherished characteristic that the authors highlighted it as one of six core virtues (the others were wisdom, humanity, justice, temperance, and transcendence). Courage "has an inner life as well as an outer one," the psychologists concluded. "Courage is composed of not just observable acts but also the cognitions, emotions, motivations, and decisions that bring them about. . . . We mean courage to include . . . any act of willfully overcoming into what it is so easy to slip: security, comfort, complacency. We mean doing what is right, even when one has much to lose."

Less about reckless behavior than strength of character, this kind of bravery includes standing up to or departing from group thinking, venturing into the unfamiliar, and making unpopular choices. As discussed earlier, courage is ever present among nonconformists. It is an emblem that, whether they know it or not, all cafeteria fringe wear by virtue of both the individualism that made them cafeteria fringe and the will to endure the exclusion as they continue to stay true to themselves.

Creativity. Freethinking. Resilience. Authenticity. Candor. Courage. None of these characteristics typically marks the collective popular crowd in schools. This is not to say that populars don't possess these characteristics, or that their own set of qualities, like negotiation skills and savvy, won't benefit them in the future. But they are perhaps less likely to exhibit them than, say, the geek, loner, punk, floater, freak, nerd, rebel, or outsider. If a student is marginalized at school, he likely already possesses at least a few of these traits. In the quest to have a satisfying post-school life that earns respect and appreciation, therefore, the cafeteria fringe are already ahead of the game.

Although the inner qualities that lead a student to be excluded or that inform his reaction to being excluded may carry over into adulthood, the exterior label doesn't have to. While scientists, doctors, writers, entrepreneurs, and various other professionals represent quirk theory, in this chapter I have focused mostly on celebrities to illustrate that popularity in adulthood is based on different factors than popularity in school. Consider this abridged list of celebrities who told the media they were excluded in school:

Judd Apatow, director, producer, screenwriter (*Superbad, Knocked Up, Freaks and Geeks*): "I think that everything I do tends to root for the underdog. I always felt as a kid that I was under-appreciated, invisible, or weird, but I've always secretly thought people would one day appreciate what is different about me. I'm always putting that message out there. Eventually the nerds and the geeks will have their day."

Actress **Angelina Jolie:** At school, "I was the punk outsider," she has said. "I used to cut myself or jump out of airplanes, trying to find something new to push up against because sometimes everything else felt too easy. I was searching for something deeper, something more. I tried everything. I always felt caged, closed in, like I was punching at things that weren't there. I always had too much energy for the room I was in." In adulthood, Jolie has channeled that energy into her award-winning humanitarianism efforts.

Actor **Zac Efron:** "I wore goofy hats to school and did musical theater. Most people thought I was a total weirdo."

Singer-songwriter **Ne-Yo:** "I was kind of the outcast weird guy" in school.

Rapper **Drake:** "I was an outcast in school."

Singer **LeeAnn Rimes:** "I was a bit of an outcast in school because I was a singer, and I would get picked on. I would literally cry and cry for days."

Actress **Megan Fox:** "I was unpopular when I was in high school. I was a loner. You learn, at an early age, that it's okay. It's fine. I could go for days without talking to another human being. I know myself, and I know that there's more to me than you know, and you don't need to know." She has also said, "The things I was made fun of for in school are the things that people now like about me and appreciate about me."

Owl City singer **Adam Young:** "I was an outcast in high school and the people who made fun of me now want to go out to eat."

Dixie Chicks (and **Court Yard Hounds**) Emily Robison and Martie Maguire were "orchdorks."

Actress **Vanessa Hudgens** has said she was an outcast; "I was totally the girl who had no friends. . . . While everyone else was playing, I would sit on the lawn and stare up at the clouds."

Actor **Chad Michael Murray:** "I was kind of an outcast in high school. I had no friends. I was a nerd. . . . Because I didn't have a lot of money, while everyone else was getting into trends and fashion, I would wear Payless shoes, a pair of jeans, and a white T-shirt every day, which only kind of excluded me further."

Actress **Sarah Michelle Gellar:** "I've always been the nerdy, geekish outsider who still remembers how a lot of my classmates used to torture me. Growing up, I always felt different from other kids and they would always tease me about my work in commercials or TV as a way of putting me down."

Actress **Busy Philipps** was "a freak [who would] wear bizarre costumes to school."

Artist **Andy Warhol,** actor **James Franco,** and actresses **Barbra Streisand** and **Mena Suvari** were loners in school: "I just didn't relate to anybody," Suvari has said.

Journalist **John Stossel** has said he was a dork. **Barbara Walters** cried throughout high school. **Al Roker** was a "nerd"; he has said, "I was on the AV squad, and I made stop-action movies with Gumby puppets. I used to record TV shows on audiotape and then splice them together. So I'd splice together Superman with Batman, stuff like that. I was an odd kid."

Amy Van Dyken, whose severe asthma and chlorine allergy made swimming difficult, was tormented by her high school swim teammates, who said she was too slow. In 1996 she was the first American woman to win four gold medals at a single Olympic Games; at her press conference she said, "This is a victory for all the nerds out there." In 2008, Van Dyken was named to the U.S. Olympic Hall of Fame.

Actresses **Nicole Kidman** and **Heather Locklear** were teased because of their looks—Kidman for her height and Locklear for her chest.

Actor **Anthony Hopkins**, who was ostracized at school, has said that the way other students treated him led him to his success as a movie star.

TV and radio host **Ryan Seacrest**, actress **Zooey Deschanel**, actor **Taylor Lautner**, singer **Christina Aguilera**, and actor **Dustin Hoffman** have said they were teased or bullied in school. Deschanel, who had a "horrible" seventh grade experience, has said that being teased in school made her more ambitious.

Winter

Outcast Profiling and Other Dangers

Chapter 6

CHALLENGES

BLUE, HAWAII | THE GAMER

ate one night, Blue drove to Jackson's house to retrieve his fight stick, which Jackson had borrowed but never used. Jackson had been rude to Blue lately. Blue didn't think he even liked Jackson much anymore, but he relished the chance to be out at night with company.

For a while, they talked about nothing. Then, in a filmy haze of sleepy confidence, Blue said, "You still never told me why Nate's an asshole."

"What?! No!" Jackson said. "If I tell you, you'll either not believe me or get mad at me."

"Just tell me what you were gonna say."

"Okay, well . . . for example, I'll mention that I'm gonna hang out with you, and Nate says, 'Oh, you're hanging out with the homo?'"

Blue didn't respond. He refrained from reacting beneath the weight of Jackson's words.

"Mark? . . . Mark? . . . Blue."

Blue's arm covered his face. Real life was harsher than any video game.

"Blue . . . Mark." Jackson took a deep breath. "Don't worryyy. He still thinks you're cool and everything. You're still his *friend*. . . . Do you hate him now?"

Blue pondered this. *Do I hate him? Do I still like him?* If Blue wasn't sure who Nate was anymore, how could he know how to feel about him? *I am so conflicted. I just want someone to be there for me.*

Jackson sighed again, impatient.

Blue made up his mind. "I'm sad now," he whispered.

Jackson looked at Blue. "What? Fine. Do you want a hug or something? Here's your chance." Blue was unresponsive. "No? Okay, then don't ask me ever again."

At the end of winter break, Blue tried to turn to Jackson again. Tired of sitting around the house, Blue found him online at 5 A.M. and asked if he wanted to do something. Jackson needed to go to Best Buy, anyway. "Sure," he said. "Just ask the others."

Blue deflated. He called Ty and Stewart, who made excuses.

Blue gave up and passed time by watching *Evangelion*, an anime series. Blue had a theory about anime and manga. He believed that "secluded kids who indulge on anime and manga—the *otakus*—do it because it gives them an opportunity to feel emotions that they may not be able to feel through their own life. That hits very close to home to me, and I think you could apply that to anything: gamers, geeks, nerds, social outcasts. People outside of that culture don't understand," Blue said. "It's just easier to call us losers."

That night he called Jackson, who didn't answer his phone. Blue tried again an hour later. Still no response. Blue went online. He found Jackson playing MW2 with Stewart. Blue messaged Jackson, "When do you want to go?"

"I'll let you know," Jackson said.

This always happens. Blue slammed his laptop shut. *All anybody wants to do is play that stupid game now. When did it become such a homewrecker?* He would try to organize outings to the beach, town, or pool hall, but his friends—even Ty—would reply, "I just want to play MW2." "I'll go if someone else goes." Or, Blue's favorite, "Can you get online? I don't want to talk on the phone."

Ty's shaky "best-friend"ship essentially meant that he let Blue spend time with him at Ty's convenience; Ty was often glued to Jackson anyway. Blue said, "They are conformist assholes, no backbone and no direction. They're just empty shells to me. Why is it that these people are the ones with the most friends?"

∽ BLUE'S CHALLENGE ∽

Blue's unhappiness made this an opportune time to spring his challenge on him. As I told all of the main characters, each of them had a different challenge, but their rules were the same: They could approach their task however they liked, though I was available as a sounding board; and they could not tell anyone at school about the challenge (Noah's girlfriend was an exception because I sought her advice in devising his assignment).

Blue deeply wanted to connect with someone who would make him feel comfortable and cared for. He also was desperate to graduate so that he could start a new life on his own terms. I combined these goals by challenging Blue to switch to a "nerd"-like friend group. I hoped that he would fall in with people who appreciated him, and that in connecting with intelligent students who did well in school, he would also find the motivation to complete his assignments and the stability he craved.

When I told Blue about the challenge, he had trouble coming up with a group that he wanted to be a part of. "Ty is the only person at school I can relate to, the only person who actually listens to me," he said.

"You *think* he's the only one you can relate to," I said. "You don't know that you don't relate to anybody else."

"Oh yes I do," Blue insisted. "I've hung out with everybody in school at least once."

"Once is not enough to give someone a chance."

"But there are no 'groups of Tys.' I'm not saying that those groups are bad; I actually like a lot of them."

"What is it about Ty that you relate to so well? Because he hasn't shown himself to be a one hundred percent devoted friend whether you relate to him or not."

"I know. But, I mean, we understand each other. Like we can make anime references constantly. He actually enjoys doing things with me, like going downtown and stuff. And he lets me teach him things. Really *scary* things, like when I taught him how to speedboard. That takes a *lot* of trust."

"You've been friends with him all year and that didn't stop you from feeling incredibly lonely at times."

"Yeah," Blue said. "I just don't know whom I'd branch out to. Even the nerds think I'm crazy."

"Crazy like how?" I asked.

"Well, for one, the most obvious thing is that I'm gay. And just in general, I'm really different from other people. I wouldn't be able to stand hanging out with a bunch of underachievers. I need people who will help me keep moving up, not bring me down, like Jackson."

"Yes," I said. "That was exactly my thought when I said nerds or 'smart kids.' "

"Well, then I'd ideally be hanging out with Angelique more, but even that group of people thinks I'm a big weirdo. That's the smart kids. A majority of them are in AP Gov. They could never see me hanging out with them," Blue said. "I'm at a point in my life where I'm trying desperately to find my place in the world, you know?"

"Yes. But how can you find your place if you don't at least peek at other places?"

"You're making it sound like I haven't tried over nine thousand things. Ever since I was in middle school, I've gone from popular jock to anime freak to hardcore skater to overachiever to computer builder and all back again," Blue said.

But he was willing to try once more.

DANIELLE, ILLINOIS | THE LONER

Danielle was doing homework in the dining room when her mother returned home from parent-teacher conferences. She called Danielle into the den. Danielle sat down on the couch and stretched her long legs onto the ottoman, curious about what her teachers had to say this time.

Danielle's mother recapped the meetings. The AP Government teacher reported that Danielle was doing well on homework and tests and that she was a strong writer, but she was so quiet that he couldn't hear her when she spoke from her seat in the corner. Because class participation counted in both AP Government and Spanish, Danielle's reticence was dragging her grades down to high Bs, while in her other classes, in which participation didn't count, she had all As.

Government was especially difficult because Tabitha was in that class. The day before the conferences, Tabitha had volunteered to be the group discussion leader and did not call on Danielle, who raised her hand a few times. Danielle didn't feel comfortable interrupting the discussion without being called on, so she waited for the right moment to make a point—but that moment never came. Danielle earned zero points for the day. Her teacher called her a church mouse.

Danielle's mother told her that the Spanish teacher provided similar feedback. For the first time, Danielle was pulling a B rather than an A in Spanish, because of class participation. The teacher told Danielle's mother that while Danielle had never been good about speaking in class, this year she was doing worse. Students frequently paired up to work on projects or discussions, and the teacher had noticed that once Danielle chose to go to the restroom at precisely the moment that students were coupling off. The teacher didn't think the timing was coincidental.

The teacher also mentioned to Danielle's mother that she was scheduling a class trip to South America for the following year. Even though Danielle had expressed interest, the teacher said she was concerned that Danielle might not get much out of the trip if she couldn't talk to the locals. The teacher was surprised when Danielle's mother told her that Danielle had no problem speaking to adults in various countries. On a flight home from Ireland a few years before, Danielle had stood in the galley for hours talking to a woman who was too claustrophobic to sit down. When Danielle returned to her seat, she'd chatted for another two hours with a man from Northern Ireland about the problems in his country.

"Once again, class participation is your biggest issue," Danielle's mother said.

"It shouldn't be important if I can do the work!" Danielle argued, scowling. She had gotten straight As so far this year.

"Danielle, I might have agreed with that when you were a freshman, but now that you're getting close to college, you have to be very comfortable talking in class."

"I don't like the kids at my school," she said. "I don't feel comfortable talking to them."

"Why?"

"They're stupid."

"Well, you're ranked at about the tenth percentile in your class, so apparently some of them are pretty smart," her mother said.

"They're academically smart, but stupid in how they act," Danielle replied. She slouched further into the sofa. "They're immature."

"If you really feel they're immature, then you should feel more comfortable with yourself," her mother said. "Maybe you should even have some sympathy for them."

Danielle rolled her eyes.

"Danielle, I've thought a lot about getting counseling for you so you can talk to someone."

Danielle grew adamant. "There is no reason to go to a counselor to talk about getting along with people I have absolutely nothing in common with," she retorted. She tromped back into the dining room to finish her homework.

∽ DANIELLE'S CHALLENGE ∽

Designing a challenge for Danielle was easy; hers would be the most straightforward one in this book. At the same time, it was important that all of the challenges focused on improving the students' circumstances by changing other people's perceptions of them without directly altering their uniqueness. Danielle's solitude was an important part of who she was. But she wasn't content with her tiny social circle, and her diffidence was threatening her grades. I challenged Danielle to make a strong effort to converse with people other than Camille, Paige, Mona, and Nikki, with the goal of finding one new friend to socialize with outside of school.

While she tried to pretend to be up for it, Danielle was "uncomfortable about the implications that making new friends has," she said.

"If I can avoid talking, that's what I do. I don't really need any help in the conversing-with-adults area, but I can't relate at all to people my age." Her pushback made me realize that the most straightforward challenge of the book could be the most personally difficult.

NOAH, PENNSYLVANIA | THE BAND GEEK

Noah was convinced that if he was going to qualify for the swimming district championships, he had to do it early in the season. To qualify, individual swimmers had to beat preset times at official meets. For Noah, qualifying was more than just a résumé line. Making the cut would validate that he was an athlete, even though he didn't always feel like one, and prove that he wasn't "just all about studying and school."

At warmups for the second swim meet of the season, Noah tried to psych himself up. He gave a pep talk to a nervous sophomore. "In order to swim like a district swimmer, you have to *be* a district swimmer," Noah said. "You have to think and act with confidence." When the sophomore's race was called, Noah cheered from the end of the pool. Less than a minute later, the sophomore had qualified.

As Noah stepped behind the block in lane five for the 50 Meter Freestyle, he realized his preparation for this race had been inadequate. He hadn't slept enough. He hadn't trained enough. The cut to make districts was 23.60; Noah's fastest time this year was 24.20. Swimming practices had been unproductive and unenjoyable, nothing like the camaraderie of band rehearsals. A few days earlier, when Noah walked into the locker room where several teammates were getting changed, Frederick called out to him. "Hey, look who it is! Did you fuck Leigh yet? I bet you he"—he gestured to a teammate—"gets ass before Noah."

Noah tried to ignore Frederick and put on his suit. Underclassmen were hanging onto Frederick's words.

"C'mon, let's hear it," Frederick sneered. "How far have you gotten with her? I bet you have a *huge* dick—you know, being that you're *Chinese* and all."

The swimmers laughed, except for Jiang. Noah's face burned. He wanted to tell Frederick to shut up, but he assumed any response would only provoke him. *One of the first techniques in dealing with bullies is to ignore them,* he reminded himself. *If they lose interest, they'll leave.* He silently thanked his parents for planning a trip to California that overlapped with the next team party.

Noah knew he and Leigh were both seen as good kids, even though they didn't view themselves that way. He never shared intimate details about their relationship. He didn't understand why sex was such a popular conversation topic; sex was something for two people to share with each other, not with a bunch of obnoxious, meddling teammates. Noah walked silently to the pool deck.

At the starting block, Noah inhaled deeply. As he did before every race, he cupped his hands around his nose and mouth, cleared his mind, and flexed his scapulae. He scanned the crowd for Leigh, who was cheering with his parents. He exchanged grins with Jiang in lane three.

When the blue strobe light flashed, Noah dove into the pool with as much force as he could muster. He raced down the lane. At the wall, he flipped hard, shoving through the water, kicking as forcefully as he knew how. A quick peripheral glance revealed that he was ahead of Jiang by about a body length. Noah's angle was too sharp for him to see the other swimmers. He remembered a lesson he had learned as a sophomore: "Breathe less, don't think." He decided to take two breaths instead of three. *Don't let up,* he told himself. *Pretend this is the last swim of your life.* Coaches had told Noah's team repeatedly, "If you leave everything in the pool, you can have no regrets." Now he clung to that.

Noah took his second breath and shot forward through the last fifteen yards. He slammed into the wall and looked up at the scoreboard. Lane 5: 23.51. First place. Noah leapt with joy and fist-pumped. He shook hands with Jiang, who placed second but hadn't qualified. Noah had done it. He was a district swimmer.

∞ NOAH'S CHALLENGE ∞

Noah's challenge was not easy to devise. He wanted to get to know more people at school, to improve his self-worth, and to convince classmates to view him as a leader. I told him that, similar to his swimming pep talk, for people to see him as a leader he had to act like one. When I explained that I was issuing each person a challenge, Noah was willing but nervous. "Redsen is pretty cliquish, and some of those cliques just don't cooperate," he said. Even the elected student government officers hardly acted like leaders. The class officers hadn't held a meeting in months. It was no wonder, he said, that Redsen seniors were no longer allowed to go off campus for lunch, go on a cool class trip, or leave school early when they were finished with classes. Nobody was lobbying for the privileges.

I thought about how Frederick picked on Noah, football players physically shoved him, and other classmates made fun of him. Noah wasn't their only target. I asked Noah to think about a way to rally as many other disenfranchised students as possible toward one cause.

In our next conversation, Noah asked if he could use his recycling program to unite students across clique boundaries. I thought that was a great idea. If Noah could get enough marginalized students to work together, they might see him as a leader, and they could prove that nonpopular kids could do as much as or more than the populars for the school; plus, if the program were successful, perhaps the administration would agree that Noah's class was responsible enough to deserve senior privileges. Most important, acting like a leader could boost Noah's crumbled social self-esteem. If Noah felt like a leader, maybe it wouldn't matter so much that he couldn't get elected to student government.

Whitney, New York | The Popular Bitch

In the car on the way to a restaurant, Bianca, Giselle, and Madison—all size zero—complained that they could never find the perfect pair of jeans. "All three of us are thin, so we all share the same problem!" Madison exclaimed. *I'm right here*, Whitney thought. Whitney was a size six.

Whitney believed she should be grateful that the preps still allowed her to hang out with them, despite her recent return to her hippie wardrobe and her continued relationship with Luke. "No one wants to be friends with a [former] prep," Whitney explained. "That's why when there isn't room for me in the party car, I have no choice but to stay home. I have no other friends."

Whitney had observed firsthand what happened to girls whom her clique turned against. The twins moved away because the populars had ensured that they couldn't make any friends at school. Now the clique targeted Irene. Without a popular boyfriend, she had no real connection to the group. Desperate, she wore anklets like Bianca's and concocted stories about her past to try to sound cool. She constantly told Bianca how pretty and funny she was and how the two of them were so alike that they could finish each other's sentences. She dug up juicy gossip to whisper into Bianca's ear, and continued to steal her mother's alcohol for the preps.

Her efforts didn't save her. First the preps stopped including her in plans. Then they filled up the seats at their cafeteria table so that she was stuck on the end, and they turned their backs to her until she moved. When Irene still followed Bianca around, Bianca finally banished her from the group for good. Bianca and Giselle were sitting on a bench in school one day when Irene joined them and complimented Bianca. "You know, Irene, you really are fucking annoying," Bianca said. Irene walked away. Now Irene could count only one friend at school: a punk girl who was nice to everyone.

After dinner, the prep girls went to the mall. They planned to browse for a few minutes in Spencer's Gifts just before closing. A Goth-looking girl behind the counter groused, "You guys seriously have four minutes." The populars left the store within three.

Whitney was the last one to leave. As she walked out, she heard the Goth say to her coworker, "I hate girls like that. They think just because they're tan and skinny, they can do what they want. They come in here when they know the mall is closing, and they don't care about anyone but themselves."

That hadn't been Whitney's intention. But the Goth girl's impression was a stereotype that Whitney had to deal with often. In Spanish class that week, the students had to write about things that annoyed them. Most people chose to write about obvious peeves, such as liars or people who chewed with open mouths.

As Whitney wrote her essay about "selfish and fake people," Caroline, an emo girl in the corner, raised her hand and asked, "How do you say preps in Spanish?"

GRADUALLY WHITNEY BECAME AWARE that the populars were leaving her out of activities. Bianca sent public Facebook Valentine's Day gifts to Giselle, Madison, Kendra, and Chelsea, but did nothing for Whitney. Through Facebook, Whitney learned they went to the movies, the diner, or parties without her. Whitney was aghast to find herself making up rumors so that she could "talk trash about people, especially Chelsea, to make it seem like I'm providing gossip. That part sucks about being in this clique. You have to lie a lot, especially about your own happiness. Everything is fake when you're in a clique."

Kendra had a party to which she didn't send Whitney the Facebook invitation she sent everyone else. Whitney was hurt less by the omission than by the fact that her so-called friends didn't object to it. "*True* friends would have talked to Kendra and been like, 'Hey, can Whitney come?'" Whitney said later. "But since my friends only care about themselves, they were just happy they got an invitation." To ease the pain of exclusion, she spent even more time with Luke.

The morning after Kendra's party, Giselle's father called Whitney's house looking for his daughter. Giselle had told him that she was staying at Whitney's. Whitney was furious that Giselle had used her house as a cover for an all-night party that Whitney wasn't even invited to. She Facebook-messaged Giselle that she was a terrible, worthless person. When Giselle called Whitney's house, crying hysterically, Whitney's mother picked up the phone. Giselle told her what had happened.

After they hung up, Whitney's mother came into her room. "Whitney, you need to stop being so mean if you're going to make any friends in college," she said. "You need to be nice to people or you're going to end up very lonely. Wish for your happiness, not the unhappiness of others." Whitney stared at her blankly, even though she knew her mother was right.

∽ WHITNEY'S CHALLENGE ∽

Whitney was certain that without the preps, she would have no one. I wasn't so sure. She was gregarious and energetic, and I thought perhaps she could use her interpersonal skills for good. She wanted to be open-minded and meet new people, but as a prep she felt constrained from doing so.

When I told Whitney that I wanted her to participate in an experiment, she was immediately game. I asked her to attempt to de-clique herself and become a floater, breaking out of the prep group to mingle with various other—and, according to the preps, lesser—groups of students. Furthermore, I said that she could not be mean to any students for the rest of the school year.

Whitney was eager to get started. I got the sense that she was the most enthusiastic of the characters to embark on a challenge because it gave her a legitimate excuse to escape the grip of populars who mistreated her and others. Whitney was most excited to get to know the punks.

———

FACEBOOK AND MYSPACE: ONLINE CAFETERIAS

"One thing that really emphasized how unpopular I am was when I was on Facebook," an Indiana senior told me. "I had just gotten a new account and there were some people I was hesitant to friend. I decided to send friend requests in case I ever needed to contact them for a project. More than one deleted the post saying they had friended me. It was a slap in the face. I know I'm not popular, but am I that socially devastating to be associated with?"

According to the 2010 Pew Internet & American Life Project national report, 73 percent of online teens and 82 percent of wired fourteen-to-seventeen-year-olds use social networking sites, a quickly rising population that increased by nearly 20 percent in three years. Between PTA panic and headlines in the popular press, sites such as Facebook and MySpace have drawn ire for sending unwary kids straight into the cyberclutches of predators. But studies of social network sites (SNS) reveal that most kids aren't going online to meet strangers.

They are spending time on these sites in order to connect with the people they already know. According to Pew, more than 90 percent of teens who visit SNS say they use them to maintain their current friendships and nearly three-quarters use them to make plans with friends.

Social media researcher Danah Boyd has pointed out that social network sites could be considered mainstream gathering spaces. After World War II, companies began marketing directly to teens, resulting in public arenas—dance halls, roller rinks, bowling alleys—where they could socialize unchaperoned. These venues have largely disappeared; SNS have filled the void. "By allowing youth to hang out amongst their friends and classmates, social network sites are providing teens with a space to work out identity and status, make sense of cultural cues, and negotiate public life," Boyd wrote.

In this sense, SNS can serve the same function as the cafeteria, a place at which to socialize outside of classes and a mostly unsupervised area that has the potential both to create new friendships and to segregate students further.

SNS opponents decry the demise of traditional communication, worrying that kids are becoming disconnected screen zombies, faces alit by the blue glow, unable to tear themselves away. Well, not so fast. The stereotype of the adult computer addict—up at all hours, immersed in virtual reality, cruising for cybersex, trapped in an on-line gambling addiction, or creating various falsely representative alter egos—largely does not apply to teens. A 2009 Nielsen report claimed that U.S. teenagers spend "far less time" on the Internet than adults.

Usually students don't intend their online profiles to be separate from their real identity. High schoolers told me that SNS can ease introductions among classmates. A recent survey found that college students spent more time with SNS friends in person than online. Additionally, a telecommunications study of college students set out to determine "whether offline social capital can be generated by online tools." Social capital involves the abilities to form new relationships, maintain current social connections, and integrate into a community. The researchers concluded that their findings "demonstrate a robust connection between Facebook usage and indicators of social capital. . . . Internet use alone did not predict social capital accumulation, but intensive use of Facebook did."

Facebook and MySpace profiles are not only mechanisms to connect with other people; they also provide a canvas onto which a student can project his desired identity. Students can reveal opinions, interests, and activities that they don't get the chance to share or don't feel comfortable publicizing at school. As a shy Texas senior explained, a profile "allows me to learn new facts about a person who I normally don't talk to, which naturally spills over to the way I treat them in person."

The identities displayed on SNS are also constructed by the network of a person's friends. This feature not only visually maps out connections but also, thanks to the Top Friends application, orders them in a public hierarchy. Or exposes attempted social climbing; some kids use the term "friend eaters" to refer to people who collect online friends to pad their network and create an illusion of popularity. In a study conducted at Louisiana State University in Baton Rouge, undergraduates reported having an average of 455 Facebook friends (the maximum was 2,000 and the minimum was 4). Yet these same students averaged seven close friends. "In choosing [Top Friends], teens write their community into being, which is precisely why this feature is so loved and despised," Boyd observed.

The dangers of SNS are less commonly media-driven fears of predatory adults than the same exclusionary behavior prevalent in the cafeteria. Consider the photos. "Pictures on Facebook are vital for high school," a Florida senior said. "People can feel betrayed if they weren't invited to a party. As soon as a new album is added, *everyone* looks at it, so within minutes everyone's outfits are critiqued. If you were to look through the average girl's Facebook inbox there would be hundreds of links to bad pictures of people with messages like 'OMG what is she wearing' or 'AHAHA, IS SHE SERIOUS.'"

Pictures, comments, and status updates also let students keep tabs on each other, a common pastime called falking, or Facebook stalking. "It's like you never really get away from your peers," said a Massachusetts scene kid. "It's like they're always watching you." A New York junior said this issue causes her social anxiety. "Although I love Facebook, I think it was quite possibly the worst invention in the world," she said. "On Facebook, I prepare myself to find something that I didn't want to know."

These sites can take Boyd's idea of writing oneself into being even farther, as words on a profile instantaneously can fuel widespread gossip. "It's practically minute-to-minute on who's breaking up and hooking up," said an Iowa overachiever. A Long Island outcast added, "You'll hear a conversation in the halls, 'Did you hear they were going out?' and the other person will say, 'No way, don't believe that. Facebook didn't say it yet.' It's as if Facebook is the God of the school, and nothing is official until Facebook says it's true."

Naturally teens are bolder in the online cafeteria than they are when face-to-face. Students nationwide told me about Facebook groups devoted to insulting a classmate, much like the I Hate Danielle club. Students at a New York school created a fake Facebook profile for a girl and posted racial slurs and nasty comments about her. Within the first week, the phony profile already had fifty "friends" signed up to make fun of the girl. Certain Facebook applications expand the artillery for kids who want to bully a classmate. Students told me about quizzes that publicly ask questions such as "Does [insert name]'s breath stink?" or "Is [insert name] ugly?" An application called "Friend FAQ" asks people questions about their friends and posts the answers. An eighth grader in the Midwest learned from this application that a friend thought she needed to lose weight. "Facebook can totally ruin people's lives," she said.

Indeed, studies have found that the frequency with which teenagers use SNS affects their self-esteem and well-being. At a time when students are most influenced by feedback from peers, sites like Facebook and MySpace serve as constant vehicles for such assessments. Kids can feel pressured to turn their profiles into never-ending commercials for themselves. Remember the imaginary audience discussed in chapter 4? Researchers have said that teenagers "tend to overestimate the extent to which others are watching and evaluating, and, as a result, can be extremely preoccupied with how they appear in the eyes of others." The problem with online cafeterias is that the audience turns out to be not so imaginary after all.

REGAN, GEORGIA | THE WEIRD GIRL

At the LGBT youth center, Regan approached the volunteer coordinator's desk to say hello. The coordinator's eyes lit up when he saw her. "We're going to have an opening for a facilitator! You'll be perfect!"

After months of sitting at the front desk, welcoming kids and signing them in, Regan would now be a moderator for a regular girls-only group discussion. The position was ideal for her; she hoped to do something similar next fall, when she planned to teach English at a school in Bangladesh. The school was run by a women's organization that hoped an education would prevent girls from getting caught up in trafficking.

Regan was especially thrilled about the youth center promotion and her Bangladesh trip because she loved working with adolescents. "I'm really interested in what teenagers have to say. They are an often overlooked demographic," she said. "They're sort of idealistic, and a lot of people try to stifle that, but I think it's important to cultivate that attitude. If we all had the ideas and drive of teenagers, a lot more could get done in the world."

∽ REGAN'S CHALLENGE ∽

By resigning at the end of the school year, Regan worried that she was leaving many of her students without a teacher to whom they could turn for nonacademic help or advice. She wanted to find a way to leave a legacy that encouraged students to accept people who were different from them. When I challenged her to form a Gay-Straight Alliance (GSA) at James Johnson, she readily agreed.

"I know I'm going to be met with a lot of negativity, but I also feel that a GSA should be available in every high school," Regan said. She knew what it took to start up such a club; she had founded the GSA at her own Vermont high school. "It's amazing that, of all people, my demographic of students is completely judgmental of a marginalized group. They are incredibly hypocritical, complaining about injustices due to race, yet calling each other 'gay' and 'faggot.' School is supposed to be a safe place for *all* students, and I'd like that to be true."

Many of Regan's colleagues were vocally unsympathetic toward

LGBT students. One teacher, telling Regan about a flamboyantly gay student in her class, whined, "I'm just so over it. Can't he keep it to himself? I mean, we all know, okay? Get over yourself." Several teachers spoke about a transgendered student "like she's weird and deserves to be ridiculed by her peers," Regan said. Recently she had walked by a classroom in which students were screaming "faggot." Regan asked them to stop. Then she saw that there was another teacher in the room, sitting at her computer, ignoring the students' behavior.

Regan hoped she could use her position as the head of Johnson's all-faculty Diversity Committee to start the GSA. At the next meeting, the group debated how to utilize a main bulletin board to demonstrate the school's diversity.

"We could put up flags for each country that's represented here," one teacher said, as if suggesting a completely original idea. The other committee members nodded.

"Maybe we could put up a map and use pushpins to show where different teachers are from," another teacher suggested.

"Well, we'd have to revise that because we can't have pins readily available to students," an administrator interjected. "That could be dangerous."

Regan wondered if she was the only committee member who thought these ideas were boring. "That's great," she said, "but diversity is more than just national origin. Maybe we could do something for religious diversity and family diversity."

"I would be uncomfortable doing anything religious," a teacher said. "If we're going to put up symbols of different religions, then what about the kids who are Satanists? Do we have to include them?"

Regan thought that argument was ludicrous, but before she could say anything, the administrator spoke up again. "I would be really wary of putting anything on a bulletin board that deals with religion."

Surprised that the group considered religious diversity to be controversial, Regan didn't fight the point. "What about family diversity?" she suggested. "Adoption, single moms, two dads . . ." The group ignored her, instead resuming discussion of the map.

This committee isn't going to help Johnson at all, Regan thought. She kept quiet for the rest of the meeting.

Not long afterward, when Regan was walking past the main office, she did a double take. Right there was a prominent bulletin board devoted to the school's Christian fellowship. The bulletin board featured images of a cross and a Bible.

ELI, VIRGINIA | THE NERD

Eli's mother had been urging him for about a month to go shopping with her at JCPenney. "It's seventy-five percent off!" she said. "We can get you some winter clothes and clothes for college!"

Eli reluctantly agreed, although he expected such an outing to be a disaster. The last time they had gone out, she had insisted on taking him to the optometrist to tighten his glasses because, she told the doctor, "he's always pushing them up." But he liked his glasses the way they were.

Eli browsed through a row of T-shirts without designs or logos. He picked up solid blue, yellow, and orange tees and continued wandering around the section. Hesitantly, he approached a rack of plaid button-down shirts, their sleeves already rolled fashionably. He mostly wore only plain T-shirts, *but maybe*, he thought, *I can try stepping out of the box.* He picked up a black, white, and gray plaid shirt and headed to the fitting room.

Eli methodically went through the solids, briefly looking down and checking the fit for each one. When he tried on the plaid button-down, he left the top button undone over his white undershirt and peeked in the mirror. His eyes widened. *Hey, this looks good!* he thought. Shopping for clothes that gave him a thrill—this was new to Eli. Encouraged, he decided to pick out a second plaid button-down, or perhaps even another clothing item he'd never worn before.

As Eli sauntered out of the dressing room, he saw his mother riffling through shirts sporting logos. "What did you find?" she asked.

Eli proudly held up his discoveries. His mother hesitated, then heaved a disappointed sigh. "You couldn't find anything else?" she said. "Honey, orange is not a guys' color. Don't you want to mix it up? We could go to Hollister if you want."

"Hollister is the last place I want to go."

His mother looked frustrated. "Then tell me: Where do you like to shop?"

"No, let's just go. 'Cause obviously this never works out." Eli's confidence in the button-down had faltered. They went home without purchasing a thing.

Just before dinner that evening, Eli's mother told him, "You can't go to college wearing [your usual] shirts! You need normal clothes."

Eli already was counting down the days until college. He had decided to attend Westcoast University even if he received other acceptance letters in the spring. Through a Facebook group for incoming freshmen, he had begun to meet some of his future classmates. He was pleased with his efforts to chat with them. He already had so many questions: "What should I bring to class the first week?" "How early should I get to class?" "How am I going to meet people?" He knew better than to post these on Facebook.

∾ ELI'S CHALLENGE ∾

When I told Eli about the challenge, he said he was "kinda overwhelmed." He liked the idea of it, but he had already given up on having a satisfying social life in high school, and therefore he wanted to get through the remaining months "as quickly as possible." He didn't want to do a challenge that involved interacting with people at school, whom he assumed had already written him off. For an outside-of-school challenge that would provide him with skills he could use in school, I suggested that he take an improv class—he could take it in a different town, with adults, if he liked—to help him with his speaking insecurity and his fear of being laughed at.

"Ohhh my goodness," he said. "It's improv. And I'm kinda worried about the convenience of it." He was busy with schoolwork, his job as a restaurant busboy, Academic Bowl, and Model UN, and he was already studying ahead of time for AP exams he would take in May.

A few days later, Eli got back to me. "Okay, I've thought a little," he said. "Could the challenge be more internal, without the need to really involve anyone else?"

When I said no—the point was to change perceptions, not the

person—Eli declined to attempt a challenge because he didn't think his social life could change.

Joy, California | The New Girl

In PE, Joy noticed that a group of three Mexican girls frequently shot dirty looks at her. Having never spoken to them before, Joy ignored them. Within a week, the girls began eyeballing Joy resolutely as she crossed the street to school in the mornings. Between class periods, they followed her down the sidewalks, calling her a bitch, ridiculing her looks and clothing. Joy IMed a friend in Jamaica.

> **Joy:** yea man, sum ppl want 2 beat me up
> **Friend:** hahahaha lmao
> **Joy:** big man ting (a Jamaican phrase meaning "seriously")
> **Friend:** lmao
> **Joy:** sum mexican gyal ah gang ah dem
> **Friend:** wow yow avoid dem dem crazy. Yea man Joy be careful . . .

A few days later, Joy was running the mile in PE when she accidentally brushed past one of the Mexican girls. "Sorry!" Joy said as she continued her run.

"Fucking bitch!" one of them yelled back. On each of Joy's subsequent laps, the girls repeated the phrase.

That afternoon, Joy worried that the girls were going to come after her. She wouldn't be able to handle all three of them at once. She called her stepfather and asked him to pick her up. After school, Joy stood outside of the school office, waiting for her stepdad, when she saw the three girls. They stared daggers at her, as if gearing up to attack.

Joy adopted her best unperturbed expression. *You're wasting your time,* she thought, feeling sorry for the girls. *Someday, we're going to be at very different places in life. They don't know any better how to behave. What can I do, say, "Let's hug?" I don't think so.* She smirked.

"What the fuck is she looking at?" said one of the girls.

"I don't know. Fucking bitch," another said.

The girls lurked while Joy waited patiently for her ride. When her stepfather arrived, he insisted that she report the girls to the adminis-tration.

The vice principal was sympathetic. "Joy, I'm sorry to hear this is happening to you," Mr. Cruz said. "You're a nice person. I don't see why you should have issues with anyone."

"I've never spoken to the girls; they've just decided I'm a target," Joy replied. "I understand if I was rude to them I would deserve that treatment, but they don't know me. And to be standing and watching me, I don't rate that." Joy used the Jamaican term for respect.

"I need you to write a report," Mr. Cruz said. "Bring it to me first thing in the morning and we'll have this dealt with. Citygrove has a zero-tolerance policy for indiscipline. We believe every student should be comfortable."

Joy filed the form in her binder. "Thank you, Mr. Cruz. I hope this will all be over soon."

At the end of the week, Joy was in PE again, waiting for the teacher to take attendance. The leader of the mean girls stood nearby, talking loudly to a classmate. "I'm gonna fuck up the bitch that's talking shit about me to the principal's office," she said. She shot Joy a piercing stare. "I'll deal with her ass after class."

When Joy changed into her gym clothes, the three girls glared at her again. Joy grew uneasy. Was today going to be the day they tried some-thing? As they left the locker room, Joy whispered to Anisha about what the girls were doing. One of the girls bumped Anisha roughly on her way out the door. "You have to tell [the teacher]!" Anisha whis-pered back.

Outside, the girls called Joy degrading names, trying to provoke her. Other girls gathered closer, circling as if they expected a fight. Joy had never been in a fight before. These girls weren't playing, and Joy was too skinny to put up much of a defense. The PE teacher led the group to the track for their weekly mile run. Joy slowed down and waited for everyone else to pass her so that she could talk softly to the teacher.

In sixth period, campus security called her to Mr. Cruz's office. Just outside the doorway, Joy realized that the other girls were already in the room. She could hear them laughing. When Joy walked in, the girls, who sat in a row facing the vice principal, smiled at her for show.

Joy sat in the empty chair next to Mr. Cruz's desk, facing the girls. Mr. Cruz told them that if they continued to harass Joy, there would be consequences, which could range from suspension to a school transfer. The girls' leader avoided Joy's eyes, instead chomping on gum and humming what sounded like a Spanish song.

Mr. Cruz told Joy that Mia, one of the girls, had gone through a similar ordeal at the beginning of the school year. Another girl had threatened to beat her up. Surprised, Joy glanced at Mia, who squirmed.

"I understand," Mia whispered to Mr. Cruz. "I won't sweat her no more."

The other two girls slouched and hummed, narrowing their eyes at Joy. Mr. Cruz sent the bullies out of the room. He turned to Joy. "I spoke to them and they say they understand," he told her. "I told them you're a nice girl who's never done anything to upset them."

"Why did they start this whole thing?" Joy asked. "I've never even spoken to them."

"They said they thought that you're too sophisticated, intelligent, and professional to talk to and because of that, they thought you hated on them."

"How can I possibly hate on someone I don't know? They shouldn't be so quick to judge."

Mr. Cruz ended the meeting by telling Joy that if anything else happened, she should tell him immediately and the girls would be suspended.

When Joy left the room, the other girls were in the main office. Two of them were still humming and laughing. Joy made eye contact with Mia. She looked sad. "Bye," she mouthed to Joy.

Joy pitied the girls. She understood them. When Joy was about nine, back when her father was abusing her, she suffered from low self-esteem. "So I used to be mean to others and tease them," she explained. "I was angry. I couldn't understand why other people could live happily yet I had to deal with my father's abuse. For a young child, that's a lot to take, so other people were my targets. I wasn't the best person I could be, not living up to my potential completely. I wasn't going to become another woman who was bitter because life broke her down, so basically I built my strength and changed myself. Most bullies were hurt at some point and don't want people to see that they're weak."

At citygrove, a woman gave a presentation and held a workshop for a select group of students about Rachel's Challenge. Rachel's Challenge was a program encouraging a "chain reaction of kindness and compassion," based on the writing of Rachel Scott, the first student killed at the Columbine school shootings in Colorado. As Joy listened to the presentation, she wept soundlessly. She remembered an incident she hadn't thought about in a long time.

It had happened when Joy was twelve, on a sunny June day in Jamaica. Joy remembered that the sky was so clear that every outline—of trees, people, blades of grass—was sharp and clean. About five minutes after school let out for the day, Joy was laughing with friends beneath a shady tree near the soccer field when they heard a pop. "Probably some eediat bwoy wid im foolishness, yo dem need fi stop, in di name ah Jesus," said one of Joy's friends.

Then there was another pop, this one louder, closer, and followed by screams. Concerned, Joy and her friends walked toward the school building. Students were pouring out of their classes toward the buses. Then—pop—again. Screams. Hundreds of students scurried like ants in every direction. "Him have a gun, him have a gun, yo run, yo run!" someone shouted.

Joy lost sight of her friends and ran around frantically looking for them. Someone from Drama Club saw Joy sprinting toward the drama building stairs and pushed her down to the ground. "Stay down," he said. "Come on, get it together. You need to help yourself. Stay low. It's gonna be okay." Three more gunshots pierced the air, this time close enough that Joy heard ringing in her ears. Tears streamed down her face. *Am I going to die?* she wondered. *Is the gunman coming after someone? Is it judgment day?*

"She dead, she dead," wailed a girl Joy knew. "A gyal get shot up, yo run, dem ah come!" Panicked, Joy sprinted upstairs toward the drama classroom. Two seniors saw Joy at the gate to the building, looked around furtively, ducked, and pulled her inside the room. Two more shots rang out. Then it was quiet.

Later, Joy went downstairs to search for her friends. They reunited and wept on one another's shoulders. "Don't cry, Joy," one of them said, hugging her. "It's okay. You're okay, don't worry." They heard sirens. Near the school office, police handcuffed a naked man the students had never seen.

Joy learned that only one child was injured, an eleven-year-old whose neck was punctured by glass from a bus window. She survived. But the ordeal was draining. It was "heart-wrenching, the fear knowing that you might die, and you say, 'Today I will die and will never see my friends and family,'" Joy said later. "It's one of the most unexplainable feelings one can have, hearing those bullets, the screams, the cries. When my face was down in that dirt, I said, 'This is it.' I couldn't help but wonder if the person came to kill me, what would I do, just sit there and take it? Wait for it to be over and pray to God I would not die? It makes you value life and value what you have."

Joy was struck by one of Rachel Scott's quotes: "If one person can go out of their way to show compassion, it will start a chain reaction of the same. People will never know how far a little kindness can go." Joy vowed to herself to continue the chain with what Joy called "positive thinking." She started an online group dedicated to this purpose; for the group's description, Joy wrote, "I want people to know that one bad experience doesn't direct our lives; things can get better, if only we have the will and drive to try." She encouraged people to share their negative experiences, in the hope that others could help them to see the positive things that could result from those experiences. She shared her own. Joy believed that the bad things that had happened to her—the school shooting, her father's abuse—had shaped her into the person she was today, a person who "found good in all things bad, [which] made me stronger."

∽ JOY'S CHALLENGE ∽

Because Joy was so inspired, I made compassion the cornerstone of her challenge. When I asked her what she hoped to improve about school, she replied, "I basically want to be able to communicate and connect with people better. I don't think I'm a negative person, but at times the worst gets the best of us."

Joy was an incredibly articulate and expressive fourteen-year-old, but I could see what she was getting at. Sometimes she didn't practice the open-mindedness she preached. This tendency might have been typical for a high school freshman, but Joy prided herself on her ability to look beyond the surface of people, as she put it. So I asked her to give students of various cultures a chance to know her better by breaking the ice with acts of kindness. Eventually, she could work up to giving one of her bullies the opportunity to befriend her—and herself the chance to broaden her network. Joy loved the idea. She happily accepted the challenge.

————

THE "WHO'S MOST LIKELY TO BRING A GUN TO SCHOOL" GAME

Midway through her sophomore year at a Delaware public school, Annmarie, a quiet girl who spent class time writing short stories or drawing chimera-like creatures, told me a secret she had never told anyone else. Well into high school, Annmarie had no friends. Students ridiculed her for her weight, her clothes, her atheism, and her love of literature. They thought she was weird because she watched anime, was obsessed with zombies, and listened to metal instead of rap. There was a time when the ridicule brought Annmarie to her breaking point. Classmates stole her belongings and hid them. A boy in four of her classes called her psycho on a daily basis. "Those were really bad times in my life. No one liked me," Annmarie said. "But I would dread coming to school because it was always the same thing every day: He would say I was crazy and that I would shoot up the school and try to kill everyone. That was one of the few people I actually wanted to hurt, though I never did."

I asked her what she meant.

"When you hear that kind of stuff over and over again, it really hurts, and you want just a little bit of vengeance. It was every day for half of the school year and only one person in the class really defended me—my teacher—but it didn't stop him," Annmarie answered. "I used to have daydreams in gym class about coming in there with a gun or something and just killing him. Of course, I would never do something like that, but I thought about it, and that was what scared me, so I never told anyone."

Annmarie's secret, though she never made plans to act on it, combined with her image at school, could have landed her in a great deal of trouble. In the aftermath of the 1999 shootings at Columbine High School, in which the student gunmen killed twelve students and a teacher and wounded more than two dozen others before shooting themselves, campus perception of outcasts shifted from objects of derision to potential murderers. Because Eric Harris and Dylan Klebold wore Goth-like fashion, demonstrated technological sophistication, and were social outcasts, each of those characteristics came to be suspect in other students; the combination became a dreaded stereotype. "We needed to know who was a good guy and who was a bad guy, and nerds and geeks seemed to be mostly in the enemy camp," psychologist David Anderegg observed. Columbine "changed the world in many ways but one of the most immediate ways was a nationwide persecution of Goths, nerds, geeks, and perceived misfits of all kinds. . . . The nationwide panic that set in after Columbine had all the characteristics of a witch hunt."

Panicked and pressured to implement politically expedient measures to prevent further massacres, schools mobilized to root out potential killers. Administrators across the country began identifying students who were "different," and then proceeded to "keep them under surveillance, remove them from the school, or subject them to intensive therapy until they are able to be like everybody else," social psychologist Elliot Aronson detailed in *Nobody Left to Hate*. Further, schools enlisted students in the campaign. "By asking the 'normal' students to point out the 'strange' ones," Aronson wrote, schools were "making a bad situation worse by implicitly sanctioning the rejection and exclusion of a sizable group of students whose only sin is unpopularity." Within short order, schools were expelling outcasts simply for being outcasts.

More than ten years after the massacre, that attitude has not disappeared. A semi-popular senior in Maryland described emos to me as "the ones you point out during a boring class when you and your friends play the 'who's most likely to bring a gun to school' game." When I met with editors to propose this book, one of the first subtopics one of them suggested was the "danger" of outcasts, as in "when good outcasts go bad."

From one perspective, the evil outcast theory may have seemed sound. When the masses send impressionable youth to conceal in dark corners the activities they should be comfortable if not proud to exhibit in the open—expressing exuberance, watching anime, building robot models, dressing uniquely, playing games, reading for pleasure, loving someone of the same gender—they seal off crucial outlets. If you contain a force of energy in a tightly enclosed space, eventually the container will explode. So, too, the emotions of a stifled teenager. Especially when that teenager is being tormented day after day. Like Annmarie. Like Blue.

When the pain of losing the club he founded was still raw and Herman and his followers were rubbing salt into his wounds, Blue unwittingly found himself thinking about how much he wanted to kill them. He had a passing daydream about taking his former friends and Mr. Pakaki "into the desert, with a CZ 75 in my pocket, bullets in their heads." When he admitted this, months later, we talked about this feeling more in-depth. "I know very well how much the anger welling up inside me could hurt somebody. But sometimes I feel that it's too much to contain," Blue said. "I'm scared of myself in a way. It's not that I'm going to hurt somebody that I worked hard on getting to know. It's that I don't know what would happen, but I do know something would. And it could be violent. It could be anything, really."

"Should I be concerned?" I asked.

"I'm confident in myself that I have enough self-control, really," Blue concluded. "Those [thoughts] are just really annoying."

The error in the evil-outcast theory is that it assumes that only social outcasts can develop into Columbine-like killers. Identifying the outcasts and tossing them out of schools is akin to singling out a Middle Eastern passenger for extra airport security screening, or stopping a driver because he's Latino. Just because a kid listens to screamo doesn't mean he's angry. Just because she plays Warhammer doesn't mean she's violent. Just because her face is pierced doesn't mean she's disrespectful. Just because he wears all black doesn't mean he's sad. This practice is what I call **outcast profiling**. It is counterproductive, it is bad policy, and it is discriminatory.

I selected a handful of popular students who appeared to be well-adjusted and asked them a delicate question: "Have you at any time day-dreamed, fantasized, or even had just a passing thought about physically hurting someone at school?" A surprising number answered yes. "When I'm really mad at someone," answered a Midwestern female jock. "At least once a day," said a popular Louisiana boy.

Even the students whose popular cliques ruled their schools answered affirmatively. "Most definitely," said a Canadian queen bee. "The thoughts are mostly fleeting but they're there, usually about hurting losers or bitchy girls." A Southern boy who dominated his high school said, "I used to think about pushing people I didn't like down the stairs, just because I could. Kids tend to think about using aggression to solve a lot of problems and popular kids, I think, tend to be a little egotistical, and that leads to thinking you can hurt other people without retribution. At least I did."

Sometimes it's the populars, the kids who seem to have it all, who are struggling with the most explosive issues, forcing them down beneath a smooth-as-plastic surface where they percolate impatiently, biding time. A mid-Atlantic overachiever said she often thought about hurting people at school. When I asked her to elaborate, she said, "The needs of students are often ignored by the administration. Violence is a way to get people to notice that you're angry, sad, or scared, so it definitely crosses my mind. Often, the kids labeled 'at risk' are the only ones on adults' radar, which isn't fair; everyone can have terrible things happen in their life, regardless of what kind of person they are. I've thought about using violence to make others feel guilty for how they treated me, even though rationally I know this will do more harm than help. But it still crosses my mind when I'm in tears after an unnecessary comment or lying awake unable to sleep because of anxiety regarding school."

Recent studies have called the link between relational aggression and perceived popularity "robust" and "remarkable." Psychologists point out that high-status cliques teach the exclusionary behavior that may be the foundation for eventual racism, anti-Semitism, sexism, and other forms of bigotry.

Eric Harris, one of the two Columbine murderers, had a secret too. He wasn't raised in Columbine; his family moved there from Plattsburgh, New York, where he played soccer and Little League baseball, earned good grades, and was a boy scout. In Plattsburgh, administrators would not have singled out Harris as a potential school shooter. Harris's secret? Before he moved to Colorado, he was popular.

Chapter 7

MISPERCEPTIONS

REGAN, GEORGIA | THE WEIRD GIRL

At a Diversity Committee meeting, Regan announced that she wanted to start a Gay-Straight Alliance.

"A *what?*" asked another teacher.

"A Gay-Straight Alliance," Regan repeated.

"Ah." The teacher rolled his eyes.

"I'd love to start one, but because I'm leaving after this year, I can't start it alone," Regan continued. She asked if anyone would be interested in helping her. The committee members either stared at her or looked down. No one answered.

WHEN A FRIEND FROM college gave Regan money to get a new tattoo, her excitement was a welcome contrast to the helplessness she felt in school. "I'm here for a tattoo!" Regan announced to the guy behind the tattoo shop desk. She opened the book on the counter and pointed to a banner presenting the word *Love*. "I basically want this, but instead I want it to say SXE." She detailed a few other changes. The guy gave her a clipboard and told her to fill out a form.

Crystal was sitting on a couch, playing with her phone. "So, explain this to me again," she said.

"It stands for 'Straight Edge,'" Regan replied. "Basically, no smoking, no drinking, no drugs."

When Regan had first identified as Straight Edge, after learning about the movement in middle school, she felt validated by the label. She believed that if she could explain her anti-substance lifestyle in one word, she would avoid excessive pressure from classmates. In high school and college, when she was invited to parties or offered alcohol, she simply said, "I'm Edge," and students accepted her answer.

Unlike at James Johnson, where colleagues mocked Regan for not drinking, many other people had told her how much they admired her commitment to a substance-free lifestyle. A friend who was married to a Rasta said that Regan inspired her to stop drinking and smoking. In college, a member of Regan's theater group thanked her for being Straight Edge because, although he wasn't, he didn't enjoy drinking. "It's nice to have someone sober to hang out with at cast parties," he said.

In fact, Regan initially had bonded with her best friend, whom she met in college, because neither of them drank. Instead of going to fraternity parties on weekends, they hung out with other SXE girls who went to art museums, plays, dance performances, ethnic restaurants, and sometimes just for walks around town (all activities that Regan enjoyed now with Crystal). Though Regan and her best friend, who still lived in Vermont, had since found additional reasons that made them believe they were "BFF soul mates," it was the SXE connection that first kindled their friendship.

A heavily inked tattoo artist called Regan's name. She wiped her hands on her jeans. In the back room, Crystal rolled her chair to Regan's side and grabbed her hand. Regan heard the whiz of the needle. She took a deep breath.

The series of sensations Regan experienced while getting a tattoo never varied. The first few times the gun brushed her skin, it didn't hurt at all. Typically her nervous anticipation of the process was worse than the reality. After a while, though, the outlining would become painful. Regan closed her eyes. She usually didn't have company when she got a tattoo. She let go of Crystal's hand, opting instead to grip the wooden back of the chair as she usually did. She peeked at her pelvis. The tattoo artist had barely begun. *Oh, God,* Regan thought, and laid her head on her arms.

By the time the artist began the coloring stage, Regan was used to the sting. Coloring was uncomfortable, like cat scratches, except when the gun traveled over a bone, which made Regan wince. Then the artist had to go over a spot multiple times, rubbing already open wounds with a needle. Just when Regan was ready for the process to end, the artist would begin adding his own flair to the piece, embellishing details, darkening a shade, adding color.

Regan had waited until adulthood to get the Straight Edge tattoo because, she said, "I've known too many Straight Edge kids who get SXE tattoos and then stop being SXE. Then they feel stupid and regret the tattoo. I figured when I got older, I'd stop holding on to the title so tightly. I thought it'd be better to wait so that the tattoo was a celebration of how being SXE has positively affected my life rather than an affirmation of my SXE pride." For similar reasons, she had waited until age twenty to get any tattoos at all.

———

A DIFFERENT KIND OF PRESSURE

Drug and alcohol peer pressure today is not the "It'll make you feel real good" variety that cracked up students during assemblies in the "Just Say No" era. It's both more subtle and more blatant a nudge. Because social events among the popular crowd seem to involve drinking and/or recreational drug use, willingness to participate can directly affect social status. "It's really down to the people that drink and the people that don't," a "weird kid" said about social divisions at her Georgia private school. "And then it goes to whether they're on a sports team or not (and if they're good). And if they go to parties or even get invited."

Alcohol and drug use often become a means for students to try to prove that they can manage a social life in addition to schoolwork, sports, or other extracurriculars, without seeming stressed about maintaining a balance. A popular Pennsylvania junior tried smoking weed and a hookah for this reason. "I did it because I wanted to be able to say I had done so," she said.

Students are trying alcohol at younger ages, which means the pressure to imbibe can start early. Lana, now a junior, was part of the popular clique in her Chicago middle school—until she refused to drink. "On the south side, you start drinking around seventh or eighth grade and if you don't, you're considered a huge loser. My dad's an alcoholic, though, so drinking was never a big thing on my list. But I wanted to be popular, so I'd pretend to drink at parties," Lana said. When her friends realized she wasn't drinking, they kicked her out of the group. To get back in their good graces, she started to smoke marijuana. She was twelve.

Some students are able to resist the pressure because classmates are accustomed to them doing their own thing. An offbeat junior in Washington, D.C., was not happy with her group's plans to drive to the homecoming dance after pregaming. (Pregaming, a term that refers to drinking socially before an event, trickled down to high schools several years ago.) Consequently, she ditched her group, including her date, and instead went out to dinner with a friend. "I'm not a Mormon; I don't mind drinking," she said. "It's the drinking and driving that bugs me, and that everyone feels they have to pregame a school event."

Other students have been harassed for being brave enough to challenge the perceived norm. Cindy, a bookworm in Syracuse, was distressed to see her best friend, Becca, a straight-A student and an athlete, use drugs. Concerned, she wrote Becca a letter, saying she wasn't "going to stand by and watch [her] kill herself" and that their friendship was "going to be [her] first consequence of drugs," although she would be available if Becca needed help. Becca mocked the letter in front of crowds at school.

As a result, when Cindy opened her locker, pro-marijuana pamphlets spilled out. She had to change her phone number to stop the prank calls. Students whom Cindy once counted as friends texted her death threats. "You're an awful person who makes everyone feel like shit," one text said. "You're not leaving school unless it's in a body bag," said another. ("It's amazing how creatively sixteen-year-old girls will come up with ways to kill you," Cindy told me.) At school, someone tried to push her down the stairs, but she caught herself on the railing.

Before long, Cindy was spending weekend nights alone. "Drinking is such a social event that if you don't go, you're an outcast," she said. The only girl who came to Cindy's defense was equally vilified. "You should just go kill yourself; the world would be better off without you, since you're friends with that bitch," a girl texted Cindy's friend. Another wrote, "You are a whore who deserves to be shot and killed because you're sticking with Cindy."

When Cindy asked a guidance counselor for help, the counselor told her, "Keep your thoughts to yourself about drugs and alcohol." Becca lost her scholarship to a prestigious college and moved in with her twentysomething boyfriend, an alleged drug dealer. Her mother found the letter that Cindy had written to her. She apologized to Cindy for her daughter's behavior. "You're the best friend Becca ever had," the mother said.

Many students told me that drinking and drugs have become so prevalent that teenagers who abstain are the rare exception. "The drinking divide is one of the biggest ones in our school," said Bethany, considered "a good girl" at her Connecticut public school. When Bethany began dating her first serious boyfriend, a popular guy, she felt pressured to go to the populars' parties. She wasn't a drinker, but at her first party, she had a beer. At school that Monday, people treated Bethany differently. Popular students high-fived her. Soccer teammates were pleased she "wasn't the good girl they'd imagined," Bethany said. "I felt awful [for caving in]. But almost *everyone* drinks, and if you don't, you're considered weird or awkward."

Bethany's assumption, a view that students echoed repeatedly to me, may be the key to helping teenagers resist the pressure they are so sure is inescapable. Why? Because that premise is absolutely incorrect.

Teenage drinking has been declining since 1999, but students vastly overestimate their classmates' use of alcohol, drugs, and cigarettes. For example, a study conducted at a Midwestern high school when teenage alcohol use was peaking found that students believed that 92 percent of their peers drank alcohol and 85 percent smoked cigarettes. When researchers surveyed the school to unearth the actual statistics, they learned that 47 percent of students had consumed alcohol and 17 percent smoked. (Another study led by the same re-searcher noted that parents and teachers also significantly overesti-mated student use.) Even college students wildly overestimate the frequency and amount that peers drink.

Study after study has shown that perceived peer drinking plays an enormous role in a student's decision to consume alcohol. The more anxious a student is to fit in, the greater the likelihood that he will be influenced by these supposed norms, especially boys, for whom heavy drinking may carry less of a stigma than for girls. Experts say that the factor that most strongly predicts both the initial age and future use of alcohol and drugs is a student's normative beliefs (perceptions about the pervasiveness and acceptability of a behavior among peers).

Why is there such a discrepancy between perceived and true stu-dent drinking? One answer could rest in the types of kids who are doing the drinking. Studies show that not only do student athletes have "significantly higher levels of perceived drinking" than non-athletes, but also they actually drink more. This could be because sports teams develop tight groups and therefore more stringent behav-ioral norms, or because jocks are often considered popular, which means they are more likely to be invited to social events involving alcohol. Remember, two of the hallmarks of a perceived popular stu-dent are that he is visible and influential. If the populars say that "ev-eryone" is drinking, then many other students will be exposed to this opinion.

Fortunately, one method of prevention is designed to curb risky behavior specifically by addressing these misperceptions. FCD Educa-tional Services, a small nonprofit, is one of many organizations that uses social norms to change behaviors and attitudes toward substance abuse in schools. Most of FCD's programs begin with a survey about students' own actions and their perceptions of peers. "In every single school, almost every single kid grossly overexaggerates peer use of alco-hol and other drugs," said Renee Soulis, FCD southeast regional officer and senior prevention specialist.

FCD, which has "an enormously high success rate" of changing behaviors, then reveals the actual numbers to students, driving the message home with presentations, school-wide marketing campaigns, and/or classroom activities that reinforce healthy attitudes and debunk the myth that "everyone" is drinking. In some communities, FCD uses high school data to improve middle school attitudes. "The middle schoolers think that everyone drinks in high school. We get nondrinking seniors to talk to eighth graders with the survey data. You can see the false perceptions start to shrink," Soulis said. FCD also addresses parent and teacher misperceptions. "Parents feel isolated so much of the time," Soulis said. "When they realize the vast amount of parents who are working with this [and feel the same way], they feel empowered."

Regan discovered another way to use social norms to resist the pressure to drink: She publicly identified herself as part of a group that has a substance-free lifestyle as its norm. Straight Edge began as a movement among punks; the hardcore punk band Minor Threat coined the term in a song of the same name. Straight Edge kids often wear the group's symbol, the letter X, on clothes or the back of a hand, co-opting the sign that clubs and bars use to mark underage patrons. (SXE and XXX are other common Straight Edge variations.)

For Regan, Straight Edge was both a validation and a defense of her lifestyle. "I like having a term to identify myself," she said. "I know I'm not the only one resisting. When you offer someone chocolate, and they say they're diabetic, you don't ask again. Straight Edge affords me that same respect."

JOY, CALIFORNIA | THE NEW GIRL

A new girl arrived in PE, assigned to the gym locker next to Joy's. Her clothing and shoes were ripped, her body odor was strong, and she had bruises on her arms and legs. Joy noticed her pretty blonde hair and nice teeth. "Hi, are you new here?" Joy asked gently.

"Yeah."

"Welcome to Citygrove! Where are you from?"

"I'm from El Dorado." The girl positioned herself as if to hide the contents of her locker.

"Did you get in a fight?" Joy asked, eyeing the girl's bruises.

"Yeah," she answered. "Three girls beat me up. If I get in another fight, I'm going to juvie."

A hyper classmate came running toward her locker, put her PSP down on the bench next to Joy, and dashed off. A few seconds later she ran back. "Hi!" she said.

The new girl glanced at the bench. "You should pick up your PSP," she said. "Don't leave anything around me. I've been known to have sticky fingers."

Over the next several weeks, Joy got to know Ariana, a foster child whom social services had taken from the trailer park where she lived with her mother. She had transferred schools after her third fight. She confided to Joy that she used and sold drugs, cut herself, and shoplifted. She said that her foster parents barely fed her and her brother. Once, Joy was afraid Ariana was going to die because she was shaking so badly when she got to PE. It turned out she was high. Her brother had given her a new drug as a joke. Ariana was fifteen.

Joy's AP English class, covered by a substitute teacher, was supposed to be working, but the students were restless. The girl next to Joy, a talented artist, put her pencil down on her desk and sighed. "I'm just gonna draw." She scratched out an anime character on a piece of paper.

Joy smiled. Sara, an Asian-American, didn't usually talk to her. "I used to be like you, sitting and drawing all day. It used to be my passion," Joy said.

"I don't draw that much," Sara said.

"You draw every time you're in this class," Xavier chimed in.

"What do you wanna be when you grow up?" Joy asked.

"My parents want me to be a doctor," Sara said.

"A doctor!" Xavier said in surprise.

"A doctor," Joy mused. "When drawing is clearly your passion, you're going to become a doctor."

"Joy, you're so mean!" interrupted Keisha, a girl who had been hostile to Joy lately. "Why do you want to destroy her dreams?! If she wants to become a doctor, then let her become a doctor!"

"Hold up, did I say that she couldn't become a doctor?!" Joy snapped. "How exactly am I destroying her dreams? You want to tell me? How will I get in the way of her aspirations?"

Joy didn't know why Keisha, who had been nice to her in the fall, had changed her mind about Joy. When Joy spoke in class, Keisha would stare at her as if she spouted gibberish.

"Nothing," Keisha said. "If I argue with you, I'm not going to win." They had crossed words before. *She's not a bad person; she just loses her bearings*, Joy reminded herself.

"I want to be an artist," Sara admitted.

"I can see you doing that," Joy encouraged.

"But no, I'm going to become a surgeon," Sara said, resigned.

"Because of your parents or do you want to?" Joy asked.

"I can be a surgeon and carve anime into people's faces!" Sara joked.

"I don't think that's the best idea," Xavier said.

"I can be a tattoo artist," Sara said, brightening.

"Yeah, you could do that! And you can make a lot of money, if you do the intricate tattoos," Joy said. "People would pay good money for that!"

A boy in front of Joy turned around. "Why the hell should she become a tattoo artist?!" he said. "Why would she downgrade from being a doctor to a tattoo artist?!"

"Maybe if you weren't so small-minded, you could see that art is something she loves," Joy said. "And she can make money being a tattoo artist. The more complicated the pieces, the more money she gets."

"Why should anyone do crap like art when they can be a doctor or lawyer?!" the boy said.

"You are so ignorant!" Joy shouted. "Maybe if your parents didn't embed that level of thinking within you, you could see there's more to life than being just a lawyer or doctor. You need to seriously wake up."

"Don't argue with her," Keisha warned him. "She'll go on and on until she proves her point."

In Jamaica, Joy had spent hours drawing, acting, and writing poetry. Since coming to America, she had neglected her artistic side because Citygrove didn't encourage creativity like her Jamaican school did. After the conversation with Sara, Joy returned to spending her free time writing poetry and creating skits to practice her acting. Many of her poems expressed her feelings that the more she grew accustomed to her American surroundings, the more they stifled her.

Noah, Pennsylvania | The Band Geek

Weeks went by without Noah mentioning his challenge. When I finally asked him if he had made any progress, he said he hadn't. With a bit of prodding, the truth came out. Noah didn't want to talk to certain crowds in school because he disapproved of the choices they made outside of it. "There's a reason I don't befriend them," he said.

"You can still be friendly without being best friends," I said.

"Yeah, I agree with what you're saying." He seemed dubious.

Several days later, I checked in with him again. "Do you feel like you've done anything outside of your comfort zone? Or approached anyone you wouldn't have approached before?" I asked.

"I'm not really sure," Noah said. "I just . . . I'm not sure how to do it."

"Why can't it be as simple as just going up and talking to people in different groups as much as you can? You want people to see you as a leader . . ."

"Part of the problem is that people at our school don't listen. They just put on their headphones and tune out the world. It's intimidating."

"Sure it's intimidating, but you won't know that they don't listen unless you try."

"Yeah, I dunno, I feel like I don't know how to do it," Noah said. "People aren't motivated. The problem is, people that aren't popular have a few friends and they are perfectly content with that bubble. It's really infuriating."

Eli, Virginia | The Nerd

In Spanish class, the teacher asked for volunteers to read a passage aloud from a textbook. "Chan! Chan!" Eli shouted, to his friend's feigned annoyance.

"Okay, Chan, why don't you read for us?" the teacher said.

When Chan finished the paragraph, he looked up with a vindictive gleam. The next paragraph was about forty lines long. "Eli!" he exclaimed. "Let Eli read!"

Immediately Eli turned bright red and started sweating. "No, that's really okay. I don't think so," Eli said.

"Come on, Eli. You can do it," said the best Spanish speaker in the class.

"How about you only read half?" the teacher said.

"Okay," Eli sighed, "I'll do it, I'll do it."

He started to read, but most of his classmates were chattering. He stopped and waited for the class to quiet, then read another line, then stopped. He waited again for his classmates to simmer down. When he resumed reading, he heard some girls giggle, he guessed because of his accent. Sweating heavily, Eli continued reading, trying to speak over the swell of the other voices in the room. About three-quarters of the way through the paragraph, the jabbering grew loud once more. He stopped and waited, tried to read the next line, and halfway through, stopped reading again. While Eli was mostly glad that no one was paying attention, a small part of him was frustrated that he wasn't being heard. Every person in the room was engaged in a side conversation. Even his teacher was talking to a French teacher who had stopped by. *Nobody's listening to me,* he thought. *Story of my life.* Eli was so fed up that he uncharacteristically exploded. "IS ANYONE EVEN LISTENING TO ME?!" he shouted.

Everyone stopped talking and stared at Eli in shock. Then some of the students laughed. "I'm listening, Eli, keep going!" said a girl.

"Even the teacher isn't listening to you!" someone else said.

"No!" the French teacher protested. "She was just saying how great of a reader you are!"

"Yeah! No, really!" Eli's teacher said, pleading.

Embarrassed, Eli resumed reading, but got through only two more lines before the room grew loud once more. Now students were laughing openly, but Eli realized they were laughing with him, not at him. Eli laughed too. "Okay, I have five lines left," he said. "Can we please just get through this?!" Eli read through the final lines, then looked up when he finished. Unexpectedly the entire class gave him a thirty-second round of applause. Eli gave a modest seated bow and, still blushing, looked down at his textbook.

That class period was one "of my favorite moments in all of high school," he said later. "I think it kind of summarized my whole high school experience in one little event. No one listens, then I think everyone's laughing at me, but maybe I just need to laugh at myself some more, or realize that people are laughing with me."

That afternoon, Eli was overjoyed to receive a text from Tad, his neighbor, asking him if he wanted to hang out. Tad, a freshman in college, showed up at Eli's dad's house with Willis, another neighbor whom Eli had known for years but hadn't seen in months. The boys walked around the neighborhood catching up on their lives. They drove to Taco Bell so that Eli could pick up some dinner before going to his busboy job.

On the ride back, Willis asked Tad, "Do you drink or smoke a lot?"

"Nah, not too much," Tad answered. "I drink more than I smoke. You?"

"Me, too. I think the last time I smoked a lot was Halloween."

Eli was disappointed. Were drugs and alcohol really that prevalent? He knew his neighbors drank, but he considered smoking to be pointless and abhorrent. "Wait," he said from the driver's seat, "are you talking about cigarettes or pot?"

"Pot," Tad replied.

"Okay, they're both disgusting," Eli said.

Tad and Willis seemed amused by Eli's emphatic opinion. "Sorry to disappoint you," Willis said from the backseat.

As much as he liked these guys, who had always been nice to him, Eli *was* disappointed. Their conversation worried him. He said later, "Personally, I don't know how I'm going to fit in in college without smoking or drinking. Then again, it's not like I want to be with those people anyways, so I guess I'll have to find a small group of friends who also don't smoke or drink? I mean, I don't think I'd mind going to parties, even if people are drinking there, but I won't drink. But I think going to a party where people are smoking is too much for me."

. . .

THE GIRL WHO SAT in front of Eli in calculus turned around and asked, "Eli, are you really going all the way [across the country]?"

"Uh, yeah."

Josephine tuned in to the conversation. "But won't you miss your family?" she asked.

Eli shrugged. "Not really. I mean, are you going to live with your parents forever?"

"No," said Josephine, "but, like, you'll just be so far away. Won't you miss them?"

"It's not like I'm really close with my family, anyways. I don't hate them or anything, but it's not going to be difficult."

He was surprised to see Josephine, who was usually aloof toward him, flash a sympathetic look.

Later that week, Eli was at home rummaging through photographs of himself for a scholarship application. He found his sophomore school picture and, pleased, laid it aside. To his delight, he had just been accepted into WCU's business program. This had been a good day.

His mother walked by. "What's that for?" she asked. She pointed to the photograph.

"A scholarship application," Eli said.

"No! Don't use this one! You look like you're in eighth grade!"

A half hour later, when Eli was watching TV, his mother broached the subject again. "Why don't you ever change your haircut?" she asked.

"Does it really matter?" Eli said. "You aren't the one living with the haircut."

"It just looks like a t-t-t-" She stopped herself.

"A t-t-t- what?" Eli asked.

"Well, a typical geeky haircut."

Eli tried to brush off the comment by baiting her until she grew frustrated. "Mom, why don't *you* think about changing your hair? Maybe some black? Black hair? Hmm? A little change? Dye it black? Some black hair, maybe?"

She didn't understand that this was what he often felt like in her company. When she insulted his hair, he explained later, "I felt . . . diminished. I mean, this is right after all this exciting college stuff happening, so it just feels like she's saying, 'Yeah, that's great, but what about what other people think about what you look like?' That just *really* pisses me off. It's a depressing social commentary. It's a lonely feeling more than anything."

The conversation reminded him of a recent afternoon when he was playing the Wii while his mother tidied his room. She was gone for a long time. Eli went to his room to see what she was up to. When he poked his head in, she was still making his bed. "Oh, I thought you were going through my homework or something," he said.

Eli resumed playing Mario Kart. His mother followed him and sat next to him on the couch.

"I knew this would happen," she said. "I knew when you signed up for five APs that you'd spend all your time doing homework." Eli said nothing. His mother was bugging him about doing too much work while he was playing a video game.

"Why don't you want to have any friends over?" she continued.

"I just want to rest and take it easy!" Eli said.

"What kid doesn't want to hang out with his friends?! That's weird! I just wanted you to have a normal senior year, but you had to take these five AP classes!"

Eli concentrated on his game. He would have loved to be hanging out with friends. He couldn't say to his mother, "No one wants to hang out with me." There was a lot he could not say.

———

PARENTS AND "NORMALITY"

In my standard interview questions for this book, I did not ask students specifically about their parents; this is, after all, a book mainly about the dynamics and targets of exclusion at school. But as a considerable number of students raised the topic, I realized that if there is a single factor that spells the difference between cafeteria fringe headed for greatness and those doomed to low self-worth, even more than a caring teacher or a group of friends, it is supportive, accepting parents who not only love their children unconditionally, but also don't make them feel as if their idiosyncrasies qualify as "conditions" in the first place. "My mom likes to compare me to the rest of society, or at least how she perceives it to be, and I just want her to stop," Eli told me. "I want her to accept me for who I am."

Throughout my years of lecturing at schools, my biggest surprise was a parent who, even after listening to a talk about how children's health and happiness should be prioritized over prestige and accolades, asked me how to force her children to follow their mom's dreams. At a high school outside of Seattle, she asked me, "What if my only dream for my kids is that they go to either Stanford or Yale?" Later, as the principal drove me back to my hotel, I told her about the encounter. The principal knew the woman. Her oldest daughter, she told me, was at Yale. Her younger daughter still attended the high school. "There's a middle daughter, too," she told me. The mother hadn't mentioned her. "Where is she?" I asked. The principal named a small college. At that moment, my heart broke not only for the daughter who already was forced to become her mother's alarmingly narrow ideal, but also for the middle daughter who knew that in her mother's mind she had already failed.

"All parents want their kids to be popular," psychologist Lawrence Bauman has claimed. "Popular kids seem to be a vindication of all the early years of support that parents have given and the effort they have made in raising their kids."[3] In this respect, there may be scant difference between parents who push their kids to get into a prestigious college and parents desperate for their kids to be cool. Both sets of parents, intentionally or not, restrict their children by jamming them into a specific mold. Both sets might seek some sort of brag-worthy validation of their "successful" parenting. Both sets might make their children feel as if they aren't good enough—or worse, that they are deficient or failures—the way they are. Certainly some parents push for popularity because they want to spare their children the pain of friendlessness. But what's tragic about students in Eli's situation is that rather than assure

---

[3] *I disagree with both statements.*

children that there's no such thing as normal, some parents are telling them that they aren't—and then making them feel like they should want to be. Too many parents fail to understand that there is a difference between fitting in and being liked, that there is a difference between being "normal" and being happy. High school is temporary. Family is not.

"Normal" is a loaded, slippery word that signifies different standards for different groups. Eli, for his part, told me he didn't "distinguish between normality and conformity." An important observation of normality comes from psychologist David Anderegg: "When you try to identify people who are psychologically normal, the one reliable thing that seems to distinguish them, above all else, is that they *define* themselves as normal. They squeeze out any and all weirdness, because they don't want it. To these aggressive mental centrists, nerds and geeks are not normal."

Parents who rely on their children's peers to dictate normality are venturing into particularly perilous territory, even apart from the idea that defining normality by teenage trends produces standards that are arbitrary and ultimately meaningless. When parents equate normality with popularity, they encourage behavior that is of much more concern than unpopularity.

Students reported that their parents' preoccupation with their social status can go beyond the bounds of trying to disguise or smother their quirks. A New Jersey junior didn't drink alcohol frequently, but happened to tell her mother that most students at her school did. Seemingly disappointed, her mom fretted, "Oh . . . well if everyone's drinking, does that mean you aren't cool?" In condoning alcohol use, parents may be hoping to be "the cool parent" among their children's friends, expecting to boost their children's popularity. Yet studies show that students perceive parents who have *negative* attitudes about alcohol and drugs to be more caring.

Parents' attitudes toward drinking can be more dangerous than they realize, whether they throw parties with alcohol for teenagers, or allow them to drink alcohol in their homes while they look the other way. "The permissiveness of parents who want their kids to be popular can lead to tragic consequences," according to Joseph Califano

Jr., former U.S. Secretary of Health, Education, and Welfare. The permissive parent debate runs hot and fierce. Some parents insist that because teenagers are going to drink anyway, they might as well drink at home. "High school kids drink. . . . It's going to happen," the Cato Institute's Radley Balko wrote in the *Washington Post*. "Surely there are more pressing concerns for the Washington area criminal justice system to address than parents who throw supervised parties for high school kids. These parents . . . know that underage drinking goes on and take steps to prevent that reality from becoming harmful. We ought to be encouraging that kind of thing, not arresting people for it."

Actually underage drinking is harmful to begin with. Health risks aside, numerous studies show that children whose parents allow them to drink at home are at a higher risk for developing alcohol problems. By contrast, teenagers who don't drink at home are less likely to drink anywhere. Balko's view is shockingly common. In a long-term study, Connecticut high school students told researchers that their parents were much more tolerant of substance abuse than they were of rudeness, academic failure, and stealing. It is unclear, however, whether Balko bothered to research his op-ed before pontificating in a major newspaper, given his erroneous claim that kids are going to drink anyway and his suggestion that if they drink at home, they won't drink elsewhere. In fact, teenagers whose parents provide alcohol for parties are three times more likely to binge drink. Penn State's Prevention Research and Methodology Center found that "the greater number of drinks that a parent had set as a limit for the teens, the more often they drank and got drunk in college." Conversely students whose parents strongly disapprove of underage drinking are less likely to drink heavily in college. Experts say college drinking can cause far worse problems than alcoholism. One wonders what, for Balko, could possibly be a "more pressing concern" than the health and safety of children?

While encouraging substance abuse is extreme, parental pressure to conform to other social standards is no less damaging to an impressionable teenager's psyche. Too many teens have to deal with parents' constant criticisms about their weight. Practically everything about Eli—his clothes, his interests, his mannerisms, his hair—was under fire. The mother of Wade, a New Hampshire junior, tried to change his sexual orientation. The only openly gay student at his school, Wade experienced only sporadic harassment from classmates in his conservative community. But when the topic came up at home, his mother immediately signed him up for counseling because, Wade said, "she believed I had been sexually abused to make me the 'way I am.' At least at school, there is room for me to breathe."

Imagine what it must be like for teenagers like Wade or Eli, who don't feel they have room to breathe in their own homes. If you are a parent reading this book, you care about your child. If she is quirky, unusual, or nonconformist, ask yourself whether you are doing everything you can to nurture her unusual interests, style, or skills, or whether instead you are directly or subtly pushing her to hide them.

The same day that Eli told me about the "geeky haircut" conversation, he mentioned that he had set a goal to sell his possessions and take off to travel the world by 2020. Eli's command of geography was impressive, his hope for adventure wistful, but I could not shake the image of this earnest but jaded boy searching the globe for the unconditionally accepting safe haven he could not find at home. Meanwhile, he couldn't wait to attend the college he had applied to mostly because it was as far across the country as he could get. I realized then that his mother's desperate attempts to convince her son to be "normal" resulted in a consequence that, to many parents, would be a far worse fate than having an idiosyncratic child at home: She drove her child away.

Late Winter to Early Spring

**Being Excluded Doesn't Mean That
Anything's Wrong with You**

Chapter 8

A BRIEF INTRODUCTION TO
GROUP PSYCHOLOGY

WHITNEY, NEW YORK | THE POPULAR BITCH

In February, Whitney walked into her new economics class, saw a sea of black, and did a double take. Since eighth grade, she had taken honors and college-level classes with the same students. But Riverland offered only one level of economics. Whitney scanned the room. All of the students were punk, emo, or losers. She checked the room number to make sure she was in the right class, then sat next to punk girls who looked at her strangely. Whitney was wearing her cheerleading warmups and a large bow in her hair because it was a game day.

"Whitney," said a skanky punk, "you need to leave right now." Populars categorized the punks as "okay punks" or "skanky punks," a division based entirely on money. The skanky punks were poor.

Startled, Whitney asked why.

"Because you're too smart to be in this class and you'll make us all look stupid." The other students cracked up.

Whitney laughed nervously. When Chelsea walked in, Whitney dashed across the room to sit next to her, finding a small sense of security in the vicinity of another popular. "Ugh," Chelsea whispered to Whitney, "here we go again."

After a brief introduction to the class, the teacher said, "Raise your hand if you have a car." Almost everyone raised a hand.

"Who pays for your own car?" Whitney and Chelsea put their hands down. Their classmates' hands were still raised.

"Okay," the teacher continued, "whose parents pay for their car?" Only Whitney and Chelsea raised their hands.

"Whose parents pay for gas?" Chelsea's hand lowered.

Whitney was the only student with a hand in the air. Her classmates stared at her and muttered, "Oh my God." Blushing, Whitney quickly lowered her hand.

"Wow," one boy shouted, "I wish I was her." The students laughed.

Later that day, in advertising (another class without preps), the students discussed which magazines to use for a project. When Whitney said she wanted to use *American Cheerleader*, the other girls in the class gave her dirty looks.

Whitney tried to focus on happier things. She had been selected as first chair flutist in the all-county band, for example. Whitney liked the flute, which she had played for nearly a decade, partly because she believed she could express herself more truthfully through music than she could at school. The preps had discouraged her from playing because rehearsals often conflicted with social plans, but Whitney was committed. She attended every rehearsal for the following month's concert, even skipping a cheerleading competition for one of the band practices. She also had been accepted to her first-choice college. But her social issues overshadowed these triumphs.

―――――

WHY GROUPS DON'T GET ALONG

Throughout the year, Eli wondered repeatedly, "Why can't we all get along?" He couldn't figure out why, by senior year, cliques couldn't just set aside their quibbles and coexist peacefully. One answer to Eli's question lies in the psychology of group identity.

In the early 1970s, social psychologist Henri Tajfel showed an audience of fourteen- and fifteen-year-old boys slides of abstract paintings. Tajfel told the boys that they would be divided into two groups, depending on which paintings they preferred. He lied. In reality, Tajfel and his team randomly assigned the groups. The psychologists then ushered the boys one by one into cubicles, gave them a list of each group's members identified only by code numbers, and told them to distribute virtual money to everyone. Even though the boys did not know what membership meant, they were so eager to adopt an us-versus-them mentality that they showed favoritism, a hallmark of group identity, toward their own random, meaningless group.

Researchers have replicated these results, using more minimal fake group assignments. Students showed group favoritism even when they were told that the groups were assigned by the flip of a coin. To rule out the idea that group members played favorites because they believed they had something in common with their groupmates, researchers split people into groups by lottery and told them so. The results didn't change.

The need to belong is one of the most powerful human motivations. We are naturally drawn toward forming and sustaining groups. There are evolutionary reasons for this drive; groups offer survival and reproductive advantages. Group membership improves odds of finding a mate, hunting successfully, and defending against predators. Groups can more easily compete for and store food and other resources than can lone individuals. Children have a better chance of survival when they are part of a group that cares about their welfare, feeding them, protecting them, and babysitting them.

Groups can also be beneficial from a cognitive standpoint. Tajfel's social identity theory said that people are quick to form and affiliate with groups because groups help us to define our social identities. We see ourselves as members of social categories that enable us to visualize our supposed place in a social structure. Groups satisfy our brain's natural inclination to make sense of the hordes of people we encounter and observe. This quality is so inherent that children intuitively understand the need to form groups without adults having to teach them.

When children first begin to sort out their social world, their groupings are broad and oversimplified. Toddlers as young as one year old might, for example, call all children babies—even if they're twelve. By first grade, children typically have split into distinct social circles, but are probably still blissfully unaware of perceived popularity. At about the age of seven, children have developed the cognitive ability to apply several categories to someone (tall, friendly, good at sports). As children age, they get better at analyzing which categories are relevant to various contexts. For example, they learn that when needing someone tall to reach a cookie jar, it would be a mistake to ask people only from their own gender, race, or grade because the tallest person may be in a different group. By fourth grade, students recognize status differences and can pinpoint each other's social positions.

Henri Tajfel didn't actually set out to prove that teenagers would identify with groups formed randomly. His purpose was different: He wanted to understand what caused people to play favorites with their own group (psychologists call this "in-group bias"). To accomplish this goal, Tajfel decided to begin with experimental groups that were so insignificant that their members couldn't possibly feel the need to show favoritism. He was surprised when his first random group and every subsequent group played favorites. Tajfel's unanticipated finding is generally hailed across fields as a seminal discovery.

More recent research has argued that people's trust in their groups doesn't necessarily mean they *dislike* outsiders, only that they may discriminate against them. Students may become cafeteria fringe merely because they don't happen to fit neatly into groups that have already formed. People assign more favorable characteristics to their own group and assume that their groupmates' beliefs are more similar to theirs than are outsiders' beliefs. They usually process information about outsiders in simplistic ways, then bond over their generalized stereotypes of non-group members.

Not all groups experience in-group bias the same way. High-status groups (populars, for instance) display more group favoritism, evaluate their group more positively, and critique other groups more negatively than do low-status groups. Members of low-status groups, meanwhile, might attempt to feel better about their identity by copying high-status groups (such as wannabes who dress like populars); using the social creativity strategy, meaning they find different factors on which to base their comparisons ("They will work for me someday"); or comparing themselves to other low-status groups, much like Eli's list of nerd sub-species.

Group favoritism seems intuitive, but how does it lead to clique warfare? In 1954, social psychologist Muzafer Sherif invited twenty-two eleven-year-old boys to a three-week summer camp in Robbers Cave State Park, Oklahoma. The boys were well-adjusted, middle class, Protestant Oklahoma City residents with similar IQs and no history of social or academic problems. Sherif randomly divided the boys into two groups and positioned them at opposite ends of a 200-acre campground outfitted with hidden tape recorders. Sherif's team of observers served as camp staff. Sherif himself, disguised as the camp janitor, watched how events played out.

For the first several days of camp, the two groups were unaware of each other. The boys instinctively formed group identities, naming their groups the Eagles and the Rattlers. Toward the end of the first week, the camp staff told each group that there was another set of boys on the campgrounds. When the Eagles heard the faraway sounds of the Rattler boys at play, one of the Eagles, knowing nothing about the Rattlers, called them "nigger campers." Each group requested to compete against the other.

During the second week, Sherif set up a tournament of competitions—baseball, touch football, tug-of-war, tent-pitching—in which only the winning group received rewards. Tensions between the groups skyrocketed. They sang derisive songs and continued the name-calling. The Eagles set fire to the Rattlers camp flag. Camp staff forcibly broke up fistfights. The Rattlers, decked out commando-style, raided the Eagles' cabin, ripping through mosquito netting and stealing or vandalizing some of the Eagles' possessions. Adults had to prevent the Eagles from attacking the Rattlers with rocks.

Tajfel's paintings experiment illustrated that random, meaningless groups can adopt an us-versus-them mentality. Sherif's Robbers Cave experiment demonstrated that those groups can quickly turn hostile, even when they haven't met face-to-face, and that in a competitive environment the hostility can escalate. Now step up the intensity of both of those scenarios: Nonrandom groups formed exclusively and bonded over time are placed in a setting in which they repeatedly must compete for resources, prestige, adult approval, and limited spots in various desirable organizations. When presented that way, it should come as no surprise that these groups might have difficulty getting along. When presented that way, it sounds a lot like school.

JOY, CALIFORNIA | THE NEW GIRL

Because of her challenge, Joy decided to try conversing with some of the most aggressive girls at Citygrove. Joy was walking with Cleo when she saw the girls a ways off. "I wanna talk to them," Joy said.

"Who, them?" Cleo asked, surprised.

"Yes."

"I can't talk to them with you!" Cleo said, laughing, as if it would be preposterous for her to approach black girls known for their attitude.

"That's why I'm gonna go to them with Latrice."

Joy and Cleo were still laughing as they passed by the girls. The girls stared at them.

The biggest one frowned. "You got a problem?" she said to Joy.

Uh-oh. "Do *you* have a problem?" Joy retorted.

The girl stepped forward. One of her friends was watching, while the other one danced, earbuds in her ears. Cleo and Joy stood their ground. "Yeah, I got a problem. I got a fucking problem with bitches looking at me."

"Oh really now," Joy said.

"Yeah, fucking bitch. If you got a problem with me, come and handle," the girl said.

The girl who had been dancing took out her earbuds. "Who?" she asked.

"That one, the one in the pink," answered the leader.

"Who is she?" asked the dancer. "She looks cool."

"No," said the other girl. "Fucking ugly bitch."

Intimidated, Joy and Cleo walked away quickly. Perhaps, Joy thought, she should approach her challenge less ambitiously.

Meanwhile, Latrice, the black student Joy spoke to most frequently, continued to ask Joy to tutor her in biology. "Aw, Joy, please. You're so smart," she wheedled. Thanks to the biology teacher, students were well aware that Joy was the highest-scoring student in the class. She usually scored 100 percent on tests.

Latrice could be flaky, and Joy wasn't sure if she wanted to invest the time if Latrice would be too distracted to digest Joy's lessons. But one night before a big test, Latrice called again. "Help me!" she pleaded. "I can pay you! Please, I need to get my grades up."

Joy sighed. She knew that Latrice could do better if she tried. "It's okay, you don't have to pay me. I'll help you." That night, at Joy's apartment, Joy taught her the entire ecosystems chapter in four hours.

When the teacher handed back the tests, Latrice gasped. "Oh my gosh, a *B*! This is great!" she exclaimed. "Joy, Joy! Look! You're so smart! Thank you! *I* feel smart!"

"You should always feel smart," Joy said. "You're an intelligent person. You just need to get guys off your mind."

"Aw, no, I can't do that. They're so luscious!"

"Well, I'm here if you need me," Joy said. Latrice hugged her.

Over the next weeks, Joy got to know Latrice, tutoring her occasionally, doing homework with her in the library, hanging out with her in classes and during breaks throughout the day. Eventually Latrice joined Joy, Anisha, and Cleo for their lunches in the biology room. Latrice confided that it had taken her a while to work up the nerve to ask Joy to tutor her. She said she'd wanted to be friends with Joy from the time they met in Joy's first English class, but, while now Joy was easy to talk to, back then she thought Joy was distant. Joy was glad that Latrice was honest.

Joy was also glad to have a black friend at Citygrove. Sometimes D'Arnell, a congenial sophomore, also made small talk with her, but most of the other black students still scowled at her. Joy liked to think she was the type of individual who could "look past skin color and see the person, but sometimes," she said, "you can't help but feel more comfy with people who are like you."

A few weeks later, Joy was walking to Ross to shop for clothes when she ran into Ariana, the foster girl from PE. "Hey! How are you doing? Where do you live?" Joy asked.

"I'm okay," Ariana said. "I live like two hours away."

"So you're going to the bus stop?"

"No, I don't have money to take the bus."

"Oh." Joy wanted to give her cash, but she didn't have any and her mother was already at the store. "You're gonna walk all the way?"

"Most of the way. My brother has a bike. Maybe if he catches up with me I'll ride on the back."

As they walked together, Joy kept up the conversation. "So . . . what are you going to do with your life?"

"Well, I'm gonna move in with my mom," Ariana answered. "So I'm gonna leave. When I'm sixteen, I'm gonna quit school and work at Kmart with my mom."

"You're going to what?!" Joy was flabbergasted.

"Work at Kmart."

"I'm not saying that's a bad job, but seriously, your education is the most important thing right now! You should truly focus on that. You have the potential to be anything you want. You just need to work hard," Joy said.

Ariana looked surprised. "Wow . . . well I don't know, I guess."

"You bet I know! I have so much faith in you! You can become something huge. Just finish school and focus on your life. I'm sure you don't want to work at Kmart for the rest of your life."

"Yeah . . ."

"Please, listen to me. I know some of your friends think I'm a know-it-all bitch, but I'm not. I care. At least take some of my words with you. You have the ability to be anything you want. All you need is hard work and perseverance."

"Thanks, I'll think about it."

"You better think about it," Joy said. "I want you to make something of yourself and become a somebody. You are somebody."

BLUE, HAWAII | THE GAMER

About once a week, when Blue woke up early or couldn't sleep, he caught the bus to the beach. It was nicest around 4 A.M., when the darkened sky was so clear that he could see shooting stars. On shore,

strange algae glowed green just before dawn. In this quiet nether-
world, Blue would swim laps, gaze at the horizon, and daydream
about a fictional person who would listen to him, would know him,
would keep him company just to be with him. The relationship didn't
have to be romantic. All he wanted was a connection.

Blue was supposed to play in the upcoming Modern Warfare 2 state
championships with Jackson, Ty, and Stewart. But at the most recent
tournament, Jackson had defied every order Blue gave as captain and
the team lost because of it.

The MW2 finals were the same day as the Simulated Congressional
Hearings (SCH) state championship, in which Blue's AP Gov class
would compete. Although he hadn't thought much about SCH before,
Blue made the decision to skip the gaming tournament for the hearings. By leaving the MW2 team, Blue would lose his sponsor and
eliminate his chances to compete in Sweden over the summer, which
he had been looking forward to for months. He explained, "I wasn't
going anywhere with what I was doing. Not that I wasn't going anywhere with gaming per se, but the people who I surrounded myself
with, I mean. I wasn't happy with my 'place.'"

When he told Jackson, Jackson was furious. After yelling at Blue in
the doorway of Blue's house, he said, "Are you jealous of me?"

Blue was confused. "What would I be jealous about?"

"I have friends, girls who like me. Are you mad at me? Orrr is it
that . . . are you gay for me?"

"What?!"

"Yeah. I think you're gay for me."

"Don't flatter yourself."

"No, I think that's exactly it. You're mad because I don't like you
the same way. Am I right?" Jackson laughed cruelly. When Blue shot
him a look, he continued. "Fine, then tell me why, if I'm wrong. I'm
not leaving until you tell me. Hmm?" He tapped his foot.

Blue worked up his courage. "You're a shitty friend and I deserve
better than you," he said. "I'm sorry, but I can't be around someone
who just brings me down anymore. I actually have goals in life."

Jackson cackled at him. "You can barely pass high school." He was
still laughing when Blue shut the door.

Because of his lack of Algebra 2, Blue's only chance to get into the University of Hawaii was the Undergraduate Assistance Program. UAP's purpose was to assist applicants who were "academically under-prepared [or] economically disadvantaged" by admitting them to the university and shepherding them through freshman year and scholarship arrangements. UAP applicants had to write essays and undergo interviews, much like a college admissions process.

"Have a seat," Blue's interviewer said, gesturing to a chair in front of her desk. "Your reading and writing test scores were off the charts. Way beyond college levels. What else makes you different from other students?"

"Like, anything?"

"Yes, anything. Doesn't matter what it is."

Blue was quiet. How could he encapsulate in a pithy admissions-interview line all of his unique ideas and interests?

After a silence, she said, "It can be anything."

"I know, but that's such a hard question. I don't want to make myself sound . . . conceited, you know?" He laughed self-consciously.

"I know," she said, "but you still have twenty minutes left. Take your time."

Hoping to diffuse the awkwardness of his silence, Blue started to answer. "I guess I tend to look at things a lot differently than other people. I can always look at both sides . . . the big picture, and draw my own conclusions. I'm very . . ."—he stumbled—"global."

"That's great!" she prompted. "Anything else?"

"This is still such a hard question."

"No, that was great. We can move on if you want."

"Okay," Blue said, though he didn't want to move on. There was so much more that he wanted to tell her about himself.

"How have your last two years in school been?" She looked at his report card. "You have a lot of absences. And you're not doing so well in some classes." From where he sat, Blue could see the Fs in English and French. "But then in classes like autos and AP Gov, you're great. Why's that?"

"Well, for a while my priorities were a little off. But I've gotten a lot better. I've arranged conferences with my counselors and teachers and we've been working on it."

Several questions later, she asked, "So how is life at home, Mark? Do you live with any siblings?"

"No, it's just me and my mom. My brother lives in France now."

"Do you get along with your mom?" she asked.

Blue's voice weakened. "Well . . . not really."

"Really," she said, looking concerned. "What's that like?"

"Well, my mom and me have conflicting opinions on what I should do with my life. Our goals don't match up. She doesn't think I can go to college, so she wants me in the military."

"I see."

"But I usually don't listen to her. It's not that I don't like the military, don't get me wrong, I just feel that I won't . . ." He paused. "I don't think I'll reach any sort of potential. I won't be able to make something that lasts beyond my own lifetime. And if that doesn't happen, I'll never be happy with myself."

"That's admirable," she said. "So on a scale of one to ten, how badly do you want this?"

"Ten," Blue answered instantaneously.

She wrote something down. "What would you do if this doesn't work out?"

"Probably go to [the local community college] and transfer here or . . ."

"Let's change gears for a second," she said. "How would you be a positive influence on other UAP students? If you aren't going to classes in high school, how can I trust you'll go to classes in college? Because I have that problem with my group right now."

"I guess you could say I've grown up a bit. Last year, I had over thirty-eight unexcused absences in one quarter, but somehow I passed," he said. "I was engrossed in doing things that really mattered to me, namely gaming. But this quarter, I've been going to my classes, even if they aren't necessarily interesting. I've got perfect attendance so far."

She glanced down at her papers. "Right, I see. But how could you get the kids I have now to go to class?"

"Well," Blue said, "I think they haven't found what they really want to do yet."

"Exactly! But they still have to go to these boring classes. Not all of your classes are going to be interesting, so how do I know you'll actually go?"

"The only thing I can say is that I've grown up."

"Okay. By the way, what's the hardest class you've ever taken?"

Blue didn't hesitate. "AP U.S."

"And the easiest?"

"AP Gov." That class inspired him by challenging him.

She looked surprised. "Interesting." She chewed her pen. "This is what I'm going to do. I'm going to pass you on to the final interview with the committee. Usually I say, 'Thanks, but no thanks.' But you're obviously very different from others, so I've passed you on to the final step. Are you excited?"

"I guess so!" Actually he was somewhat disappointed that the questions hadn't been more probing.

She leaned back. The air lightened. "What do you want to major in?" she asked.

"Futurology."

She nodded. "Well, bring this to the front desk and they'll give you the rest of the forms."

"Okay, thank you," Blue said. The woman behind the front desk looked at the papers Blue handed her. "Congratulations!" she said. Other applicants fidgeted as they waited their turn.

Blue left the building, still underwhelmed. The impact of the interview didn't hit him until his mother came to pick him up. As he got into the car, he realized that UAP was his ticket to a new, inspiring life—and he was only one interview away from getting in.

DANIELLE, ILLINOIS | THE LONER

Danielle sat in the librarians' office for the first meeting of the book-selection subgroup of Stone Mill's Summer Reading Committee. The staff and three students were tasked with compiling the list of books that students would choose from to read over the summer and discuss at school in the fall. At first Danielle was hesitant to speak up, but as the deliberations went on, she grew increasingly disturbed.

Danielle had joined the committee determined to get some good books onto the list so that her school didn't end up with the inanities that comprised the previous summer's list. She thought it was pathetic how few Stone Mill students liked reading for pleasure.

"We have to pick books that students would be interested in," one teacher pushed.

"All of my students keep talking about *Twilight*," said another teacher.

Danielle watched incredulously as the librarians added *Twilight* and another YA book to the list. Danielle didn't understand why every summer book had to be "targeted to idiots." *Shows a lot about how Stone Mill views its students*, she thought. *These books are as stupid and as shallow as a puddle.* She tried to counter some of the books the teachers recommended with classier fare, but the librarian in charge said, "No, we need something more interesting and less literary." Most of the books Danielle suggested drew reactions such as, "That's an *adult* book."

When an English teacher suggested *1984*, Danielle was relieved. Finally a decent literary book for the list. "Or *Animal Farm!*" she suggested.

"I don't think *1984* is a good idea because it's too much of a school book," said the teacher who headed the committee. Danielle bristled. Stone Mill didn't even teach Orwell.

When the discussion moved on to books that would appeal to Hispanic students, Danielle piped up again. "What about *Blindness*? It's by José Saramago," she said. Despite a teacher's protest that the books for Hispanic students had to be more relatable to Hispanics, a librarian tentatively added *Blindness* to the list.

Another teacher suggested a book that she said "glorifies gangs." Danielle rolled her eyes as the librarians brought up similar titles. The idea that Hispanics could relate only to books about gang life was both ridiculously stereotypical and insulting. *Because you're Hispanic, you're Mexican*, Danielle thought. *Because you're Mexican, you're in a gang and have a really low IQ and reading level.*

"What about Gabriel García Márquez?" Danielle asked a librarian. Danielle loved *One Hundred Years of Solitude*.

The librarian looked at her condescendingly. *She thinks all of my suggestions suck*, Danielle thought. "We're trying to get books for lower-level students, so we need books that are less literary," she said.

Danielle was speechless. *What's the point of having a summer reading program if the students are just going to read crap?* she thought. She didn't make any other suggestions for the rest of the meeting; instead, she kept fighting for *Blindness*.

After the meeting, Danielle lent a teacher her copy of *Blindness* to prove how good it was. She was determined to get at least one of her book suggestions onto the list.

The day after the meeting, a librarian distributed the minutes to the committee members. She added an editorial: "Remember, the books have to appeal to lower-level readers." Danielle knew the reminder was directed at her. No one else had repeatedly suggested classic literature.

A week later, the teacher returned *Blindness*. "It was too difficult for me to get through," she said. "The writing was so confusing!"

AFTER A SHORT VISIT to her father's house in Florida, where she learned to ride a RipStik (a skateboard shaped like a snowboard), Danielle was back at home watching television when the phone rang. Danielle checked the caller ID. Stone Mill High School again. Someone from Stone Mill had been calling repeatedly, but Danielle had ignored the calls, presuming they were about registration or something else that she shouldn't have to think about on a nonschool day. This time, Danielle picked up, if only to stop the calls.

"Hi," said an unfamiliar voice. "I'm from Stone Mill High School. Is Danielle home?"

"Yeah, this is Danielle."

Without preamble, the woman told her that Emily had died. "There's going to be a wake on Friday," she said. "Counselors will be at school if you need to talk to anyone."

Danielle was rattled. She hadn't been sure what was wrong with

Emily, but she didn't realize it would kill her. Emily was so young to die. Danielle had known Emily for only a few months, but she still felt sad and somewhat hollow. It was "like losing something that you never really paid a lot of attention to, but when it was gone you wish it were still around." Danielle wasn't a crier, but Emily's death was so unexpected that she got slightly misty-eyed.

When Danielle nervously walked into the funeral home, she recognized only one girl, who had come with someone else. As Danielle waited in the long line to talk to Emily's parents, she looked around the room. She felt out of place. She thought it was important that she pay her respects, but she had no idea what to say to parents whose child had just died. She glanced at the open casket and tried not to look again.

After half an hour, Danielle reached the front of the line. "I am sorry for your loss," Danielle said to Emily's mother.

"Who are you?" the mother asked.

"I'm Danielle. I worked with Emily in school."

"Oh!" the mother exclaimed. "That's so nice of you to come! We always get the papers that you guys fill out about yourselves, but we rarely get to meet anyone." She smiled at Danielle. "Did you come here by yourself?"

"Yeah." Danielle shrugged. "I only live a couple of blocks away so it was easy to walk here."

Emily's mother tapped her husband. "She came here all by herself!" she said to him, sounding touched. She turned back to Danielle. "That's so nice of you!" She enveloped Danielle in a long hug. Danielle awkwardly hugged her back. She gazed at the plain white wall behind Emily's mother and waited until the woman pulled away.

"Thank you so much for coming," Emily's mother said as she let Danielle go.

"Yeah, no problem. I'm sorry again." Danielle shook Emily's father's hand and walked away.

On the cold walk home, Danielle shoved her hands in her coat. She treaded carefully along icy sidewalks, thinking about the open casket. It would be easier if you couldn't see the dead person's chest, she mused, because then you wouldn't keep waiting for a breath that wouldn't come.

When Danielle got home, she called her mother at work. "Am I weird?"

"Why would you say that?" her mother asked.

"Emily's mom was really surprised that I went there by myself. I don't see what's so strange about that."

"Well, most girls your age always need to go places with someone else, but you've never really been like that." Danielle's mother sounded proud.

————

WHY SEVENTH GRADE IS THE WORST

It is likely no coincidence that the I Hate Danielle Club formed in the seventh grade. Students nationwide told me about the anguish of their seventh-grade year. Parents told me about seventh graders' tendencies to give out personalized apparel (like sweatshirts listing the attendees) at bar mitzvahs, such that on Mondays at school, uninvited students feel excluded again from the same event.

On the first day of biology, Laura, a Californian, made the egregious mistake of sitting next to Brittany, whose best friend, Dana, was the most popular girl in the seventh grade. Brittany and Dana ridiculed Laura, and persuaded other popular kids to join in. They made fun of her red hair, her parents, and her clothes. When she wore a sweater with a fake-fur collar, they called her an animal killer. When she explained the fur was fake, they mocked her for wearing a cheap sweater. They wrote notes with expletives on blackboards and signed Laura's name. As Laura tried to erase a note, Dana shoved her to the floor. Brittany called her a loser. Laura couldn't talk to the teacher; Dana was the teacher's pet.

Dana and her friends continued to torment Laura daily. Laura's grades dropped and she became depressed. Dana's boyfriend shot staples into her ear. When Laura stood up, the substitute biology teacher told her she had something on her back. As Laura pulled off the KICK ME HARD sign, the class laughed and pointed. Laura tried not to let them see her cry. The substitute did nothing. Even after Laura talked to administrators and switched to another class, she remained a pariah. Laura's social life didn't begin to improve until high school.

Middle school has the potential to shake up a kid's world, thanks to external and internal factors hurtling toward each other that happen to collide in approximately seventh grade. Externally, the transition from elementary school to middle or junior high school brings many changes, whether it begins in sixth or seventh grade. Elementary school children typically stay in one classroom, or travel the hallways in a teacher-led line. Except for lunch and recess, they regularly interact with the same group of classmates and within the confines of a room under adult supervision. By the end of elementary school, their social circles have been established.

Then middle school splices those circles. Middle schools begin to divide students by academic performance, separating them into tracks in various rooms with various teachers. Students have to be more responsible for themselves. Middle schools might sponsor afterschool social events, such as sports, concerts, and dances, which heighten the emphasis on having something fun to do and someone to do it with.

All of these changes would be scary enough. But perhaps the most powerful adjustment in the middle school setting is the shift from socializing during classes to socializing between them. Students are no longer anchored in one consistent classroom, which may lead them to seek that consistency in a friend group. Because they have to navigate hallways several times a day, many of their most important interactions outside of the cafeteria occur in crowded, unsupervised territories. These are the easiest areas in which students can get away with being cruel; it was in the hallways that students bullied Eli.

The middle school social scene accentuates the insecurity and confusion that students are experiencing internally. As preadolescents are thrown into this larger, complicated social pool, their cognitive abilities haven't yet caught up to their environment. They react to certain situations with a different part of the brain than do adults, which leads to more frequent emotional gut reactions.

One of the major cognitive changes at this age is that students frequently reflect about themselves and absorb other people's perspectives.

The problem is, they don't yet have the ability to organize these thoughts properly. At the same time, peer influence peaks from age eleven to thirteen. Middle schoolers are more likely to ask, "Where do I belong?" than "Who am I?" Their identity is so collective that one psychologist called it a "wego" instead of an ego. Students often don't recognize that in trying to form an identity independent of their families, they end up shaping that identity with the characteristics of their social group. This is one reason why children this age believe that group membership is crucial.

Social circles are most homogenous during middle school because to define themselves by their group, students want to view that group as having clear characteristics. Therefore, they are more likely to adhere to group norms and to demand that other group members conform. Psychologists have said that this period is characterized by a "strong, if not totalitarian, press for conformity to the peer group's expectations." These are then the standards by which middle schoolers judge each other and reorganize their social categories.

At the same time, the standards for conformity aren't necessarily static. Students this age change their minds about everything from fads and fashions to goals, values, and dreams. They can be rigidly idealistic without knowing how to define their ideals. Worse still, they haven't yet developed all of the skills necessary for group problem-solving, making it more challenging for their group to agree on a standard of conformity in the first place. Concordia University psychology professor William Bukowski warned, "As this consensus is elusive, the struggles for power within groups may provide nearly perfect conditions for some group members who upset a tenuous consensus to be victimized."

Puberty then complicates all of these dynamics. Middle schoolers are more likely to hang out with older students, form opposite-sex friendships, and enter romantic relationships. They might date, play hormone-driven party games, and, as the media is fond of reporting, engage in sexual activities. With puberty comes an increase in sexual harassment and harassment about gender nonconformity (boys wearing eyeliner, girls with short hair, etc.). Furthermore, children don't hit puberty at the same rate, which means that both early maturers and late bloomers are at risk for being seen as different.

And different, in this intransigent world in which strict group boundaries reign, can have powerful repercussions. A thirteen-year-old Midwesterner pinpointed seventh grade as the year in which her ex-boyfriend and his friends daily made fun of her breasts. "[He] would call me man chest and wrote poems about me that made me cry every night. [Another] guy called me pepperoni face because I had acne. Everybody thinks we're the perfect blue-ribbon school and we're all friends, which isn't true."

Early adolescents report more antagonistic interactions both within their groups and with outsiders than do younger and older students. The rate of cyberbullying peaks in middle school. Antagonism is strong during these years because groups most want to separate themselves from other groups when the importance of group membership peaks. They create this separation by using hostility. "Kids in middle school are, in a social sense, fascists," psychologist David Anderegg has written. "Desirability of all kinds is rigidly circumscribed by what is seen as 'normal.' . . . Since they cannot impose any regularity on their bodies, they impose a rigid regularity on each other. Although this social hazing now starts earlier and earlier . . . , seventh grade is at its peak. It is a time in most kids' lives when being different from the agreed-on norm is an absolute guarantee of social death."

It is also a time in which students are increasingly sensitive to negative evaluations from others, and the aggressive kids vocalizing these critiques are increasingly admired. Many studies show that early adolescents value dominance and aggression, which they associate with high social status. For girls, the association of popularity with these negative behaviors plateaus in the seventh and eighth grades, at about the same time that the social goals for both genders often shift from likeability to perceived popularity.

Popularity is paramount in middle school. At no other time of life is it so important to students to be in a popular group. Yet during the grades when they are most susceptible to peer influence and most concerned about social status, they are also most prone to exclusivity—meaning, groups become most important at precisely the time when it's hardest to get into them.

High schoolers might more easily find a home. More subcultures exist in high school than in middle school, offering more places in which to belong, and the presence of older students can create a more supportive environment. Upperclassmen are less likely to feel like they have to conform to group norms because their group boundaries aren't so strict. In addition, their social understanding has broadened enough for them to make more sophisticated distinctions among individuals and to begin to discount stereotypes when forming opinions about their peers.

By the end of high school, students are usually less concerned with popularity and group membership. They become more self-reliant and more interested in individual friendships or romantic relationships than in traveling in a pack. They are not as vulnerable to peer influence and are less bothered by criticisms. So the sting of seventh-grade exclusion is sharper than the same treatment might have been at age six or sixteen.

With all of these issues in mind, it's no wonder that decades of studies indicate that students experience a drop in self-esteem in early adolescence, at the time that they make the transition into middle school. When these various external and internal factors converge, the resulting panicked confusion can cause some kids to take desperate coping measures to restructure their worlds—which might explain why seventh graders were so desperate to belong that they formed a group so expansive that the only person excluded was Danielle.

Chapter 9

WHY LABELS STICK: THE MOTIVATIONS OF THE NORMAL POLICE

After only a few days or weeks of unsuccessful attempts to find a table at which to fit in, some of the cafeteria fringe opt to escape the lunchroom entirely. At lunchtime, Blue ate in Ms. Collins' room, Joy went to biology, and Danielle usually went home. Eli was fortunate to find fellow "nerds" in his senior year lunch period; as a junior, he ate in the library. Noah sat in the cafeteria, but was unhappy there.

Why do so many students believe they must sit at the same cafeteria table with the same people every day? Why don't they view lunchtime as an opportunity to socialize with new people? Why are students convinced that once they are part of a group or cafeteria table—or shunned from one—they cannot change their situation?

Trey, a senior at an all-boys school in Connecticut, is, to his classmates, a musclehead. They use that label because he works out, takes protein supplements, talks frequently about lifting, tends to pick up heavy items—and people—and because he sometimes doesn't think before he acts. Trey doesn't always mind the label, however, because some classmates admire him for his strength. But there is more to Trey than weightlifting. Few people know, for example, that in his free time he sings and writes poetry.

Sometimes people exclude Trey from activities because they're afraid he'll hurt them. They tell him he hugs too hard. He doesn't mean to. He doesn't know his own strength. "Watch where you're going, you lummox!" a student shouted when Trey turned a corner and accidentally knocked him over. Some classmates call him Caveman, insinuating that he is "big, stupid, and hairy." For years, Trey's older brother called him Lenny in front of his friends and said that Trey couldn't hang out with them because he was "too much like Lenny." Trey didn't know what his brother was talking about until he read *Of Mice and Men*, and was crushed. His brother was calling him a clumsy oaf who broke or killed practically everything he touched. The worst part of the name-calling, Trey said, is that "once you gain a label, you can't really lose it, no matter what."

Teenagers change their minds about a lot of things. They change their minds about their favorite songs and TV shows and regularly ricochet from crush to crush. But they do not easily allow each other to change their minds about social labels. Why do those labels stick?

Many studies show that once students slap a label onto someone, they don't want to remove it. It can be difficult for the child who was socially awkward, nerdy, timid, or odd in elementary or middle school to change his reputation, even if he alters his behavior—and especially if he attends a small school. The major exception occurs when one's status drops; classmates are only too eager to acknowledge a peer's downward mobility by demoting her to a so-called freak, slut, or loser.

In the early 1900s, a German gym teacher told the popular students in her class ahead of time to defy her classroom instructions. When the teacher asked her students to raise their right hands during a calisthenics exercise, the popular children instead raised their left. After class, students recalled that the *un*popular students were the ones who disobeyed the teacher. Subsequent experiments conducted by psychologists have had similar results.

Here's why. As previously discussed, when social circles form, group members inevitably develop stereotypes about each other and about outsiders' traits and behaviors. They might initially base these assumptions on first impressions—and first impressions cling. Beyond those impressions, as University of Pennsylvania education professor Stanton Wortham has written, people " 'rent' categories from the society in order to make sense of themselves and others. These categories of identity often come packaged in larger models that show habitual characteristics, relationships, and events involving recognizable types of people."

One reason labels stick is that when we place someone into a category, we expect him to behave in a way that's consistent with that category. That's why students who defy those expectations might become cafeteria fringe or further marginalized. For some groups, the inconsistency is too confusing to handle. As a result, they also tend to interpret inconsistent behaviors more negatively than might be warranted. Many students told me a version of this description: "I feel like I have to act and look the way I am perceived. I can't wear anything too low-cut because I'm the 'innocent one.' I can't goof off because I'm the 'smart responsible one,'" said a California junior. "In most ways I *am* those things. But sometimes, when I do things that are unlike me, I get looks as if I'm not acting like I *should* act."

This reaction to inconsistency can apply to racial stereotypes as well. A Maryland high school teacher said, "Students who break away from stereotypes are often somewhat ostracized from the 'race group' as a whole. When black or Hispanic students do things that are considered 'un-black' or 'un-Hispanic,' they tend to lose friends," an observation supported by many of my student interviews.

Labels stick because people *want* them to stick. It's easier to sort out your social world when everyone stays in her place. Consistency is less taxing than inconsistency. It's less work for the brain. Several studies have shown that teenagers are more likely to remember behavior that conforms to stereotypes than behavior that doesn't. Similarly, it's easy for our brains to misremember behavior that does not conform to our expectations, which explains why the German students assumed it was the unpopular students, rather than the popular, who had disobeyed instructions.

Psychologists have a name for this set of expectations based on social status. "Reputational bias" typically surfaces during elementary school, as children address their need to begin compartmentalizing their social environment. Adults, too, have this type of memory process. Canadian researchers asked experienced judges to score the short programs of fourteen figure skaters. Six of the judges had heard of only half of the skaters; the other six knew of only the other half. The judges gave significantly higher scores to the skaters whose names were already familiar—particularly for technical merit, a supposedly objective measure. "Why is the exact same skating performance being given higher marks when it is evaluated by judges who know the positive reputation of the athlete versus when she is unknown?" asked the researchers. The answer, they concluded, was that a reputational bias exists, despite clear official guidelines that judges should evaluate "without bias . . . uninfluenced by audience approval/disapproval, the reputation and/or the past performance of the skater."

Our brains like to utilize reputational bias because it keeps the status quo intact. Once people establish labels, those labels become cues for how they "should" treat each other. That treatment then perpetuates the labels, turning reputation into perceived reality. Reputational bias keeps the populars popular and the outcasts outcast. As reputational bias expert Shelley Hymel wrote, "Popular children acquire a 'positive halo' and unpopular children acquire a 'negative halo,' which color how their behavior is perceived, evaluated, and responded to by others."

The halo effect is one of the oldest known phenomena in modern social psychology. It's also highly relevant to social labels in school. The halo effect is the tendency to let one characteristic, even an irrelevant one, influence the total judgment of someone or something. This accounts for our inclination to judge attractive people as more talented, intelligent, and friendly than they might actually be.[4] It is also a reason that many people assume an item is durable, cool, and of good quality simply because it carries a prestigious designer label. It explains why the iPod revitalized Apple's other products. How guys can use puppies as successful chick magnets. And why we think someone is better-looking once he or she acquires celebrity status.

The halo effect also explains in part why the "cool" crowd stays cool. Because these students were crowned with high status, the halo effect extends that alleged superiority to other traits. The clothes they wear, the ways they act, the trends they follow, the words they favor,

---

[4] "There is actually not much difference in the social qualities of attractive and unattractive individuals," Psychology Today reported in 2010.

even the color of their hair can be cool simply because of the association with high status. This distinction between the populars and the cafeteria fringe doesn't indicate that the latter are in any way inferior. They simply might not happen to be the beneficiaries of the halo effect, which creates an arbitrary, illusory, and ultimately meaningless aura of coolness.

An interesting aspect of the halo effect is that it has been proven that we don't realize when it's kicking in. So when Trey's classmates assume that he is clumsy, stupid, and one-dimensional merely because he is labeled a musclehead, they likely don't realize that their minds have taken a huge, improbable leap. They are unaware of the series of mental cop-outs they have taken to brand Trey with a label and let the resulting reputation color their views about his personality, character, and identity. And they have no idea that, by refusing to peel back that label—and refusing to mix up their cafeteria seating—they might be missing out on their next best friend.

WHITNEY, NEW YORK | THE POPULAR BITCH

Whitney decided to cast aside the preps' aversion to Dirk, the leader of the punks. She had always admired him; her challenge would be a good chance to get to know him better. In the small advertising seminar they took together, they gradually grew closer. They IMed outside of school. Eventually, rather than the awkward eye contact they used to make in the hallways, they purposely bumped one another or gave playful shoves, teasing, "Ew!" If Whitney weren't exclusive with Luke, she would have wanted to hook up with Dirk.

But as Whitney got to know the punks, chiefly through Dirk and his best friend, she was surprised to discover that they shared some of the preps' characteristics. Many of the punks were promiscuous, or spent their spare time getting high. The girls shunned Whitney when she chatted with Dirk. The guys badmouthed other students. *Maybe all cliques are the same,* Whitney thought. *They all have their own drama, their own backstabbing, their own conformities. How they treat people outside the group differs, but the insides are all the same.*

When she realized that the punks weren't the unique, free-spirited individuals she'd assumed they were, she was disappointed. "I've lost all hope in people. No matter what clique you're in, you're still in a clique and you still have to be fake and conform," she said. "I don't know if it's even worth [branching out from the preps]. Like, the punks really aren't as nice and laid-back as I thought. If I hung out with them, I would still have the same conformity problems. Because punks conform to their things too."

A few days later, Whitney learned that Dirk had told a punk girl that Whitney disliked her—which was true, but Whitney had hoped those sentiments would not become public. Then Dirk promised Whitney he would text her about a party, but never did. *I guess punks are just as unreliable as populars sometimes,* she mused, and decided to go to the movies with the populars instead.

In the midst of Whitney's social turmoil, the boys' basketball team qualified for the state tournament. Unfortunately the playoff game— Whitney's last chance to cheer during her high school career—fell on the same night as a mandatory all-county band rehearsal.

Whitney found her band teacher in the hall by the band room. "Hey, um, I need to talk to you," she said. "So I just found out that the boys play Monday night." Whitney's heart pounded; she was worried her teacher would be angry.

"Oh," the teacher said. "This is a problem."

"Yeah."

"Let me email the all-county president and see what he says. The rules say only sickness, weather, or death in the family are excuses for missing rehearsals. But I'll see if there can be any exceptions."

Later that week, Whitney asked the teacher if the president had responded. Whitney was optimistic. The president knew who she was. She had always gotten her way at school functions.

"I talked to him and it doesn't look good."

Whitney's heart sunk. "Oh . . . really?"

"Yes. I explained that you couldn't have known when the game was going to be scheduled and you can't do half-and-half since they're at the same time. And I explained that you're captain and you already chose band over cheerleading for another event. But he said he can't make an exception."

"So, I have to choose?" Whitney asked.

"Yes," said the teacher. "I really hate giving guilt trips, but as a musician, I have to say you're more easily replaced in cheerleading than you are in band, since now they have to find a new first chair. . . ." He trailed off as Whitney started to cry.

Whitney agonized over her decision: miss her last all-county concert, letting down the band that had rehearsed with her as first chair, or abandon her last cheerleading game of her career, letting down the squad. She asked Luke for advice. "I think you should go to the game, because it will be a better memory for you to look back on," he said.

Whitney agreed, but for other reasons. This year alone she'd been hospitalized twice for minor injuries sustained during cheerleading stunts; if those didn't stop her, she didn't think a scheduling conflict should. But even more, she wanted revenge on the all-county organization for its rule. "I wanted to make them scramble to find a replacement," she explained later. She chose the game.

EVERY YEAR IN HIGH school, the preps had been in charge of Class War, the culmination to Spirit Week. Class War was a grade-versus-grade battle of silly games, relay races, obstacle courses, and skits performed in front of most of the town. The preps planned activities and decorations and decided who would participate in each event. When they discussed who should represent the class for tug-of-war, Bobby cracked, "Basically it could just be Fern and we would win."

"Asshole," Whitney muttered. Since the twins had moved, Fern was the only new student left in the class. Students continued to alienate her, a fate she seemed to accept passively from her usual spot in the corner.

A few days later, the preps were in a classroom painting Class War banners along with a smattering of other students. Because they were seniors, some non-preps decided they wanted to be involved, for once. Bianca came into the room. "Ew," she said. "I heard people saying they don't do Class War because they're afraid of us."

Jessica, the Future Farmers of America student who had run against

Whitney for class treasurer, looked up from her banner. "Well, it's true. The same little group runs it every year and you guys *are* intimidating to the rest of the grade." She left to refill her paint cup.

The preps looked at each other. "What is she talking about?" one asked.

"Yeah, because we're *so* scary," Chip said, his voice dripping with sarcasm.

"We're not intimidating," said Bianca.

The teacher looked at the populars as if to say "duh." "Uh, yes you are," she said. "You guys scare the rest of your grade away from being involved in Class War, since you run the show. Not everyone gets your sarcasm, and some people get offended."

Bianca grew defensive. "I am *not* fucking scary," she said to the teacher. "People are just pussies."

As usual, the teacher didn't bat an eye at Bianca's language because Bianca was a prep, and preps could say what they pleased. "You're bossy," the teacher said.

"I just like things done in a certain way, that's all. I don't scare people," Bianca sniffed. "That's so stupid."

The rest of the preps remained quiet. *I need to make an even bigger effort than I realized to get away from that reputation*, Whitney thought. *And I only have three months to do it.* She had her work cut out for her. Even the wannabes weren't sucking up to Whitney like they used to.

Whitney had a small lunch period attended mostly by preps, band kids, and freshmen. One day, she sat at the band kids' table, where she was surprised that they acted as if it were natural for someone from another clique to join them. They chatted about Spirit Week; it was Costume Day. Whitney took pictures of Shay (the frizzy-haired band kid she used to ignore) and Shay's friend Grace in costume. When the band kids left the lunchroom, Whitney rejoined the preps. The group stopped whispering as soon as Whitney sat down. Bobby looked at her pointedly, glanced at the empty band table, looked at Whitney again, and snorted.

That afternoon, Whitney overheard the honor society advisor telling an administrator that Fern, whose family didn't have a car, had no way to get to the honor society's induction ceremony. *I should help her,* Whitney thought. *Anyone else would tell the whole world Fern doesn't have a car.*

The next day, Whitney approached Fern in Spanish class. "Hey, Fern, do you need a ride to the honor society thing tonight?" Whitney asked. Chelsea shot her a perplexed look.

Fern looked stunned, then nodded and smiled broadly.

"My mom knows where you live so she'll give me directions. Can I have your number in case I get lost?"

Fern wrote down her number and handed it to Whitney. Whitney turned to Grace, a neighbor. "Grace, you need a ride too?"

"Sure, Whitney!"

"Okay, I'll get you after Fern," said Whitney, making the quick decision to go out of her way to pick Grace up last so she wouldn't see that Fern lived in a broken-down apartment building. Whitney assumed that Fern would be more comfortable if fewer people saw her neighborhood.

On the ride to the ceremony, Whitney made small talk with Fern while Grace sang along with the radio. "Do you like Riverland?"

"I'm afraid to like it too much because I'm leaving soon."

"I know what you mean."

"I have a hard time making friends. So I don't want to put the effort in when there's only half a school year left, because it takes a lot of effort for me to make friends."

"Yeah," Whitney agreed. "I'm starting to drift away from my friends, so saying good-bye will be easier." Whitney thought to herself that she was grateful she had friends, even if they were mean.

WHITNEY WAS HANGING OUT with Luke when Steph texted her. Steph sometimes hung out with the preps, even though she often told Whitney how much she hated them. She had transferred to Riverland from a school that the preps called "mad ghetto" because of its diversity. "My mom is going away," Steph texted. "I'm having a small party and you're invited."

"I'm down," Whitney texted back. When Bobby invited her to the movies with the preps, she told him she had plans.

That evening, Steph called to give Whitney directions to her house. "Is Bianca going?" Whitney asked.

"Ugh, no. She's so annoying and cocky," Steph said. "I'm not inviting her." Giselle, the only other prep invited, was going to the movies instead.

All of the other partygoers went to Steph's old school, and most were black or Latino, drastically different demographics from Riverland. The guys wore hats with flat brims, baggy pants tucked into puffy Nike sneakers, and oversized zip-up hoodies. They rapped along with the background music. At Riverland, these attributes would classify the students as gangstas (or, as Chelsea later said to Whitney, "guido-ish").

In the past, Whitney would never have gone to a gangsta party. Now, she was open-minded, uninhibited, and engaged, or at least acting that way, later calling it a "pretty cool culture shock." She introduced herself to each new person who walked in the door.

The students were friendly, even as they chatted about dramas involving people Whitney didn't know. She listened and laughed along anyway. Close to midnight, she heard one girl say to another, "I really like Whitney." Whitney was having more fun at a gangsta party full of strangers than at most prep parties with friends. Better still, she felt at ease. She had been afraid that the gangstas would peg her as a prep as soon as she walked in the door, and ignore her for the night or ridicule her hippie fashion like the preps would. But they didn't. The gangstas appeared to accept her without prejudice.

When Bianca found out that Whitney had gone to Steph's party, she acted as if she'd been invited too. "Yeah, I didn't want to drive all the way out for that," she told Whitney.

DANIELLE, ILLINOIS | THE LONER

Danielle wanted to fulfill her challenge by starting small, but rejected my suggestion that she begin by smiling at people in the hallways rather than trudging with her head down. "It's just plain weird to smile at someone you hardly know in the hallway. Chances are, you won't be getting a smile back, and if you do, it's one of those polite, awkward smiles, and they'll be thinking, 'Why is she smiling at me?'" she reasoned. Instead, she decided to start by saying a few extra sentences to people in class, even if only about that day's homework.

On the last snow team trip of the season, Danielle sat alone in the front of the bus, silently berating herself for forgetting her iPod. Danielle was surprised to hear Shelby, the snow team president, calling her name from the back of the bus.

"Danielle! Come back here and be social!" Shelby shouted.

Danielle hesitated. She couldn't think of anything to talk about with Shelby and her friends. And the only empty seat happened to be diagonally across from Margaret, a girl who annoyed Danielle. But Danielle was trying to turn over a new leaf. "Okay," she said.

Shelby and her friends made no further effort to include Danielle. She wasn't sure why Shelby had summoned her in the first place. When Shelby switched seats to talk to other students, Danielle returned to the front of the bus and spent the rest of the ride looking out the window. She had come alone on every snow team trip this season. At least, undistracted by socializing, she had improved her boarding skills. At one of the snow team resorts, she could now negotiate the black diamonds. At the other, she was able to tackle some of the hills that she couldn't even go down on skis, and she had been skiing for years. She couldn't do tricks yet, but the teacher in charge of the snow team said she was good enough that she could attempt tricks next year.

On the lift, Danielle recognized a couple of juniors from the bus, Stone Mill potheads who were fantastic boarders. One of them turned to her. "So how long have you been boarding?" Caleb asked. Danielle answered him.

"Where do you live?" he prodded.

"I go to Stone Mill," Danielle said. Clearly, they didn't recognize her.

"Wait, were you on the bus?"

Danielle smiled sheepishly. "Yeahhh."

"Oh, I didn't even notice!" Caleb said.

Danielle flew down the hills. She loved snowboarding; she loved the crisp pivot of the board on sharp turns, the risk that she could crash if she hit the smallest bump. Danielle wasn't nearly as skilled as the boys, but she managed to keep up with them. Her confidence soared.

They got on the same lift again and talked during the three-minute ride up the hill. Danielle noticed Margaret on the lift in front of them. When Margaret was getting off the lift, she fell, rolling down the small mound of snow in front of her chair.

Both boys laughed. Danielle had some misgivings, but said, quietly enough that Margaret couldn't hear, "When I took lessons, she wasted the entire lesson just falling," she said. "She screwed me over because I never learned how to turn."

The guys laughed. "What a loser," Caleb said.

Danielle went down the hill first, and the guys caught up to her. They shared a chair on the lift going back up the blues. When the lift stopped suddenly, Caleb's friend said, "God, I bet that fat girl fell again!"

"We should send her up to the top of the black diamond and she'll just roll!" Caleb said.

Danielle didn't respond this time; she felt uncomfortable referring to Margaret as fat and she didn't want to make fun of her.

After another ride down and back, Danielle decided not to get on the lift again with the guys. She didn't want them to think she was stalking them. They looked disappointed. *I guess they kind of liked boarding with me*, Danielle thought. *I must not have been that bad at conversation.*

Danielle went alone to the black diamonds.

BLUE, HAWAII | THE GAMER

Blue began spending more time with the AP Gov students as they prepared for Simulated Congressional Hearings. To Blue's surprise, they welcomed him. Rather than disdain his unusual theories, they praised his unique perspective and integrated his ideas into their work.

One afternoon in AP Gov, Blue called out, "So who wants to go to the beach with me?" He wasn't expecting an answer, but he was tired of going alone.

"Really? 'Cause I'll totally go," Leilani replied.

"Seriously?" Blue asked.

"Yeah. I'm down if you are."

"Bro, that does sound really good," Angelique said.

"Jess, you should come too!" Leilani said.

"Okay!"

"Are you guys all serious?" Blue said.

"I wanna go!" said Kaia.

"Wow, uh, all right."

After school, Blue drove them to their houses to pick up swimsuits and towels, then to a small stretch of golden sand lined with large black rocks, in a cove tucked into the mountainside. The girls gushed over the beach, which they had to themselves. They could jump off the rocks into turquoise waters, watch turtles grazing nearby, and follow vibrant fish at a reef just offshore. The edge of the rocks formed a blowhole that sprayed when a wave passed through, bathing the group with a cool mist that felt blissfully refreshing in the hot sun.

A while later, Blue led the girls up a winding path to a nearby park where they could shower, then through a maze of questionable alleys in town to his second-favorite spot to watch the sun set. He guided them through a residential area to the top of a little-known mountain pass. The girls were astounded by the view. They mostly watched the sunset in silence, taking in the moment.

On the drive home, Leilani said to Blue, "You have all this edgy new music and take me places I've never been. I love how we just went on a full-on adventure out of nowhere."

"Yeah!" Jess agreed. "I've never done anything like that before."

"Well, I go out pretty much every day. You're welcome to come," Blue replied.

"Oh my God, are you serious?" Leilani asked.

"I don't see why not. I just never thought anyone would want to go with me."

"That's so sad!" Jess said.

"Aw, but we're your friends!" said Kaia.

Blue was momentarily speechless.

"Fine, then I guess we aren't," Kaia added.

"No, it's not that," Blue said. "I'll show you guys something cool tomorrow too."

Blue was overcome with warmth, as when Ty had called him his best friend, except this time was somehow different. *This feels natural,* he thought.

Over the next few weeks, more AP Gov classmates joined Blue on his adventures. Blue liked them all. He appreciated that they had intelligent discussions; all eight of them were class valedictorians (Kaloke granted valedictorian status to all students with a 4.0 GPA and a senior project). He had known Angelique for years. He was drawn to Jess, whose innocent image masked a vulgar wit, and Leilani, a laid-back surfer who happened to have one of the highest GPAs in the class. He was especially partial to Michael. Smart, ambitious, and disciplined, Michael was also a good listener. Blue grew comfortable talking to Michael about nearly anything. Once, they had a three-hour phone conversation while Blue was longboarding. As they quickly became close friends, Blue developed a crush on him, even though he had heard Michael mention his ex-girlfriend. Blue knew crushes on straight guys were futile, but he was glad for Michael's company nonetheless.

As Blue helped the team prepare for the SCH state championships, his enthusiasm for the project grew. He thrived in the "constant intellectual environment that never seems to stop," he said. "I can't get enough of it. I feel good about myself when I'm in it, like it isn't a waste of time. And people praise me for my work."

For the SCH competition, teams split into six units that appeared before judges who grilled them about topics relating to the Constitution. While other schools had thirty to forty team members, Kaloke had only nine, the entire AP Gov class. In other words, Blue's team had to do nearly triple the work of the other teams' students, and each team member had to master two units. Blue's favorite was Unit Six, which dealt with challenges the U.S. would face in the future. Enthralled by the topic, Blue wrote almost all of his group's potential responses.

Blue's teammates were under no illusion that they would win. Waipouli, a school with four times as many team members and heavy parent involvement in SCH preparations, had won states and traveled to the national competition in Washington, D.C., for twenty-five consecutive years.

When the judges called Unit Six, Blue stepped up to the judge's table with Michael and Kaia. As the judges asked questions, Blue took over, spinning his answers into broader-reaching observations. He was able to turn the format into a dialogue with the judges, rather than a one-sided interview. He told them that the Internet was tearing communities apart, that people were "outsourcing their relationships, becoming unengaged citizens," that misplaced priorities and increasingly insular, self-serving associations were turning the United States into a "monster."

After the presentation, the judges spoke directly to Blue. "I've never heard such insightful thinking from someone at your grade level," one of them said.

"Your answers were original and beyond graduate-level analysis," said another.

"I think we all know who's the wordsmith here," said a third judge.

Ms. Collins pulled Blue aside and hugged him. "I'm so proud of you. That's exactly what this competition is about," she said, her eyes tearing. "I just want to let you know that you're making this all worth it."

Blue's team surrounded them. "When you were talking, I seriously had goosebumps," Jess told him.

"Everything you said was exactly what I've always felt deep down, but was too afraid to say," Leilani said.

All of the schools convened at tables in the auditorium for the announcement of the winners. While most teams filled several tables, Blue liked that his team was so tiny that everyone fit at one table, "like a close-knit little family." As the announcer listed the winners of the individual unit competitions, Kaloke slumped in disappointment. The awards were dispersed equally among Waipouli and two other schools.

Kaloke barely paid attention when the announcer prepared to reveal the overall winner. "There's no way we got anything," Kaia said.

"This was a big waste of time," Michael added.

Blue said nothing. *I gave up probably winning a Modern Warfare tournament—and my friends—for this,* he thought.

"Second place goes to Waipouli!" the announcer shouted. Gasps reverberated through the room. Waipouli's streak was over. The Waipouli students looked confused as they accepted their plaques, as if someone had played a joke on them. The other two dominant schools shuffled excitedly in their seats. "The first-place winner of this year's competition is . . ."—the announcer paused.—"Kaloke!"

As his teammates shrieked and hugged, Blue could not stop laughing at the ridiculousness of the moment and the jolt of unexpected happiness it brought him. The announcer continued. "This small but *mighty* team has demonstrated to us today an incredible knack for unconventional understanding of the world around us. Let's give them a round of applause."

From the stage, Blue could see Waipouli students crying with disappointment. *I've finally found something worth working for,* he thought as he hugged his delirious teammates. *I finally have a place to belong.* Blue and his new friends were headed to nationals.

NOAH, PENNSYLVANIA | THE BAND GEEK

Noah was walking past the locker room showers on his way to the pool when Frederick called out, "Hey, wait up." Noah turned.

"Listen," Frederick said, "if I've ever said anything about your hair that seriously offended you, I'm sorry."

Noah looked at him quizzically but saw that Frederick was serious. "Thanks, Frederick. I appreciate it." Noah never learned what brought on the apology.

Districts passed by in a blink. Noah swam personal bests in his races, but wasn't fast enough to qualify for states. He got over it. There were too many other activities for him to focus his energy on, like the Chess Club and Ultimate Frisbee team. Socially, he wished he could hang out with more people outside of school; he could talk to students beyond his friend group, but didn't feel comfortable suggesting after-school plans. Academically, Noah's counselor had informed him, to his dismay, that his class rank had fallen to number five.

Noah and Leigh waited in a physics classroom at the appointed time for their first recycling meeting. They had plastered signs around school advertising that Redsen's recycling club would meet three times a week. A few minutes after the final bell, six students entered the room: Adam, a popular guy in Noah's English class, with a jock friend; a senior pothead; and a few artsy girls who knew Leigh.

After a short question-and-answer session, Noah and Leigh explained the program's logistics. Students were to encourage classmates and teachers to recycle, using bins in forty classrooms. Once a week, they would collect the bins and drive the paper to a Dumpster at Noah's church. The volunteers would receive community service credit, and the revenue the students earned from the recycling center would go into a scholarship pool divided into thirds. The volunteer with the most hours (excluding Noah and Leigh) would automatically get one-third of the scholarship money. The names of the other volunteers would be entered in a raffle for each of the remaining two-thirds. "At the very least," Noah said, "you can help by spreading the word." The group seemed enthusiastic.

Over the next few weeks, the artsy girls disappeared because of scheduling conflicts, but the boys became recycling regulars, along with Noah, Jiang, and Leigh. Collecting the bins, which used to take an hour, now took fifteen minutes.

In English one day, when another popular boy threw a piece of paper into the trash can, Adam said, "Hey, man, you gotta recycle that!" Adam removed the paper from the can and put it into the recycling bin. "Come on, guys, you should help me and Noah with the recycling thing after school. It's good!" Noah's spirits lifted when he realized that a popular kid whom he had "had notions about" was so willing to help. Noah pledged to himself to fulfill his challenge. He was determined to finish the year on a high note.

REGAN, GEORGIA | THE WEIRD GIRL

After one of the community theater's last performances, Regan waited at the exit with her castmates for the audience meet-and-greet. Her castmates complimented her, as they usually did, on her emotional scene in the middle of the show. The woman who played Regan's mother usually ended the scene in real tears because, she told Regan backstage, Regan's commitment to the role made her believe she loved Regan like a real daughter.

As the audience filed out the door, an elderly man stopped in front of Regan, took her hand, and held it still as he looked into her eyes. "You have a lot of intensity," he said kindly. "You're going somewhere."

Regan thanked him and thought about his compliment for days. Since high school graduation, her love of the theater had brought all good things. In college, her drama group had voted her club president. "Art is funny. You do it, and you try your hardest at it, of course, but sometimes it affects people in ways you wouldn't expect," she said later. "To have a stranger come up to you and let you know that you inspired him in some way is an amazing thing, and probably the reason why I continue to do theater."

REGAN WAS CHECKING EMAIL at school when she saw the message. An assistant principal wanted to meet with her immediately.

"What did I do this time?" Regan wondered aloud. Every week there seemed to be another issue of contention. Just last week, Francesca had tattled to an administrator that Regan didn't turn in an analysis she hadn't realized she was supposed to do. This week, at a faculty meeting, as soon as Mandy saw Regan sit down, she nudged Francesca and both of them mean-mugged Regan.

Regan's troubles with her colleagues were not going to help with her challenge. She had met with an administrator and emailed a guidance counselor, the only faculty member she could think of who might be willing to help start a GSA, but the woman said her schedule was full. Regan wondered if trying to form the club would further marginalize her. "There's this theory that people have about 'the gay agenda,' the bullshit idea that gay people want to push their ideas on other people (as if you can convert to gayism)," she said. "As the only truly *out* faculty member, I know that people are going to look at me like, 'Figures.'"

Regan found the assistant principal in her office. "Rumor has it that you are selling CDs?" The administrator's inflection lifted, making her accusation sound more like a question, but Regan knew better.

"Yeah," Regan said. She wasn't about to lie. Crystal's band had released its first CD, so Regan was selling it at school. She wasn't profiting, only trying to spread the word about the band. Besides, her students had asked her to update them, and because the music wasn't yet in stores or on iTunes, the only way they could get a copy was through Regan.

"You know that's illegal?"

"Seriously?" Regan asked. "No, I didn't know that. Say no more. I got you. Done and done."

"No, not quite," the assistant principal said. "[The principal] would also like to meet with you. Are you available at three?"

"Three? Yeah, I can do three," Regan said.

"Great. We'll see you then."

"Okay! Not a problem."

After school, Regan sat fidgeting in the main office. "I've never been to the principal's office before," she texted her mother. "It's nerve-racking." Finally the secretary called Regan in. Regan sat down across from the principal and assistant principal.

"It is entirely wrong to expose students to work that is deemed inappropriate," the assistant principal said, "and from what I understand, the CD had both profanity and cover art that featured the artists scantily clad. Not to mention the message was inappropriate."

This bothered Regan. If the administrators had actually listened to the album, they would understand that the songs had strong values and preached morals that were the opposite of hip-hop culture stereotypes. The cover art featured the band wearing underwear that concealed more than a bathing suit would. Regan explained later, "The message of the album is a good one: It deals with nonconformity. It begs teenagers to look deep within themselves to find out who they really are instead of following trends. The cover art was in reference to Eden. Culture tells us to be ashamed of who we are naturally, and the group says that we shouldn't be. So I'm being persecuted for individuality and liberalism."

Regan replied to the administrators, "Why is it okay to expose students to inappropriate language in text? I mean, teachers teach books here with language that's worse than on the CD," she said, thinking of *The Catcher in the Rye* and *The Adventures of Huckleberry Finn*. "Is it just because they have been approved as having literary merit? How can we determine that this album doesn't have merit?"

The administrators eyed each other and gave a stumbling explanation that because the books had been "proven" to be appropriate for students, they were acceptable.

Who makes that choice? Regan thought. "Okay," she said. "Another thing. There's a piece of student artwork in the English hallway that features magazine pictures of people in their underwear. Why is that allowed?"

"I'd have to see it," said the principal. "I'm sure it is permissible."

"I have a picture," Regan said, grabbing her camera out of her bag. She had come to this meeting prepared. She showed the administrators the photo. They said the art should be taken down.

"I'm not trying to get anyone else in trouble," Regan said. "I just want to understand why I'm being singled out for 'inappropriate' activity. Not to mention, I was told this morning that I had broken a law, and I don't believe that I did." She took out a copy of the school's Code of Ethics. "It says here that if soliciting results in 'personal financial benefit,' then it's against the rules. But I made nothing out of this. I was simply doing my friends a favor."

The administrators told Regan that she couldn't do such favors if they exposed "inappropriate" material. "You're young," the principal said. "I just wanted to make you aware of the issue because I know that young people make these mistakes."

"It won't happen again," Regan said, resigned. "I'm sorry. Thank you for explaining it to me."

"Do you have any other questions?" the principal asked.

Regan shook her head and started to gather her belongings.

"Oh, there is one more thing," the assistant principal said. "You know that administrators receive the backlash of whatever students go home and tell their parents. I'd really rather avoid those phone calls." Confused, Regan raised an eyebrow. The administrator continued,

"Whatever you do in your personal life is fine, but leave it out of school."

Later, when Regan told her mother what happened, her mother protested, "They told you not to tell anyone that you're gay? You're out to people and all of a sudden, you're getting in all sorts of unnecessary trouble, and you think that's a coincidence?!"

Word spread quickly around school that Regan had been reprimanded again. Her students rallied around her. One student offered to tell the administration that the CD sales were his fault (Regan declined). Another wanted to organize a protest. Another asked, "How come everyone is trying to bring you down in school?" to which a classmate responded, "Because she's the coolest teacher, and everyone else is jealous."

"You're one of the only teachers in this school who legitimately cares about kids," said a sophomore.

The class nodded. A junior said, "It's a teacher's job to try to help kids any way they can. You're the only teacher I have who does that. How come other teachers aren't getting in trouble? Why are you getting in trouble for making class interesting?"

"Yeah, what do they have against you?" another student asked.

Regan didn't know.

Eli, Virginia | The Nerd

The Academic Bowl coach began to ask a question: "Indo—"

BUZZ. "Jakarta," Eli said.

"Right!"

"I didn't even know what he said!" a teammate complained.

The coach continued. "The Parisian mus—"

BUZZ. "The Louvre," Eli said.

"How could you get that?!" another teammate whined. "He only said two words!"

Eli grinned. Sometimes it was fun to be a nerd.

After school the next day, Eli approached his locker to retrieve his books. Three students Eli identified as "ghetto people," wearing baggy pants and chains, were standing at a nearby locker, blocking Eli's way.

"Excuse me," Eli said to the student directly in front of his locker. The student did nothing.

"Excuse me," Eli repeated.

"Dude," said another boy. "Move out of his way."

"Oh, sorry," the first kid said. He stepped forward only slightly, his backpack still obstructing Eli's access.

Eli had to stand to the side of his locker, and could open it only partially. As he tried to maneuver his books out of the narrow crack, he heard the third student say to the first, "Why are you standing so close to me?"

"That kid's at his locker."

The third student lowered his voice. "Who cares? Look at him, he's a nerd."

"I know, but . . ." Eli missed the end of the conversation as the group walked away.

Eli sighed. *Okay, you're ghetto, I'll leave you alone; I'm a nerd, leave me alone,* he thought. *Why can't we just stay in our own separate spheres?*

At the next Academic Bowl practice, Eli managed to run the entire National Parks category (prompting a teammate to say, "Do you just spend all your time staring at maps or something?"). But he wasn't as quick as usual, and neither was the rest of the team. When they missed a few easy questions, the coach jumped out of his chair and shouted, "What is wrong with you guys?! You laugh now, but just wait 'til we get our asses kicked by Arrington." Arrington had won several championships. "They practice five days a week, and after I said some things to their coach after the first round"—which Eli's team had won—"do you think they're going to let us get off easy? You guys have got to get faster on the buzzers and stop missing easy questions. I'm not losing to Arrington. They're from the freakin' ghetto."

As the rest of the students tried to stifle their laughter, Eli listened somberly to his coach's warning about the upcoming final round.

The following night, Eli's mother asked him, "Why don't you get some friends together and go see a movie or something this weekend?" At his look, she added, "I just thought you'd want to get out and do something on the weekend."

"Okay, I'll think about it."

"Well, you say that all the time. I talked to Dad and he also says you never go out on the weekends."

"Okay, just please leave me alone then."

That night, he emailed a friend, "I'm both excited and nervous for college, but does that necessarily mean big changes? There is just so much I want to do—skydive, travel the world, run a marathon—but is [this] the beginning of these dreams or just the beginning of a lifelong realization that maybe everything isn't as I expect it to be? Will moving to the other side of the country really open me up to people? What will I do if I don't make friends? The more I think about it, the more doubt, uncertainty, and more than anything else, loneliness, plagues me. As depressing as that sounds, I'm still gonna go into all this with an optimistic outlook. There is still a teeny-tiny part of my soul holding on and thinking the best is yet to come. But right now, with a zero social life, depressing family situation, mounds of schoolwork, and questioning who I am, I'm just doing all that I can to keep pushing on."

WHY STUDENTS EXCLUDE

Experts attribute exclusion to a fundamental concept. As Duke University psychology professor John Coie has said, "The dynamics of group life require that someone be rejected." You can't have positive space without negative space to define its outlines. You can't crown a winner without others to defeat. This idea isn't new. Emile Durkheim, a prominent sociologist at the turn of the twentieth century, theorized that society needs "deviants" in order to define the boundaries of normality. Social psychologists tell us that deviant group members are those who stray from prevailing group norms. A group might assume that alienating these nonconformists will lead to a more cohesive group, a more consistent group image, and group decision-making that's tidy and conflict-free.

The deviants, however, are powerful. The role of the deviant can be such a catalyst that it can cause a group to reverse its in-group bias. In 1988, researchers discovered an anomaly they dubbed the "black sheep effect." First, they found that students evaluated likeable fellow group members more positively than likeable outsiders, as expected. But then they unearthed something strange. Those same students evaluated unlikeable outsiders more positively than similar, unlikeable insiders.

How can the black sheep effect so clearly flip the concept of in-group bias? Group members, consciously or not, may want to manipulate group dynamics in the group's collective best interest. According to one theory, a deviant member is more of a threat to the group than a deviant outsider because he goes against group norms, which are in place to distinguish that group from other groups. If a group member rebels against group norms, then he challenges the group's belief that it is better than other groups. A deviant outsider, however, not only poses no threat to the group, but also validates group norms because the group adheres to them and the outsider does not. The preps nearly drove Whitney out of their group for wearing her own distinctive hippie-chic style. Yet when a non-prep wore a similar fashion later in the year, the preps complimented her.

So who are these deviants? They may be people with unusual interests and opinions, like Eli or Blue, students who do not fear being alone, like Danielle, or guys who are unafraid to express their emotions, like Noah. Some groups choose to exclude a classmate for no significant reason at all. I heard from dozens of students whose cliques or "best friends" turned on them for no apparent cause. There may be a psychological explanation for this sudden 180: Attacking a third party makes people believe they have something in common. Australian psychologist Laurence Owens observed, "Bitching, gossiping, or storytelling serves to bind the friendship together and create intimacy for those who are *in* as against those who are *out*." This method of exclusion is particularly common in schools. As a drama kid in Georgia put it, "Gossip is like word vomit here."

The good news is that if people are left out because a group needs a scapegoat, they are not doomed to a life of social rejection; they should, according to Coie, "experience some relief when they join new groups in which they are not cast in this same deviant role." As with the black sheep, these scapegoats illustrate another case in which a student might be excluded not because his or her behavior is offensive per se, but because of its potential effect on the group as a whole. Is that, then, what exclusion is all about—not necessarily cruelty for the sake of cruelty, but a valid way for kids to coordinate and organize their social environment? That's what Stacey Horn, a University of Illinois psychology professor, wanted to know. Horn conducted a series of studies about exclusion to investigate how adolescents view group status and social identity issues.

In one study, Horn surveyed freshmen and juniors at a large Midwestern high school where the low-status groups included Goths, druggies, and dirties (a label, used there, for smart kids who wore grunge and sometimes participated in delinquent behavior). Horn presented the students with hypothetical scenarios about Goths, druggies, and dirties excluded from various activities because of their label. In one scenario, preppies didn't want a classmate on the student council specifically because he was a dirtie. Horn asked if it was all right or not all right for the preppies to want to exclude the dirtie from the student council. Students in both grades said the exclusion was acceptable.

Horn's work led her to conclude that students regard exclusion and teasing as "a legitimate way of regulating behavior that they viewed as deviant or weird." Teenagers try to enforce the categorizations they use to make sense of the world around them. If kids see themselves as the Normal Police, then exclusion is one of their most powerful weapons.

During the second stage of Horn's study, she provided a new detail about the low-status student to make the situation less ambiguous; for example, the dirtie was involved with high school activities. This descriptive variable led students to say they believed the exclusion was more wrong than before they knew anything about the boy besides his label. Ninth graders were more likely than eleventh graders to use stereotypes, rather than moral reasoning, to justify the exclusion. But a number of students still thought that it was fair to exclude someone just because of his label. Horn concluded that stereotyped group labels "function as social categories by which adolescents can judge their peers without having actual information about them." Thus many students are excluded only because classmates don't get to know them. It's easier on the brain to lump outsiders into a general category.

In a follow-up experiment, Horn wanted to see how far teenagers would go to rely on stereotypes over morality when making judgments about someone. She and her colleagues asked high school freshmen to judge whether it was all right to punish a particular group of students for wrongdoing even when there was no evidence that they were to blame. The result? A significant number of the freshmen said that it was okay to punish the group—if the group's stereotypes fit the crime. They agreed that it was more acceptable to penalize football players for damaging property at a school dance than to punish them for hacking into the school computer system, even if there was no proof they committed either transgression. In scenarios consistent with group stereotypes, the freshmen were more likely to judge based on those stereotypes than on issues of fairness or rights.

Does it matter if a dirtie isn't on the student council? Or if a Goth doesn't make the cheerleading squad? Some kids, and even adults, may view this type of exclusion as relatively harmless because it seems reflective of a school's natural order. At many schools, like Whitney's, class officers are usually preps.

But what if the peer group categories were more incendiary? What if a student was excluded from the student council not because she was a dirtie but because she was a girl? What if students were punished, without evidence, for destroying school property because they were black? Horn's mentor, University of Maryland professor Melanie Killen, interviewed diverse nine-, twelve-, and fifteen-year-olds about hypothetical situations in which a child was excluded from friendship, school, or a music club based on gender or race. Almost all of the students said that excluding a child from school because of race or gender was wrong. Their opinions changed, however, when it came to friendship and club membership. In those cases, the students said, exclusion was more acceptable because they should be able to choose their own friends. They rationalized that the club would function better if the club members were more alike.

Similarly Killen told first, fourth, and seventh graders that they hypothetically had to choose either a black or white student for a basketball team or a math club. The seventh graders were more likely than the younger students to use stereotypes when making their decision, choosing the black student for the basketball team and the white student for the math club. The seventh graders also tended to justify their choice by explaining that their selection would make the group work better.

In situations in which little personal information is available, teens often rely on stereotypes when drawing conclusions about a person. Even if, as they age, adolescents become more aware of discrimination issues, their stereotypic expectations also tend to increase. This confusing combination of changes can make it even more challenging for them to evaluate people—and can cause them to de-prioritize fairness and morality when they decide to exclude. Exclusion is common behavior. But that doesn't make it unchangeable. And that doesn't mean that anything is wrong with the cafeteria fringe.

Spring

Quirk Theory's Origins: Why These Issues Are Hardest in School

Chapter 10

CHANGING PERCEPTIONS

Danielle, Illinois | The Loner

Danielle remained unenthusiastic about her challenge. The girl who had no trouble careening down black diamonds and who had just plunged into below-freezing water with her mother for a charity event, was scared, especially to talk to the students she referred to as "supernerds." (She later remarked, "People freak me out more than potentially life-threatening activities.")

Danielle liked what she called "my little bubble where I don't have to talk to anyone or feel compelled to do anything that someone else wants me to do." Her creative writing teacher had described "building a fortress around your heart and shooting down anyone who tries to climb it." Danielle identified strongly with that metaphor. "I don't really trust anyone, so the idea of trying to be friends with them is really unappealing," she explained. "I don't like feeling responsible for relationships, which is probably why all of mine suck. And I'm kind of worried that no one else will really get me like my friends now do. They all make fun of me for doing things like spontaneously laughing in class because I remembered something funny from earlier, or just being completely random, but they at least accept it and think it's funny, while other people might think it's really weird. Also the idea of having to talk is not something I'm happy about."

Nevertheless, she had accepted the challenge, which she termed "Operation Outcast," because, she said, "I'm not happy being so secluded, either. I don't want to be someone with a million friends, but I don't want to be so uncomfortable talking to people. I hope to be able to not be so completely socially awkward. It's embarrassing that I can't even keep the most basic of conversations going, and that will inevitably hurt me later on. I don't want to be like people my age, because I like being different, but I should be able to talk to them. Making friends is a skill that I'll most likely need, and I can't relate to people older than me forever. (They're going to die eventually.)"

Furthermore, National Honor Society elections were coming up, and Danielle hoped to run for Webmaster. Having honed her HTML skills on MySpace since eighth grade, she assumed that she would be good at updating the Web site. In order to run for the position, however, she would have to do some minor campaigning. Which meant she would have to talk to people.

Danielle wasn't sure how to chat in class, when teachers' lectures took up entire periods. She didn't talk to students between classes because the atmosphere was so chaotic that she feared saying something unimportant would seem pathetic. As she put it, "I hate saying things that are stupid and don't need to be said, so I usually won't say anything if I don't have to."

But she tried. Over the next week, Danielle managed to ask a supernerd a question about a homework assignment. In government, she discussed a test with a classmate. In math, she talked to Camille's preppy friend Trish, who sat in front of her. At a reading committee meeting, she asked another outcast why, after the one meeting Danielle had missed, *Blindness* had suddenly disappeared from the list.

In creative writing, she sat next to a student she knew from the school literary magazine, for which she had devoted time to evaluating student submissions. The guy was both weird and well-liked; he was an excellent writer, painter, and gymnast. They talked about food and pop.

In late March, Danielle decided to get a job to earn money for college and for the long list of books she wanted to buy. Her first stop was Dairy Queen. As a teenager, Danielle's mother had worked at McDonald's for several years, which had helped her to get over her own fear of people. Danielle hoped that a fast-food job would help her too. Plus, she was a big fan of ice cream, and her mother would be tickled if she regularly brought home Cherry Mr. Misty floats.

A Stone Mill supernerd—the girl who would probably end up being class valedictorian—stood behind the counter. Danielle asked for an application. Normally she would have left immediately, but instead she attempted small talk. "When you work here, do you ever want to eat the food?" she asked.

The girl smiled. "Yeah, sometimes! Not usually, though."

Danielle left, pleased with the nonessential exchange.

As Danielle grew bolder (on the Danielle scale) with potential friends she hardly knew, her current friends gave her a hard time. On St. Patrick's Day, Danielle wore a green T-shirt; she loved the out-of-the-ordinary giddiness that holidays inspired. All day, Nikki and Paige rolled their eyes at her, muttering, "I can't believe you wore green." Even so, Danielle gave up her free period to go to lunch with the group. At Camille's house, Nikki said to Camille, "Did Mona tell you about Saturday night!?" They whispered to each other. Danielle could tell that Paige knew what they were discussing.

On the walk back to school, Danielle stopped to wait for Nikki and Camille. "Go away, Danielle," Nikki said. "Me and Camille are talking."

As far back as Danielle could remember, even in elementary school, the group had never explicitly excluded anyone else but Danielle. Danielle remained friends with the girls because, she said, "I don't really have anyone else to be friends with. Also, whenever they aren't being bitches, they're really fun to hang out with, so I guess I overlook the mean stuff. And with them, you can't just quietly stop being friends. Because if you start to pull away, they find a reason to turn against you and it completely blows up in your face."

She didn't know why the group made fun of her, rather than, say, Mona. Maybe, she thought, they did it because they knew that she wouldn't retaliate. "After all, if they don't tell me something, what am I supposed to do? They don't have to tell me if they don't want to," she explained. "I just want to find new friends that I can hang out with, at least until the end of high school, who don't know Paige, Mona, Nikki, or Camille."

That night, Danielle received a Facebook message from Camille's friend Trish: "Want to go to lunch tomorrow?" Danielle was surprised. Trish was outgoing, friendly, and obsessed with Facebook and TV, none of which applied to Danielle. *What would we have to talk about?* she thought. *This could be really awkward.* Because she didn't want to be rude by making up "a creepy excuse," she hesitantly agreed. This would be the first time Danielle went out with someone she didn't know well without the company of her usual friends.

The next day, Danielle drove Trish to McDonald's. At first, it was strange to be alone with Trish; they had barely spoken without Camille. But she was happy to be hanging out with someone new. Also, knowing that it would piss off her friends that she went to lunch with Trish instead of with them gave her a different sort of satisfaction.

During the ride, Danielle filled the silence by venting about their math teacher and vocalizing her road rage ("Come on! You can't move up a couple of feet?!"). Trish brought up a girl they both knew from math class.

They sat outside at a picnic table, eating ice-cream sundaes near the parking lot. Trish noticed someone in the car next to theirs. "That old man is watching us eat!"

Danielle craned her neck. "I think that's an old lady," she said.

"That's so sad! She's just sitting there alone."

"Maybe she's waiting for someone," Danielle said.

"What if some old man stood her up?!" The girls concocted stories until it was time to leave.

After school, Danielle had her Dairy Queen job interview. She made sure not to say "uh" and attempted to make peppy small talk. Later, she couldn't stop mentally replaying a particular question for which she hadn't been prepared. She wasn't sure if she had heard the manager correctly over the noise of the fan, but she had thought the question was something like, "If a customer complains about her Peanut Buster Parfait, what do you do?"

"Well," Danielle said, stalling. "I would probably first talk to my manager, but if that wasn't an option, I guess I would . . . make them a new one?" The interviewers looked at her with expressions that told Danielle that the question she had heard was not the one they had asked.

When she got home, she looked up blogs about fast-food interviews that recommended techniques for interviewees—which Danielle hadn't used. Fifteen kids had applied for five slots, and she was convinced she wouldn't get the job.

As Danielle complained to her mother about the interview, the phone rang.

"Hi Danielle, this is [the manager] from Dairy Queen."

"Oh, hi."

"We were wondering if you would like to work for us."

"Oh, wow. Yes, I would. Definitely."

"Would you be able to come in this Saturday at three thirty for a training session?"

"Um, Saturday . . . Yeah, I think I'm free then."

"Okay, Danielle, we'll see you then."

"Okay. Thank you so much!"

Danielle hung up the phone and grinned. She couldn't believe it. Maybe she wasn't so bad at interviews after all.

In Danielle's creative writing class, each student was assigned a day to bring in snacks. On her day, Danielle came in late. When she walked into the room with a box of cookies, the teacher looked up and said something, but Danielle was too embarrassed about arriving late to pay attention to him.

That period, Danielle made an effort to be more social. She talked to Max, a sophomore whom classmates saw as loud and somewhat obnoxious. Danielle thought he was funny and smart; he read books on Taoism and got As on Spanish tests without studying. She sat by him for a while as they waited for the computers to boot up. He seemed receptive.

At the bell, two preppy sophomores, Bree and Kristy, walked out of the room in front of her, glancing at her and laughing. They were also in Danielle's Spanish class, but she hadn't talked to them before. Danielle couldn't make out what they said through their laughter.

Bree turned around. "You know what we're talking about, right?"

"I think so," Danielle answered. She did not.

"When you walked in, we didn't know that you had cookies," Kristy said. "So when [the teacher] said, 'Mmm! More deliciousness!' we thought he was talking about you." The three of them laughed.

When Danielle walked into Spanish the next day, Bree and Kristy cracked up. "More deliciousness!" they exclaimed in unison. Danielle thought she might as well talk to the sophomores if it made the class go by that much quicker. But over the next several days, she still couldn't break through her shyness to initiate conversation.

BLUE, HAWAII | THE GAMER

Despite their shared class, Blue's teammates previously hadn't hung out together as a group. Now that Blue regularly took them on adventures around town, however, they were gradually leaving their old social circles to form a new one.

The first time the group convened at Blue's house, the students were amazed.

"This room is so nice!"

"Look how organized!"

"Look at the cable management!"

"Oh my God, look at his computer," Michael said. He fingered the customized headphones that Blue had designed and surveyed the others, which hung neatly in frames on the wall, each pair illuminated by picture lights. "Wow, your headphones are like artwork."

The girls peeked into Blue's walk-in closet and gasped in admiration at clothes and shoes meticulously organized by color and style. When they saw his mechanical models, they called his craftsmanship "impeccable." They were riveted when Angelique made him demonstrate a speedrun of Portal.

The smart kids' reaction to Blue's room was the polar opposite of that of his old friends. Jackson, Stewart, Ty, and the rest of them incessantly made fun of Blue's cable management, high-end electronics, and room decor. Blue was astonished that these new friends actually liked him *because* of his differences. When they weren't preparing for SCH, they accompanied Blue to beaches or to the playground to stargaze. With this new group, Blue was happier than he had imagined he could be. As his spirits rose, so did his motivation. He didn't want these students to think he was the equivalent of his low GPA. He tried to follow their lead. When Michael suggested that Blue ask his French teacher for help, he did so, because if a valedictorian could ask for help, then it was okay.

One night, Michael came over to Blue's house to work on Unit Six. Blue suggested they take a walk. They strolled to a nearby playground, where they ran into some of Blue's skater friends. Blue felt cool in front of Michael as the skaters asked him to teach them his newest tricks on the board.

As they walked to the playground, talking about skating and cars, Blue gently bumped into Michael, his hands in his pockets, to test whether Michael would flinch. He didn't. They lay on a bench, hands behind their heads, and stargazed. Blue tried not to shiver in the brisk night air as they talked about family and friends. Ty had been frustrating Blue lately, he told Michael, because he was "an inconsistent friend" whom Jackson easily influenced, and because he had started to drink and smoke pot.

Michael listened, then asked, "So how long have you and Ty been going out?"

Blue turned to him in surprise. "What?! No, no, Ty is just a friend! We just hang out a lot."

"Oh," Michael said. "So . . . are you seeing anyone right now?"

"Nope. I really wish I was," Blue said. "It sucks to be me."

"Why?"

"Because in heterosexual relationships you have tons of examples. Rules, even. So you know what to do. But in homosexual relationships, there are no rules. It's confusing. That and you can never really tell who is and who isn't, you know?"

"Yeah, that makes sense."

They were silent for several minutes. Then Michael asked, "Would you be able to tell if I was gay or not?"

This was interesting. "No, I don't think so," Blue replied.

"Well, that's funny, because . . . I am."

Blue was astounded. *Wait, what?!* he thought. The guys Blue liked were always straight. He never had a chance with his crushes. Blue stared at Michael, who was still gazing up at the stars. He looked proud of himself. He looked sincere.

"Really?" Blue asked.

"Mmhmm."

Blue lay his head down again. "Huh. Really." *He just came out to me?!* After a few minutes, Blue said, "Aww," and patted Michael's chest reassuringly.

"Thank you for that."

"Does anyone else know?" Blue asked.

"No, not really."

"So all of that stuff with your girlfriend. What's that about?"

"Well, I did like her but I just like guys more, you know? I just don't have any experience with a guy."

"Me, neither," Blue said.

More silence. Blue pondered his situation. He was lying next to a crush who had just admitted he was gay and seemed to be interested in Blue. Blue shivered violently, unable to control his nerves. "Fu-fucking cold," he stammered when Michael looked at him quizzically. "Time to get up."

While they talked, Blue realized that since Michael had come out, his voice had been cracking, as if he were holding back tears. Blue looked into his eyes and saw they were watery. "Hey," he said, nudging Michael. "Don't be sad! Why are you sad?"

"I don't know, I just feel stupid now. Don't know what I'm doing."

"Oh. Well cheer up, man." Now Blue was sure. *I'm gonna have to save his sappy ass*, he thought. He took a deep breath, summoned all of his courage, and said, "Don't tell [the team] that I told you, but I've kind of had a crush on you for a while."

Michael's face lit up. "Really?!"

"Yeah," Blue said.

"Can I tell you something? I've had a crush on you too."

"That's convenient." Blue nudged Michael, and in a quiet voice that was so awkward it embarrassed him, said, "We should go out."

"Yeah," Michael said. They smiled at each other.

"So . . . why exactly do you have a crush on me?" Blue asked.

"You're kind of cute? And, I don't know, I just feel good around you. I think it's cute how you're really into comics and anime and games and stuff. You're a massive geek, basically."

"True," Blue said. "And the part about me being attractive: also true."

Michael laughed. "Let's see, what else. You're really smart. And different from other people. You always have something new to say, not like all those other dumbshits. You're always calm and collected, more mature than the rest of us. And you have a real sense of humor. The super-funny kind that everyone likes. Like, not too much where you're blatant but not too little where you just sound immature. You're perfect." Michael paused. "What about you? Why did you like me?"

"I guess I've been comparison shopping lately, trying to find people that don't bog me down, people that help me up in life. Compared to my old friends, well, you're just light years ahead of them. And I just . . . I feel happiest when I'm with you."

Following more silence, Blue looked at his watch discreetly. Michael's curfew loomed. Blue sighed audibly, then said, "You know, you probably don't want to leave until you kiss me, but you aren't doing anything because you know it would be awkward with my hat on. Am I right?"

Michael leaned in. They tilted the same way. Blue corrected his angle. The bill of his baseball cap bopped Michael on the forehead.

"Oh, damn this," Michael said, and took off Blue's hat. Blue's first-ever kiss gave him butterflies. He felt like he was smiling the whole way through.

When Michael left to go home, Blue decided to conduct a self-test. He hadn't played MW2 in months, but he knew he was still good at it. Was he too disoriented to play well? "If I really liked him, I'd play shitty," Blue later explained. "And alas, I played shitty."

WHITNEY, NEW YORK | THE POPULAR BITCH

In Spanish, rather than chatting exclusively with Chelsea, Whitney talked to Shay. Shay was generous and affable; when Whitney was sick, she offered to lend her movies and books. Within days, they were having extended, open conversations. Whitney also decided to be friendly to Irene once she realized she alienated her only because the preps did. She didn't have anything against her personally.

Whitney even tried to be nice to Elizabeth, a wannabe who disliked her. In advertising, she struck up a conversation. "Hey, Elizabeth, where are you going to college?" Whitney asked. Elizabeth looked up, startled, and answered.

"What are you going to major in?" Whitney asked.

"I want to do sociology or advertising, but my mom wants me to do education," Elizabeth said.

"It's your life, so you should do what you want, not what your mom wants," Whitney said. "I took a sociology class junior year. I think you'd really like it."

As Whitney walked through the halls now, instead of strutting with her nose in the air, she greeted anyone who made eye contact with her. She also made a concerted effort to stop gossiping—or, at least, to cut back.

At the end of speech class one day, the teacher announced that the class had to go to a speaking event. When the bell rang, stuck behind a group of slow-moving students, Whitney climbed over a desk and headed for the door. When she saw Fern trying to reach her, Whitney turned around and maneuvered against the traffic.

"Can you let me know when you're going and maybe give me a ride?" Fern asked, her head down and her voice barely audible.

Whitney was gratified. For Fern to come up to her in public surely was a sign that she was becoming more approachable, not a traditional prep hallmark. "Yeah, sure!" Whitney said, in a perky voice that annoyed even herself as she used it.

"Thank you," Fern whispered.

During her free period, Whitney was in the mostly empty library with Giselle and Steph, watching Bianca rush to finish a major economics project due the following class period. By now, the prep clique had begun to splinter: Bianca, Madison, Chelsea, and Kendra were the senior preps, while Whitney and Steph had become more independent. Giselle fluctuated between Whitney and the preps.

Whitney, Steph, and Giselle lounged on the couch, watching as Bianca typed frantically on a computer and bossed Chelsea around.

"Chelsea, fix the printer!" she said, and Chelsea rushed to do it. "Chelsea, run and get me a glue stick!"—and Chelsea was off, sprinting to the front desk to find one. Bianca turned to the couch. "Steph, go and get me scissors!"

Steph snorted. "Uhh, no?" she said.

Bianca rolled her eyes. "Ugh, I hate you," she said, passive-aggressive and half-jesting.

Steph mimicked the tone. "The feeling's mutual."

For the next few minutes, Whitney, Steph, and Giselle told Bianca what they really thought of her, but they did it jokingly so that Bianca couldn't get angry.

"Bianca, you suck at life. Your project sucks just like you," said Steph.

"Steph, you are so ugly," Bianca shot back.

"Haha, not as ugly as you and that project," Giselle said.

"Giselle, I hate you," Bianca said.

"Bianca, you think you own the world when you don't," Whitney said.

Bianca didn't say anything else the rest of the period.

Joy, California | The New Girl

In PE, some boys were fooling around, refusing to listen to the teacher. Visibly upset, the teacher sat at a table bordering the basketball court, muttering to himself. "These kids are so immature. They don't respect anyone, they don't respect me. I don't know why I waste my time . . ."

Joy scrawled a note on a piece of notebook paper: "There'll always be a negative aspect," she wrote. "Just think positively and know that there's always a better outcome, and at the end of the day know that you're valued. Joy." She climbed down from the bleachers and handed him the note. "Here," she said, and walked away.

The teacher read the note and smiled. Joy could see that he cared about the students and generally liked his job. She thought he needed to be reminded that some of his students cared about him.

Friday was Ariana's last day at Citygrove. She had decided to drop out of school and move in with her mother, where they would work together at Kmart. In between classes that day, Joy saw her on the sidewalk. "Hey, Ariana, I got you something!"

"Really?! What?"

"I got you this monkey." She handed Ariana a furry blue monkey that she had persuaded her stepfather to buy.

"Oh my gosh! You're the first person to ever give me anything!" Ariana said, hugging the monkey. "I love you, I love you, I love you so much!"

Joy laughed and showed her the stuffed animal's tag, on which Joy had written her email address and the message, "You can be whatever you want. You can achieve anything in life."

"Hey look, if anything, send me an email," Joy told her. "I want to hear from you, so here's my email address. Take care of yourself, and listen to what I said."

"I love you," Ariana said. Her eyes welled up. "You're so nice! You're the nicest person I've ever met! Thank you, thank you so much!"

"Anytime. No biggie," Joy said. As she went into her classroom, she glanced back and saw Ariana watching her, squeezing the monkey tightly.

A few days later, as Joy's English class watched a movie, Xavier teased Keisha. Joy noticed that Keisha, who sat next to her in the front row, looked upset. "Are you okay?" Joy asked. "Don't pay attention to him. He doesn't know what he's talking about."

Keisha dismissed her. "I'm fine. It's nothing," she said.

"I don't think it's nothing. You look like you're going to cry."

Keisha shot her a look that said "Go away."

Joy tried to speak sternly but compassionately. "I'm not as bad as you think," she said. Keisha's eyes widened.

Joy watched the movie for a few more minutes, then scribbled a message onto a piece of notebook paper: "To Keisha: Sometimes things aren't supposed to be easy, whatever it is just look past it and try to have a clear perspective. Just think positively. Have a good week! :)" She folded the paper and handed it to Keisha, along with an apple lollipop she had bought at a fund-raiser earlier that day.

Surprised, Keisha read the note. Soon, she passed a note to Joy:

"That's so sweet, thanks a lot, this really helped me. I'm sorry for act-ing like a bitch. PS are u sure you don't want ur sucker?"

Joy wrote back: "It's okay, we all have our days, you're a smart girl just work towards what you want, and yeah, keep it. I was thinking you'd need it."

They resumed watching the movie. Keisha wasn't cold to Joy again.

Joy was determined to inject "positivity" into other people's lives. Eventually, she hoped to become a psychologist (broadcasting on the radio or TV) specializing in adolescents dealing with abuse or suicidal thoughts. "I don't think society focuses on that so much because of a taboo," she later explained. "I mean, I grew up with abuse and people don't address it because of fear or not knowing what to do. My deep-est passion actually is acting; there's just something about relating my emotions to another person that completely captivates me. So I'd also love to act, but I need to help people. I have the drive and the passion for it. I know I will be something big."

She believed this career path was an obvious extension of her na-ture. "People tend to run away from becoming more than what they know they can be," she said. "I like to make people recognize who they are and show them that someone has faith in them. The way I do it is by making the person see the good in themselves, talking to them on a personal level."

Joy's PE class was gathered for attendance-taking when the teacher announced that the class wasn't going to change into gym clothes be-cause of the rain. The students relaxed. Joy chatted with Christine, a Filipino girl who was also in her Spanish class. She and Christine had bonded because other girls "hated on" them for being naturally skinny.

As they chatted, Joy could hear Mia, the Mexican girl who had been bullied, repeatedly asking classmates, "What did [the teacher] say?" The students ignored her. Mia's friends were busy gossiping.

Finally Joy turned to answer her. "He said that we don't have to change and that we should go to the gym," she called out.

"Oh, really? Cool, thanks!" said Mia.

"No problem," said Joy. "You're welcome." She recognized an opening, and crossed the room to stand next to her. "So," Joy began, "are you gonna start talking to me now? Are we gonna act like civilized human beings?" They both laughed.

"Yeah, we can," said Mia. "Are you used to it here yet?"

"Um, I'm getting used to it. I'm not as professional anymore."

"So have you started chillin' with people? You speak or understand slang yet?"

"No, I don't. But I can try," Joy said.

"It's cool. Me and my homegirls just thought you had a problem with us."

"I have a problem with no one. I'm a cool person. I don't like to judge," Joy said.

"That's good. We should talk!" Mia said.

Joy was relieved she wouldn't have issues with Mia anymore. "Of course!" she replied.

The girls went their separate directions. Mia's friends crowded her. "What's up with her? What she say?" one of them asked, pointing and watching Joy walk away.

Already Joy was ashamed about the assumptions she had made about Mia back when the girls harassed her. Because of the other Mexicans she had encountered at Citygrove, she had assumed that the Mexican girls in PE were ignorant. For the rest of the month, Joy and Mia greeted each other whenever they passed by.

REGAN, GEORGIA | THE WEIRD GIRL

Late at night, Regan was surfing Facebook when she received an IM from a student who had graduated last year. The student wanted to go away to college, but her boyfriend asked her to stay in town with him. "What's the right thing to do?" she asked Regan.

"You have to do what's right for you," Regan answered. "I know you don't want to hear this, but you're young. Chances are, your relationship isn't going to last anyway, and if he can't stay with you while you do what you need to do, then it's not worth it. But I know that love doesn't work that way. If you love him, even if you know it might not last, you're going to want to stay with him, so I know this is hard."

They talked for a while longer. At the end of the conversation, the student thanked Regan profusely for being there for her. "Love you for real, Davis," she wrote.

Regan glowed. "It made me remember how amazing and important my job is," she said later. "In the end, teaching isn't about anything except the students. Forget all of the administrative bull and the bureaucracy. Teaching is about kids. I find myself spending a lot of time with students, giving them advice on life issues more so than on Shakespeare. And although administration would argue that means I'm not doing my job, I disagree."

Regan was the kind of teacher whom students sought out for non-academic discussions. Regularly in the morning or during her planning period, she received visitors who would drop their books on her desk and say, "I've been looking all over for you. I need help."

Delilah, a fellow English teacher who Regan liked, once asked her, "Why do kids love you so much?" Delilah had several of Regan's former students in a new class, and those students had asked whether she ran her class like Regan did. "It was like *Freedom Writers* in there!" a student told Delilah.

"I don't understand it," Delilah said to Regan. "They flock to you. How do you manage that kind of rapport?"

Regan couldn't say for sure, but gave her best guess of an answer: "I listen."

In the spring, some of Regan's students participated in the Mr. Johnson pageant, an inter-grade competition among Johnson boys. Regan spent her Saturday night at the pageant—which Mandy supervised—to support the students.

On Monday, when one of the boys, a senior, walked into second period, Regan said, "I went on Saturday, and I waited for you to come out from backstage, but I never saw you!"

"Aw, man," the senior said, appreciating her support. "I tried to put you on the thing, but she said no."

Regan asked him to clarify. He explained that contestants could name "sponsors": adults whose names were listed on the program as people who had been supportive. "I wanted to put you down as my sponsor, but [Mandy] said I couldn't because she doesn't like you."

Regan's jaw dropped. *What?!* "She didn't actually say that, did she?" Regan asked.

The senior looked uncomfortable. "I'm just playin'," he said, but then added, "Why don't you two like each other?"

Obviously he isn't playing, Regan thought. "No. *She* doesn't like *me*," she replied, against her better judgment. "I have no problem with her."

"I need to try to end y'all's problems," the senior said.

Briefly, Regan considered confronting Mandy about involving students in their drama, but she concluded that such a discussion would only make the situation worse.

A few days later, when Delilah asked if Regan and her first-period class wanted to accompany her class on a movie field trip, Regan jumped at the chance. James Johnson did not have the budget for frequent field trips; the opportunity to leave school grounds was rare and welcome.

Two weeks later, Delilah approached Regan with bad news. Because of the number of classes wanting to go, there was room for only a few chaperones. When Delilah had gone to the teacher in charge— who was part of the black clique called "The Seven"—to discuss the dilemma, her immediate reaction was, "Let's take Davis off, then."

Regan stared in disbelief. Delilah avoided eye contact. "Why?" Regan asked.

"I don't know," Delilah said. She was not convincing.

When Regan asked who was still on the list, Delilah mentioned four teachers. All of them were black. And one teacher's class wasn't even going. It made no sense. Why did the administration refuse Regan, whose class was going on the trip, in favor of a teacher whose class wasn't?

Later that day, Delilah walked in on Regan, who was sitting in an empty classroom and talking on the phone to her mother. When Regan hung up, Delilah asked what was wrong. "The field trip thing," Regan said. "I feel like they took me off the list 'cause I'm white."

"It's not that," Delilah said.

"What is it, then?" Regan asked.

"Stay after school and I'll tell you."

After the last class of the day, Delilah found Regan and said, "We need to have a serious talk." She listed other English teachers' grievances against her: Regan had too many absences, they claimed, and she had taken her girlfriend to the emergency room during the school day for a minor injury. "It's not just because you're white. I was supposed to talk to you about this a while ago," Delilah said.

Regan flipped out. "I'm not about to be punished because I had to go to the emergency room. If it had been someone's husband or child, no one would have said anything," Regan said. "I don't care about the field trip, but I don't want my kids to be punished. They are a great class and they deserve to go out. So take me off the list, fine, but let my kids go."

But she did care. On the drive home from school that afternoon, she cried hysterically to her mother—the first time she had cried all year. ("It's not just because you're white," Regan repeated Delilah's words. "Oh, what, because you're gay, too?" her mother replied.)

Regan hated that her colleagues were petty and immature. She was tired of being picked on. When she got home, she did what she considered to be the professional thing to do: She called the head of the English department to ask that her class be able to go on the field trip even if she couldn't chaperone.

Over the next few days, gossip spread among teachers that Regan was "trying to cause trouble," and that she had "tattled." Eventually Regan's entire class was kicked off of the field trip list. "I seem to be the scapegoat of the department this year. Fine. Whatever. But I don't see why people have to make this so difficult, knowing I'm leaving at the end of the year. People are just taking their misery out on me. If that's what makes them feel better, so be it," Regan said later. "I don't start trouble; that's just not who I am. So I hate having people start trouble with me. Why am I the person who everyone is against when I'm the nicest person in the department?"

Even Regan's faculty evaluation, which she had received recently, included a personal dig. The ratings of her teaching were good. Regan's only "Needs Improvement" was in the category about her appropriateness with faculty and students. "My administrator wrote that I shared too much about my personal life with my students, and that I need to learn to use more discretion—which was a direct reference to my telling the kids that I'm gay," Regan said. "I really wanted to demand an explanation as to why that isn't appropriate, and yet Mandy and Wyatt could tell all of their students that they were dating, but I didn't want to argue. I'm just so over it."

At this point during the year, Regan and I agreed that because she hadn't been able to find a GSA cosponsor and her job security seemed at risk, we would let the challenge die. Not even the Diversity Committee would touch gay issues. Instead Regan focused her efforts on working outside of James Johnson to promote LGBT tolerance. She started a blog and web community as a safe space in which twenty-something lesbians could interact. Within days, grateful emails from blog readers flooded her inbox.

ELI, VIRGINIA | THE NERD

Eli rejoiced when Kim—a girl from his lunch table whom he liked talking to—and a few of her friends invited him to play board games with them in the library on early-release days. Eli laughed more often than usual with this group, even though he couldn't help thinking, *I should really be doing schoolwork right now*, while in the midst of a game.

During a game of Apples to Apples, Kim was having a side conversation with a friend. "Watch," she said, smiling. "Eli, when did you turn in your college apps?"

"October," he said.

"See?" Kim said to her friend. "When did you finish your gov vocab?" The homework was due at the end of the week.

"Two weeks ago," Eli replied.

"See! He's such a nerd. And he worries too much."

"Yeah, you are kind of OCD," said another friend.

Eli didn't mind the ribbing. The board games in the library were the only social events he'd attended in months.

ELI WAS BOTH EXCITED and anxious to walk into the auditorium for his last high school competition. He had higher expectations than usual. Strattville had not boasted any successful Academic Bowl teams in recent memory, but this year the team was decent—and was entering this final round with more points than most of its opponents.

Eli scanned the posters draping the five tables onstage. His heart sank. Not only would Strattville be competing directly against Arrington, but also his team's table was the farthest from the moderator, which could lead to difficulty hearing the questions.

Students from ten schools packed the auditorium; the schools from the morning round hadn't scored enough points to threaten Strattville's contention for the title. Students practiced trivia or did homework as they waited for the moderator to take the stage. Near Eli's team, in the back of the room, a few students from another school practiced slapping imaginary buzzers.

The moderator called the teams to the stage and explained the competition format. Questions were worth ten points apiece. Each round would consist of two sets of toss-up questions, during which teams would buzz in to answer, and two series of questions directed to each team separately. Each student could compete in only one round. Because Strattville didn't have enough members for four students to compete in each round, however, two of its groups, including Eli's, had to proceed with only three students.

Eli's group was up first. Eli sat in front of the buzzer, hoping that his round would be a geography round. As the moderator began with science questions, Eli's team was silent. Then, "What is a talisman?" Eli buzzed in, then hesitated. What was the judge looking for? "A . . . charm?" Eli asked.

"Correct. Next question. "What's the derivative of $yx = 19$ with respect to x?"

Buoyed by his success, Eli buzzed in quickly. "-y over x."

"Incorrect." Eli kicked himself. He hadn't answered with respect to x.

His teammates answered a few other questions. When the judge directed questions to Eli's team, Eli leaned forward in concentration.

"Who was the only nonelected president?"

"Ford," Eli answered with confidence.

"Correct." Eli's teammates patted him on the shoulders.

"Where do Creoles live?"

"Louisiana," Eli said.

In the final toss-up round, the moderator finally asked the type of question Eli had been waiting for. "What is the largest artificial lake in the United States?"

Eli slapped the buzzer. "Mead," he answered.

"Correct."

When Eli's group returned to the audience, teammates cheered. The coach said they had tied for the highest points scored in the round. Eli was slightly disappointed, though. He could have done better. As the second round began, Eli was dismayed to realize that this was the round that focused on geography questions. He answered every geography question correctly in his head. On stage, Arrington, the perennial champion, wasn't dominating the questions. Frostpike, another nearby school, was pulling ahead. Soon, it was apparent that Strattville and Frostpike were the leaders.

"In the Old Testament, what is the fourth of the Ten Commandments?" the moderator asked. From his seat in the auditorium, Eli triumphantly raised his fist in the air. Strattville's most devout Catholic happened to be on stage. She buzzed in immediately. "Thou shalt honor your mother and father," she said.

"Incorrect."

"What?" murmured Eli and his teammates.

"No, she's definitely right!" a Catholic girl whispered to Eli. As the game progressed, Eli's teammates tapped their cell phones. Apparently there was some debate over the text of the fourth commandment, but enough sources agreed with Strattville that they believed they had grounds to contest if needed. For now, it was so unlikely that ten measly points would matter that they remained silent in their seats.

After the last round, Eli and his team were on edge while the moderator conferred with the judges. They hadn't kept track—the questions passed too quickly—but they thought they had done well. They knew they had beaten Arrington, which was a major victory in itself. In fact, they thought, they might even have won for the first time in school history.

For Eli, this moment was bittersweet. He would miss Academic Bowl. Nowhere else did he feel like a leader, the kind of guy to whom people turned for advice and companionship. He hardly saw his Spanish camp friends anymore. He hadn't been able to reach Dwight in months. The board game hours continued on early-release days, but the conversations didn't veer toward the personal. Eli had the lingering feeling that even his supposedly close friends didn't get him. They considered him odd for not wanting to go to prom because he thought the dance was "a waste of hard-earned money." Eli didn't mind that he wasn't going, but he did mind that his friends made such a big deal about it, trying to fix him up or warning that it was a mistake to miss his only prom. In addition, they repeatedly questioned why Eli was going to Westcoast University when he had been accepted to more prestigious schools. Eli would shrug amiably and daydream about going to a university where students would appreciate him.

Finally the moderator returned to the stage. "The winner"—he paused, "with five hundred sixty points is"—he paused again and surveyed the audience—"Frostpike!" Frostpike erupted in cheers. "In second, with five hundred fifty points . . . Strattville."

"What?!" Eli's team exploded in muffled outrage. As soon as the moderator completed his remarks and presented the trophy to Frostpike, the Strattville coach marched to the judge's table to protest the ten-point Bible question. Eli and his team remained in the now-emptied auditorium while the judges conferred. They said they had to check their "official sources" and that they would email Strattville by the end of the day. The email never came.

On the bus ride back to school, the team members concocted excuses for their narrow loss. "People shouldn't have been applauding; we couldn't hear." "We couldn't hear anything because we were the table all the way at the end." "Our math bonus was calculus, but everyone else got Algebra 2 or geometry questions."

The coach broke in. "There's no reason to place all of the blame on anyone else," he said. "You all had at least one question you should have answered right and you know it, and that would have made us the winners."

He's right, Eli thought, recalling a few of the questions. Eli felt better.

Strattville had placed second in the Academic Bowl championships, had trampled its rival, and performed well enough to deserve first place. Leading his school to its best ever season was not a bad way for Eli to end his career.

The Strattville administration never once acknowledged the victory.

———

HOW SCHOOLS MAKE THINGS WORSE

In nine classes at a Midwestern summer-school program, researchers randomly divided elementary school-age students into yellow and blue groups and gave them corresponding T-shirts to wear. Six of the nine classrooms (three classes formed the control group) displayed posters supposedly of the prior summer's attendees. Posters about athletic contests and a spelling bee showed that five of the six event winners wore yellow shirts. In three of those classrooms, over the course of the summer, teachers did not mention the groups. In the other three classes, teachers were instructed to make use of the color labels and organize activities using those groups, without favoring one group over another. By the end of the program, the only children who developed stereotypes and biases were the kids whose teachers referred to the yellow and blue groups. Even when surrounded by posters conveying implicit messages about color group status, the children didn't categorize the groups unless the teacher acknowledged them.

Students are not solely to blame for creating cafeteria fringe or for the selection of which students are treated as such. Whether intentionally or not, many administrators, teachers, and school policies or traditions foster the same results as the teachers who distinguished yellow from blue. Over the last several years, students have shared with me ways in which this discrepancy occurs at the academic level. A Massachusetts "flirt," for instance, said that at her public school, "The honors students use their rigorous academic record as justification that they are better than the [non-honors] kids. The school encourages this distinction. My math teacher once said, 'The same amount of energy it takes to teach all thirty-five of you guys is how much it takes to teach eighteen [non-honors] kids.' This type of comment isn't unusual."

Neither is a more controversial form of neglect. An Illinois middle school teacher described a number of instances in which students singled out English Language Learner (ELL) students and ridiculed them in front of their lunch tables. This behavior continued for months until ELL teachers notified administrators, who did nothing other than reprimand the offenders. Business as usual, perhaps—except the teacher believed the offenders were modeling teacher behavior. "Sometimes teachers and staff treat these kids differently," she told me. "Administration is slow in reacting toward situations regarding ELL students being wronged. And I have heard [colleagues'] comments about generalizations toward certain ethnic groups. The biases and stereotypes are there, and of course that comes out in their teaching, no matter how subtle. Kids usually catch on to how teachers act toward them."

In this manner, teachers play a role not only in perpetuating stereotypes, but also in alerting students to them. A Texas teacher said that at his school, "The veteran teachers and administrators tend to treat students according to dress. The emo kids sometimes are kept at arm's length or are chastised about piercings. The openly gay kids have complained that some of their teachers have stopped lessons to lecture them in front of their peers about sexual morality and not being able to 'enter the Kingdom of God' if they don't change their 'ways.'"

Psychologists suggest that teachers are influenced by students' cliques and vice versa, fueling a cycle that keeps certain groups atop the social hierarchy. One study described how this phenomenon can cause an achievement catch-22: Rather than vary student pairings, "Teachers may take the social structure of the class into account in making ability group assignments in an effort to utilize student friendships to promote learning. As a result, the presence of cliques can affect a teacher's decision regarding the number, size, and composition of tracks and ability groups in a school. These grouping characteristics, in time, affect student achievement."

Educators can be just as guilty as students of affixing labels and then refusing to look beyond them. Teachers across the country discussed colleagues who treated students poorly for this reason. An Iowa teacher reported that a coworker gave some students "the same grade all four years she had them because she didn't believe they could change after freshman year." At this school, a few days before classes started, the administration briefed new teachers on the "troubled" students. "We were told horror stories about attitudes and that these kids should be thrown out of class and sent to the office immediately if needed," the teacher said. "Since they are labeled the troublemakers of the school by the administration, a lot of the faculty has bought into that and will automatically send them to the office. Those students are immediately suspected to be guilty of anything. Sometimes they deserve it, but a lot of times the teacher could handle it without intervention."

One of the students labeled "troubled" by the administration was simply a quirky girl who liked anime. "I have never had a problem with her in my class. She's a good kid who just got an unfortunate label. Other faculty talk about her like she's the worst troublemaker they've ever met and I wonder if they've actually ever paid attention to her or know anything about her, because I just don't see it," the teacher told me. "I was taken aback that we were warned about these particular students and weren't given the chance to make up our own minds. The students don't really put a label on the 'troubled' students. That's the label the administration puts on them. They seem to be targeted for bad behavior that other students mostly get away with."

Several students told me they have experienced this treatment first-hand. Dawn, a freshman in Florida, was in class when a cheerleader sniped to a teacher about her, "I think you should write her up for being ugly." Dawn retorted, "I think you should be written up for being stupid." The teacher kicked Dawn out of his class and gave her an in-school suspension, while the cheerleader got off scot-free. "Because I'm known as a crazy and emo kid, I was the only one who got in trouble," Dawn said. "Because she was a cheerleader, she couldn't get in trouble."

Teachers blame their colleagues for wedging students so tightly into categories that they get stuck there. "*Very* often, a teacher will think that once a kid is a troublemaker, he is always the one on the wrong side of a problem. This keeps the kid from learning to make the right choices (what's the use?) and to trust adults for advice," said a Connecticut teacher. "Colleagues make a borderline-negative kid a confirmed troublemaker when they treat him with a lack of respect. Those kids will go out of their way to be 'good' for me because I tell them they have it in them. The best way to get a kid to be a leader is to give him something to lead." Or at least to believe that he has potential. Studies have shown that teachers' and coaches' subjective views about a student can affect the way they grade him or her. Regardless of actual performance, some teachers give higher grades to students whom they *expect* will do well than to the students for whom they don't have high expectations.

Teachers and students nationwide told me that educators give popular students preferential treatment, much like Whitney and her fellow preps experienced at Riverland. An Arkansas teacher has seen coworkers "let the in-crowd get away with more." Her coworker, for example, has a reputation for "paying a lot of attention to the popular crowd," she said. "It's widely known that she writes these kids passes to skip their regular classes to come sit in her class. She has even texted a student while the student was in my class." A teacher at a school for juvenile offenders told me about administrators and teachers favoring popular, typically wealthy kids, "not expecting them to follow the same rules as the general population and allowing them off-periods to socialize and schmooze with the adults." A counselor in Tennessee said that some of her colleagues joke around more with the "cool kids."

Some teachers apparently take the jokes too far. Pennsylvania high school junior Beth Anne observed, "I see teachers participate in this social conformity as heavily as students do. In class, teachers are as merciless towards the unpopular kids as their peers are. In elementary school, teachers offered protection. If someone hurt you, made fun of you, the teacher was there to protect you. Now I see them participate in the demeaning of self-esteem."

On a broader level, school practices can exacerbate social issues among students. Many schools tend to give honors and awards to the same groups of students every year. An Oklahoma teacher said, "Administrators favor the families who are big-money donors or board members. Those are the students who win the year-end awards and are often warned of Facebook pictures or behavior that could hurt their chances at recognition. The outcasts are just suspended." Students said that members of the in crowd are handed student government positions, leads in plays, team captainships, and other distinctions that are selected by teachers rather than students.

The ways in which schools attempt to address problems among cliques can end up bolstering the same stereotypes they are trying to eradicate. Several students pointed out that many of the programs that schools implement for this purpose limit the number of participants. "It disgusts me to think that the school has spent thousands of dollars so we can go through these school-bonding lectures and nothing comes out of it," said the Massachusetts flirt. "[One] program is supposed to create a more welcoming school environment. To be in the program, students have to be recommended by their teachers and take a Friday off every other month to play bonding games all day. Students not invited to participate become frustrated when their friends don't have to take tests or attend class and they do. The students were asked to make a list of new people to invite in. It's a type of invitation-only club."

Even administrators with the best intentions can unwittingly contribute to students' perceptions that some kids should be elevated while others should be shunned or ignored. Many students and teachers mentioned their schools' emphasis on athletics, and within that group, a prioritization of specific sports. Some schools let certain athletes (like Giselle) out of detentions for practices or games, whereas nonathletes can't escape detention for any reason. Schools might issue a no-homework night for the boys' basketball championships so that students are free to attend the game, but then don't offer the same privilege for the girls' soccer championships. Cheerleaders or poms perform only for certain teams. Just as Noah's band, which was talented enough to represent the state in the Macy's Parade, had to practice in the school parking lot so as not to damage the football field, a Texas middle school band had to step aside for what the band teacher called "preferential treatment of the athletic program." The teacher said, "One of our concerts, scheduled eight months in advance, was moved with two weeks' notice because an athletics banquet was scheduled on top of our performance. Three weeks ago, our classroom was taken over, and my principal did not provide our classes with an alternative space in which to hold class. We performed outside."

Students with even less common interests are out of luck. At a New England technical school, students in the environmental technology shop said that administrators discriminate against their program, which helps solidify their status as "the reject shop." And over the last several years, schools across the country have eliminated or drastically reduced music, art, and science programs in order to devote more time to preparation for standardized tests in reading and math.

Meanwhile politicians bemoan the comparative lack of North American–produced scientists. The most recent Trends in International Mathematics and Science Study reveals that U.S. students have shown no gain in science scores since 1995. As a result, government officials are scrambling to find solutions that will encourage students to become scientists and engineers. But has anyone bothered to consult students about how their school culture leads them to think about these career paths?

Those hoping to analyze the age-old rift between jocks and nerds cannot overlook the ways in which schools themselves signify whose endeavors are more meaningful. It's no wonder that interest in the sciences can carry a stigma for many students. If schools celebrated student scientists the same way they celebrate student athletes, more students would be encouraged to pursue the subject. Instead, science is considered nerdy because schools help students to paint it that way.

Similarly, if Eli's school gave the same attention to his Academic Bowl triumphs that it gave to athletic victories, perhaps his classmates would have been more likely to admire his wealth of knowledge rather than make fun of it. Few, if any, administrations throw schoolwide pep rallies that give equal billing to athletes and mathletes. Simply stated, schools effectively control which students are eligible to achieve the visibility and recognition that pave the path to perceived popularity. Too often they glorify the wrong people. A Hawaii middle school teacher said, "I have seen adults treating non-in kids differently. I've seen it with teachers and coaches. It kills me because they should know better—that we all are different somehow and if we didn't have kids who thought apart from the crowd, then we'd never have innovators and people willing to take risks."

Another distressing aspect of schools' elimination of programs, classes, and attitudes that would encourage imaginativeness is their timing. Studies have found that the dopamine system, which plays a large role in developing the ability to innovate, reaches its peak in activity during the teenage years. In addition, gray matter density in the posterior temporal and inferior parietal lobes of the brain increases until approximately age thirty. These areas of the brain are related to perception, which is "the most plastic and adaptable of all cognitive functions," according to the book *Iconoclast*. "This may explain why so many of the early adopters [of new ideas] tend to be young adults. In addition to a robust dopamine system, their perceptual processes are more open to seeing the world in new ways." From a biological perspective, the schooling years are the most important years in which to foster creativity, individuality, and open-mindedness. And what that means is, our schools are dissuading teens and young adults from pursuing critical educational paths at precisely the best time for students to do so.

Chapter 11

TWO STEPS FORWARD, ONE STEP BACK

JOY, CALIFORNIA | THE NEW GIRL

I n PE, Joy's class was running the mile when Joy passed Lupe, one of the Mexican girls who had harassed her. She was alone and looked upset. Joy slowed down. "Are you okay?" Joy asked, jogging in place.

Lupe looked surprised, then smiled. "Yes," she said.

Joy smiled back and ran on. Lately Joy had made a valiant effort to befriend students of various cultures. She talked to D'Arnell, the sophomore, between classes sometimes. She had resumed chatting with Natalie, who even sought Joy out occasionally, despite her friends' disapproval. She also had become close friends with Christine, the Filipino girl in two of her classes.

A few days later, Mia approached Joy in PE. "What up with it? How you kicking it, mami?" Mia asked.

Joy raised an eyebrow. "What does that mean?!"

Mia laughed. "It's what's up, or what's up with you."

"That's funny," Joy said.

"You're funny!" Mia said. "It's cool, though. You don't speak Spanish, right?"

"No, I don't, but I'm trying to learn. I'm terrible at it!" Joy said. "I've been doing it since grade two."

"Wow," Mia said. "So how do you say what's up in Jamaica?"

"Wah gwan," Joy replied.

"¡¿Qué?!"

Joy laughed. "Wah gwan. It's really dialect."

"Oh. Jamaican isn't a language?"

"It's a language—I mean, we speak it—but we call it a dialect because it isn't recorded as a language. The real name is patois."

"That's cool," Mia said.

For the final weeks of PE, Joy and Christine debated which sport to sign up for. Christine insisted they swim, even though Joy couldn't swim well. As they handed in their choice cards among a swarm of students, Joy said, "Come on, let's switch to dance."

"No, Joy!"

Joy laughed. "You bitch! Please!"

"Your mom," Christine said.

"You hobag!" Joy said.

Lupe and Mia, who stood in front of them, turned around. "You curse now?!" asked Lupe.

Christine laughed. "She always cursed."

"You're different than I expected," Lupe said.

"I'm not that different," said Joy.

"Hey, so which activity are you doing?" Mia asked.

"We're doing swim," said Joy.

"Hey, me too," Mia said. "We can talk."

"Of course!" Joy said.

A SUBSTITUTE TEACHER WAS playing hip-hop music on the AP English teacher's computer. The students couldn't believe it. "He's playing music! Is he allowed to do that?!" one student whispered.

This quarter Joy's assigned seat was by the door, behind a girl named Pooja, who kept turning around and glaring at Joy. Joy stared back. *What's she looking at?* Joy thought. She was in a bad mood to begin with. In PE the day before, students on the opposing volleyball team decided the game would be more fun if they pegged the ball at Joy's head. A skater had hit her, hard.

Xavier asked the sub to play another song, but when the teacher realized the lyrics were explicit, he paused it. "I can't play any songs that are dirty," the sub said. "I'll put on this one." He turned on a Sean Paul song.

Joy laughed. The sub had chosen a song containing multiple sexual references. "You just don't think it's dirty because you don't understand Jamaican," she said.

"And you do," the sub said sarcastically.

"I think I would, since I'm from Jamaica."

"You're from Jamaica?! That's so cool," the sub said. He asked her to recommend other Jamaican musicians.

Joy spelled out names for the teacher. "E-t-a-n-a. There's also Queen I-f-r-i-k-a." The sub typed in the names but couldn't find their songs.

Joy thought of another. "Type in S-i-zed-zed-l-a."

Xavier turned around. "What's a 'zed'? Do you mean 'zee'?"

"Yes, that's what I mean. Same difference," said Joy.

"Who the heck says 'zed'?! So weird," Xavier said. "Say 'zee.' That's the correct pronunciation."

Joy bristled. "I don't need to change my speech to accommodate you. I say zed, you say zee. Get over it!"

The class quieted, watching Joy and Xavier like a tennis match. *Sly mongrels want to suck up every last drop,* Joy thought. The teacher observed silently.

"You're American now," Xavier said. "Speak English."

"I *am* speaking English," Joy retorted. "You're so ignorant!"

Xavier adjusted his glasses. Pooja twisted around in her seat, her fingers clutching the back of her chair. "What's your problem?! Why do you hate everybody?" Pooja shrieked.

I hate someone?! Joy thought. *For God's sake, I don't even hate my father!* On other days, Joy might have just brushed her off. But not today, she thought wearily. *No sirree, not today.* "I don't hate anyone," Joy snapped, reverting to her Jamaican accent. "I just have a problem with people like you!"

As Pooja gasped, it sounded like the entire class held its breath. People didn't speak to Pooja that way. The teacher finally stepped in. "You guys, relax. What's going on? This is supposed to be a room full of positive energy and peace."

Joy, still fuming, raised her hand. "May I go outside?" she asked. As she left the room, she thought, *If you want to talk to me, don't insult my culture. Just talk to me. I know I'm outspoken, but I can be really sweet to you, if you don't screw around with me.*

About ten minutes later, the sub came outside to check on her. "What was going on in there?" he asked.

"Nothing, just a little blowup."

"You look really upset," the sub said.

"Yeah, that's 'cause I am. I'm tired of having to change myself and my culture for these people."

"You shouldn't change. It's great that you're from a different place!"

Joy switched to her strong Jamaican accent, the one she took pains to disguise at school. When she was upset, she slipped back into it because it was easier to use her first dialect. "It might be cool to people who appreciate it, but I don't like having to change my accent, or my letters, or anything about myself just 'cause others aren't used to it."

"You see that right there? I love your accent! You know how many people *wish* they were Jamaican? That they were different? Just ignore it. People must like seeing you upset. I mean, I did," he said.

"I don't normally let things get to me, but sometimes you need to put people in their place for them to understand, or to have an ounce of respect." A tear rolled down Joy's cheek. She hurriedly wiped it away.

"I don't understand why they behave like that," the sub said. "They should be trying to learn more about your culture."

"That's just how AP kids are. They believe they are elite. My mother always taught me that no matter how far you reach in life, no matter how intelligent you are, have respect for others and recognize that you're equal to them. We never know, we might end up scrubbing their toilets," Joy said.

"Well, what you have right there is so cool, and no one else has it. You just be you, and love who you are," he said. "Do you want to go inside?"

"Thanks," Joy said. "I think I'll go inside and give them more to talk about."

When Joy returned to the room, Pooja again turned and glared. Joy ignored her.

That afternoon, Joy's biology teacher conducted an oral quiz. He kept picking on Joy specifically, asking her several questions before he'd asked other students one. Joy grew frustrated. "I don't *know*," she said.

As the teacher strode down the aisle in the middle of the classroom, he said, "What's wrong with Joy? Joy used to be the best. She used to be able to answer everything. Now she's becoming like all the other Americans."

"She used to be the best," a few students parroted, laughing. "*Used to be.*"

He didn't say anything about Joy's classmates. The teacher had told Joy previously that he pushed her like that to motivate her. "Joy, you're a smart girl, and I don't do it to hurt your feelings," he said once. "Sometimes you need to be pushed. You're not second best; you're the best! Plus, I like making you upset; it's fun hearing you go back into your Jamaican . . . Mi irie, mon!"

The teacher called on a few other students, then returned to Joy. When she didn't know an answer, she said so, and the teacher resumed his banter. "What's wrong with you, Joy? You becoming American or what?"

Joy grew increasingly irritated, rapping her fingers against the desk. The teacher thought he was joking around, but Joy was angry. Although she liked America, she wasn't American. She was Jamaican and proud! Why should she change for anyone?! Next to her, an abandoned textbook lay on the corner of an empty desk. Joy hit the book as hard as she could. The book dented. The class was shocked that Joy had hit the desk. She had never been physically violent before in her life. Joy felt better.

That evening, Joy told herself that this was her home now and there was no going back, so she'd just have to make the best of it. "I recognized that I lost touch with myself because I wasn't being the best me," she said. "I was neglecting the very being that makes Joy Joy! I love myself and should try not to be cranky. I'll return to my accent. I behave like a Jamaican. I stick to my roots and don't try to conform to societal pressures. And if someone's rude to me, I will put them in their place."

———

CONFORMITY IN SCHOOLS

Amelia, an excellent student in southern Missouri, had a special relationship with her dad. When she was six years old, however, he died of brain cancer. Just before she began seventh grade, with her mother's permission, Amelia dyed her blonde hair pink, which she called "the cancer color," as a tribute to her beloved father. When she showed up for school, administrators sent her home. "You're suspended until you change your hair," they told her. The twelve-year-old was concerned about falling behind in classwork, but pledged to make her father proud by fighting to express her individuality. Only after the ACLU got involved did Amelia's middle school revoke the suspension.

Why would a school try to control the color of a student's hair? Amelia's principal told a local television station, "We want it to be equal for everybody, nobody getting any more attention than anyone else, and we just go on with the process of education." Since when is equality identical to conformity?

In the 1970s, fewer than 25 percent of U.S. residents lived in counties in which the presidential candidate won by a landslide. Thirty years later, that percentage had nearly doubled. Political partisanship, an example of the homogenization of U.S. communities, is also a force powerful enough to perpetuate sameness, politically and socially. The existence of political majorities deters minorities from voting, just as the preps' perennial dominance of the student government at Whitney's school caused most nonpopular seniors to skip the elections. But the impact doesn't end there. Those voting minorities also withdraw from volunteering and other local social activities. The community loses exposure to diverse philosophies and consequently becomes more uniform. "What had happened over three decades wasn't a simple increase in political partisanship, but a more fundamental kind of self-perpetuating, self-reinforcing social division," Bill Bishop wrote in *The Big Sort*. "The like-minded neighborhood supported the like-minded church, and both confirmed the image and beliefs of the tribe that lived and worshipped there."

One might assume that the more educated a person, the less likely he will prefer such a narrow existence. University of Pennsylvania political science professor Diana Mutz's findings illustrate a different reality: Well-educated Americans are the *least* likely Americans to engage in political discussions with people who hold different views. The higher the level of education, the more homogeneous the conversations. The people who experience the most diverse political networks are poor, nonwhite high school dropouts.

At first glance, that finding doesn't make sense. Aren't schools supposed to enlighten students by teaching various manners of thought, problem-solving, and expression? They're not, students say. Junior Beth Anne Katz wrote in a column for the *Intelligencer Journal* in Pennsylvania, "Elementary school taught us that variety is what makes the world beautiful. In high school, variety is weird and conformity is survival."

Schools are so focused on conformity that administrators panic over students who stray even slightly outside of the box. Across the country, for example, schools have squelched efforts to display cultural pride at commencement ceremonies. For American Indians, eagle feathers, imbued with deep spiritual meaning, are sacred, traditional gifts that honor accomplishments or sacrifice. In Oregon, a tribe member arrived at her high school graduation with eagle feathers sewn into her cap, feathers she had carried since age five. School officials plucked them off. An Idaho school removed a boy from his graduation procession because he wore an eagle feather. A Maryland school withheld a Cherokee student's diploma to punish him for wearing a bolo tie— symbolic Native American formalwear—instead of a necktie. Schools are also punishing gender nonconformity. Examples abound of administrators suspending crossdressers, with an Atlanta school going so far as to tell a student that he had two choices: dress more "manly" or stay home.

But the issue of conformity in schools concerns much more than appearances. The overemphasis of standardized tests forces teachers to teach the same restricted, uninventive curriculum. Longtime educator

Brent Evans has said that today's schools are organized as assembly lines, "(running at a set speed) and with each worker (teacher) at designated places (grade levels) on the assembly line performing predetermined actions on products (students) considered to be somewhat generic (one-size-fits-all) and passive (waiting to be filled or formed to the desired shape)."

That this assembly-line metaphor is used frequently makes it no less apt. Marketing expert Seth Godin told *Psychology Today*, "The school system was invented by industrialists, and its only function was to train people to work in factories. When you slap on top of it standardized testing and No Child Left Behind, what you are left with is a system optimized for compliance—the opposite of what we need. What we need to teach is how to solve interesting problems."

As schools whitewash their populations into a sterile sameness, creativity fades. Schools impose a hierarchy on subjects, with unequal credit requirements for arts, sciences, humanities, physical education, languages, and mathematics. Rather than using interdisciplinary curricula designed to encourage learning related to students' interests, skills, and learning styles, many schools overlook the fact that not all students learn best the same way.

Schools' prioritization of conformity over creativity is a global problem. In 2009, two schools in Ireland were sanctioned for discriminating against boys by suspending them for coming to school with hair that fell past their collars. One of the schools hired a barber to measure; one boy violated the dress code by only an inch. The school refused to lift the suspension. The *Toronto Star* reported on a Canadian school system that "values conformity and control" and in which "many get suspended simply for opposing authority." (A professor who works with at-risk youth said, "That's sort of like saying, 'Okay, we're suspending you because you're fifteen.'")

A Scottish health services report cited a study illustrating that children's "capacity for divergent thinking (a good proxy for creativity and imagination) declines steadily from 98% at age 3-5 to just 2% at age 25 as we progress through the education system," leading the report's author to conclude, "We teach conformity." In England, a government-commissioned study found that British schools were extinguishing the creativity of students and teachers alike. Sir Ken Robinson, a former arts education professor who chaired the inquiry, said, "All children start their school careers with sparkling imaginations, fertile minds, and a willingness to take risks with what they think. Education is the system that's supposed to develop our natural abilities and enable us to make our way in the world. Instead it is stifling the individual talents and abilities of too many students and killing their motivation to learn."

In response, the British government implemented Creative Partnerships, a program designed to focus on creative learning by partnering schools with creative professionals including artists, performers, multimedia developers, architects, and scientists. The program was so successful that England's Art Council allocated £75 million (more than $90 million) to create a new national organization called Creativity, Culture, and Education, to operate from 2009 to 2011.

Meanwhile, U.S. students acutely feel the effects of a system whose priorities fall on the opposite end of the spectrum. "School doesn't encourage creativity and imagination," said a Texas freshman. "I think this is why lots of creative-type people, like musicians and artists, are sometimes seen as outcasts. If you don't behave like everyone else, most likely you'll be an outcast."

Student populations blatantly conform their clothing, hair, and other features. A Florida senior noted that, "All the girls fake tan, and you know when a dance or big party is coming because the whole school is orange." Several redheads told me they were picked on merely because of their standout hair color.

Many teens feel pressured to match an ideal body type. A freshman boy in Georgia said, "Right now, my forearms are about as big as my biceps, because I run and don't work out. I look around and see all these big guys walking around school and there's definitely pressure to look ripped, because when you're small, you're usually labeled as a nerd." An Indiana thirteen-year-old added that students are much more likely to pick on boys who are underweight than overweight.

Cliques of girls tend to share levels of depression and self-esteem, as well as body mass index. In the first study to examine eating disorders within friendship groups, psychologists discovered that cliques of high school sophomores shared extreme weight-loss behaviors, body-image concerns, and dietary restraints. The researchers could even predict a girl's rate of extreme weight-loss behaviors simply by gauging the rates of other girls in her group. "I've struggled with anorexia and bulimia since eighth grade and that's not even rare," a semi-popular Maryland senior said. "I've gone into the bathroom towards the end of lunch to fix my makeup and heard girls vomiting in the stalls. And no one talks about it, ever. Because that would be abnormal, and no one can afford to be that."

Conformity is a mask behind which students can hide their identity or the fact that they haven't yet figured out their identity. "I disguise how little of a life I have outside of school by wearing cute, fancy, expensive clothes," said a Texas sophomore. "I pin myself as a 'mess in a dress' because although I look pretty on the outside, I feel awful on the inside."

More troubling than accessories that can be removed at will are group standards for attitudes and behavior that can't be so easily changed. Students in gangs, for example, might be pressured to fight or to act belligerently in school. In a group discussion, several minority students from various states told me that they felt they had to "act white" to be accepted by teachers and administrators.

Other students repeated the sentiments of a New York junior, who said that in her school there's an unspoken rule prohibiting frequent class participation. "In math, someone told my friend that I ask too many questions and that I'm a bitch trying to be a teacher's pet. I asked two questions that day. Now I don't even bother raising my hand."

A sophomore at a school in rural Pennsylvania hides her religious beliefs from evangelical Christian friends. She said, "With some of my friends I have to undermine my true beliefs so I can maintain a good relationship. I think high school is similar to the political atmosphere of today: Tailor your image to the audience around you for your best benefit. I find it funny when adults say that teens don't think before they speak, because when it comes to social situations, everything you say and do has an impact, and teens definitely realize this."

NOAH, PENNSYLVANIA | THE BAND GEEK

Leigh was collecting bags of recycling for Noah to shuttle to volunteers' cars. On Noah's second trip back, he saw several students helping Leigh—and not just the regular volunteers. One of the least popular students in school lugged two heavy bags to the curb. *People may not like him, but he's willing to help,* Noah thought.

The next day, Noah saw the unpopular boy sitting alone in the library. Noah went over to him. Students avoided the boy only because he seemed to be in his own world, an indoor street musician playing his guitar in the halls. "Hey, I wanted to thank you for helping us out the other day," Noah said.

The boy smiled. "Oh sure, no problem. You're awesome, Noah Giancoli!"

Noah was shocked that he knew his name. They had never spoken before. Within minutes, Noah recruited him as a regular volunteer.

Slowly, Noah's year was improving. Volunteers were finding fewer pieces of trash in the recycling bins, an encouraging sign. Noah had persuaded a popular girl, a nerd, and a quiet boy from his calculus class to join the club and a student with autism in the school's special needs program signed up. Nearly every week, administrators asked Noah how the program was going. He was proud to inform them that students had recycled more than four tons of paper.

Bolstered by his success with the recycling program, Noah turned his attention to another interest. He was spearheading an effort to persuade the administration to set up a dual-enrollment program with a local university for Mandarin and Arabic classes. Two outcasts whom he didn't know approached him in the hall. "Can you explain what the whole Chinese thing is about? Is it a class? Do I sign up?" Several other students asked him similar questions.

Noah explained the process. He added, "If you have any other questions, let me know. I'd be happy to talk with you." *Maybe it'll only be one or two people at a time,* he thought, *but hopefully, I'll come to be known by more people.*

In English, Noah noticed Bill, a wannabe jock, throwing a tissue into the recycling bin. Bill was a heavyset boy whom athletes harassed because he was on JV. "Hey, Bill, c'mon, read the sign," Noah protested. "We can't recycle those."

"Oh, sorry. I didn't realize it was such a 'big deal,'" Bill said, lifting the tissue from the bin.

"Well yeah, it's a big deal because the environment is important, and we're trying to start our new program. You know Adam? He's getting volunteer hours and bidding for our scholarship!"

"Whoa, really?" Bill seemed genuinely interested in hearing more.

At that point, two jocks put Bill in a headlock and gave him noogies. "Oooh, Bill's gonna be a tree-hugger! How gay are you?!" one of them said. Bill wasn't laughing.

Offended, Noah scowled at them. "All right guys, that's enough," he said. He tugged Bill from the headlock. Noah wasn't sure whether he interpreted correctly that the jocks glanced at him with a silent respect before they walked away.

"Thanks, Noah," Bill said as he dusted himself off.

"Bill, you shouldn't hang out with them. Seriously, they just bully you."

"But, like, we're teammates. Next year it'll be better!"

Noah couldn't remember the last time he had been bullied. Frederick had left him alone since the apology. In fact nobody had picked on him for anything—the band, his ethnicity—for months. Mostly when non-friends approached Noah these days, it was to ask him a question about recycling or the Chinese class. Soon, Noah had more than double the signatures he needed on the petition for the Chinese class, and Bill had joined the recycling club.

Within days, Bill backed out of the club, citing schedule conflicts. Noah was dispirited. "I just want to apologize for how my challenge has gone downhill," he told me. "I've been canvassing people at lunch, asking them to help, and it's just not working. They smile, they laugh with me, we get into discussion. I'm getting to know people, but they just don't show up to help."

Noah was certain he was failing his challenge because the number of recycling club members was not increasing significantly. He didn't realize that simply by mingling among various lunch tables, he was befriending people in different crowds, weaving together the fringes of the cafeteria.

DANIELLE, ILLINOIS | THE LONER

Danielle practiced her conversational skills frequently. At her Dairy Queen orientation, she chatted with Autumn, a trainee who had been on the softball team with her freshman year. Nikki had told Danielle that people didn't like Autumn. Nevertheless, Danielle asked her questions about homework.

"Why aren't you doing softball anymore?" Autumn asked her.

"I don't know. I didn't really like it, and Nikki told me [the coaches] said they wouldn't even let me try out, which I didn't believe, but I don't know . . ."

"She did? That's not true at all!"

Danielle hadn't been spending much time with her friends lately; they were busy, and Danielle wasn't itching to hang out with them. She continued to visit Viv once a week. She went to lunch with Trish again. They sometimes chatted on Facebook, but rarely ran into each other in school anymore.

Meanwhile, National Honor Society elections loomed. Danielle wasn't sure how to campaign. One day in the hall, she approached an emo from her sophomore year English class. "Soo. . . I'm running for Webmaster. Want to vote for me?"

"Oh, wow. That was really random," the girl responded.

"Oh, yeah . . . sorry," Danielle said, turning red. "I'm just trying to get votes."

She was surprised that some people were nice about telling her they would vote for her. As she put it, "Everyone I asked said they would vote for me. So I guess not *everyone* in high school is that bad."

In government, Danielle was assigned to partner with Logan, a senior, for a mini-discussion about civil liberties. Normally, after that type of task, Danielle would fall silent and return to her desk. But

Danielle figured she might as well practice talking with someone new, and she had a fallback conversation topic. By coincidence, her mother had recently learned through Facebook that Danielle's stepfather had grown up in a small Missouri town with Logan's mother. The conversation flowed smoothly enough, however, that Danielle didn't need to bring up the connection.

By mid-April, Danielle, too, was frustrated because she didn't think she had made any dramatic progress on her challenge. She was tentatively treading outside of her comfort zone, but felt as if she were taking one step forward and two steps back. "I want to come out of this with at least one good friend," she said. "Though I'm still not doing so hot in the friends area, I have gotten better at talking to people. I'll actually talk to a teacher instead of running away at the first opportunity, and I'll at least try to continue the conversation with people my age rather than falling silent. Unfortunately, as much as I may talk to someone in class, it doesn't seem like I'll ever hang out with them outside. I want to come out of this project less socially inept than I was before."

In Spanish, she partnered with Max, Bree, and Kristy for a game in which the teacher showed a student Spanish flashcards that she would have to describe so that her team could guess the accompanying vocabulary words. As they waited their turn, Danielle and her group tried to think of clues ahead of time.

Kristy brought up one of the vocabulary terms, the Spanish word for failure. "What do we say if the word is *el fracaso*?" she asked.

"Max," Danielle muttered to herself. When she joked, she did so quietly because she didn't think people usually got her sense of humor. It was too embarrassing when she said something she thought was funny and no one reacted.

The girls burst out laughing and Kristy gave Danielle a high five.

"You may laugh now, but I'm going to go home and cry," Max said, mock-hurt.

After their turn, Danielle's group watched the other students play. They saw the teacher flash "*el error*" at a student. Max looked at Danielle. "Max!" he said. Kristy and Bree laughed and high-fived Danielle again. The teacher kept glancing at Danielle's group. Danielle was delighted that, for once, she was part of "that group"—the students who disrupted the class because they couldn't stop talking.

When the National Honor Society held its vote for club officers, Danielle learned she was running for Webmaster unopposed. She was pleased to get the position, but slightly disappointed to win it automatically. She peeked around the room at students' ballots. People who didn't like her hadn't voted for her, even though she was the only candidate, but she noticed that some people whom she never talked to had voted for her. So that was something.

At the NHS luncheon celebrating the newly elected officers, Danielle was excluded once again. When she walked into the room, students were eating at tables pushed into a large square. Every other student had been on the NHS board since middle school. As they gossiped, seemingly all old friends, Danielle didn't say a word. She sat at a corner of the table, observed the group, and texted her mom. After lunch, the officers went outside to take photos. The group formed a large circle. Danielle was the only student outside of the circle, leaning against the wall.

One day, Max mentioned to Danielle that he was learning how to play tennis. "We're playing tennis sometime, okay?" he asked her.

"All right," she said.

Unsure whether Max was sincere, Danielle was hesitant to ask if he wanted to play at a specific time. Playing tennis would be an easy way to hang out with someone outside of school. *I can always make fun of him for sucking, so I won't have to struggle to think of something to say*, she thought. Max talked to her frequently now. Almost daily, he'd ask, "Hey, Danielle, how was your day?" Not even her friends asked her that. Another thing Danielle liked about Max was that he seemed to pay attention to her. She could tell Paige and Mona something fifty times and they still wouldn't remember. She could tell Max something once, and a week or two later he would bring it up.

The next day in Spanish class, Danielle casually leaned against her desk. She was nervous, even though she had overthought this interaction in advance. "Do you have volleyball today?" she asked Max.

"I have a game," he answered.

"Man, no one can play tennis today!" Danielle said.

"I might be able to around one," Max said. "Give me your number." Danielle ripped a piece of paper out of her notebook, scribbled her number, and handed it to him.

"Whoooaaa," said a student nearby.

Max kept a straight face. "Oh, yeah, we're dating," he said. Danielle cracked up. The idea of her dating Max was absurd. He was immature, she wasn't interested, and she was convinced she had commitment-phobia, in any case.

After school, Danielle waited for Max to call. By 1:30, she gave up. "That's another reason why I don't hang out with new people, or even my friends very often," she told me then. "I can't trust them to actually do what they say they will. So it really doesn't matter if it was hard or not to ask Max, because it didn't work out anyways."

This single incident caused Danielle to be dejected about her challenge once again, sure that there was no way she could make a new friend who would spend time with her outside of school. "I don't think people are ever that interested in talking to me, especially since most people have this preconceived notion that I'm a bitch," she said.

DANIELLE'S AND LOGAN'S MOTHERS had emailed back and forth for weeks. Because both families were going to be in Florida for spring break, they exchanged phone numbers. Logan's mother emailed that Logan wanted to hang out with Danielle. Danielle's mother nudged her to call, although Danielle hadn't called someone new in years. Danielle put it off.

The day before break, Danielle was in an English teacher's classroom, typesetting the accepted submissions for Stone Mill's literary magazine. Danielle was the only student who showed up to help. She was surprised to see that one of her submissions was given the highest possible score by the other student staff members. When her creative writing teacher had assigned the class to write a submission, Danielle had dashed off a poem about her dislike of poetry. And here it was, selected for publication. Unfortunately she had turned it in as "Untitled" by "Anonymous."

More than an hour after school let out, Danielle was still typing as the teacher reviewed other submissions. "I can take some of these with me to type over spring break, since I'm just going to be sitting around in Florida," she told the teacher.

The teacher looked up. "Really?! You wouldn't mind that?"

"No. I want to try to get tan, so I can just type the stuff while I'm sitting by the pool."

"That would be great!" the teacher said, then left the room for a moment. Danielle continued to type. When the teacher returned, she asked, "Would you like to be the editor next year?"

Danielle was stunned. She had always assumed that one of the two boys who attended every meeting and who had been in the club for much longer would be the new editor. "Oh, wow. Yeah, I would. But . . ." She was about to mention the boys, then thought better of it. "Uh, yeah, that would be cool."

Already, she had come a long way from freshman year, when she was too shy to join any clubs at all. Next year, she would be vice president of the snow team, a position the advisor had created just for her; a senior on the varsity tennis team; NHS Webmaster; and now the editor of the literary magazine. Not bad for someone who rarely talked.

In Florida, Danielle worked up the nerve to pick up the phone. She didn't know what to say. "Uh, hey, Logan, it's Danielle. Your mom said something in an email to my mom about you guys wanting to do something . . ."

"Yeah, we're going to the beach tomorrow if you want to come," Logan said. Just like that, Danielle had a planned outing.

When Logan and two other Stone Mill seniors picked up Danielle, Logan hopped in the back of the van to talk to her. Danielle recognized Juliana; she didn't know Tracy, who was driving. To Danielle's surprise, conversation flowed naturally about teachers and local restaurants. Even when the friends talked among themselves, sometimes Danielle chimed in.

At the beach, Danielle jumped waves with Tracy in chest-high water, while Logan and Juliana stood closer to shore. When Tracy said she wanted to swim out to touch the buoy, Danielle joined her. The afternoon passed quickly. The girls watched dolphins swimming by the pier, ate ice-cream cones, and shopped for souvenirs. On the ride home, Danielle again sat in the back with Logan. The conversation came naturally.

A skateboarder passed in front of the van. "I really want to learn to skateboard," said Danielle.

"Hah, why?" Logan asked.

"I snowboard a lot during the winter, so it seems like it would help me get better over the summer. Although I'm not really too crazy about the falling on the pavement and getting a bunch of cuts part. . . ." Danielle trailed off. "So do you know what you want to major in?"

"I don't know. I'm torn between two things. I really want to be a vet, but I also want to work with sharks."

"Working with sharks would be really cool!" Danielle said. She liked Logan even more now.

"How about you?"

"I'm stuck between two things also," said Danielle. "There are a lot of things I want to do actually, but the main ones are archaeology and medicine."

They talked about their parents and the book they had to read for government. Logan told Danielle to give her a call if she needed any help. When the seniors dropped Danielle off, Tracy thanked her for coming.

"Thanks for inviting me," Danielle replied. "Bye!" She hurried into her backyard, self-conscious about the girls watching her walk up to the house.

When she was out of sight, Danielle realized that she was proud of doing something social with new people. Maybe, Danielle thought, she wasn't as socially awkward as she had assumed. She wondered if she could muster the courage to hang out with Logan again. She didn't count the beach outing as part of her challenge because her mother had set it up.

Whitney, New York | The Popular Bitch

In Spanish, Shay asked Whitney, "Are you doing anything tonight?"

"Nah," Whitney said.

Shay spoke tentatively. "Could you work for me at the pool this week?" Shay and Whitney were lifeguards at the public pool. "I have choir practice."

The timing wasn't convenient, but Whitney figured she could use the extra money. "Yeah, of course," she said.

Chelsea watched the conversation carefully.

Whitney and Shay were growing closer. Shay helped Whitney with a speech assignment. When Shay pulled ahead of Whitney in the class rankings, instead of holding a grudge as she would have in the past, Whitney allowed herself to be genuinely happy for her.

For an economics group project, the teacher placed Whitney in a group with Shay, a loser, a punk girl, and a badass. Whitney asked their opinions and incorporated their ideas instead of snootily blowing them off as the old Whitney would have done. She tried to temper her bossiness, and she chatted about nonschool subjects like iPhones and baseball. The group shared ideas equally and ended up with the best presentation in the class. A week later, Whitney acknowledged all of her former groupmates in the halls. They said hello back. ("That's huge, trust me," Whitney said later.) When Whitney greeted them while standing with preps, the preps stared at her. She was certain that they disparaged her as soon as she walked away.

Whitney, Shay, and Chelsea were huddled at a table in the library, working on an English group project, when Bianca and Giselle walked in and sat on the couch. A few minutes later, Chelsea stood up and, without a word to her partners, joined Bianca and Giselle for the rest of the period. "Dude, what the fuck?!" Whitney vented. "That's so annoying." She began a tirade about Chelsea's selfishness. Chelsea had wormed her way into the preps' circle. She had been savvy enough not to try too hard, as Irene had. Chelsea, for example, knew better than to wear anklets as Bianca did.

"Calm down," Shay told her. "Let it go, it's not a big deal. She wasn't helping us anyway." Whitney liked that Shay didn't let minor matters bother her. Generally Whitney agreed with classmates' assessment of her as a melodramatic, high-strung girl. When she was with Shay, though, she felt more relaxed.

The next day, when Bianca and Giselle entered the library, Bianca yelled across the room, "Chelsea, you know you want to sit with us." Chelsea seemed thrilled that Bianca had gone out of her way to invite her over. The following day, as Whitney again worked with Shay on their project, out of the corner of her eye she saw Chelsea sneak into the library and bolt into the other room, where Bianca lounged with Steph.

Outside of the cafeteria, Whitney hadn't hung out with the preps as a group since February. The only Riverland students she socialized with after school were Giselle, Giselle's boyfriend, and Steph. Otherwise, she spent much of her free time with Luke. In school, Whitney was gradually branching out. In Spanish and speech classes, Whitney started to chat with Caroline, the emo who, when asked to write about something that annoyed her, chose to write about preps. The first time Whitney spoke to her, she pointed to Caroline's Bullet for My Valentine shirt. "I like them. Are they still touring in Europe this summer?" she asked.

Caroline eyed Whitney suspiciously as if to say, "Why are you acknowledging me?" When she realized Whitney was sincere, she answered, "I think so."

"Oh my God, [our Spanish teacher] is, like, so crazy," Whitney said, and told a story that made Caroline laugh. Over the next several weeks, Whitney made an effort to ask Caroline questions and smiled at her in the hallway. (Whitney stuck to "small gestures because she's emo, so she doesn't like people.")

For advertising class, Elizabeth and another wannabe were putting on a children's rock concert. The advertising teacher had asked Whitney to emcee the concert because of her charisma and because she didn't mind speaking in front of large groups.

When Whitney got to school Friday night, she helped Elizabeth iron tablecloths for a vendor's booth. As they waited for the audience to arrive, Whitney told Dirk about her latest fight with Giselle. Elizabeth and her partner came over to hear what Whitney was talking about. Realizing that she was upset, they sat down, listened to her, and offered advice. Whitney couldn't believe that girls who used to hate her were being compassionate. Dirk spent most of the night trying to convince Whitney to go to a punk party. Whitney declined. Partying didn't seem all that important anymore.

Later, another so-called loser initiated conversation with Whitney. In the past, Whitney would have shot her a why-are-you-talking-to-me look—or the girl would have waited for Whitney to deign to talk to her. Now Whitney engaged in the discussion, talking about school and the girl's crush on Dirk. In return, the girl smuggled over free cookies from another booth. As she waited to go onstage, Whitney played hangman with Dirk and Elizabeth. Preps wouldn't have been caught dead playing hangman. Or eating cookies.

ONE NIGHT, WHITNEY AND her mother were finishing up dinner before an honor society event. "I'm going to leave in, like, fifteen minutes to pick up Fern," Whitney said.

"You should call her before you leave," her mother replied. "While you're in the shower, I can do it."

"No, it's okay. I don't mind calling her house."

Whitney's mother put down her fork. "You know, I'm really proud of you and how much more grown up you've become this year. This is the most pleasant you've been basically since you were born."

As Whitney showered, she reflected on what her mother had said. She had not stopped to think that in the process of improving her social world, maybe she had also bettered herself. She hadn't realized that people would notice her efforts.

At the honor society event, students—mostly band kids and nerds—chatted in small circles backstage. Whitney stood in a circle with three band kids, listening to them talk about a concert. While she pretended to be interested, she saw Fern timidly approach a different circle, teeter on its perimeter, and then back away because no one thought to let her in. She tried another circle. Same deal. And another. Whitney's heart broke. She excused herself from her group and approached Fern. "Hey, so you pumped for college?" Whitney asked.

Fern looked pleased. "Yeah, I have family who live near there."

While they continued to chat, Whitney slowly herded Fern toward the band kids. Whitney stepped into the group and shifted to create an opening for Fern. As she included Fern in the conversation, the boys did too. The group talked until the ceremony began.

On the drive back, Whitney racked her brain for a topic for the twenty-minute ride to Fern's house. She settled on a girl who had been the meanest girl at Riverland before she transferred to Fern's old school. They talked about the girl the entire ride home. Whitney's stories made Fern laugh. Whitney had never seen Fern laugh before.

At an honor society meeting a few weeks later, Whitney noticed Fern sitting in her usual spot at the back of the room. "Fern! What are you doing?!" Whitney shrieked. "Get over here with us right now!" Fern beamed as she sat down with Whitney and the rest of the group.

————

WHY SCHOOL UNIFORMS DON'T ERASE CLIQUES

Some schools have attempted to ease clique tensions, such as those at Riverland, by requiring school uniforms, to create the illusion of sameness among the student population. Students I interviewed, however, said that uniforms don't work. "There's still pressure to act and look a certain way," said a senior at an all-girls school in Arizona. "If you don't have the new Vera Bradley design as your backpack, or you're not wearing the cutest flats or the cool Vans, then you're not popular. People spend crazy amounts of money on their shoes, backpacks, and designer earrings. The uniforms were supposed to stop girls from spending too much time worrying about clothes or what they look like, but [they] do just the opposite."

In a study of a Southern middle school's incentive-based voluntary uniform policy, within the first three weeks the number of students wearing uniforms dropped from 70 percent to less than 40 percent. Eventually fewer than a fifth of the students complied, and even then, mostly on days the school rewarded them for it. At many schools with uniform policies, shoes and accessories end up playing the same roles as clothing does at non-uniform schools. "The people who don't care wear Birkenstocks (I do)," said a Florida senior. "If you wear fake Uggs, you get made fun of. If you wear other boots, you get made fun of. And if you wear black boots, you get looked at weird."

If students experience such a strong urge to conform, then why do they resist standardized clothing? The answer returns us to the battle between the group and the individual, the dichotomy of hoping to stand out yet striving to blend in. As writer-performer Quentin Crisp wrote in his 1968 autobiography, *The Naked Civil Servant*, "The young always have the same problem—how to rebel and conform at the same time. They solve this problem by defying their parents and copying one another." Although people conform as a way to belong to a group, they nonetheless want that group to seem unique and special. This need to be distinct from other groups can even overtake the desire for a positive group image, which may partly explain why some cliques pride themselves on being mean.

You've seen this phenomenon before. Popular students might stop using catchphrases once nerds adopt them, celebrities move on to new designer denim when trickle-down versions arrive on discount-store racks. Men are less likely to order a small steak when it is labeled a "ladies' cut." British fashionistas deserted Burberry caps once they became ubiquitous among soccer hooligans.

A basic tension exists between the opposing drives for similarity and distinction. According to marketing professor Jonah Berger, "People resolve [this tension] by defining themselves in terms of distinctive category memberships. When people feel overly similar, their renewed need for individuation drives them to emphasize distinctive group memberships (e.g., band member rather than Plainsville High student); when people feel excessively different, they emphasize broad, generic social category memberships (e.g., Plainsville High student rather than Chess Club member). Membership in small groups allows people to feel similar and different at the same time: similar because they are part of a group and different because the group is separate from the masses." Freud referred to the hostilities that can arise from the perceptions of some of these smaller distinctions as "the narcissism of minor differences."

The social process that results from this need for distinction is called divergence. Except in the case of perceived upward mobility, groups generally don't want to be mistaken for one another. Scene kids don't want to be misidentified as preps. Geeks aren't interested in mimicking the punks. Even as Bianca insisted the preps conform to her fashion standards, she wore anklets as a way to distinguish herself.

In an intriguing divergence experiment at Stanford, Berger and his team distributed yellow Livestrong wristbands to freshmen in a target dorm and a control dorm. They told the students it was "wear yellow" month and asked them to wear the bracelet in the upcoming weeks in support of cancer awareness. One week later, the team made the same request of students in a reputed geek dorm located near the target group. During the week after the geeks began wearing the wristbands, 32 percent of the students in the target dorm abandoned the trend, as opposed to only 6 percent of the students in the control dorm, which was on a separate part of campus. Berger's other divergence studies yielded similar results.

The reputation of a low-status group can have a reverse halo effect, or forked-tail effect, on the trends it adopts; because the dorm was considered geeky, its geekiness spread to wristband wearing. Notice that the effect didn't go both ways. The geeks were happy to wear wristbands, even though the target dorm had been wearing them for a week. Berger didn't interview the geeks, but, he said, people "may want to be treated like members of other groups and, to reach this goal, may poach the cultural tastes of those groups." Or maybe the geeks cared more about the cause than about the superficial image of the trend.

REGAN, GEORGIA | THE WEIRD GIRL

From the middle of the crowd, Regan watched Crystal's band perform its last show before Regan left Georgia. As she listened to her girlfriend rap, Regan already missed her. After a year of dating, Regan and Crystal thought of each other as spouses. They planned to conduct their relationship long-distance until Regan returned from Bangladesh, at which point both of them hoped to move to the East Coast. "We can make it through anything because we can tell one another the truth," Regan said.

Regan knew that Crystal loved every bit of her, quirks and all. Once, Crystal had written Regan a list entitled, "100 Reasons Why I Love Regan." Crystal happened to list many of the same qualities that Johnson teachers had made fun of: Regan's refusal to drink, for example, her "love and respect for all living things," her intelligence, her honesty, her independence, her vegetarianism, her creativity, her feistiness, her self-pride, her ability to be profound one minute, silly the next, the inner strength she called upon to stand up for what she believed in, even her love of dinosaurs.

"You're so sure of yourself," Crystal wrote. "You're always ready to take the lead. I adore that about you. I love that you are open-minded alongside strong convictions. You stay true to what you believe. You aren't afraid to tell me straight up. I love that you have the most vivacious personality I have ever come across. I love that you're going to Bangladesh to stand up for something that matters. It's beautiful that you want to live as they live and learn outside of what 'us' Americans are used to. . . . Regan, I would actually give you the world if it was mines."

Crystal took the mic and announced the next song. Regan gave the stage her full attention. Crystal had told Regan in advance that this new song was about her. As the lyrics unfolded, Regan melted with love and pride. Crystal had captured Regan in lyrics, poetically summarizing some of the items from her list and even throwing in a Shakespearean reference. The song expressed something that Crystal had told Regan often: What Crystal loved most about her was her individuality and the way that she followed her heart.

The song meant a lot to Regan. "When I was a teenager, I had a hard time with people wondering why I didn't want to take the easier path," Regan said later. "Only as I've grown older have I found that people find this characteristic attractive. I think it's mostly because most people *don't* follow their hearts. Most people do what is expected of them; most people take the path well-traveled, just to get by. Now, in the adult world, when someone meets me, they tend to admire me because I know what I want, I know who I am, and I *go* for it. Every day when I wake up, I know that my dreams are just beginning." It did not escape Regan—to whom I had not yet explained quirk theory—that the precise qualities that caused people to exclude her in the school setting were the same ones that people admired outside of it.

DURING LAST PERIOD, WYATT knocked on Regan's office door. "Got a minute?" he asked. He plopped down in a chair. "So what's the plan?"

"I'm going to live with my parents for the summer. Then I'll be in Bangladesh for three months. Then grad school." She bustled back and forth from the printer to her desk.

"Where are you going?" he asked.

"Well, I don't want to say I don't want to teach anymore because that's not true. But I don't want to be in public education, I guess. So I found this place for community-based education. Sex education." Regan hoped to work with small organizations to teach students about sexuality, date rape, and other important issues.

"Where did *this* come from?"

Regan sat down. "When I was in undergrad, I almost switched my major to human sexuality. Then I took this education class that talked about everything that's wrong with the system, and I thought, 'I have to be part of the change.'" She scoffed, mocking her idealism.

"So what happened?" he asked.

"This place."

"Yeah," Wyatt said. "I get that. I just had a racial issue the other day. And I heard about your issue with [the movie]."

Regan rolled her eyes. "The whole thing is just so stupid. Someone came up to me and flat-out said, 'People don't like you.' It's ridiculous to have someone say that to you. So now, what, I go to work every day, worried about who hates me?"

"I don't think anyone hates you, Davis. I think the problem people have with you is that you're . . . Well, you put yourself in the front of the class, so to speak. You've got a personality. And you don't try to hide it, and you don't try to please anyone, and people just don't get that. I mean, you came into school with bright red hair, you've made some odd decisions. People can't understand it."

"I get that," Regan said. "It's been that way my entire life. Do you

think this is something new to me? Because it's not. I'm just disappointed that at the end of the day, it's adults acting like this."

"Do you really think that anyone in our department could be classified as an adult?"

"No," Regan said. "That's what's scary to me. It's gotten to the
point that I don't trust anyone. I hate to say this, but talking to you
right now, all I'm thinking is, 'Who's he gonna tell?' And I think that's
awful. That's not the kind of place I want to work at."

"Hey. Are we past that?" he asked.

She couldn't meet his eyes. "Yeah," she said, but she wasn't sure.
"Yeah, you know me: overcome, adapt, improvise. I get over things."
She tried to change the subject. "I just don't need people going around
talking about me when they don't even know me. You know, I had a
student tell me that someone said they didn't like me."

Wyatt shook his head, knowing Regan referred to Mandy. "Jesus.
You've got to be kidding me. She didn't."

"Oh, she did," Regan said and explained the story. "I think I'm a
pretty good person and I don't go out to hurt anyone, so I don't know
why people want to hurt me."

"She's the school bully," Wyatt said. "She feeds off of fear. She
makes herself known by scaring people."

"I'm not *scared* of her," Regan said. "I just don't like what she does."

"She doesn't know what she's doing."

"How can she not? How can she look in the mirror and not see
that she's awful? Did you hear about what happened at that faculty
meeting?"

He rolled his head back and looked at the ceiling. "Yes. We got
into a fight over that."

"What?!"

"She told me how Theodore mistook her for you, and how she
screamed at him. And I said to her, 'What is *wrong* with you?' She was
like, 'What do you mean? She's a bitch.' And I said, 'No, *you're* a bitch.
She's done nothing to you.' That's when I realized that girl is *poison-
ous*. I told her, 'I want nothing to do with you.' I don't want people to
associate me with her."

When Regan recovered from her surprise, she said, "I just don't get it. I mean, in this little competition she has with me that's in her head, didn't she win?"

"No, she didn't. How did she win?" he asked. Before Regan could answer, he continued, "You're prettier. You're younger. You have more going for you. Her insecurities make it impossible for her to see that she's just jealous of you. It's easier to call you a bitch than to own up to her own issues."

Regan nodded, speechless, as Wyatt continued. "That's how the end of she and me sort of started. I started thinking, with you it was easy. It made sense from the get-go." He looked up toward Mandy's floor. "She's poison."

Regan fiddled with paper, moving it from her desk to her lap and back again.

"But us? We're good?" Wyatt asked.

"I, um," Regan stuttered, tears pooling in her eyes before she could stop them. Wyatt grabbed a box of tissues. "I'm going to hate myself for saying this later, but it's just that before, I couldn't take you seriously when you were with her."

They sat in silence, neither one making eye contact.

"I think I really needed to hear that," Wyatt said. "Talking to you, I realize I should've come straight to the source all along, instead of listening to everyone else. Our department is messed up. It's so divided." Wyatt checked his watch and stood up. It was two minutes until the bell. "Hey, Davis," he said before he left, "it was good talking to you. Oh, hey, are you friends with Cesar on Facebook?"

"Yeah."

"Well, he's been Mandy's source, just so you know, about stuff about you. Do you have naked pictures up there?"

"What? On Facebook? I'm friends with my *dad* on Facebook."

He shrugged. "Well, that's what I heard, that's all. That's what's going around." Wyatt closed the door.

BLUE, HAWAII | THE GAMER

Blue was more content than he could ever remember. Not only did he now have an interesting, playful, caring group of friends who liked spending time with him, but, more significantly, he had found his connection. Blue believed that Michael complemented him perfectly and Michael said he felt the same. Michael admired Blue's edginess, innovation, calmness, dedication, optimism, and sense of fun. Blue admired Michael's discipline, stability, aspirations, and focus.

One day when they were driving to the beach, Blue asked Michael, "Can you do me a massive favor?"

"Mmhmm, sure."

"Can you bribe me somehow to do my homework?" Blue asked. He was a month behind in English. "I can't bring myself to do any of it. I have no idea why."

"Okay. What did you have in mind?"

"I don't know. You choose."

"I'm not good at choosing!" Michael protested. "You're the fun person here, the idea guy, remember?"

"But I think it'd be better if you chose."

"Fine. Let me think." After a few minutes, Michael said, "How about this: I'll take you out somewhere nice for dinner. Like a real date."

Blue scrunched his face. "Lame. That kind of stuff isn't important to me."

"Ugh." Michael was silent for another few minutes. "Okay, how about this: I'll come out to AP Gov only if you do your homework."

Blue leaned back in amazement. "Oh, oh, ohhh. You're pretty slick. Pretty crafty. Wow, that's a sick deal. Thanks."

Blue pulled an all-nighter and nearly caught up on all of his homework. Homework felt like unimportant busywork compared to the hours he was putting into preparation for SCH. He savored the chance to share his perspectives, to connect the dots of politics, economics, social science, and abstract philosophy, to show that he was much more intelligent than his grades reflected.

Increasingly, "the smart kids" turned to him for help. Blue was able to grasp SCH's complex concepts more instinctively than the valedictorians. Gradually, Blue's paternal instinct kicked in. He soothed internal gripes among team members. When they tried to exclude a devout Christian teammate, Blue made them stop talking about her behind her back and welcomed her warmly to the team. The others followed suit. They constantly told him "You're the only mature one of us" because he never gossiped, and they admired him for it. He emailed pep talks to bolster the team's enthusiasm for nationals and organized meetings and deadlines for their preparation. He set up a Wiki and a Facebook page through which the group regularly shared ideas. He spent much of his free time reading works that would help their presentation, such as Slovenian philosopher Slavoj Zizek's writings, the Federalist Papers, and notes on every major political debate of the 1850s.

Ms. Collins told Blue that she wanted the team to distinguish itself from those of other states by demonstrating that original, independent analysis was important for the health of the country. The team didn't expect to place because it was so small. A win for Team Hawaii, she said, would entail upsetting some of the judges by challenging traditional thought, rather than telling them what they wanted to hear. She told Blue she was counting on him to make it happen.

Meanwhile Blue held weekly AP Gov parties at his house. As his friendships deepened, even Blue's mother couldn't lower his spirits. She didn't talk about college anymore. She told him that he would work at McDonald's and live on the streets. She didn't believe that the Undergraduate Assistance Program was real. He hadn't bothered to tell her he had made it to the final admissions round.

Blue was already skittish about the looming interview. "I'm so scared I won't get into college," he said. Except for English and French, he had As and Bs.

The night before the interview, Blue stayed up late reading political and philosophical books, taking notes for SCH arguments. Blue's interview happened to be scheduled at the same time his teammates had a practice run-through with the state judges. He wanted to make sure they were ready. At 4 A.M., he noticed that three teammates were online. He asked them if they needed help, then guided them through their work. When one girl seemed to be struggling, he called her. She told him she was having family issues. He spent the rest of the night writing her answers so that she could get some sleep.

At 5 A.M., too excited to doze, Blue brewed coffee and finalized his

UAP materials, printing extra copies of his financial forms and personal essay. At 7 A.M., he stopped by school to say hello to his teammates. He handed out $150 worth of social science books he had
bought for them and explained how each book related to their units.
They wished him luck, but nobody thought he needed it. Blue was
now the team leader of a group of Kaloke's smartest students.

Blue walked into the interview room. The woman who had passed
him through to this round wasn't there. He sat in front of a conserva-
tively dressed middle-aged woman, a twentysomething woman, and
a burly man. After they read his essay, they fired questions at him:
"What is UAP?" "Name the three requirements a student agrees to in
the program." He nailed these.

Then the younger woman asked, "Do you have a significant other?"
How is this relevant? Blue decided to be honest. "Yes," he answered.

"What's her name?"

Blue paused. "Uhh . . ."

"You don't need to give me her name if you don't want to."

"No, it's just . . ." Blue took a breath. "Well, his name is Michael."

All three interviewers raised their eyebrows. "Is he okay with coed
dorms?" one asked.

"Yes."

"Have you guys talked about it? There's no issue with that at all?"

"No, it's a total non-issue," Blue said, laughing mildly to show he
was comfortable.

Then they asked bland questions that anyone could have answered.
Blue had been prepared for challenging inquiries that would give him
a chance to let these interviewers into his mind. He grew antsy as they
reread his essays and asked him questions only about his mother. In
answer to the essay prompt, "Explain how your family will support
your participation in UAP," Blue had written that his mother wanted
him to join the military. Blue's essays were completely candid, at the
advice of his guidance counselor. Ms. Pierce had told him to explain
how he was different from other students as well as the reasons behind
his predicament. He wrote about his mother's refusal to pay for his
schooling, and his peace with that. Emotionally, he wrote, "the support

will come from my own personal support group I have surrounded myself with. People who bring me up in life, and not down. These people include Ms. Collins and my newfound circle of friends from AP Gov."

"Does your mother want you to go to college or not?" the older woman asked.

"She's all for it, as long as I can pay for it myself."

The interviewers seemed to think this was an impossible task. They asked him which scholarships he was applying for, and drilled him on how he would survive college without a supportive parent. The man asked blunt questions about the nature of the $200,000 in investments listed on Blue's financial forms, which suggested that Blue's mother could afford to pay for college; she simply didn't want to.

"You do understand that we need full parental support on this, don't you?" the man asked.

"Yes, I do, but my mom—"

"Well, I don't know," the man interrupted. "Your mom needs to get on board with this for it to work out."

Hopeless, Blue began to shut down. They hadn't even cared about his essay. When the man handed him the yellow piece of paper, Blue forced himself to say "Thank you," and left the room, numb. In the bathroom, he splashed cold water onto his face, trying to ward off tears.

On the drive back to school, Blue thought about getting into a car accident, hunting for an excuse for his inability to get into college. He felt the shadow of his dark period from earlier in the year creep over him.

He called Ms. Collins, who answered her phone, excited. "How was it?" she asked.

"I, uh . . ." Blue's voice cracked. "I didn't make it."

Ms. Collins' voice changed instantly. "Oh my God. I didn't expect that. Are you okay?"

In the background, Blue could hear his AP Gov classmates reacting with surprise.

"I don't know," Blue said.

"Okay, just come here and we can talk about it."

When he walked into the classroom, his eyes were moist. Everyone else looked sad. Michael looked like he had been crying. Blue lay his head on a desk. He felt like his only chance at college—and the rest of his life—was gone. Leilani and Kaia hugged him tightly.

On the way to Ms. Pierce's office, Blue stopped by the lunchroom to see Ty and Stewart. As soon as he approached, they made fun of him.

"How's the butt sex?!" Stewart called out.

"Ew, don't touch me; you're gay," said Ty.

Blue did an about-face and walked away.

After meeting with his counselor, who was baffled as to why he had been rejected, Blue returned to Ms. Collins' classroom. He sat there, head down, and slept through the rest of his classes, tallying his first unexcused absences of the semester.

Late Spring to Early Summer

Popular vs. Outcast

Chapter 12

POPULARITY DOESN'T LEAD TO HAPPINESS

Whitney was sitting next to the preps when Chelsea said loudly to Bianca, "Hey, Bianca, I have some new information for you."

"Yeah, I got your message last night. That's some juicy stuff," Bianca replied.

"I know. I had to do some research before I found out it was true, but it totally is."

"I can always count on you as my little source of gossip about everything," Bianca said.

Madison leaned over. "Giselle, we have to talk to you about something later."

As Whitney watched her former friends talk over her, she realized that by befriending non-preps, she had become one. Until now, she had been optimistic enough to believe that she could become a floater yet still maintain her ties to the preps. Later that day, Whitney tried one more time to sit with the preps, who discussed Seth's and Spencer's prom after-party. "Too many people want to come," Seth said. "It has to be totally exclusive and only people who are invited can be let in. I made a guest list." He tossed the list onto the table and the preps looked it over. Everyone at the table was invited except for Whitney. The group continued to talk about the party in front of her.

What the fuck?! Whitney thought, stricken. *I used to be like that?!* She could understand now where Caroline was coming from. The preps *were* annoying. Still, she remained at the table as her friends discussed the party. She couldn't believe that her group was so obviously rejecting her. "I'm used to being a co-queen bee of the clique and I'm used to doing this to other girls," she said later. "It's eye-opening. They're notorious for blatantly talking about an outing in front of you even if you weren't invited. I de-cliqued myself from that group. I'm just another one of their victims now. I didn't realize how shitty-like we treat people until I'm being treated like that."

Outside of school, Whitney was again spending time with Dirk, who had introduced her to a bunch of his friends. Even Giselle had started going with Whitney to punk parties. In the cafeteria, Whitney usually sat with Shay, Grace, and the other band kids. She often talked to Fern, who had undergone a significant transformation.

In Spanish class, when Fern cracked a loud, sarcastic joke, students were surprised.

"Whoa, Fern!" said Shay. "You're totally coming out of your shell!"

"You say what you think now!" added Grace. "We like this new Fern!" Other classmates agreed.

As Fern giggled, Whitney realized that Fern had changed people's perception of her. Only a couple of months ago, she was seen as a loser who sat alone in corners. Then Whitney was her only friend for a time. Now Fern was interacting with people, making witty remarks to teachers, and sitting with the rest of the group at honor society meetings. People knew she existed.

A few days later, in speech class, Caroline suddenly stood up and ran out of the room. The preps in the class laughed at the emo.

That afternoon, Whitney saw Caroline in the hall. "Are you okay?" she asked.

"No." Caroline buried her head in her locker.

"I'm sorry," Whitney said.

Caroline sighed. She told Whitney about her awful home life.

Whitney tried to console her. "Well, you know my mom deals with that kind of stuff, so you might want to go talk to her," Whitney said.

"Thanks, Whitney." Caroline smiled gratefully. Whitney again couldn't believe how easy it was to talk to someone who used to hate her.

In seventh period, Whitney, Giselle, and Bianca finished their work early and wandered around the building. On the way to the library, Whitney saw Dirk walking upstairs. Before Giselle and Bianca noticed, she slipped away and followed him to the senior lounge.

At first, she and Dirk were the only ones in the room. Eventually a crowd of punks, badasses, and losers streamed in. When the room filled, Whitney was intimidated. She wondered if the others were thinking, "What is *she* doing here?!" Gradually, Whitney realized that they were funny and nice and laughed at her jokes. She had a much better time than she would have had with Bianca and Giselle, especially now that Bianca realized that she had no control over Whitney anymore. Whitney spent seventh period with that group for the rest of the school year.

Whitney was sure "the old Whitney" was gone. She considered herself officially de-cliqued. She felt more independent. She wore hippie clothes to school without worrying about what other people said. She talked to whomever she pleased. "I'm just myself now," she said later. "It feels so good!"

She enjoyed her friendship with Dirk, which garnered her an unexpected benefit: Because she had more fun in advertising, she had done extra work and landed a major advertising internship. "This is making me a better person," she said. "I don't feel confined anymore. I have one best friend, Luke, one really close friend, Giselle, and then a huge variety of different kinds of friends. And I'm learning things from all of them in different ways." Shay had taught her to relax and to be less dramatic, Dirk had taught her that even the most mundane things could be fun, and Fern was teaching Whitney to be grateful. "I always thought my littlest problems were the biggest things ever," Whitney said, "but she helped me to stop taking the things I have for granted."

————

IS POPULARITY WORTH IT?

The first week I started following Whitney, she mentioned that when it came to popularity, "you need to know how to play the game."

When I asked her how to play, she rattled off four steps to gaining and retaining popularity.

1) *Befriend the "right" people.* Whitney explained, "To be popular, you have to make the right friends early because it's so hard to transition friends. The game is basically do whatever it takes, deal with the bullshit and pain, and in the end you'll feel like it was all worth it when you're popular."

2) *Do what the popular kids do.* "I followed a role model. When I was in eighth grade, she was a senior and the most popular girl in school. I joined all of the clubs and sports she did. I tried to live my high school years like she did."

3) *Conform.* "To remain popular, you have to lose all your individuality. Individuals are 'weird' in high school. Every clique has a leader. Your job is to do everything the leader wants. I know from being a past leader that we thrive [on] worshipping. It makes our egos huge and [makes us] feel like we own the other people in the group. Don't disagree with the leader, don't reprimand them, and just do what they want. And do not, by any means, do something to make them mad."

4) *Sacrifice.* "In cliques, it's all about sucking up to the selfish people. I volunteer to be the driver because when I'm not the driver, I'm usually forgotten about. If you don't put yourself out there to the queen bee, you won't go anywhere unless she has a reason to take you. You need to be willing to sacrifice a lot to fit in and be accepted."

At the time, Whitney was blinded by the superficial perks of popularity. She couldn't see that each of the aspects of her social life that made her unhappy—distancing from Luke, being prohibited from befriending punks, wearing clothes that reflected her clique instead of herself—corresponded to the rules she insisted were worth following in order to be popular.

But were they?

In the 1990s, UCLA scientists conducted a fascinating experiment on twelve groups of vervet monkeys. They removed the alpha males from each group and randomly selected one of the two remaining subordinate males to inject with a drug that would increase the activity of serotonin in his brain. In every case, that monkey changed his behavior and rose in social status to become the dominant male in the group. Separately, other researchers observed that in natural settings, rhesus monkeys with high levels of serotonin were more likely to participate in grooming with peers and lived closer to a larger number of other monkeys. In short, the monkeys with the most serotonin activity became popular.

Based on the results of these studies, psychopharmacologists decided to test a similar hypothesis on humans. Teams of researchers administered to volunteers a drug to increase serotonin levels, then monitored them during a puzzle-based task with a partner. The treated individuals demonstrated an increase in "socially affiliative" behaviors, such as dominant eye contact and clear communication. More recent studies have also reported that administration of a selective serotonin reuptake inhibitor (SSRI) "can modify social status." In 2009, Michigan State University professor S. Alexandra Burt discovered that a region of a particular gene was associated with popularity ratings of teenage boys (in experimental settings), leading her to conclude that genetics may play a part in popularity, at least when it comes to the serotonin link.

The directions and findings of these experiments might lead a layperson to wonder whether scientists theoretically will have the capability to develop a popularity drug. But the more important questions are: If they do, would you take it? Would you give it to your kids?

It may be difficult to perceive all of the downsides of popularity when you are in the midst of it, but they can be pervasive, overpowering, and downright dangerous. According to a team of psychologists in Los Angeles, "popularity can incorporate notable risks for development. For example, popular youths tend to experience increases in relational and overt aggression over time." Several researchers report that students who are popular and involved in either form of aggression are less likely to do well in school. In these studies, as elementary school and high school students became more popular, their unexplained absences from school increased and their GPAs declined. Because this aggression includes not only physical fights but also the rumors, backstabbing, and mind games that seem to be commonplace among teens, one might wonder what the difference is between populars who deal with these things and populars who don't. The difference comes down to students' intentions, which brings us back to the distinction between being liked and being perceived as popular.

If a student's social aim is to build close friendships, then she is more likely both to have a positive attitude about school and to perform well. But the perceived popular student involved in aggression, according to psychologists, probably has another social goal: one of dominance, or having power over classmates. That focus is "likely to lead to disruptive and off-task behavior and low achievement," observed University of South Florida professor Sarah Kiefer. This connection is especially strong for girls and for white students. Interacting with one aggressive friend outside of the clique doesn't automatically lead to poorer academic performance. But when school disengagement is part of the popular group standard, the group, directly or indirectly, will push its members to follow that road.

This point raises another disadvantage of popularity: the pressure. The time and energy it takes to be popular—socializing in and outside of school, throwing or attending parties and other events, simply being, as explained in chapter 2, visible—not only detracts from school pursuits, but also can become a clique mandate. Bianca tried to pressure Whitney to go to a party even though she had walking pneumonia. The preps instilled a belief that people who weren't out on a weekend night were losers.

Popular students told me they felt intense pressure to change themselves. "I wanted to date a 'normal' and my friends told me, 'To date a normal is to be a normal,' so I let a good opportunity pass me by," said a popular Southern student now in college. Pressured by his clique to be aggressive and manipulative, he spiked a football player's drink with steroids, then told his coach to test him for drugs. "We crushed dreams by mocking them to death. There was a girl who was a very good poet but she had flirted with my friend's boyfriend, so we stole her poems and read them aloud at lunch and laughed [even when] she started crying. I regret being so mean because that's not the person I truly am," he says now.

For Brigitte, a popular Canadian, the pressure focused on her looks. "My weight is never good enough for any of my friends. I go to bed mad at myself for eating," she said. "I was talking with one of my best friends and we were reminiscing about the first time she saw me. She said, 'I remember seeing you and you were sooo pretty, I knew I had to be friends with you. Then we took you out with us, you drank a lot, the guys loved you, and we knew you were in.' Then she said, 'Why is it that all pretty people are friends? Like, do you think that if I was ugly you'd be friends with me?' And I honestly responded to her, 'Probably not.'"

An Illinois football player was able to hide from the rest of the populars the fact that he wore glasses—until his gym class had to go swimming. For as long as he wore glasses, his clique shunned him. "Deep down, I know it's wrong to be in a group that is convinced they are so exclusive and important. Deep down, I know that who you hang out with should not be decided by money, looks, skills, or background. Deep down, I wish I could change some of the relationships I've made with people over the years," he said.

Popular cliques are more likely to be characterized with negative traits than are other groups. Experts have linked popularity to "involvement in risky behaviors during adolescence, including sexual experimentation and alcohol use." Well, sure. If popularity involves parties, and many parties include sex and alcohol, then it makes sense that the students who go to the most parties are the people who will be more likely to engage in "risky behavior." Three of Brigitte's best friends have been hospitalized for drug use. The populars constantly tried to pressure Whitney to smoke pot; the one time they succeeded, Whitney felt horrible about herself. When Whitney refused, they either made fun of her or alienated her.

Students who are willing to play the game—to tolerate the aggression, to de-prioritize their school involvement, to deal with pressure to engage in risky behavior, and to chip away at their individuality—may nevertheless find their tenure at the top of the popularity chain to be short. Resentful wannabes could bring them down. Or their own clique could build them up and cast them out, as the preps did to the twins, Irene, and, finally, Whitney.

By the end of the school year, Whitney had changed her mind about whether playing the game was worth the status. She said in May,

"The biggest thing I want to make readers understand is that being popular isn't all it's cracked up to be. They shouldn't strive to be a part of the clique. They should strive to do what I'm doing now and be friends with everyone and be neutral. Like, I'm so much happier now without the pressure to conform. And I can just say no now: No, Luke won't buy you guys beer again; no, I won't change my shirt because we're wearing the same one, Bianca; no, I won't smoke pot with you guys; no, I won't cut that person up behind their back."

As Whitney came to realize, the primary problem with being a popular high school student, even with all of its perks—some classmates will do your bidding; you may be invited to more parties; you might find your fashions meticulously copied, your actions obsequiously praised; you can sit at a prime spot in the cafeteria; you might even be treated, as Whitney said to me after one party, "like a mini-celebrity"—is that high school ends.

REGAN, GEORGIA | THE WEIRD GIRL

As Regan tossed the remains of her lunch into the garbage, she could hear the history department having its last cookout. She grimaced as the teachers shouted about hot dogs outside her office window.

Delilah caught up to Regan on her way back to class. "I have been looking all over for you!" she shouted.

"What's wrong? You good?"

"I ate lunch with history," Delilah said, a twisted grin on her face. "And your name came up."

"Oh God. Lemme guess—"

"Mandy." Delilah relayed that Mandy had told the group Regan should be fired. Apparently, Mandy hadn't heard that Regan was leaving Johnson of her own accord.

That's it, Regan steamed. *I'm done with this.* She typed a quick memo to Mandy's administrator, asking to speak with him. During her planning period, Regan met the administrator in a break room. "Look," she began, "I want to start this off by saying I'm not a tattletale. That's just not me."

"I already don't like where this is going."

"I'm sorry," she said, embarrassed.

"No, no, it's okay. Go 'head."

Regan settled her nerves. *I don't know if I'm doing the right thing or not,* she thought. *I'm extremely conflicted karma-wise.* "I'm having some issues with a history teacher," she said.

"I can narrow this down to . . . oh, one."

"Yeah," she said. "I'm not worried about me. I don't care. What I'm afraid of is, well, I'm leaving, and if it's in her personality to be mean, then she's going to find someone else to pick on. And if she's going to do that, then I want a record to exist to prove that it's a pattern." Regan listed Mandy's multiple acts of alternative aggressions.

The administrator, seemingly unsurprised by what he called Mandy's unprofessionalism, said he would look into the matter and talk to the principal. By the final week of school, nothing had been done about it.

On the last day of the academic year, at the bell, one of Regan's classes lined up by the door so that students could hug her on the way out of the classroom, risking being late to their next class. Throughout the day, kids sought her out, asking frantically, "Is it true that you're leaving?!" and embracing her tightly.

Regan loved the students, the material, and the teaching itself, but her experience with the Johnson teachers and administrators was enough to drive her out of the field. "I discovered during my three years as a public school teacher that teenagers need more than what they get in schools, and because of bureaucracy and financial issues, they're not getting it," she said.

Regan returned to her office to finish cleaning up. She took down the student artwork that she had plastered on her walls. She removed the poster she'd made with her favorite quotes, like "When the power of love overcomes the love of power, the world will know peace" (Jimi Hendrix), and "You never really understand a person until you consider things from his point of view, until you climb into his skin and walk around in it" (*To Kill a Mockingbird*). She detached the magnets she had affixed to her file cabinet; one said LOVE, another said MAKE A DIFFERENCE.

Regan wondered how many teachers like her, beloved by students, had left teaching because of intolerant schools. She closed her eyes for a moment and wiped away the tears.

When Regan read the teacher evaluation forms that students had filled out, she saw that her ratings were excellent. Most students gave her top marks. In answer to the question "Do you trust this teacher?", one student responded, "I'd trust Ms. Davis with my *life*." Regan would miss her students fiercely.

"Ms. Davis is truly the best teacher I have had at Johnson since I been here, and I am truly going to miss her so much next year," a senior wrote. Regan smiled and read the rest of the notes.

- Ms. Davis, I love you. She's the best lady in the whole wide world.
- Ms. Davis is a real cool teacher. You always know the right words to say. Your teacher skills really rock. Thanks for being a really cool person, the best teacher ever, and a big inspiration.
- Ms. Davis is the MASTER of Lit. No one could teach it better than her.
- Ms. Davis is the sweetest, most nicest teacher in the world. I learned a lot with and from her. PS: I love this class.
- Ms. Davis is my favorite teacher. I trust Ms. Davis. I see people tell her personal things about them, and I never see Ms. Davis running off and telling other people. I know she would keep my issues secret.
- Alright man. You are like the freakin' best teacher of LIFE. You accept people's thoughts and take things into consideration. You're very open and expressive, and I think that's purrrty cool. I've had a lot of fun in your class this semester.
- Ms. Davis is an awesome teacher. So far, she has been my favorite. She has fun activities and teaching methods, and she also interacts with her students openly. She has inspired me in many ways.

Once again, Regan was praised for qualities that caused her contemporaries at school to exclude her. She *had* made a difference, she realized, to the people who mattered to her the most. And tomorrow was the beginning of another dream.

BLUE, HAWAII | THE GAMER

Blue was in limbo. Ms. Pierce asked the UAP committee members to reconsider, given Blue's special circumstances. They refused. To escape his uncertainty about the future, Blue continued to throw himself wholeheartedly into preparation for the Simulated Congressional Hearings. When he was alone, he distracted himself by reading books on philosophy. He spent as much time with the smart kids as possible.

The group quickly had become close-knit. Leilani told Blue that she thought she was her true self only around Blue and the other AP Gov kids. He felt the same way. He didn't even mind anymore when Ty and Stewart drifted by him in school. "I feel happier in this group of friends," he said. "I laugh a lot. I don't feel like I have to conform to anything. When I'm with Stewart and Ty, I feel like I need to conform to their standards of 'normal' or whatever. When I'm with these people, I can just be whoever I feel like."

At nationals, Blue's team was pleased with its performance, even though it didn't place in the top ten, because the students had managed to disquiet the judges by arguing that Hawaii was an occupied nation. The trip to Washington, D.C., was the best time of Blue's life.

On the last night of the trip, Blue quietly panicked. His disappointment that the team wasn't coming home with an award was far overshadowed by the feeling that he was coming home to nothing. He was scared that the end of SCH meant the end of everything good that had happened to him over the last couple of months. *All of the awesome progress I've made socially and intellectually ends here,* Blue thought sadly. *Now we all go on with our own lives.* Every other member of the team had a plan; Michael was going to a mainland college and the others all had scholarships to the University of Hawaii. Blue had no inkling of what was going to happen to him.

Back at home, it became apparent that Blue would have to follow the most obvious avenue remaining to him. He could go to the local community college and work his tail off so that he could attempt to transfer to the University of Hawaii. First, however, he would have to graduate.

Because Blue again was behind on homework, he was still failing English and French. With three weeks left in the school year, he appealed to those two teachers for help. He had paid attention, he told them. He moved his seat to the front of the room. "If I get an A on the final," he asked them, "will you pass me?" They agreed. "I know you're smarter than this," his French teacher said.

When Blue hunkered down to study this time, he did not hear voices screaming at him that he was an underachiever who would amount to nothing. His mother, having realized that she couldn't force him into the military, largely left him alone. Instead, Blue heard a new chorus. "You're an intellectual," he remembered Michael saying. "You have a one-in-a-million kind of mind," Leilani once told him. He got to work.

DANIELLE, ILLINOIS | THE LONER

By May, pieces of Danielle's new social life slowly clicked into place. In the school library, she studied for government with Logan. In classes, she chatted with Kristy, Bree, and Max. She went to lunch with Trish a few more times. She had become friendly with another of Camille's friends, a boy who liked *National Geographic* as much as Danielle did and had the same taste in movies. One afternoon, when she happened to spot Autumn, the Dairy Queen trainee, leaving softball practice, Danielle offered to drive her home, even though she lived out of the way. On the ride, they chatted easily about work and softball. Danielle decided she didn't care that other people called Autumn "creepy." Autumn was nice to her, and that was enough for Danielle. To Danielle's amazement, a supernerd even included her among the eight classmates he invited through Facebook to a study session. She was both disappointed and relieved that she couldn't go because of a Dairy Queen shift.

A few days later, Danielle summoned the nerve to ask the guy with whom she had discussed pop if he could burn for her the new TV on the Radio CD, which he had reviewed for the school newspaper. She expected him to think it was strange for her to ask a favor, but she wanted the CD. He agreed. The next day, Danielle passed him in the hallway and actually smiled at him. It was the first time at school that Danielle had smiled unprompted at someone whom she didn't know well. He smiled back.

To celebrate the end of classes, Danielle's creative writing teacher hosted a picnic on the soccer field for his students. Danielle rolled up her jeans, kicked off her flipflops, and played soccer barefoot in the mud. She scored a goal and even called out for the ball a few times when she wasn't teasing Kristy and Olivia, a girl she knew from eighth-grade summer camp.

After the game, Danielle, Max, and Olivia went inside to talk to their AP U.S. History teacher, who was one of Danielle's favorites. She chattered away, realizing that this was probably the most that Max and Olivia had ever heard her speak. Max and the teacher agreed that it had taken ages to convince Danielle to talk to them.

"She used to just sit in the back of the room and look like this," the teacher said, crossing his arms and adopting an angry glare.

"I did not!" Danielle protested.

Max nodded emphatically. "It took three months to get Dani to talk to me," he said. "I just kept on talking to her nonstop and eventually she started to talk to me a little."

Why'd he do that? Danielle wondered. *Most people don't bother.*

Danielle gave Max a ride home from the picnic. Still new to driving, she told herself, *Watch for the curb. Do* not *forget to watch for the curb.* When she started the engine, Max said, "Okay, Dani, we're going to play a game. You're going to drive around town until you find my house."

"What?!"

Max laughed. "I'll tell you if you're hot or cold."

Danielle saw Olivia riding her bicycle down Stone Mill's semicircular driveway. She pulled alongside her.

"Olivia!" she shouted. "Where does Max live?"

"Kjshfjklsdfhjk!" Max yelled gibberish so that Danielle couldn't hear.

"I pass his house on the way home!" Olivia shouted over Max.

"I know! Where does he live, though?"

"Um, you go right, and then . . ."

"Do you know the street?" Danielle pressed.

"DANI!" Max shouted as Danielle, too busy talking to Olivia to pay attention to the curving driveway, drove over the curb and onto the grass in front of the school.

Max couldn't stop laughing while Danielle, kicking herself, got back onto the road. "You are a horrible driver!"

"Well, I did drive through a garage door." Danielle hadn't admitted that to anyone at school.

When she pulled into his driveway, Max lingered. He goofed around, pressing buttons in the car, turning on the windshield wipers. He was still laughing about how she'd driven onto the curb.

"Get out," Danielle said, mock-angry.

"Okay!" Max chortled. "Bye, Dani! We're going to play tennis soon!"

Danielle didn't realize until she had been home for an hour that Max had turned on her hazard lights, which hadn't stopped flashing since.

WHITNEY, NEW YORK | THE POPULAR BITCH

Whitney was in the senior lounge when the class advisor asked if any students wanted to organize the senior slideshow. The show would feature childhood pictures of the seniors and would run during Senior Night, the pre-graduation ceremony during which senior awards and scholarships were announced. Bobby and Chip volunteered. Aware that if the preps were in charge of the slideshow, they would spotlight only themselves, Whitney also volunteered. The teacher gave a quick speech about how they needed to include everyone.

The next day, Whitney met Bobby and Chip in the computer graphics room, which the boys said they had never entered because "only punks and emos do stupid things like graphic design." Bianca and Giselle watched from across the room. Bianca made fun of pictures of students who were overweight as children. She said little to Whitney.

As they shuffled through the photos, Whitney began scanning

pictures of students from various groups. When she inserted a photo of a "loser," Chip said, "No, absolutely not."

"Eww, Whitney, don't include that!" Bianca said. Whitney inserted the photo anyway.

"Whitney, are you kidding?" Chip said. Bobby laughed.

"You guys are so annoying," Whitney muttered. She made sure the slideshow was accessible only under her username so that the preps couldn't change the photos later.

Whitney flipped to a picture of a group of punks. She dragged and dropped it into the show.

"You're ruining the slideshow!" said Chip, the senior class president. "It's just disgusting!" Bobby doubled over.

As Whitney continued to represent all of her grade's groups, Chip made snarky comments about most of the non-preps, while Bobby played along. "What a dome!" they crowed about a band kid with a large head.

"You guys weren't the best-looking kids, either," Whitney said.

Chip insisted that every photo of him had to go in the slideshow.

"Whatever," Whitney said, knowing she would sneak a few out. She made sure that, no matter how much the boys complained, every senior who submitted a picture was included in the show.

Two weeks later, Whitney pulled into the school parking lot for Senior Night. She couldn't remember the last time she had parked discourteously as she had done in the fall. When she and Fern stepped out of the car, Whitney saw Bianca, Giselle, and Madison a few spots away; dressed similarly in overdone formalwear, they obviously had gotten ready at Bianca's house. Whitney remembered when the four of them had sauntered together through the same parking lot before Homecoming, sashaying toward the building like stars at a movie premiere. *I used to be on the other side of Bianca right there*, Whitney thought. When Giselle saw Whitney and Fern, she waited for them, while Bianca and Madison floated by without acknowledgment.

Inside, Whitney immediately went backstage to set up the slideshow, knowing that Bobby and Chip wouldn't help even if she asked. By the time she finished, most of the seats in the auditorium were taken, and the preps hadn't saved one for her. Whitney sat in the front row next to some of the unpopular guys she had gotten to know during the last few weeks of school.

During the final speech of the night, Whitney slipped backstage. When the class advisor flashed her a thumbs-up, Whitney pressed PLAY and stood on the catwalk to watch the audience's reactions. As the first notes of Vitamin C's "Graduation Song" filled the auditorium, Whitney skimmed her classmates' faces, tilted upward and bathed in the soft glow from the screen. She watched them laughing at the pictures of themselves, or exchanging tender looks with their parents. There was a girl whose graduation party Whitney had convinced Giselle to accompany her to, even though the preps made fun of them for going. There were the band kids she'd gotten to know so well over the last couple of months. There was Fern, smiling. Fern had written in Whitney's yearbook, "You definitely made my senior year a lot easier. Thanks for making me feel comfortable even when I thought I never would be." When Whitney had shown her mother, she told Whitney that she was proud of her. "You made such a difference in someone's life!" added her mother's secretary, peering over her shoulder.

Whitney hadn't considered it that way. But she was even more surprised to realize that Fern, who would patiently listen to Whitney complain—usually about Bianca—had become a real friend.

There were the emos, with whom Whitney had started eating lunch in the hallway on occasion. The badasses looked like any other students; Whitney had learned while hanging out with them during seventh period that they weren't the thugs that classmates assumed them to be. Even the preps, knotted together in the middle of the room, grinned as they gazed at the screen. Bianca, too cool to submit pictures of herself, had told Whitney to copy some from her Facebook page. Knowing this would be the last thing she ever did for Bianca, Whitney selected elementary school photos of Bianca with non-preps, back before the class had shuffled into a hierarchy of cliques.

Whitney imagined that all of the seniors finally felt included. She was proud that she had created this moment for her classmates. She grew nostalgic too, as the occasional photo of her popped up on the screen: Whitney in elementary school, Whitney as the sixth grade queen bee,

Whitney in high school. . . . As she watched, she mused that she had occupied various roles with these classmates. "I was a hated loser when I got kicked out of the popular group, I was the queen of the school, I was a loyal follower, and, most recently, I was independent," she said. "In each of those positions I, like, learned something new and something I'll use later in life. Being in each position led to something better."

Whitney wasn't naïve enough to think that she had smoothed over relationships with all of the students she had burned in the past. She was certain that the FFAs continued to think of her as, in her words, the Antichrist. And Bianca hated her. But now Whitney knew the difference between being a popular and being *popular*.

As a prep, she realized, she had been a member of a clique that was considered "the populars" even though they comprised the group that had the fewest friends. Now, without any group affiliation, Whitney walked down the halls feeling free to sit with or talk to practically anyone in her grade. She had never been happier.

Chapter 13

THE RISE OF THE CAFETERIA FRINGE

It would be misleading to assert that group identities and exclusions disappear immediately when students go to college. Certainly, many outsiders love college right away. Other college students told me that, at first, they sensed divisions that didn't seem all that different from high school: drinkers vs. non-drinkers, Greeks vs. independents, partiers vs. studiers. Some students encounter new labels; a college freshman in Iowa learned the term "narnian," used to refer to students who don't often leave their dorm rooms. Students who look forward to a sea change in atmosphere the second they arrive on campus may be disappointed at first. But it gets better. Give it time.

Granted, it is a lot to ask a teen to wait. Geoffrey, a "smart kid" eighth grader in Indiana, said, "I'm always single, so it's tough. Never can get a girl. The smart thing repels girls. I like being smart because I breeze through school and can get a good job and make good money. That's the good thing, but the girl thing is killing me." One of Geoffrey's thirteen-year-old classmates, who was labeled a "ditz," told me, "I'm near the bottom of the food chain and I have to live with that for the rest of my life." No! You don't! Adolescence is a formative time, but it should not, as Eli worried to me once, comprise the best years of your existence.

Eventually, it passes, and, whether in college or as young adults, many individuals will come to experience quirk theory. Blue began to understand a glimmer of quirk theory when the first-round UAP interviewer told him that he was different from anyone else she had interviewed—and she passed him to the final round of admissions because of that. He experienced a hint of this phenomenon again when his new friends, especially Michael, admired him for some of the same reasons for which his old friends had mocked him.

The main characters and several of the other students discussed in this book exemplify quirk theory. To begin with, many of them already exhibit the attributes described in chapter 5 as some of the most appreciated qualities among adults. Each of them also displays additional traits that others will respect outside of school.

- Blue, creative and curious, is a freethinker with the ability to see around corners. His discipline may have been shaky, but his integrity is solid, both in his character and in his refusal to gossip. His longing to connect, diverse talents, and yearning to share them, and openness to multiple perspectives—all of which his old friends made fun of—have already begun to serve him well.

- Danielle's vow to be her own person following a shattering social blow keeps her grounded and committed to the matters she prioritizes, such as learning about global, environmental, and social justice issues. Her wealth of interests, rich literary exposure, and fearlessness to engage in activities she enjoys, even if she must participate alone, will make her a standout whether she pursues medicine, archaeology, or any of the other fields that currently captivate her.

- Noah's self-awareness and receptiveness to his emotions make him the kind of forthright, empathetic individual whom others will appreciate. He continued to grow his hair long to donate it to charity even though it made him a target for teasing. Noah's sense of devotion and willingness to shoulder more than his share of responsibility—of the band, of his brother—are qualities that are highly valued outside of the school setting. And how many other students would keep running for class office because, even if they lose, year after year, the experience will help them grow?

- Joy's ability to find the positive in even the most harrowing of experiences demonstrates resilience far more pronounced than that of many people twice her age. Her maturity, eloquence, and undaunted willingness to express herself—which led some students to exclude and harass her—along with her eagerness to help others are good signs that we will be hearing her name in years to come.

- Eli likely will find that people will respect his curiosity and his dedication to lifelong learning much more in college than his high school classmates did. His earnestness, vast knowledge, and determination to stay the course, even in the face of multi-faceted pressure to be "normal," are qualities that many adults will find impressive.
- Outside of school, Regan has already found admirers of her policy to be candid and open, even when her honesty gets her in trouble. Both personally and in her new career path, adults will continue to treasure her authenticity, outspokenness, and compassion, as well as her warm acceptance of other people's unique qualities.
- Even the traits for which the preps excluded Whitney—her ability to wear multiple hats, her refusal to continue being cruel, her alternative sense of style, the charisma that enabled her to befriend students from other groups—will benefit her in college and beyond.

All of these people also demonstrated inspiring qualities that are generally representative of cafeteria fringe across the country. For example, the outsiders did not waste time repainting their images to increase their popularity. In the end, they stayed true to themselves, asserting their uniqueness in the environment that makes it most challenging to do so. Remaining nonconformist in the face of intense social pressure, if not outright harassment, takes dedication, drive, and as previously discussed, courage.

It is not the labels themselves that make these individuals unique and admirable. Blue is not extraordinary because he is a gamer. He is extraordinary because he is Blue. But so many of the students whose labels signify their lack of perceived popularity—emos, indies, freaks, nerds, scenes, loners, floaters, skaters, punks, all manner of geeks and dorks—someday are going to derive practical and/or social advantages from attributes that qualified them for those labels in the first place. Geeks profit from their technological know-how. Emos might be in touch with their feelings and others', and unafraid to show and empathize with those emotions. Scenes and indies often influence the cutting edge of cultural movements. Gamers, adept at problem solving, engage in ventures of successful "collective intelligence," researchers say, because of their collaborative efforts, on forums, blogs, and wikis, to understand the games. As game designer and award-winning innovator Jane McGonigal has argued, these "collective knowledge–building" efforts could be applied to real-world issues.

Freaks are often creative and perhaps the boldest of the cafeteria fringe because they display their distinctions openly with pride. Skaters and punks are frequently underestimated; their sense of artistry suggests the inventiveness they could bring to other endeavors. Dorks might exhibit a childlike goofiness that endears them to adults who are young at heart, and the often-appreciated quality of not taking themselves too seriously.[5] Loners may be the most self-aware people in school, with the introspectiveness that allows them to work through identity issues long before their peers. And floaters are already skilled at adult-style social networking, able to converse and connect with different people, and instrumental in transmitting information, culture, and ideas across various groups. Indeed, the number of floaters in a school setting increases with age.

A closer look at any cafeteria fringe label reveals quirk theory at work. Consider the nerds, perhaps the most widely persecuted outcasts in school. What makes them nerds? Here is a series of descriptions from David Anderegg's book *Nerds*. They exhibit "some combination of school success, interest in precision, unself-consciousness, closeness to adults, and interest in fantasy. . . . The weird enthusiasms, the willingness to cooperate with adults, the lack of social skills—all these things seem nerdy and pathetic to sophisticated, self-conscious teenagers. . . . Nerd-labeled kids are, in fact, curiously immune from the rampant sexualization and, more generally, adultization of preteen

---

[5] *Additionally, a childlike mindset recently has been proven to boost creativity.*

culture. Here we might notice one of the very best things about nerds, or at least nerd-labeled kids: they act like children."

Unself-consciousness. Closeness to adults. Interest in imaginative worlds. Enthusiasm. Cooperativeness. Immunity from fads. None of these is a negative characteristic for adults, yet combined they form a recipe for exclusion among teens. Eventually, people come to appreciate nerdiness. With the success and popularity—actual popularity—of standout nerdy characters like those portrayed by Stephen Colbert, Tina Fey, Seth Green, Michael Cera, and Masi Oka, today's generation of adults has entered the Age of the Nerd. Movies celebrating the beta male (think Seth Rogen, Jonah Hill, Ben Stiller)—clean up at the box office. In many areas, nerds are appreciated and even beloved precisely because of the qualities that set them apart from the mainstream.

Both the nerd and geek subcultures have undergone a renaissance in recent years. In 2010, "nerd fashion"—large, thick-framed glasses, tapered pants, and argyle vests—gained favor. Even Hello Kitty sported black-rimmed glasses on Sanrio's "nerd tote bag" and other items. The rise of geek chic and nerd merch, the proliferation of nerdcore hip-hop artists, and celebrity endorsements of and appearances at the "nerd prom" known as Comic Con all contribute to what Jerry Holkins, the creator of the *Penny Arcade* webcomic and video game conference, called "the social pariah outcast aesthetic." The massive mainstreaming of spheres that once were the domains of nerds and geeks—video games, Internet destinations like Wikipedia, YouTube, MySpace, Facebook, Skype; technological gear like Bluetooth headsets and BlackBerries; the literary genres that encompass *Lord of the Rings, Harry Potter,* and *Twilight*; pop culture remixes like *Transformers* and *X-Men*; activities like forwarding or embedding viral videos and blogging—provide ample evidence that a once-stigmatized subculture is now embraced and thriving.

So, too, can teenage nerds and geeks find this acceptance. While there have been surprisingly few trickle-down effects from the adult Age of the Nerd to the student world, they have been positive. Some student bodies have acknowledged a "cool nerd" subset, for example. More important, many teenage nerds and geeks now choose to celebrate their label rather than allow it to imprison them. These outcasts are rising up, exulting in the "geek cred" that differentiates them from other groups and the knowledge and precision that, as Geoffrey suggested, eventually will enable them to profit financially (as have, to name a few, Paul Allen, Sergey Brin, Larry Ellison, Bill Gates, Steve Jobs, Larry Page, and Steve Wozniak, some of whom themselves exemplify quirk theory). They are realizing at an early age that the geeks (and loners, punks, floaters, dorks, and various other outcasts) shall inherit the earth.

Some students are fighting their marginalization by co-opting typically derogatory terms. In 2009, four twelve-to-fourteen-year-olds won the New York City FIRST LEGO League Robotics Championship under the team name Nerd Herd. The St. Edmund School students, finalists at the Robotic World Festival, told the *Gothamist* how they came up with the name: "I was looking across the lunchroom and I saw the rest of the team doing some nerdy things," said Simon Shkreli. "Now I have to make a good name. Geek Squad (NO!). Nerd Dudes (almost). Nerd . . . HERD! (YES!)"

Caitlin and her friends, seniors at a small all-girls school in North Carolina, call their group "drama dorks." Caitlin listed the following as her "dork" qualities: "I'm in my second year of AP Calculus. I'm taking AP Statistics as an elective. I work as a techie for drama, can recite *Star Wars* movies, watch anime religiously, can write Java computer code and HTML, and write fan fiction and original novels in my free time. I have a T-shirt for AP Calc that I wear in public and another one for the Math Club, even though I'm not in the Math Club. Not that I go around making the Spock 'Live long and prosper' hand signal, but basically, once you've met me you stop applying the word dork to anyone else." Because Caitlin is confident in her identity and wears her label as a badge of honor rather than someone else's stamp of disapproval, she has escaped cruelty from her peers. That and, she said, "No one is going to make fun of me if they want me to tutor them in chemistry."

Just because outcasts are excluded from certain groups or in particular environments doesn't mean that everybody will avoid them. In psychological parlance, groups expel "deviants" because they threaten group identity. But because different groups have different characteristics, a deviant in one group may be a nondeviant in another. This is why many students flourish in college, where the environment is typically more accepting of diverse qualities than in high school, and includes students who aren't already saddled with reputational bias. A college freshman in Alabama was alternately mocked and ignored in high school. "High school was so unimaginably stifling for me. I never went on a date," she said. "Since I've been in college, away from everyone who knew me previously, I've thrived. I've been able to reach my full potential, even winning a student government position. I feel like I'm finally free to pursue what I want, for me."

Laura, the redhead mentioned in chapter 8 who was tormented by students who shot staples into her ears and stuck KICK ME HARD signs on her back, eventually found similar solace in college, where she joined several clubs. "The best thing to do is find a group of people who share similar interests and stay true to oneself. That's how I've survived. I'm my own person and not defined by a large group of people," she said. Incidentally, Laura's red hair has become more of an attraction than a deterrent. "There aren't a lot of redheads, so I think people remember me. It really does pay to be different in some way."

Those differences will be appreciated someday. A teacher in Oklahoma reflected on the post-graduation aftermath of student social divisions. "The in crowd always hangs together, even after graduation. They are the ones who will become debutantes after their freshman year in college. The others tend to drift away. They don't get invited to the parties, they are laughed at because they aren't wearing designer clothes, etc.," she said. But when it comes down to the popular students versus the outcasts, the latter "are more sure of themselves (even with the ridicule), and usually turn out to be more successful and well-adjusted. I would take the outcasts in a heartbeat." So would I.

NOAH, PENNSYLVANIA | THE BAND GEEK

Near the end of sixth period, a secretary called Noah to the principal's office. As he walked down the hall, Noah fretted over the possible reasons for being summoned. *Are they going to give me detention for play-*

ing Pokémon in school? he wondered. *Are Leigh and I getting a citation for kissing in public?*

Noah's recycling efforts were more successful than he had realized. In less than two months, he had recruited about twenty regular volunteers, and had extended conversations—especially in the cafeteria—about recycling with more than one hundred other students, including jocks, populars, wannabes, quiet kids, weird kids, bandies, and a bearded student in ratty clothes whom Noah's friends thought was a hobo.

In study hall, Noah had noticed a prostitot cleaning out her binder. He was intimidated by prostitots—and this one was heavily pregnant and seemed angry. He took a breath, then stood up. "Waitwaitwait!" he shouted.

She paused, holding a pile of papers over the trash can. "What am I waiting for, your stupid comments?"

"No," Noah said, still nervous. "I was just going to ask if you'd put your papers into the recycling bin."

"What does it matter? It all gets thrown away anyways. Not like I care about some trees."

Noah walked over to her. "Here, I'll do it, then. I don't mind."

She dropped the papers into Noah's hands and returned to her seat. He placed them in the recycling bin. "Do you guys really think you're making some kind of difference?" she asked.

"Of course! We've recycled over two dumpsters. Like five tons!"

"Really? That's a lot, right?"

"Yeah, and we've been getting help from a lot of other kids to make it so good. From the kids who just recycle their paper instead of throwing it in the trash to kids who'll stay after school and recycle with us, every little bit counts."

"Oh. That's cool. I'd help, but . . ." She trailed off and glanced down at her stomach.

"We're happy to have anyone we can helping, and if you ever want some volunteer hours or a shot at a scholarship, let me know. We do work every week."

Each time Noah successfully broke through to someone about recycling, his self-esteem soared. *I might not get recognition, but maybe people really do see me as a leader,* he thought. *I'm not an aggressive, charismatic leader; I'm just trying to be nice and connect with people so that they feel welcome.* As Noah gained confidence, other areas of his life improved as well. His grades had risen, he had scored a few goals on Redsen's playoff-bound Frisbee team, and he was happy and relatively calm. Noah hadn't crashed in more than a month.

The office door opened and a popular girl exited, laughing with the principal. Noah's stomach dropped. *Everyone knows a principal can go from zero to two hundred in one second,* he thought.

"Come in, Mr. Giancoli. There's something I'd like to discuss with you," the principal said. Noah gingerly stepped over the threshold. He had never been in this room before. He rubbed his elbow anxiously as the principal sat down.

"Don't worry, you're not in trouble," she said. "I just wanted to talk to you about something called the Senior Advisory Council. Have you heard of it?"

"I've heard of it, but I'm not familiar with it," Noah said.

"It's the students who petition for class privileges."

Noah nearly screamed. *Is she asking me to be on this?!*

The principal continued: "A lot of things get done by class officers, but this is an opportunity to have another part. A legislative branch of sorts."

Noah nodded enthusiastically.

"Would you be interested? Our meetings are once or twice a month, before or after school, over food, of course."

"Definitely! I'd love to participate."

"Good, good! I'm glad. Your teachers told me that you would be a great candidate for this."

"Principal Clayton, if you don't mind, may I ask a question?"

"Of course."

"Who else is participating?"

The principal named three other students from various social groups.

"Thank you very much, Principal Clayton!"

"Well, I think we'll have a great council. I'll talk to you later," she said as she handed Noah a pass for seventh period.

Noah contained his euphoria until he reached the stairwell. Then he began to skip slaphappily toward the stairs. *Someone has recognized me and given me the chance to make changes!* he crowed to himself, bounding up the stairs. *And they've actually made a balanced council! The four of us will be able to unite, hopefully across* all *popularities, to make the school better!*

Noah tripped on the last stair, flinging his books all over the floor. He looked around to make sure the stairwell was empty, laughed to himself, brushed off his knees, picked up his books, and resumed skipping down the hall.

Eli, Virginia | The Nerd

After check-in for Westcoast University's freshman orientation, a volunteer announced that students in the business program should leave for their introductory session. Eli went outside, realized he didn't know where to go, and stopped.

While Eli had looked forward to the two-day orientation, now that he was here, he was scared. WCU was a sprawling campus, with tens of thousands of students. He wondered how many of them would judge him the same way his high school classmates did. *The only way I'm going to make any friends is if I take the first step,* he told himself. *Okay. The next person who walks out that door is going to be my friend, whoever it is.* He hoped that the excitement of "letting fate pick" a friend, as he put it, would override his jitters.

Within twenty seconds a pleasant-looking Asian girl with stylish glasses exited the building and looked around. Eli didn't give himself a chance to chicken out. *Treat this like the first days of Spanish camp,* he thought. *Just be myself.*

"Hi, are you in the business program too?" he inquired.

"Yeah!" she said.

Eli inwardly cheered. *She's friendly!* "Cool, do you know where you're going?" Eli asked as they walked down the stairs. "Because I have no idea."

"I'm not sure either."

"Well at least I feel better knowing I won't get lost on my own," he said. "I'm Eli." He held out his hand. She shook it.

"I'm Lindsey."

For the rest of the morning, Eli and Lindsey made comfortable small talk before splitting up for the afternoon elective sessions.

Just before dinner, WCU held a mandatory assembly for all incoming business freshmen. When Eli arrived at the lecture hall, hundreds of students were already seated. As he meandered up the stairs, he realized he was pleased to have chosen a university with so many students. In high school, he felt out of place whenever he looked for a seat. Here, it didn't matter if he looked a little lost. No one was judging him. Already he could see that the campus could be as small or as large as he wanted it to be. There would be plenty of potential friends from whom to choose.

Suddenly Eli saw someone waving at him from the front of the auditorium. Lindsey grinned and gestured to a seat she had saved for him. They spent much of the rest of orientation together and resolved to stay in touch over the summer.

Already Eli felt more comfortable about his prospective social life than he ever had in high school. "College will be full of Lindseys: genuinely nice people that I can become friends with," Eli said when he returned home from orientation. "I'm still scared about making friends and all that, but I just have to trust that everything will work out. Generally, I'm leaning more toward the excited than the nervous side now. 'Normality' is more defined in high school because it's smaller, but it's all relative in college. In time, I know I can find my own little niche."

JOY, CALIFORNIA | THE NEW GIRL

At lunchtime, Joy spotted Anisha and Latrice walking toward her. Except for lunches with Joy, Latrice and Anisha didn't hang out; an Indian AP kid and a black cheerleader were an unheard-of combination at Citygrove. Typically, Joy divided her free time in school among her friends. But today, these two were talking as if they'd known each other for years.

The girls found a sunny patch of grass outside the biology classroom and caught up on each other's day. After a while, Cleo knelt on the grass beside them. "We have the weirdest combination of people here: crazy Jamaican chick, Indian AP kid, cheerleader . . ." Joy said.

"And cool, white artsy chick with funky clothes!" Cleo chimed in.

"Wow," said Anisha, looking around at the group. "We're like the only people that do this! It's a cool combination."

"That's because we set our own trend," Latrice said. " 'Cause normally, the cheerleaders don't talk to the AP kids, the white girl doesn't talk to the black girl. People are left out! We move toward change."

Joy adopted a squeaky little-girl voice. "And it's all because of me!"

"Right, Joy!" Anisha said. "We love you!"

"I love you too!"

When Joy and Latrice walked away, Latrice turned to her and said, "I can tell you anything. I can trust you, and you'll never give up on me, and you don't judge me, and you're always honest with me. You're my best friend. Give me a hug, boo." Latrice embraced her.

The next morning was the first day of swimming in PE. In the middle of her first lap, Joy began to sink. She was a terrible swimmer; somehow, even in Jamaica, she had never learned how. She further submerged. Panicked, she flapped her limbs. She struggled to keep her head above the water.

Suddenly, she heard a shout. "Go, Joy! You can do it!" Joy looked up, still flapping. It was Lupe, standing at the edge of the pool. Mia joined in, cheering her on. Soon several students echoed her former bullies, shouting encouragement. "Come on, keep going, Joy!" "You can do it! Swim, swim!" Spurred on, Joy forced herself to plod to the end of the pool.

That afternoon, between periods, D'Arnell approached Joy and Latrice. He talked with them briefly, then cocked his head at Joy. "Your accent is so funny," he said. "Where are you from?"

Joy cracked up. She had known D'Arnell since January and he never thought to ask.

"She's from Jamaica, duh!" Latrice answered.

"Ohh," D'Arnell said, thrusting his arms in the air. "*You're* the Jamaican girl! Everyone's been talking about you. You're like the daily gossip, everyone asking me if I know this black Jamaican girl that moved here. Man," he continued, "you are really popular . . . and the entire time, I've been hanging out with you. Whoa!"

Joy laughed in surprise. People had called her many things, this year and always, but never once had she so much as imagined that classmates would consider her popular.

BLUE, HAWAII | THE GAMER

When Blue's class filed into the arena, the noise was deafening. The stands were so packed that people spilled into the aisles and stood along the walls. In between camera flashes, Blue could make out some of the banners, featuring messages and photographs of students that families held for their high school graduates. "*Aloha nui loa*" ("All my love"). "*A hui hou kakou*" ("Until we meet again") for a student entering the military. Blue was relieved that he wasn't headed in that direction.

When the students took their seats, the crowd sang "The Star Spangled Banner," "Hawaii Pono'i" (the state song), and Kaloke's alma mater. After various dignitaries spoke, the vice principals presented plaques to each of the school's valedictorians. Blue was proud to see all of his SCH teammates receive their plaques, but watching Michael stride across the stage gave him a special joy.

After receiving her plaque, Angelique remained on stage to give the valedictorians' address:[6] "From the vantage of someone living a thousand years from now, the [last four years] may seem negligible. What that person may not realize is that each of those days have been as precious and unpredictable as this one. The yearbooks most of us have contain images of that time passing in a certain way. They set the conditions for a nostalgic expedition. Any memories evoked by our yearbooks take place 'now' at the moment they are called up in the mind. Every memory is a re-creation, not a playback. When we remember, we focus on certain facts and emotions, and become active participants in re-creating memories. Often we are guilty of restraining ourselves because of past embarrassments or limitations. We should

---

[6] *Abridged here.*

never let those memories dictate or limit our futures; high school is not a model for the rest of our lives. It is only a stepping stone, a foundation for future success.

"Any way you look at it, what made being in school interesting is that most of us are different from one another. Isn't there something a little fantastic about that? It's those differences in who we are, and the connections we make with each other despite those differences, that will make us great as adults.

"Some of us may be at the point in our lives where we are desperately trying to define ourselves. If you think you're one of those people, look to your teachers, parents, and friends. They are and always have been, the reasons you've grown up the way you have. My teachers encourage me to think deeply, my parents teach me to be kind and fair, and my friends inspire me and share their insights with me—Mark Laurent, the muse that speaks through me tonight, is the best example of an unconventional thinker that brings out the best in other people. Just like me, your understanding of the world is shaped by the people you love, and soon your constructions of the world will guide others. . . .

"It is now time for our expedition into life after high school. Let us move forward with the intent to inspire the uninspired, so that someone living a thousand years from now will strive to follow in our footsteps."

In the cheers that followed, students nearby turned to Blue in amazement. "Oh my God, that was so good," a girl said. "Holy shit, breh, you wrote that?" a guy asked. Blue was smiling too hard to answer. He had been surprised when the valedictorians had asked him to write the commencement address. He was floored to hear the line they had added about him. In front of thousands of people, some of the smartest kids at school had validated his intelligence.

The rest of the ceremony moved quickly. Spectators threw fresh flowers and leis from the stands when students' names were announced. When Blue walked across the platform, one of the administrators cracked, "I guess you didn't drop out after all." Blue smiled, met another graduate in the middle of the stage, stopped short, and gave her an emphatic fist bump, which the jumbotron broadcast to massive cheers.

Afterward, the arena emptied onto the fields. At first, Blue looked around, feeling bare and sheepish, lost amidst reunions of families and friends adorning graduates' necks with homemade leis. Finally, Michael appeared and hugged him. Then one of their SCH teammates gave Blue a lei that she had made of pink and yellow plumeria, his favorite flower. Within minutes, streams of people sought him out—sophomores, juniors, friends from other schools—to give him leis made of fresh flowers, nuts, beads, or candy. Ty's mother gave him leis made of forty $1 bills. Even Jackson found him. "Let's forget the past," Jackson said sarcastically, but still hugged him and gave him a lei.

Two hard-core gamers approached Blue, congratulated him on the speech, and gave him leis. As they left, one of them called out, "Oh, did you get the Starcraft II beta key? Dude, you have to play with us. RED TEAM!"

Blue was gratified, knowing that so many people of various backgrounds went out of their way to find him. By the time he saw his family, he wore so many leis that his neck resembled a lion's mane. "Oh, my baby!" Blue's mother exclaimed and hugged him. "Did you really write that speech?"

"Yes," Blue said.

"No you didn't. Oh my God. No way." Blue's mother and brother, who had flown in from France, placed plumeria leis around his neck.

That night, Blue skateboarded around town with Jess and Leilani, weaving in and out of hotel lobbies, laughing and talking through the early morning hours. As the sun rose, they returned to Blue's house, giddy with possibility. "We were so happy that we wanted to throw up," Blue explained. "It was that feeling that you get right before you're about to do something crazy, right before you go into intense competition or something, that butterfly feeling. We were about to jump into our new 'adult lives.'"

Much of Blue's future was uncertain. He had not yet told Michael that he wanted to stay together even though Michael would attend college thousands of miles away. Blue's brother and his wife were moving back to Hawaii in August, but they did not yet know whether they would rent their own home, where Blue could live with them.

All that Blue knew in this moment was that he was going to work hard at community college so that he could transfer to the University of Hawaii and reunite with the best friends he ever had. The UH futurology professor had agreed to allow him in his graduate-level course for college credit. And for now, that was enough for Blue. "I always thought that surrounding myself with people who brought me up in life was good. I just never thought that it would happen so naturally, or to me, like that stuff that happens in movies," he said. "I feel a lot more secure with myself. Like I can *be* myself and there are people out there that will like me for it." And there was something a little fantastic about that.

DANIELLE, ILLINOIS | THE LONER

Danielle began her summer working at Dairy Queen and as an assistant to her tae kwon do instructor. At Dairy Queen, the managers gave her additional hours because they were impressed with her work ethic; they said that other kids tended to stand around, while Danielle worked reliably and efficiently.

In early July, Danielle's mother and stepfather had Logan's family over for dinner. Danielle and Logan spent most of the night talking to each other. They discovered they both were big fans of the Sea Shepherd Conservation Society, the BBC, and Shark Week. Danielle told Logan about the hate club. Logan listened sympathetically and said that seventh grade was her worst year too.

Later that week, Logan invited Danielle to join her and her friends for Logan's birthday. The group went out for pizza, played laser tag, then went to Logan's house to play Super Smash Bros. Brawl on the Wii. Danielle was one of the last people to leave.

The next day, Logan texted Danielle to tell her how much she loved the soundtrack Danielle had given her for her birthday. When they discussed soundtracks they liked, Logan suggested a music swap. Danielle brought her laptop to Logan's house to trade songs. In Logan's bedroom, pictures of several fish species dotted walls blanketed in fish wallpaper. A basket full of shells lay on a hutch above Logan's desk, beneath a small plastic shark.

Danielle noticed a book lying on Logan's desk: *Party of One: The Loners' Manifesto.* As she and Logan copied each other's soundtracks, they discovered they shared other tastes: *Riverdance*, a random song they both loved in childhood, the movie *The Swan Princess.* A pile of books towered next to a full bookshelf, which was smaller than Danielle's, but still impressive. They talked about Logan's books as Danielle fingered the spines. *The Snows of Kilimanjaro*—Danielle wanted to read that collection. *The Count of Monte Cristo*, one of Danielle's favorites. . . Danielle stopped short. There, on Logan's shelf, was *Blindness.*

Danielle wished they had started hanging out before Logan had graduated from Stone Mill. She realized she had more in common with Logan, whom she'd known for only a few months, than with any of her other friends, some of whom she'd known for more than a decade. Danielle was quietly overcome by a wondrous, heartwarming feeling because even though Logan would be leaving for college in a month, Danielle realized that she had finally made a new, true friend.

———

31 TIPS FOR STUDENTS, PARENTS, TEACHERS, AND SCHOOLS

When we left off with the Robbers Cave experiment in chapter 8, by the end of two weeks, relations between the Eagles and the Rattlers were so hostile that they were fistfighting. But the fake summer camp didn't end after two weeks. During the third week, Muzafer Sherif reversed the experiment, devising collaborative activities that required the participation of both groups. The boys were tasked with fixing the camp's drinking water pump and cooperating to push a stalled food truck up a hill, for example, and they were told they could go to a movie only if both groups pooled their funds. As the boys worked together, they gradually ceased the name-calling and the fighting. They began to intermingle at meals. They cooked campout food together, by choice. By the end of the week, the boys were singing together. The groups requested to share a bus back home; during a stop on the way, the Rattlers bought malted milks for all of the boys in both groups. Sherif called the turnaround "dramatic" and "striking to all observers."

The Robbers Cave experiment illustrates that even groups of people who believe each other to be despised enemies can overcome severe us-versus-them prejudice and rancor to the point of genuine camaraderie. The experiment, which has been replicated elsewhere, shows us that, even for today's students stuck within or outside of seemingly unyielding group boundaries, there is hope that perceptions can be altered.

Hope abides for another reason too. Early on in our work, Whitney said, "I would love to know what an emo or a wannabe thought about cliques and if they had the same pressures as me." Sure enough, without my ever having to ask, one by one, students of various labels voiced laments similar to something Whitney had once expressed. As a Pittsburgh senior said: "I just wish people could see me as something besides a theater geek." Dozens of students repeated the message of a New York cross-country girl: "It's hard because sometimes people forget [that] most people have more than one dimension to them. Sometimes, the thing you enjoy most isn't the thing you're best at, and sometimes you want people to know you for all that you have to offer, not just one or two things you're good at."

Although so many students have the same things to say, they cross signals in a maelstrom of misinterpretation, then lose sight of each other behind their stereotypes. A Nebraska sophomore, ostracized at school because of her high grades, said that one day the boy next to her was complaining about homework. Attempting to strike up a friendly conversation, she said that she was also swamped. "But you're smart. You like doing homework," the boy protested. The sophomore told me, "His response really got to me. Lots of students share his stereotype of smart kids. It was like he thought just because I aced a lot of tests and always remembered to do my homework, I didn't enjoy the things that normal teenagers enjoy."

Just because students are different doesn't mean that they have nothing in common. Old interests can be experienced with new people; new common pursuits can develop. As Blue learned from his SCH teammates' admiration of his room and his adventures, new friends can appreciate your interests even if, and perhaps especially if, they haven't been exposed to them before.

As much as this book is about applauding students who dare to be different, it is also about how many of them ultimately long for the same thing. More than almost anything else, everyone I followed wanted a connection, someone to listen and to care. The gamer, the band geek, the new girl, the loner, the nerd, the popular bitch, the weird girl—to be sure, they were diverse individuals. But I hope I am not too naïve to think that had they met one another, they might have been friends.

Students, parents, teachers, and school administrators can take numerous steps toward fixing the problems detailed in this book. To begin with, here is one approach not to pursue. In an article entitled "From Nerds to Normals," sociologist David Kinney wrote, "Adolescents who were unpopular in middle school and who became involved in high school activities and friendship groups were able to recover by becoming self-confident and reconstructing themselves as 'normal' within a changing school social system." No student should be encouraged—by anyone—to change himself until he's "normal," a term that says everything and means nothing.

Yet this attitude is disturbingly common. Instead of revamping school policies to welcome every child, many school systems are bent on revamping the students to conform to their schools. Some systems are so horrifyingly regressive that they deliberately retool policies to make non-in-crowd students feel *un*welcome and *un*wanted, such as the Mississippi county school board that cancelled the 2010 high school prom rather than permit a lesbian senior to wear a tuxedo and bring her girlfriend to the dance. The educational atmosphere can be so intolerant that in late 2010, five students committed suicide after being harassed because bullies believed they were gay. Two of the students were thirteen years old.

Enough of this. Too many people have lost sight of the fact that the most integral part of a school's success is the well-being of its students.

The worst aspect of the treatment of cafeteria fringe isn't the name-calling. It isn't the loneliness. It isn't even the regrettable demise of attitudes and programs that are important for fostering creativity, originality, and independence. The most heartbreaking consequence of this treatment is that so many tens of thousands of students—imaginative, interesting, impressionable people—think that they have done or felt something wrong.

Here are some recommendations for students, parents, and school personnel to set things right and reclaim their schools.

WHAT STUDENTS CAN DO

Know that being different doesn't mean you're flawed

First and foremost, there is nothing wrong with you just because you haven't yet met people who share your interests or outlook on life. Unless you are doing something unhealthy or destructive, take pride in your beliefs, passions, and values. Know that you will eventually meet people who will appreciate you for being you.

Give everyone a chance

No matter your social status, there is plenty to gain from getting to know every student beyond a first impression. Do not automatically assume that you have little in common simply because you travel in different circles. And if you really don't have anything in common with someone, don't assume that you can't be friends. Making an effort to understand and appreciate differences can be both enlightening and exhilarating.

Keep in mind that loneliness won't last forever

Loneliness can be excruciatingly painful. But it is also temporary, and is not an excuse to engage in behaviors that make you uncomfortable. If you find that it is truly impossible to make friends, in or outside of school, at least take heart in knowing that you're not the only one who feels that way and you won't always be alone. In some cases, if loneliness slides into depression, it might help to talk about your feelings with a counselor.

Try humor and confidence

A Maryland high school freshman used to get teased about her obsessive-compulsive disorder habits, such as tapping on desks, turning doorknobs, and counting. "If someone asked why I was counting the tiles on the floor, I'd just laugh it off and say, 'Because it's fun,' or 'I just feel like it.' Then they'd count or tap with me until we would both collapse on the floor with uncontrollable giggles," she said. "Once people got to know me and my bubbly personality, for the most part they wouldn't care about my little ticks and taps. My attitude saved me from withdrawing into myself and becoming completely embarrassed and antisocial because of my disorder, and helped people see me for me, and not my weird quirks." Her outlook sets a good example for anyone who is criticized for being different. If you accept your own idiosyncrasies, others may accept them as well.

A Virginia senior who has been homeschooled and, more recently, attended both private and public schools, has additional advice for peers. "I've had to make a new group of friends every year of high school, which sucks, but at the same time, I've always had a fresh start. I've learned a lot about making friends this way, and the best principles seem to be: listen to other people, be confident, act like you don't *need* friends but maybe *want* them, trust that people will like you, and definitely never think you know everything."

Stop trying to conform

There is a huge difference between being unhappy with yourself and being unhappy with your social status. I asked a Pennsylvania nonconformist who shuttled between emos and ghettos for advice for students who feel they can't be themselves in school. She replied, "Continuously pretending to be someone you aren't may end up turning you into someone you don't want to be. There is someone out there who will understand you, no matter how far out there you are."

If you spend your school years repressing your identity, someday you're going to graduate and realize that you've lost yourself only to appease a temporary crowd. Middle school and high school are the most difficult places in which to resist the pressure to conform. People who are able to battle through school without succumbing to fakery are going to be better off when they graduate.

Find an ally

In Solomon Asch's line-matching conformity experiment, he found that all seven actor-participants had to give the same answer in order to effectively push the student volunteer to conform. Even one dissident was enough to encourage the student to say what he actually saw instead of mimicking the group's incorrect answer. By extension, Asch's discovery suggests that if you can develop at least one true ally within your group, you will have an easier time resisting the pressure to conform. Another lesson from Asch's experiment is that even if everyone disagrees with you, you're not necessarily wrong.

Pursue nonschool activities

One way to avoid reputational bias is to participate in afterschool activities with students from other schools who don't already have preconceived notions about you. If you choose an activity you love to do or are fascinated by, you'll meet people with similar interests. Whether or not you end up with new friends, you can at least develop a skill and gain confidence in your abilities.

Eli called his experience at Spanish camp the best time of his life because he was able to make friends without having to reinvent himself. The knowledge that he could have those relationships, even if only for a short time, sustained him throughout his senior year and gave him hope for a college social life.

WHAT PARENTS CAN DO

Remove social status from your list of worries

Ultimately, social status does not represent a person's identity, and high social status can come at a cost. Perceived popular kids might be more likely to drink, engage in risky behavior, and be involved in aggressive incidents. It's okay to encourage your child to make friends (without pushing), but it can be destructive to put a premium on popularity.

Don't assume you know what your child wants

Your child is not you. There are many reasons to avoid imposing your social experience on your child, especially when she already might be happy with her social circle. She may want only one or two close friends, and that's okay.

Whether you were unpopular, hoped to be cool, or were and still are popular, don't expect the same experience for your child and don't let your own insecurities influence your child's social life. Before you react to or make decisions about your child, reflect on whether you are considering your own popularity or image as a factor. If so, rethink your position. Furthermore, your child's social status does not indicate your parenting abilities. It may be tempting to get caught up in a frenzy of social comparisons among parents, much as children do. Don't. Your child's social standing does not reflect your own.

Encourage individuality

When your child comes up with her own way of doing something or expresses a unique perspective or style, convey your admiration. Ask your children for their opinions and encourage them to form their own views, which you can appreciate even if they differ markedly from your own. As psychologist Lawrence Balter has suggested, "It is essential for children to learn that they need not submerge their own identities in order to get along with others. Show them that it is possible to maintain good relations with friends while not necessarily agreeing with all of their thoughts or actions. A child can learn to formulate thoughts and expressions such as, 'I like your way too, but I think I'm going to do it this way.'" Rather than compare your child to others, enjoy him the way he is.

Have faith in your child

If there is anyone in the world whom a child needs to believe in him, it's a parent. Trust that your child wants the best for himself just as much as you do. It sounds glib to say, "Love your child unconditionally." That should be a given. But unconditional love also involves being an effective communicator, able to listen to your child and provide guidance without conveying messages that you might love him less for any reason, such as if he isn't—or doesn't dress—cool, is overweight, doesn't play sports, and so on.

Your home should be a safe place where children know they can be themselves without worrying about their image. Don't badger them about what's "normal." Normality has no inherent value. You should be a source of comfort, support, and confidence. Your children should know that you will never be disappointed in them for any reason related to their social standing.

Consider switching schools

If students are tormenting your child, switching schools is a potential solution (if your child is interested). Remember, a deviant in one population won't necessarily be a deviant in another. Furthermore, several cities have schools that specifically cater to marginalized students. One alum of what she fondly called Outcast High said that she was so "crippled socially" at her first school that her academics suffered. If she hadn't switched schools, she said, she never would have made it to college.

Lobby for changes in schools

School personnel are more likely to make the changes I suggest in the following section if committed groups of parents request them and offer to help. Volunteer to work with the school staff to bring these changes about by outlining logistics, sponsoring fund-raisers, or whatever else may be necessary to relieve busy teachers and administrators of some of the responsibility for implementing these ideas.

WHAT SCHOOLS CAN DO

The most important thing a school can do is not attempt to "normalize" outcasts—they are not the students in the wrong—but rather to focus on developing an atmosphere of acceptance and tolerance among all students. Students considered cafeteria fringe should be an essential part of the tapestry that defines every school. Toward that end:

Respect the significance of the cafeteria

Lunch period is one of the, if not the, most important social times of the day; the cafeteria is a place in which students both socialize with friends and conduct psychologically harmful behavior. During a group discussion at a western Missouri middle school, students told me that limited seating in their lunchroom forces cliques into a frenzied competition. Each table is attached to eight seats, rendering it impossible for a ninth student to pull up a chair or for a small group of three to converse privately. At schools with this configuration, students have to make a mad dash en masse to the cafeteria to snatch a place at the table for themselves and their friends. The Missouri students suggested that cafeterias could offer a variety of seating configurations so that groups of all sizes could fit in and feel comfortable. In some lunchroom arrangements, setting out a handful of loose chairs for students to pull up to tables might encourage more mingling as well as varied opportunities for the cafeteria fringe.

In the same vein, a New Mexico freshman told me about a system that she believes works well at her school. On several days, her two-thousand-student school assigns lunch seating to encourage "social development." When I asked her how that went over with students, she said, "Some people want to sit with friends every day, and people don't usually become super-close friends or anything through assigned seating, but at least it gets you familiar with some people you'd usually never meet otherwise and gives you some allies, in a weird way."

Early on in school, teachers direct students to cafeteria seating arrangements. But just when students begin to turn cliquish, schools tell them that they are old enough to choose where to sit. This timing often coincides with the beginnings of outcast designations. Would it be so horrible if students were to mix up their cafeteria tables occasionally, or might they learn something interesting about a classmate? This option is worth implementing at least once a month. Annually, Teaching Tolerance, an organization that provides free educational materials to educators, leads a nationwide movement called "Mix It

Up at Lunch Day," which challenges students to sit with someone new. This concept emphasizes breaking down barriers and looking beyond stereotypes.

Encourage teachers to offer safe havens

What would Blue have done without Ms. Collins' welcoming classroom? Teachers who open their rooms (or other areas) to students who don't want to deal with the pressures of the cafeteria should be rewarded for going beyond the call of duty. This small kindness can be enormously comforting to a student.

These safe spaces aren't limited to lunches. Several teachers told me how they watched students find confidence in afterschool clubs. A Texas teacher who coaches her school's Academic Decathlon team told me that one of her team members is a gangsta (at that school a term for students who "are generally defiant and consistently make poor choices; they gain credibility by wreaking havoc"). The gangsta, she said, "is also a math nerd. His safe place to be himself is in Academic Decathlon. I have seen him go foul in the hallway to another teacher and couldn't believe it was *my* José. It was like watching a beloved pet become rabid. He is the sweetest, kindest, and most considerate kid in my class." Approach all students with the attitude that they, too, will show their best side once they find a comfortable space in which to express themselves.

Create superordinate goals

Before a football game between the University of Delaware and Westchester State University, researchers conducted a field experiment outside the stadium. Students wearing either Delaware or Westchester hats approached white adults who were obviously affiliated with one of the two schools and asked to interview them about their food preferences. When black students wearing a hat from the opposing school made the inquiry, 38 percent of adults agreed to the interview. When the students wore a hat from the same school, however, 60 percent of adults agreed to help them.

What happened here? By manipulating the adults to believe that they shared the same university affiliation as some of the students, researchers created a cohort in which in-group bias outweighed racial differences. Similarly, the Robbers Cave boys were able to reconcile because Sherif shifted their focus to joint goals that transcended group boundaries. School personnel can also use this strategy by grouping students from different backgrounds on teams, group projects, community-service events, interschool competitions, and other collaborative endeavors. Higher levels of generality can minimize lower-level differences. As one maxim in psychology goes, "The best way to achieve peace on Earth is [to have] an invasion from Mars."

Monitor for both kinds of aggression

Schools need to be just as vigilant about preventing and curbing alternative aggressions as they are about physical aggression. This charge does not lie on teachers' shoulders alone. It is up to administrators to enforce strict policies against these behaviors in class, on school grounds (including the cafeteria), and at school-sponsored events, and to enforce them fairly. In between classes, school personnel, perhaps assisted by parents, can patrol the hallways and common areas to watch for instances of aggression. Adult supervision will not eliminate alternative aggressions entirely, but it may cause some students to think twice before being cruel. If a teacher had been stationed in the populars' hallway in Whitney's school, the prep boys might not have heckled so many non-preps.

Employ social norms strategies

A proven method to reduce the drinking divide among students is to use a survey-based program that shows students that they overestimate both the amount and the frequency with which their classmates drink. These social norms programs can significantly reduce alcohol, drug, and cigarette use, as well as drunk driving.

Programs utilizing social norms can be much more effective than programs using scare tactics. Social psychologist Robert Cialdini, who has conducted many social norms studies, explained the distinction: "Informational campaigns stress that alcohol and drug use is intolerably high, that adolescent suicide rates are alarming, and that rampant polluters are spoiling the environment. Although these claims may be both true and well-intentioned, the campaigns' creators have missed something critically important: Within the statement 'Look at all the people who are doing this *undesirable* thing' lurks the powerful and undercutting normative message 'Look at all the people who *are* doing it.' It is conceivable, then, that in trying to alert the public to the widespread nature of a problem, public service communicators can make it worse."

Treat all groups equally

Schools must examine the myriad ways in which teachers and administrators, traditions, and policies help to establish a social hierarchy, thus delineating which students will dominate and which will be abased for their differences.

Look carefully at the recognition and support offered to certain groups of students, and then formulate ways to provide equivalent recognition and support to all groups. Pep rallies should promote not just sports teams but also academic, debate, and mock trial teams. If a no-homework night is offered for one team's championship match to encourage students to attend and cheer, the policy should be extended to all teams' championship matches—athletic, academic, or otherwise. If school or class competitions generally cater to certain groups, restructure the events so that all students have the opportunity to represent their class or interests. Trophies for the math and chess teams should be displayed with as much fanfare as those of the football and basketball teams. The order of clubs, teams, or organizations presented at rallies, activities showcases, and banquets should be random rather than status-based.

At St. Edmund School, home of the Nerd Herd, the robotics club's success has led to a refreshing new atmosphere. Not only have the students' attitudes changed toward science, but also the school devotes more attention to promoting the subject, celebrating even small scientific achievements and considering a robotics and engineering curriculum. The Nerd Herd is no longer uncool. Its symposiums draw dozens of students. FIRST LEGO League, said St. Edmund coach Christine Zaremba, "has done a great deal toward breaking down stereotypes by creating such a pumped-up, sporting-event, rock star–type atmosphere for what's essentially a glorified version of the math team. When we get students to come visit the competitions, I've never seen a kid leave a tournament without saying, 'I want to be a nerd!'" Students no longer make fun of the Nerd Herd, who proudly announce, "We're the kings of the nerds."

Schools that put traditionally "nerdy" achievements on par with, say, sports victories, encourage a better attitude among staff and students toward those who participate in those activities. "We're teaching our students that being smart and proud of it can bring you the same accolades and recognition that other 'traditional' activities can. That's a big motivator for younger kids, that they can be 'famous' just for being intelligent and working hard," Zaremba said. In other schools, "the stereotypes of the smart kids being losers still persists, and they're constantly being bombarded with the 'ideals' of beauty and talent. Schools that celebrate activities like robotics have a different attitude. We ignore those stereotypes and say, 'Hey, being you is enough, and we're proud of you.'"

Make credit requirements equitable

Examine the ways that students can fulfill credit requirements for graduation. If participation on a school sports team counts as a gym credit, then participation on an academic team or in a drama production also should fulfill a requirement. Will the band geek or theater tech feel that his schedule is just as individualized to him as the jock's schedule is to her?

Encourage upperclassmen to support new students

Several students told me that they would have been lost if not for the nurturing and attention of an older student with similar interests. Rather than encourage perceived popular upperclassmen to turn underclassmen into fawning wannabes, schools can create mentoring opportunities in which older students support younger ones' diverse interests and quirks. Senior nerds, for example, can steer certain freshmen toward welcoming groups and entertaining activities. In this manner, younger students can gain comfort and confidence in the interests they already have, rather than in the interests that other people want or expect them to have. Once they feel secure in the new environment, they can expand their horizons.

Encourage unexpected introductions

Joy found a close friend in Cleo after a teacher paired them together. She would not have known that Mia had been a bullying victim had the vice principal not voiced the connection. A shy senior told me a similar story. "When I moved to Dallas, my science teacher gave me my first friend. The first day in her class, she asked a student to let me sit with him at lunch. He was and still is a really nice kid, and having him as a friend saved me from the inevitable exclusion I would have felt or imposed on myself otherwise," he said.

Students may be more likely to tolerate others' differences if someone has already unlocked the gate that they are convinced divides them. Teachers can help by partnering unlikely pairs in class. "I'm just as guilty as everyone else of judging people by their appearance. Though once I get to know these people, I completely change my mind," said a New York nerd. "We have a program for very artsy people, and I won't lie, I used to think they were all weird and crazy. Then I became friends with them and realized they are just a different type of people and that didn't mean they were weird; they were just different. I was walking home from school with my friend and we saw this girl with a lot of piercings and her hair dyed funky colors and my friend said, 'Isn't that the freak weirdo girl that goes to our school?' Thing is, I had met this girl in gym class and I couldn't help but answer, 'Yeah, but she's not weird; she's actually really nice.'"

Facilitate connections rather than imposing friendships

At the same time, refrain from shoving students into friendships. Some students are just fine on their own, and others will balk if they think adults don't trust them to manage their own social life. "Sometimes adults get too focused on everyone being friends, and they forget that they probably can't even achieve this with their own coworkers," said a Pennsylvania sophomore.

Offer teachers/advisors of marginalized students the chance to be visible

A special education teacher in Tennessee told me, "I've made efforts to be more visible around school. Three-quarters of the special education teachers served as wrestling and cheerleading coaches. It's good to work with students in regular education classes because it means that these students will know me, come to my room, and interact with the students I teach. In a sense, it makes my kids feel cooler because they know some student athletes. Plus it helps the regular education kids see you as a true teacher rather than a 'special' teacher." Her suggestion could also apply to art and music teachers, academic and robotics club advisors, etc. Afford these teachers the opportunity to emcee a pep rally or host another high-visibility event.

Rock the vote

Elections for student government and class officers should be held in all classes during the same period, and ballots should be distributed to every student. At Whitney's school, not all students were encouraged to vote, which partly explained why the same set of students—who neither represented nor cared about the cafeteria fringe—won every year.

In elementary schools, a committee of teachers and counselors could select student officers, with an eye toward choosing shy or otherwise sidelined students who could benefit from the self-esteem and leadership skills associated with representing their class.

Don't punish individuals by rewarding groups

For school-related events—plays, dances, sports, etc.—don't offer ticket discounts to couples or groups. Rewarding students who can find a date or friend to join them automatically penalizes students who would go alone. Along the same lines, sponsor social events other than dances.

Reach out

Flor, the Oklahoma junior in chapter 4, credits teachers and counselors with her turnaround from high school dropout to eloquent college applicant. "It may not seem like much, but there were moments when I near lost hope, and even the smallest word meant a lot," she said. Any adult working at school can reach out to ask students how they're doing, what they need. Let them know that it's okay for them to ask you for help, guidance, or a compassionate ear. During his darkest days, Blue told me that he would have felt less disconnected if only a teacher had asked him sincerely, "What's wrong?"

Fight to promote creativity

The British government funneled millions of dollars into programs that brought creative professionals into schools to talk to students, increase their access to cultural experiences, and endeavor "to help them to discover new things, to express themselves, to develop a passion and to make the most of their talent—whether it is music, art, film, theatre, dance, digital media, exploring libraries, museums, or heritage," according to the program's Web site. Why was the United Kingdom able to invest substantial resources in this important venture while the U.S. government has reduced funding for creative learning? No wonder so many students consider creative kids—like Blue, or Suzanne and Allie from chapter 4—to be on the wrong side of conformity. By affirmatively de-prioritizing creative learning and activities, schools send the forceful message that students who value original thought and expression should be marginalized. Brainstorm methods of teaching students that creativity is useful and essential.

Schools can also send that message by experimenting with imaginative ways to address the issues discussed in this book. At Sachse High School in Texas, for example, every day for fifteen minutes between third and fourth periods, all 2,600 students and every professional staff member—including teachers, administrators, counselors, librarians, coaches, diagnosticians, and facilitators—must sit down in a classroom, pick up a book, and read for fun.

Now students who would have been ostracized in years past are no longer vilified for reading for pleasure. Everyone does it. Students' and teachers' conversations often revolve around literature, many teachers keep classroom mini-libraries, and bulletin boards are plastered with book reviews written by students for fun. Since Sachse introduced the sustained silent reading program in 2007, said assistant principal Cheryl Beard, "It has really made a difference in the culture of our school."

Improve clique relations–among staff

Students across the country told me, unprompted, that they are fully aware of what one student called "a hostile environment among school faculty." They know who among teachers and administrators are allies or enemies, and they pay close attention to teachers' cliques. If schools want to improve student relations, they would do well to begin with relationships among the adults. At the very least, school personnel (like Mandy) should take pains to disguise their animosity in front of students. In extreme circumstances, administrators should sanction the offending teachers.

Confront issues head-on

If there are divisive social issues at your school, rather than dance around the topics, ask students about them directly. "When we have special bully meetings, we read short stories instead of discussing what's actually going on in our school," said a popular Midwestern middle schooler. "We have some kids that are bullies, and reading short stories to them is not going to help." Recognize that administrative neglect is even worse than teacher neglect. A teacher who doesn't put a stop to psychological abuse might ruin the educational experience for a handful of students or classes. An administrator with his head in the sand can affect an entire school.

Have a well-known anti-bullying procedure and contact person

If schools truly want to eliminate bullying, then they must be prepared to address every aspect of the school environment. Bringing in an expert for a one-day presentation will not improve the school atmosphere if administrators don't continue to instill the messages every day. We don't teach kids about oral health by making them brush their teeth only once a year.

There has to be a plan to reduce exclusionary behavior and harassment. Even three years after two alleged bully victims orchestrated the Columbine massacre, the school still did not have an anti-bullying program in place. No matter how ineffective students claim these programs might be—and even if the programs do fall short—it is nevertheless crucial to have an adult whom kids can turn to for help. As the mother of a friend of the shooters said in 2002, "There has to be, in every school, someone these troubled kids can go to . . . Columbine does not have an anti-bullying program. One lady said to me, 'You can't expect them to do it this fast.' Well, yes you can.'" And you must.

Chapter 14

CAFETERIA FRINGE: LUCKY AND FREE

t is natural for people to want to join groups, and to do what they believe they need to do—like exclude—in order to be accepted into those groups. Groups can, of course, provide benefits. But there's a catch.

Consider the jellybean jar game, in which the person who comes closest to guessing the correct number of beans wins the jar. There is a trick to winning this game, or at least coming close. If you play once and alone, you have small chance of victory. However, if you play with a group, you have much better odds, and not only because of the higher number of guesses. When a large enough group plays the game, the arrangement of the guesses resembles a skewed bell curve (bounded by the number zero). The average of those guesses will approach the actual number of jellybeans—and usually will be more accurate than 95 percent of individual players' guesses. If you waited until all of the members of your group had guessed, averaged their answers, and submitted the result as your own guess, you would have an excellent chance at a jellybean dinner.

There's an interesting caveat, however, that makes this game relevant here. This trick works only when each group member comes up with his guess alone, without sharing information or strategies. "The more diverse the group of participants," neuroscientist Gregory Berns explained in *Iconoclast*, "the better the group's average. The only thing that matters is that the participants act independently of one another."

Groups are most advantageous when they consist of diverse members, when each person can act as an individual, bringing something different to the table. A study group wouldn't fare well if each student were an expert on the same subject. A potluck meal wouldn't be satisfying if everyone brought the same dish. Yet many perceived popular students demand that group members stick to the same bland fare. In the school setting, the higher a group's status, the more likely it is to require unanimity. "The more influence a group's members exert on each other . . . the less likely it is that the group's decisions will be wise ones," journalist James Surowiecki wrote in *The Wisdom of Crowds*. "The more influence we exert on each other, the more likely it is that we will believe the same things and make the same mistakes." The conformity that tends to characterize student social circles, then, negates many of the benefits of belonging to a group in the first place.

It is arguable that outcasts are not only courageous, not only crucial, valuable contributors to society, but also, in a way, lucky. Cafeteria fringe status can be a blessing that allows people to embrace and express their true selves because, having already been labeled as different from preconceived norms, they're not *expected* to act like everybody else. Outcasts may be persecuted or shunned, but they are also free. Just as the Straight Edge label validated Regan's decision not to drink, cafeteria fringe labels validate students' decisions to resist conformity. Cafeteria fringe status liberates them from the confines of rigid teen boxes, saving a student the time, energy, and frustration of trying to be someone he's not.

Undoubtedly the loneliness that may accompany this freedom can be a heartrending price to pay. But most people are lonely at times. As countless students—like Whitney, like Blue—have indicated to me over the years, just because a student has company doesn't mean that she's not lonely. Better to be lonely and real than to hide constantly behind a mask of self-deception. The loneliness will pass.

Geeks, loners, punks, floaters, dorks, freaks, nerds, gamers, weirdos, emos, indies, scenes—whether they choose to alter their labels or ignore them entirely, they are free to self-catalog as an identity of one. Identifying as an "I" rather than as an "us" means that there are no rules. Unshackled by strict yet arbitrary, misguided norms, outcasts can be, look, act, and associate however they want to. And in this ever conformist, cookie-cutter, magazine-celebrity-worshipping, creativity-stifling society, the innovation, courage, and differences of the cafeteria fringe are vital to America's culture and progress.

Which is why we must celebrate them.

For character updates, news, and book giveaway contests, please visit **Facebook.com/AuthorAlexandraRobbins**

To schedule a lecture, seminar, Q&A, or moderated discussion with Alexandra Robbins, please visit **AlexandraRobbins.com**

Endnotes

CHAPTER 1

high schoolers view life as "a conveyor belt": Interview.

"the Bermuda triangle of education": See, for example, Juvonen, Jaana; Constant, Louay; Augustine, Catherine H.; Le, Vi-Nhuan; and Kagonoff, Tessa. *Focus on the Wonder Years: Challenges Facing the American Middle School*, Rand Education, 2004.

Only 22 percent of U.S. youth: See Wittig, Michele A. "A Mutual Acculturation Model for Understanding and Undermining Prejudice Among Adolescents," *Intergroup Attitudes and Relations in Childhood*, Levy, Sheri R. and Killen, Melanie, eds., Oxford: Oxford University Press, 2008.

some of the highest rates of emotional problems: See Juvonen; however, I first came across this statistic in Ryan, Allison M. and Shim, S. Serena. "An Exploration of Young Adolescents' Social Achievement, Goals, and Social Adjustment in Middle School," *Journal of Educational Psychology*, Vol. 100, No. 3, 2008. In addition, a higher percentage of U.S. students than students in other countries say they are stressed in school. Health Behaviors in School-age Children 2005/2006 survey.

In 1957, theologian Paul Tillich: See *LIFE*, Jun 17, 1957. See also Tillich, Paul. *The Spiritual Situation in Our Technical Society*, Thomas J. Mark, ed. Mercer University Press, 1988. This quote is cited in Bishop, Bill. *The Big Sort: Why the Clustering of Like-Minded America Is Tearing Us Apart*, New York: Houghton Mifflin, 2008.

Author J. K. Rowling: See, for example, Dick, Sandra. "Rowling Back the Years," *Evening News (Edinburgh)*, September 19, 2001.

"a squat, bespectacled child": See, for example, Flockhart, Susan. "rowling rowling rowling," *The Sunday Herald*, November 11, 2001.

"are plainly outcasts": See Weir, Margaret. "Of magic and single motherhood," *Salon*, March 31, 1999.

Musician Bruce Springsteen: See "A Yearbook of In-Groupers, Outcasts, Strivers and Dropouts Reveals that Biggies Can Bomb in High School Too," *People*, December 25, 1978.

Television host Tim Gunn: See Gunn, Tim. *Gunn's Golden Rules: Life's Little Lessons for Making It Work,* New York: Gallery Books, 2010.

DreamHack: The video that inspired Blue: http://www.youtube.com/watch?v=o__iUR pwMWs.

The pedophile, etc. claims: A resource for students in similar situations is WiredSafety.org, which polices all forms of harassment related to technology and the Internet.

the advisor restricted Arwing's: "Now he's taking it into his own hands, and it's failing horribly," Blue lamented a few days after the meeting. "It's like, if a veterinarian said he couldn't save your dog because he didn't want to do the surgery because it would have been too complicated. So eff the veterinarian."

"hyper and squeaky": Interview.

A substantial percentage: Interviews.

keep the price tags on: Interview.

changed her e-mail address: Interview.

"We get a lot of Goths": Interview.

"Goths wear all black": Interview.

"People constantly criticize": Interview.

"head toss every five seconds": Interview.

"every song in the Apple commercials": Interview.

"usually have long hair": Interview.

"even if they aren't tardy": Interview.

Blue's table: Blue sent the table to me, unprompted. I disagree with the characterizations, but I think the perspective is informative.

"smart Asian nerds": Interview.

Jew Crew, Superjews: Interviews, group discussions. Thank you to Rani Schlenoff, Hava Shirazi Anderson, and their students for a fun and interesting discussion.

church girls: Interviews.

"they wear alternative clothes": Interview.

"underground concepts": Interview.

global warming: Interview.

who are weird on purpose: Interview.

descended from beatniks: Interviews.

"It makes me more sure about myself": Interview.

"I'm not going to eat them": Interview.

"bros": Interviews.

student bullying is up: See, for example, Elkind, David. "Playtime is over," *The International Herald Tribune*, March 30, 2010.

concept of "normal" has narrowed: This trend is occurring among labels for mental health characterizations as well. See, for example, Lane, Christopher. *Shyness: How Normal Behavior Became a Sickness*, New Haven: Yale University Press: 2008. As Lane wrote, "We've narrowed healthy behavior so dramatically that our quirks and eccentricities— the *normal* emotional range of adolescence and adulthood—have become problems we fear and expect drugs to fix."

CHAPTER 2

"I've been able to use that": Interview.

Blue's mother: Readers of *The Overachievers* will recognize some similarities between Blue and AP Frank. I was not aware of Blue's issues with his mother when I began following him. Blue, who told me he could relate to Frank, noted that in response to the pressure, Frank completed his schoolwork to escape while Blue abandoned his schoolwork to rebel.

students' involvement in extracurricular activities: See, for example, Eder, Donna and Kinney, David. "The effect of middle school extracurricular activities on adolescents' popularity and peer status," *Youth and Society*, Vol. 26, 1995.

route to popularity: Ibid.

factor that brings cheerleaders prestige: See, for example, Merten, Don E. "The Meaning of Meanness: Popularity, Competition and Conflict among Junior High School Girls," *Sociology of Education*, Vol. 70, No. 3, July 1997.

visibility: See, for example, LaFontana, Kathryn M. and Cillessen, Antonius H. N. "Children's Perceptions of Popular and Unpopular Peers. A Multimethod Assessment," *Developmental Psychology*, Vol. 38, No. 5, 2002.

nerds or geeks might not be popular: See, for example, Brekke, Kjell Arne; Nyborg, Karine; and Rege, Mari. "The Fear of Exclusion: Individual Effort when Group Formation is Endogenous," *Scandinavian Journal of Economics*, 2007.

being recognizable: See, for example, Merten.

the most frequent interaction: See, for example, LaFontana.

"children focus on the quantity": Ibid.

to be popular means to be influential: See, for example, Xie, Hongling; Li, Yan; Boucher, Signe; Hutchins, Bryan C.; and Cairns, Beverley D. "What Makes a Girl (or a Boy) Popular (or Unpopular)? African American Children's Perceptions and Developmental Differences," *Developmental Psychology*, Vol. 42, No. 4, 2006.

prefer the things they see: See, for example, Berger, Jonah; Heath, Chip; and Ho, Ben. "Divergence in Cultural Practices—Tastes as Signals of Identity," Stanford University unpublished paper, March 2005.

often able to actively maneuver their position in the social hierarchy: See, for example, Mayeaux, Lara; Sandstrom, Marlene J; and Cillessen, Antonius H. N. "Is Being Popular a Risky Proposition?" *Journal of Research on Adolescence*, Vol. 18, No. 1, 2008.

savvy about the Machiavellian methods: See, for example, LaFontana.

viewed as lacking skills: See, for example, LaFontana.

The Exclusives: Interview.

"Hair color has to be blonde": Interview.

dictionary definition of popularity: Merriam Webster defines popular as "commonly liked or approved." See Merriam-webster.com.

"a shared recognition among peers": See Schwartz, David; Nakamoto, Jonathan; Gorman, Andrea Hopmeyer; and McKay, Tara. "Popularity, Social Acceptance, and Aggression in Adolescent Peer Groups: Links with Academic Performance and School Attendance," *Developmental Psychology*, Vol. 42, No. 6, 2006.

developmental psychology literature: Ibid. Note that sociologists made this distinction earlier than developmental psychologists did. Also, thank you to Sacred Heart University psychology professor Kathryn LaFontana for discussing this issue with me.

More recently: Interview, LaFontana. See also Mayeaux. See also Rubin, Kenneth H.; Bukowski, William M.; and Parker, Jeffrey G. "Peer Interactions, Relationships, and Groups," *Handbook of Child Psychology*. Hoboken: John Wiley & Sons, 2006.

perceived popularity: See, for example, Parkhurst, J. T. and Hopmeyer, A. "Sociometric popularity and peer-perceived popularity: Two distinct dimensions of peer status," *Journal of Early Adolescence*, Vol. 18, 1998.

kind and trustworthy: Ibid.

"mean popular" and "nice popular": Interviews.

CHAPTER 3
"the girls who could model": Interview.

overt aggression and alternative aggressions: See, for example, Rose, Amanda J.; Swenson, Lance P.; and Waller, Erika M. "Overt and Relational Aggression and Perceived Popularity: Developmental Differences in Concurrent and Prospective Relations," *Developmental Psychology*, Vol. 40, No. 3, 2004.

Relational aggression: Ibid. A popular theory holds that relational aggression is the more common aggression among girls. However, Stacey S. Horn persuasively argues against dividing aggressions by gender in Horn, Stacey S. "Mean Girls or Cultural Stereotypes: Essay Review," *Human Development*, 47, 2004.

relational bullying: See, for example, Coloroso, Barbara. *The Bully, the Bullied, and the Bystander*, New York: HarperCollins, 2003.

eye rolling: Ibid.

intended to harm: See, for example, Underwood, Marion K. *Social Aggression Among Girls*. New York: The Guilford Press, 2003.

socially incompetent: See, for example, Kiefer, Sarah M. and Ryan, Allison M. "Striving for Social Dominance Over Peers: The Implications for Academic Adjustment During Early Adolescence," *Journal of Educational Psychology*, Vol. 100, No. 2, 2008.

measured a child's rates of aggression: Ibid.

undeniably strong link: See, for example, Mayeaux. Note: "Only *perceived* popularity is characterized by dominant and aggressive tendencies . . . including both overt and relational forms of aggression." See also Schwartz: "Aggression and popularity become progressively more intertwined over the course of adolescence."

associated with high social status: See, for example, Puckett, Marissa B.; Aikins, Julie Wargo; and Cillessen, Antonius H. N. "Moderators of the Association Between Relational Aggression and Perceived Popularity," *Aggressive Behavior*, Vol. 34, 2008. See also Kiefer. See also Horn, Stacey S. "Mean Girls or Cultural Stereotypes: Essay Review," which discusses the debate over whether social aggression is fundamentally negative.

"should not be seen as socially intelligent": See Goleman, Daniel. *Social Intelligence*, New York: Bantam, 2006.

"popularity cycle": See Eder, Donna. "The Cycle of Popularity: interpersonal relations among female adolescents," *Sociology of Education*, Vol. 58, Issue 3, July 1985.

distancing herself too far from old friends: See, for example, Adler, Patricia A. and Adler, Peter. "Dynamics of Inclusion and Exclusion in Preadolescent Cliques," *Social Psychology Quarterly*, Vol. 58, No. 3, September 1995.

appearing to think she's "all that": See Merten.

"Loss of popularity in this manner": Ibid. Merten also discussed what he calls "the paradox of popularity," in which popular students were also vulnerable to being labeled stuck-up and, for that reason, could lose their popularity.

His answer: Be mean: Ibid.

treating other students as equals: Ibid.

undermining their own popularity: Ibid.

"Whereas being stuck-up": Interview, Don Merten.

shows like Gossip Girl: Interviews.

Broadcast TV networks: See, for example, Wyatt, Edward. "More Than Ever, You Can Say That on Television," *New York Times*, November 14, 2009.

Today: See, for example, *Today*, October 16, 2009.

Celebrities like Paris Hilton: See, for example, Hefferman, Virginia. "Epithet Morphs from Bad Girl to Weak Boy," *New York Times*, March 22, 2005.

"Shopping at only designer stores": Interview.

relational aggression can be difficult: See, for example, Wiseman.

students reward populars: Interview, University of Missouri psychology professor Amanda Rose. See also Rose, "Overt and Relational Aggression . . ."

"I throw a lot of parties": Interview.

"We crushed their dreams": Interview.

various other groups: Interviews.

Female athletes: Interviews.

even teachers and administrators: Interviews.

keep perceived popularity: See, for example Mayeaux: "Growing evidence suggests that children's reliance on aggressive behavior increases *after* they achieve high status, perhaps as a means of protecting their status, in response to a sense of elitism, or as a way to combat the resentment directed toward them from less popular peers."

realigning relationships: See, for example, Adler.

Meanness is a language: See Merten.

"Is there anyone fighting for those rights?" For additional resources, see The Trevor Project: www.thetrevorproject.org; PFLAG (Parents, Families, & Friends of Lesbians and Gays): http://community.pflag.org; GLSEN (Gay/Lesbian/Straight Educator Network): http://www.glsen.org/cgi-bin/iowa/all/home/index.html; Lambda Legal Defense and Education Fund: www.lambdalegal.org; and information and discussion boards at The Gay Youth Corner: http://www.thegyc.com and Queer Attitude: http://www.queerattitude.com. Thank you to Evan Cook for his assistance compiling this list.

the ruling clique there: Interviews.

"usually the cheerleader or good-old-boy types": Interview.

"this is how I felt in high school": Interview.

"It was the most disturbing": Interview.

other administrators and teachers openly: Interview.

Teachers in various states: Interview.

"The labels are the 'veterans' ": Interview. Many other teachers also mentioned this distinction in interviews.

"There were the 'haves' ": Interview.

secretaries who gossip: Interviews.

"the distinct impression": Interview.

an intimidating drama teacher: Interview.

"as if I am special ed. also": Interview.

"mean-girlish" teachers: Interviews.

"I have seen teachers try": Interview.

cliques palming off: Interviews.

"the worst part about cliques": Interview.

hostilities among teachers: Interviews.

"teacher gossip frenzy": Interview.

rationalize them by saying: Interviews.

"get together over margaritas": Interview.

mechanical model: for a photo of Blue's model, please visit www.facebook.com/pages/AuthorAlexandraRobbins.

CHAPTER 4

"Eccentric, over-the-top": Interview.

"The sci-fi convention": Interview.

"The otaku, or odd person group": Interview.

"Socially awkward and totally irritating": Interview.

"They're completely different": Interview.

"freaky kids, drama kids": Interview.

Suzanne, Laney, Allie, Flor: Interviews.

DIY: Indies are not the only group to identify with the DIY ethic. See, for example, Traber, Daniel S. "L.A.'s 'White Minority': Punk and the Contradictions of Self-Marginalization," *Cultural Critique*, No. 48, Spring 2001.

"stands out": Interview.

groups to form judgments: See, for example, Manstead, Antony S. R. and Hewstone, Miles, eds. *The Blackwell Encyclopedia of Social Psychology*, 1996.

polarization occurs for three reasons: Ibid.

juries whose individual members: See Myers, D. G. and Bishop, G. D. "Discussion effects on racial attitudes," *Science*, Vol. 169, 1970. See also Bray, Robert M. and Noble, Audrey M. "Authoritarianism and Decisions of Mock Juries; Evidence of Jury Bias and Group Polarization," *Journal of Personality and Social Psychology*, Vol. 36, No. 12, 1978.

study of civil liberties decisions: See Walker, Thomas G. and Main, Eleanor C. "Choice Shifts in Political Decisionmaking: Federal Judges and Civil Liberties Cases," *Journal of Applied Social Psychology*, Vol. 3, No. 1, 1973.

group polarization in France: See Moscovici, Serge and Zavalloni, Marisa. "The Group as a Polarizer of Attitudes," *Journal of Personality and Social Psychology*, Vol. 1, No. 2, 1969.

group polarization can make students: See, for example, Myers and Bishop.

evaluations of faculty: See, for example, Myers, D. G. "Discussion-induced attitude polarization," *Human Relations*, Vol. 28, 1975.

modify individuals' perceptions of themselves: See, for example, Swann, William B., Jr.; Milton, Laurie P.; and Polzer, Jeffrey T. "Should We Create a Niche or Fall in Line? Identity Negotiation and Small Group Effectiveness," *Journal of Personality and Social Psychology*, Vol. 79, No. 2, 2000.

Unable to separate: See, for example, Harter, Susan. "Self and Identity Development." In *At the Threshold: The Developing Adolescent*, Feldman, S. Shirley and Elliott, Glen R., eds. Cambridge, MA: Harvard University Press, 1990.

"imaginary audience": See Elkind, David. "Egocentrism in Adolescence." *Child Development*, Vol. 38, 1967.

Asian girls were subtly reminded: See the Tufts University experiment cited in Vedantam, Shankar. "With Subtle Reminders, Stereotypes Can Become Self-Fulfilling." *The Washington Post*, December 11, 2006. Along similar lines, "Exposure to words related to the elderly makes people walk more slowly; words related to professors make people smarter at the game Trivial Pursuit." See Haidt, Jonathan. *The Happiness Hypothesis*, New York: Basic Books, 2006.

parents and teachers to influence: See, for example, McNulty, Shawn E. and Swann, William B. Jr. "Identity Negotiation in Roommate Relationships: The Self as Architect and Consequence of Social Reality," *Journal of Personality and Social Psychology*, Vol. 67, No. 6, 1994.

"called me the 'happy freshman' ": Interview.

classmates viewed them as nerds: Interviews.

"it's a lot better than being a nobody": Interview.

group polarization is not so different: See, for example, Myers, David G. and Lamm, Helmut. "The Group Polarization Phenomenon," *Psychological Bulletin*, Vol. 83, No. 4, 1976.

"a pattern of thought": See Merriam-webster.com.

the responsibility is shared: See, for example, Moscovici.

"the mindless sinking of personal identity into the group of Us": See Wrangham, Richard and Peterson, Dale. *Demonic Males*, New York: Houghton Mifflin, 1996. Wrangham added, "That it also produces irresponsibility and deeply unpleasant behavior is only relevant from the point of view of Them."

in the midst of a crowd: See, for example, Billig, Michael. "Social Psychology and Intergroup Relations," *European Monographs in Social Psychology*, Vol. 9. Billig also notes Freud's description that a group consists of "a number of individuals who have put one and the same object in place of their ego ideal and have consequently identified themselves with one another in their ego."

a susceptibility: Many psychologists refute Gustave Le Bon's concept of a "mental unity," however. See, for example, Baumeister, Roy F. and Leary, Mark R. "The Need to Belong: Desire for interpersonal attachments as a fundamental human motivation," *Psychological Bulletin*, Vol. 117, No. 3, 1995: "Wegner (1986) noted the irony that traditional theories of the 'group mind' tended to assume that all members would essentially think the same thing, because much more far-reaching advantages could be realized through a group mind if each member was responsible for different information, thereby enabling the group to process considerably more information than any one person could." I address this issue in Chapter 14.

"crowd contagion": See Canetti, Elias. *Crowds and Power*, New York: Farrar, Straus, & Giroux, 1960. Cited in Goleman.

"Usually one person starts making fun": Interview.

"The human brain takes in information": See Berns, Gregory. *Iconoclast: A Neuroscientist Reveals How to Think Differently*, Boston: Harvard Business School Press, 2008. I would like to take this opportunity to thank Gregory Berns. *Iconoclast* was fascinating and fun to read.

the group and the individual: See, for example, Bettancourt, B. Ann and Sheldon, Kennon. "Social Roles as Mechanisms for Psychological Need Satisfaction Within Social Groups," *Journal of Personality and Social Psychology*, Vol. 81, No. 6, 2001.

"the satisfaction of one tends to come at the expense of the other": Ibid., which cites Brewer, M. B. "The social self: On being the same and different at the same time," *Personality and Social Psychology Bulletin*, Vol. 17, 1991.

"groups require consensus, homogeneity, and cohesion": See Bukowski, William and Sippola, Lorrie K. "Groups, Individuals, and Victimization: A View of the Peer System," in Juvonen, Jaana and Graham, Sandra, eds. *Peer Harassment in School: The plight of the vulnerable and victimized*, New York: Guilford Press, 2001.

CHAPTER 5

longboarding has more of a graceful flow: For an example of this sort of artistry and athleticism, please visit www.facebook.com/pages/AuthorAlexandraRobbins.

drawn to peers who are similar: See, for example, Hartup, Willard and Abecassis, Maurissa. "Friends and Enemies," *Blackwell Handbook of Childhood Social Development*, Smith, Peter K. and Hart, Craig H., eds. Malden, MA: Blackwell Publishers, 2002.

From the age of five: See, for example, Nesdale, Drew. "Peer Group Rejection and Children's Intergroup Prejudice," in *Intergroup Attitudes* . . .

"I have to be the same as everybody else": Interview.

Note: As children spend time with each other, in the course of their interactions they often become more alike. See, for example, Poulin, F. and Boivin, M., "The role of proactive and reactive aggression in the formulation and development of boys' friendships," *Developmental Psychology,* Vol. 36, 2000.

levels of academics: See, for example, Cairns, R. B.; Cairns, B. D.; Neckerman, H. J.; Gest, S.; and Gariépy, J.-L. "Social networks and aggressive behavior: Peer support or peer rejection?", *Developmental Psychology,* Vol. 24, 1988. Cited in Xie.

more conformist: See, for example, Gavin, Leslie A. and Furman, Wyndol. "Age Differences in Adolescents' Perceptions of Their Peer Groups," *Developmental Psychology*, Vol. 25, No. 5, 1989: 827–834.

experience more negative behavior: Ibid.

In the mid-twentieth century, psychologists: This group included Muzafer Sherif, who later conducted the Robbers Cave experiment.

gauge levels of conformity: See Asch, Solomon E. "Opinions and Social Pressure," *Scientific American*, Vol. 193, No. 5, November 1955.

likes to cheat: See, for example, Gilbert, Daniel. *Stumbling on Happiness*, New York: Knopf, 2006.

"the more measurements you make": See Berns, Gregory.

deferring to the group: Ibid.

"We observed the fear system": Ibid.

"unpleasant nature of standing alone": Ibid.

brain emits an error signal: See Klucharev, Vasily; Hytönen, Kaisa; Rijpkema, Mark; Smidts, Ale; and Fernández, Guillén. "Reinforcement Learning Signal Predicts Social Conformity," *Neuron*, Vol. 61, Issue 1, January 2009.

financial loss or social exclusion: See, for example, Landau, Elizabeth. "Why so many minds think alike," *CNN*, January 15, 2009.

triggers a process: See Klucharev.

"Deviation from the group": See Landau.

debuted at number four: See Pomerantz, Dorothy and Rose, Lacey, eds. "The Celebrity 100," *Forbes*, June 28, 2010.

"When I see somebody like Gaga": See Lauper, Cyndi. "The 2010 TIME 100: Lady Gaga," *TIME*, April 29, 2010.

"I didn't fit in in high school": See *The Ellen DeGeneres Show*, November 27, 2009.

"nerdball in theater and chorus": See Herndon, Jessica and Dyball, Rennie. "Totally Gaga: What You Don't Know About Pop Star Lady Gaga," *People*, June 22, 2009.

teased for her eccentric style: See LadyGaga.com.

by age twenty: Ibid.

"This is really who I am": See *The Ellen DeGeneres Show*.

a comprehensive review: Included countless books and articles, most of which are not quoted in the section, too many of which to name here.

record for Emmy nominations: See, for example, Taylor, William C. and LaBarre, Polly. *Mavericks at Work: Why the Most Original Minds in Business Win*, New York: William Morrow, 2006.

HBO executives ask themselves: Ibid.

Southwest Airlines, which distinguishes itself: See Taylor. In 2002, *Money Magazine* reported that Southwest was the best-performing stock in the magazine's history.

Senior Executive Service: Interview.

"The work that matters most": See Taylor, William.

Steven Spielberg: Incidentally, Spielberg's fifth grade teacher complained to the principal about his "obsession with filmmaking." "He was driving her nuts," principal Richard T. Ford recalled. "He did some filming at the school and he was always talking about it." See McBride, Joseph. *Steven Spielberg: A Biography*, New York: Simon & Schuster, 1997.

"a real nerd": Ibid.

"I got smacked and kicked": See Weinraub, Bernard. "Steven Spielberg Faces the Holocaust," *The New York Times*, December 12, 1993.

'weird' and 'independent-minded': See McBride, Joseph.

"he always saw things differently": See Weinraub, Bernard.

shy, introverted, and ostracized: See McBride, Joseph.

"He was my nemesis": Ibid.

"the most bankable director in the business": See, for example, Barnes, Brook. "A Director's Cut," *The New York Times*, July 27, 2008.

"Big ideas come from big thinkers": See Taylor, William.

In 1896, French naturalist: See Fabre, Jean-Henri. *The Life of the Caterpillar*, New York: Dodd, Mead, and Company, 1916.

Fabre observed the caterpillars: Ibid.

Manager of the Century: See, for example, "Fortune Selects Henry Ford Businessman of the Century; GE's Jack Welch Named Manager of the Century," *Business Wire*, November 1, 1999.

"the ability to see around corners": See Welch, Jack. *Winning*, New York: HarperCollins, 2005.

view multiple angles: Also note: In the legendary book *How to Win Friends and Influence People*, one of Dale Carnegie's principles is "Try honestly to see things from the other person's point of view." Carnegie, Dale. *How to Win Friends and Influence People*, New York: Pocket Books, 1982.

The Google Story *coauthor*: Interview.

The Writer: See DeLillo, Don. *Hungry Mind Review*, Fall 1997.

"was inclined to separate himself": See Isaacson, Walter. *Einstein: His Life and Universe*, New York: Simon & Schuster, 2007.

"Play and playmates were forgotten": Ibid.

Einstein was slow to speak: See Isaacson, Walter. *Wired*, March 2007.

"When I ask myself how it happened": Ibid.

"a lively sense": See Isaacson, Walter.

Einstein: Contrary to popular belief, Einstein did not fail math. In fact, Einstein said, "before I was fifteen I had mastered differential and integral calculus." See Isaacson, Walter. *Einstein: His Life and Universe*.

"He comes in entirely as an outsider": See Falk, Dan. "Einstein's science genius wasn't just about IQ," *Boston Globe*, March 15, 2005.

"Other scientists had come close": See Isaacson, Walter. *Wired*.

first African-American admitted: See, for example, edelman.sfsu.edu.

her secret to success: See, for example, Kimbro, Dennis. *What Makes the Great Great*, New York: Doubleday, 1998.

"the hardiness factor": See Collins, Jim. *Good to Great: Why Some Companies Make the Leap . . . And Others Don't*, New York: HarperCollins, 2001.

resulting feeling of abandonment: See, for example, Johnson, Allan. "Only Lately Has Freddie Prinze Jr. Begun Getting Over His Father's Death," *Chicago Tribune*, January 28, 1999.

as he stepped onto his school bus: See Pearlman, Cindy. "Fresh Prinze: Freddie Jr. making name for himself, family," *Chicago Sun-Times*, January 24, 1999.

found comfort in Stan Lee's characters: See "Today's People: Prinze Gets Serious About Comic Books," *Charleston Daily Mail*, April 11, 2000.

related to the X-Men: See Johnson.

"I would always pretend": Ibid.

"running and diving": Ibid.

Students called him freak: See Vincent, Mal. "From Nerd to Prinze Charming," *The Sunday Telegraph*, October 15, 2000.

weirdo: See, for example, Garner, Jack. "Despite big-screen image, Prinze was a high-school recluse," *Rochester Democrat and Chronicle*, January 29, 1999.

Bullies threw rocks at him: See Vincent.

"Kids thought that was really strange": See Johnson.

"The quirks that made him": See Berlin, Joey and Revel, Dera. "art2," *Los Angeles Times,* January 25, 1999.

being quiet and sensitive: See Valdes-Rodriguez, Alisa. "Don't Label This Prinze," *Los Angeles Times,* January 20, 2000.

creating plays for girls: See Pearlman, Cindy. "Steady Freddie: Prinze more than just pretty face," *Chicago Sun-Times,* June 11, 2000.

"vulnerable humanity": See Valdes-Rodriguez.

"a male Julia Roberts": See Vincent.

"He's just an incredibly natural actor": See Valdes-Rodriguez.

"I was considered weird and a freak": See Berlin and Revel.

"People think I'm cool now": See Gordon, Bryony. " 'They told my mom I was a schizo': From class geek to husband of Buffy the Vampire Slayer—how did Freddie Prinze Jr. do it?" *The Daily Telegraph,* January 16, 2003.

"I look at it like this": See Valdes-Rodriguez.

"The more faithfully you listen": See, for example, Blank, Warren. *The 108 Skills of Natural Born Leaders,* New York: AMACOM, 2001.

"enables us to stand apart": See Covey, Stephen R. *7 Habits of Highly Effective People: Restoring the Character Ethic,* New York: Free Press, 1989.

worth more than $5 billion: See, for example, Taylor, William.

down-to-earth "nerd values": Ibid.

"wearing a plastic pocket protector": See craigslist.org.

although they didn't always know: See Cohen, Ben and Greenfield, Jerry. *Ben & Jerry's Double Dip: Lead With Your Values and Make Money, Too,* New York: Simon & Schuster, 1997.

"social progress for the common good": Ibid.

met in school as shy boys: See, for example, Long, Joyce Rainey. "Green Middle School serves up Ben & Jerry's videoconference," *South Side Leader,* May 13, 2010.

"Self-awareness is fundamental to leadership growth": See Blank.

"the kings of emo": See "Playboy interview: Pete Wentz," *Playboy,* October 1, 2008.

"an entire generation": Ibid.

"a giant pop-culture idea": Ibid.

dyed his hair blue: See, for example, Thompson, Phillip. "Boy Crazy; Fall Out Boy—Chicago's pretty in punk success story—always reflects on where it all began," *Redeye,* March 30, 2006.

talented soccer player: See *Playboy.*

"a solitary guy": Ibid.

"Wentz's deeply personal": See Cripps.

"equal parts protector": See Thompson.

Jay-Z dubbed it, a movement: See Cripps.

"it's okay to feel down": Ibid.

"confessional bravado": See, for example, Ulaby, Neda. "Fall Out Boy Rewrites the Gender Roles of Rock," *All Things Considered*, November 30, 2007.

wrote a comic book series: See, for example, "Pete Wentz Named UNICEF Tap Project National Spokesperson," *PR Newswire*, February 22, 2010.

first record went platinum: See, for example, Ulaby.

VH1 named Wentz: See, for example, *PR Newswire*.

"I'm happy to be part of a culture": See *Playboy*.

making good on promises and fulfilling expectations: See, for example, Covey.

Integrity: Warren Buffett has said, "In looking for people to hire, you look for three qualities: integrity, intelligence, and energy. And if they don't have the first, the other two will kill you. You think about it; it's true. If you hire somebody without the first, you really want them to be dumb and lazy." Also note that Buffett said that in high school, "I was just sort of nothing." Lowe, Janet. *Warren Buffett Speaks: Wit and Wisdom from the World's Greatest Investor*, New York: John Wiley & Sons, 1997.

"Integrity also means": See Covey.

"Lack of candor basically blocks": See Welch. Benjamin Franklin also highly valued both candor and integrity. In his 1726 essay "Plan for Future Conduct," he wrote, "To endeavor to speak truth in every instance; to give nobody expectations that are not likely to be answered, but aim at sincerity in every word and action—the most amiable excellence in a rational being."

in a twenty-seven-second phone call: See, for example, Sandell, Laurie. "Bombshell in Blue Jeans," *Glamour*, August 2009.

"She listens to her heart": See Goodspeed, John. "Swift puts heart in work," *San Antonio Express-News*, February 6, 2009.

"The farther away you get": See "Best Buy," *Journal of Technology & Science*, August 30, 2009.

"became a people-watcher": See DeLuca, Dan. "Taylor Swift, focused on 'great songs,'" *The Philadelphia Inquirer Daily Magazine*, November 11, 2008.

When she sat down: See, for example, Hammerstein, B. J. "Names & Faces," *Detroit Free Press*, December 25, 2008. Swift also discussed this isolation with Katie Couric on a Grammy special that aired February 4, 2009.

"The kids at school thought": See Waterman, Lauren. "Swift Ascent," *Teen Vogue*, March 2009.

"in middle school there really doesn't": See DeLuca.

"It was so healthy for me": Ibid.

moved to Nashville: See, for example, Goodspeed.

at fourteen, became the youngest: See Taylorswift.com.

"showed up, wearing my T-shirts": See Waterman.

In 2008 and 2009: See Taylorswift.com.

top-selling digital artist: See "Nielsen SoundScan Lists Taylor Swift as the Top-Selling Digital Artist in History," *PR Newswire*, January 7, 2010.

"What does it matter": See Goodman, Jilian J. "Taylor-made for group hug," *Omaha World-Herald*, August 10, 2009.

When Yahoo! executives evaluate: See, for example, Taylor, William.

number one most influential business thinker: See White, Erin. "New breed of business gurus rises," *The Wall Street Journal*, May 5, 2008.

"You must marry a thorough understanding": See Hamel, Gary. *Leading the Revolution*, Boston: Harvard Business Press, 2002.

he was a loner and a "misfit": See Chouinard, Yvon. *Let My People Go Surfing: The Education of a Reluctant Businessman*, New York: Penguin, 2005.

"the godfather of ice climbing": See Boardman, Peter. *Outside Magazine,* in a review of Chouinard's book *Climbing Ice*, Sierra Club Books for Children, 1978.

A craftsman at heart: See, for example, Gordon, Michael. "Riding out the storm on a new wave," *Sydney Morning Herald,* April 18, 2009.

One of the first green companies: See, for example, Burke, Monte. "Wal-Mart, Patagonia Team to Green Business," *Forbes*, May 24, 2010.

Patagonia annually gives: See, for example, Patagonia.com.

Walmart, Nike, and Gap: See, for example, Archer, Michelle. "Founder of Patagonia became a businessman accidentally," *USA Today*, October 31, 2005.

forty employees take paid: See, for example, Greenhouse, Steven. "Working Life (High and Low)," *New York Times*, April 20, 2008.

Solar panels power: Ibid.

built using 95 percent: See Earnest, Leslie. "Patagonia's Founder Seeks to Spread Environmental Gospel," *Los Angeles Times*, October 9, 2005.

the most fuel-efficient cars: See, for example, Greenhouse.

lunchtime yoga and Pilates: Ibid.

Patagonia covers 100 percent: Ibid.

"Only those businesses operating": See Chouinard.

"the coolest company on the planet": See *Fortune*, April 2007.

Character Strengths and Virtues: See Peterson, Christopher and Seligman, Martin E. P. *Character Strengths and Virtues: a Handbook and Classification*, Oxford: Oxford University Press, 2004.

in more than seventy countries: See, for example, Max, D. T. "Happiness 101," *New York Times Magazine*, January 7, 2007.

"those abiding moral traits": Ibid.

"the good life": Peterson and Seligman make a disclaimer: "We also believe that positive traits need to be placed in context; it is obvious that they do not operate in isolation from the settings, proximal and distal, in which people are to be found. . . . Situations of course make it more or less difficult to live well, but the good life reflects choice and will." Separately, I like University of Virginia psychology professor Jonathan Haidt's paraphrase of Aristotle: "A good life is one where you develop your strengths, realize your potential, and become what it is in your nature to become."

"has an inner life": See Peterson, Christopher and Seligman, Martin.

"even when one has much to lose": I also like how Peterson defines "strengths of courage": "Strengths of courage entail the exercise of will to accomplish goals in the face of opposition, external or internal." See Peterson, Christopher. *A Primer in Positive Psychology*, Oxford: Oxford University Press, 2006.

Judd Apatow: See IMDB.com.

Angelina Jolie: See Rader, Dotson. "Angelina Jolie: Taming Her Wild Heart," *Parade*, July 11, 2010.

Zac Efron: See Zuckerman, Blaine. "Zac Efron Answers Your Questions," *People*, April 27, 2009.

Ne-Yo: See Arroyave, Luis. "About Last Night . . .", *Chicago Tribune*, August 22, 2009.

Drake: See, for example, Carter, Kelley. "Drake: Influenced by the south, this Canadian rapper earns his cool and command of hip-hop," *Jet*, September 20, 2010.

LeeAnn Rimes: See Cioffi, Adrianna; Cioffi, Lauren; and Salto, Christine. "Kidsday," *Newsday*, September 30, 2003.

Megan Fox: See Vincent, Mal. "Bombshell," *The Virginian-Pilot*, June 18, 2010. Fox also told *People* that she was picked on and made fun of at school; a classmate even dressed up as Fox for Halloween. See "I Wasn't a Mean Girl," *People*, October 5, 2009.

Adam Young: See Dawson, Kim and Cabooter, James. "I'm on Fire!", *Daily Star*, February 9, 2010.

Emily Robison and Martie Maguire: See Dennis, Alicia. "Dixie Duo," *People*, May 24, 2010.

Vanessa Hudgens: See *Nylon*, April 2010.

Chad Michael Murray: See Crook, John. "One Tree Hill's Cast Starts Branching Out," *Los Angeles Times*, September 28, 2003.

Sarah Michelle Gellar: See, for example, *Post* staff. " 'Other Kids Picked On Me': Buffy," *New York Post*, August 3, 2001.

Busy Philipps: See Freed, David A. "New kids in the box," *Chicago Tribune*, September 12, 2005.

Andy Warhol: See, for example, Curtis, Dawn Marie. "Pop Artist Was Born in Pittsburgh," *Pittsburgh Post-Gazette*, January 16, 2002.

James Franco: Interview with Lindzi Scharf. Lindzi.com.

Barbra Streisand: See, for example, Churchill, Bonnie. "Streisand Relishes 'Complete Control,'" *Christian Science Monitor*, December 13, 1996.

Mena Suvari: See Lee, Luaine. "An All-American Actress: From 'American Beauty' to 'American Pie,' Mena Suvari Grows as a Woman and a Star," *Scripps Howard News Service*, September 16, 2001.

"I just didn't relate": Ibid.

John Stossel: See Stossel, John. "The 'In' Crowd and Social Cruelty: Exploration of what causes popularity and unpopularity in children and adults," *ABC News*, June 3, 2002.

Barbara Walters: See *People*, 1978.

Al Roker: See Getlen, Larry. "Today Is Always a Busy Day When Your Name Is Al Roker," *CityScoops*, 2008. See also, King, Larry. "Al Roker Discusses His 'Adventures in Fatherhood," *Larry King Live*, June 16, 2000.

Amy Van Dyken: See, for example, Ford, Bob. "Van Dyken Wins Butterfly for U.S.," *The Philadelphia Inquirer*, July 24, 1996.

was tormented by her high school: I interviewed Van Dyken on this topic several years ago.

first American woman: See, for example, Allen, Karen. "U.S. swimmers haul in records," *USA Today*, July 27, 1996.

"this is a victory for all the nerds": See, for example, Brant, Martha. "Pool Sharks," *Newsweek*, August 5, 1996.

U.S. Olympic Hall of Fame: See, for example, Meyer, John. "Golden girl Van Dyken joins U.S. Olympic Hall," *The Denver Post*, April 16, 2008.

Nicole Kidman: See, for example, King, Larry. *Larry King Live*, September 26, 1997.

Heather Locklear: See Kovanis, Georgea. "The Official Encyclopedia of Heather Locklear," *Detroit Free Press*, September 25, 1995.

Anthony Hopkins: See, for example, Williams, Tryst. "New Role for Hopkins's Old School," *Western Mail*, September 18, 2004. Students called him "Mad Hopkins." See, for example, McCarthy, Phillip. "Full marks for Anthony," *The Age (Melbourne)*, February 12, 1994.

Ryan Seacrest: See, for example, "Would They Have Dated in School?", *US Weekly*, August 16, 2010.

Zooey Deschanel: See, for example, O'Hearn, Amanda. "The Nature of Zooey Deschanel," *Mean*, 2000.

Taylor Lautner: See, for example, Strauss, Neil. "Teen Wolf," *Rolling Stone*, November 2009.

Christina Aguilera: Aguilera told the *Observer Magazine* that she was bullied and ostracized because classmates didn't understand her: "I would get a lot of cold shoulders because there was just no way they could relate to what I loved to do. You know, it's not really normal for a child to just want to be in front of the camera and on stage. It's not something that all kids want to do—they want to play in the playground. . . . That was my form of release without my even knowing it at that young age. You know, it was hard for me to relate to other kids because I didn't have the same interests. I was even more the oddball, I felt, because of that." See Day, Elizabeth. "I'm not there to parent anybody's children," *Observer Magazine*, November 23, 2008.

Dustin Hoffman: See *People*, 1978.

"horrible": See, for example, O'Hearn.

made her more ambitious: Ibid.

CHAPTER 6

"One thing that really emphasized": Interview.

73 percent of online teens: See Lenhart, Amanda; Purcell, Kristen; Smith, Aaron; and Zickuhr, Kathryn. "Social Media & Mobile Internet Use Among Teens and Young Adults," *Pew Internet & American Life Project*, Pew Research Center, 2010.

in three years: See Lenhart, Amanda; Madden, Mary; Smith, Aaron; and Macgill, Alexandra. "Teens and Social Media," *Pew Internet & American Life Project*, Pew Research Center, 2007.

the cyberclutches of predators: Also, many adults have raised this topic at my lectures. I do not mean to imply that cyber predators aren't a danger; only that teens are more likely to use SNS to connect with friends than strangers.

people they already know: See, for example, Nyland; See also Lenhart, 2007: "The vast majority of teens who use social networking sites say they use the sites to maintain their *current* friendships." (emphasis theirs)

more than 90 percent: See Lenhart.

After World War II: See Boyd, Danah. "Why Youth ♥ Social Network Sites: The Role of Networked Publics in Teenage Social Life." *Youth, Identity and Digital Media*, Buckingham, David, ed. The John D. and Catherine T. MacArthur Foundation Series on Digital Media and Learning, Cambridge, MA: The MIT Press, 2008.

"By allowing youth": Ibid. See also Nyland, Rob; Marvez, Raquel; and Beck, Jason. "Myspace: Social Networking or Social Isolation." Paper presented at the AEJMC Midwinter Conference, Reno, Nevada. Feb 23–24, 2007. Note that "This does not mean that face-to-face communication is being displaced," British psychologist Sonia Livingstone said. "The simple distinction between offline and online no longer captures the complex practices associated with online technologies as they become thoroughly embedded in the routines of everyday life." See Livingstone, Sonia. "Taking risky opportunities in youthful content creation: teenagers' use of social networking sites for intimacy, privacy, and self-expression," *New Media & Society*, Vol. 10, 2008.

"far less time": See Nielsen Report. "How Teens Use Media," June 2009.

time with SNS friends in person: Ibid. See also Subrahmanyama, Kaveri; Reich, Stephanie M.; Waechter, Natalia; and Espinoza, Guadalupe. "Online and offline social networks: Use of social networking sites by emerging adults," *Journal of Applied Developmental Psychology*, Vol. 29, 2008. The Nielsen report announced, "To teens, social networks are a key source of information and advice in a critical developmental period." See Nielsen Report, June 2009.

"whether offline social capital": See Ellison, N. B.; Steinfield, C.; and Lampe, C. "The benefits of Facebook 'friends': Social capital and college students' use of online social network sites," *Journal of Computer-Mediated Communication*, Vol. 12, no. 4, 2007.

"allows me to learn new facts": Interview.

"friend eaters": Interviews.

average of 455 Facebook friends: See Sheldon, P. "I'll poke you. You'll poke me! Self-disclosure, social attraction, predictability and trust as important predictors of Facebook relationships," *Cyberpsychology: Journal of Psychosocial Research on Cyberspace,* Vol. 3, no. 2, 2009.

"In choosing [Top Friends]": see Boyd, Danah.

"Pictures on Facebook": Interview.

falking, or Facebook stalking: Interviews.

"It's like you never really get away": Interview.

"Although I love Facebook": Interview.

"It's practically minute-to-minute": Interview.

"You'll hear a conversation": Interview.

devoted to insulting a classmate: Interviews.

a fake Facebook profile: Interview.

quizzes that publicly ask: Interviews.

"Facebook can totally ruin": Interview.

frequency with which teenagers: See, for example, Valkenburg, P. M.; Peter, J.; and Schouten, A. "Friend networking sites and their relationship to adolescents' well-being and social self-esteem," *CyberPsychology and Behavior,* Vol. 9.

"tend to overestimate": Ibid.

Rachel's Challenge: See rachelschallenge.org.

Annmarie: Interview. Note: By the time I contacted Annmarie, she was happy and comfortable in a crowd of gamers.

student gunmen killed twelve students: See, for example, Pevere, Geoff. "Mass murder as performance," *The Toronto Star,* April 18, 2009; See also *CNN,* April 20, 2009.

wore Goth-like fashion: See, for example, Anderegg.

"We needed to know": Ibid.

"keep them under surveillance": Brief interview, Elliot Aronson. See also Aronson, Elliot. *Nobody left to hate: teaching compassion after Columbine,* New York: W. H. Freeman and Company, 2000.

"the ones you point out": Interview.

Blue: Blue and I had enough discussions about this topic that I believed that he was not realistically any danger to himself or others.

A surprising number answered yes: Interviews.

"The needs of students": Interview.

"robust" and "remarkable": See Puckett. See also Rose and Swenson. See also LaFontana. See also Andreou, Eleni. "Social Preference, Perceived Popularity and Social Intelligence: Relations to Overt and Relational Aggression," *School Psychology International,*

Vol. 27, 2006, which states, "Relational aggression may predict increased perceived popularity."

the foundation for eventual racism: See, for example, Adler and Adler, 1995.

his family moved there from Plattsburgh: See, for example, Belluck, Pam and Wilgoren, Jodi. "Shattered Lives—A special report," *The New York Times,* June 29, 1999.

played soccer and Little League: Ibid.

earned good grades: See, for example, Florio, Gwen; Lelyveld, Nita; and Jones, Richard. "Looking into the Souls of Teens En Route to Ruin," *The Philadelphia Inquirer,* April 25, 1999.

he was popular: See Aronson.

CHAPTER 7

"It's really down to the people": Interview.

to prove that they can manage: Interviews.

"I did it because I wanted": Interview.

trying alcohol at younger ages: See, for example, Mays, Darren; Thompson, Nancy; Kushner, Howard I.; Mays II, David F.; Farmer, Derrick; and Windle, Michael. "Sports-specific factors, perceived peer drinking, and alcohol-related behaviors among adolescents participating in school-based sports in Southwest Georgia," *Addictive Behaviors*, 35, 2010.

"On the south side": Interview.

"I'm not a Mormon": Interview.

a bookworm in Syracuse: Interview.

"The drinking divide": Interview.

declining since 1999: See, for example, "Morbidity and Mortality Weekly Report," *Surveillance Summaries*, CDC, June 4, 2010.

study conducted at a Midwestern high school: See Haines, M. and Christensen, S. "Communities Use a Social Norms Approach to Reduce Teen Alcohol and Tobacco Use: Two Case Studies," Conference presentation at The National Conference on the Social Norms Model, Boston, MA, July 17, 2003. In addition, people tend to evaluate their participation in high-risk behavior by comparing themselves to other people. So if students believe that classmates are drinking more than they individually are, they tend to underestimate their personal risk. See, for example, Sessa, Frances M. "Peer Crowds in a Commuter College Sample: The Relation Between Self-Reported Alcohol Use and Perceived Peer Crowd Norms," *The Journal of Psychology*, Vol. 141, No. 3, 2007.

college students wildly overestimate: See, for example, Pedersen, Eric R.; LaBrie, Joseph W.; and Lac, Andrew. "Assessment of perceived and actual alcohol norms in varying contexts: Exploring Social Impact Theory among college students," *Addictive Behaviors*, Vol. 33, 2008.

the more anxious a student is: See, for example, Neighbors, Clayton; Fossos, Nicole; Woods, Briana A.; Fabiano, Patricia; Sledge, Michael; and Frost, Deborah. "Social Anxiety as a Moderator of the Relationship Between Perceived Norms and Drinking," *Journal of Studies on Alcohol and Drugs*, January 2007.

a student's normative beliefs: See, for example, "Does Prevention Work?" *FCD Educational Services.*

"significantly higher levels": See Mays.

they actually drink more: See, for example, Lewis, Todd F. "An explanatory model of student-athlete drinking: the role of team leadership, social norms, perceptions of risk, and coaches' attitudes toward alcohol consumption," *College Student Journal*, Vol. 42, Issue 3, September 2008.

Sports teams develop: See, for example, Mays. See also Martens, Matthew P.; Dams-O'Connor, Kristen; and Duffy-Paiement, Christy. "Comparing Off-Season with In-Season Alcohol Consumption Among Intercollegiate Athletes," *Journal of Sport & Exercise Psychology*, Vol. 28, 2006.

FCD Educational Services: Interview, Renee Soulis.

social norms: While most social norms programs are geared toward preventing substance abuse, schools also have used the approach to tackle seat-belt use and sexual assault prevention. Social norms marketing is also the strategy that hotels recently began using to convince guests to reuse towels. Powerhouse social psychologist Robert Cialdini, an Arizona State University professor, conducted a study in several hotels in which he displayed different versions of the "Reuse your towels" message in the bathroom. One placard asked guests to "Help save the environment." A sign explaining that the majority of hotel guests reuse their towels was 26 percent more effective than the first. A placard stating that the majority of guests in that room, specifically, had reused their towels was nearly 30 percent more effective.

"In every single school": Ibid.

"an enormously high success rate": Ibid.

"The middle schoolers": Ibid. Parent surveys reveal statistics such as the number of parents who are talking to their children about these issues or allowing them to drink at home.

Straight Edge: Note: Some Straight Edge kids also avoid promiscuity and animal products and others debate whether caffeine consumption also qualifies as "breaking edge." See, for example, Guzowski, Stephanie. "Rutgers students share reasons for becoming Straight Edge," *Daily Targum*, November 15, 2006. See also Bartlett, Thomas. "Studying Rock's Clean, Mean Movement," *The Chronicle of Higher Education*, September 29, 2006.

a movement among punks: See, for example, Valenzuela, Beatriz. "Straight edge: 'Stay punk, stay clean' is the anthem they live by," *Daily Press*, June 1, 2008.

the group's symbol: See, for example, Carroll, Ed. "Straight edge lifestyle helps some achieve goals," *The Independent Collegian*, January 18, 2007.

school outside of Seattle: These conversations occurred after a lecture I gave based on *The Overachievers.*

"All parents want their kids": See Bauman, Lawrence. *Ten Most Troublesome Teenage Problems and How to Solve Them*, New York: Kensington, 1997.

"When you try to identify": See Anderegg, David. *Nerds*, New York: Tarcher, 2007.

"if everyone's drinking": Interview.

parents who have negative *attitudes*: See, for example, Nash, Susan G.; McQueen, A.; and Bray, J. "Pathways to adolescent alcohol use: Family, environment, peer influence, and parental expectations," *Journal of Adolescent Health*, Vol. 37, 2005.

"The permissiveness of parents": See Califano, Joseph Jr. *High Society: How Substance Abuse Ravages America and What to Do About It*, New York: PublicAffairs, 2007.

"High school kids drink": See Balko, Radley. "Zero Tolerance Makes Zero Sense," *The Washington Post*, August 9, 2005.

underage drinking is harmful: See, for example, Van der Vorst, Haske; Engels, Rutger C. M. E.; and Burk, William J. "Do parents and best friends influence the normative increase in adolescents' alcohol use at home and outside the home?", *Journal of Studies on Alcohol and Drugs*, January 1, 2010. See also Fergusson, David M.; Lynskey, Michael T.; and Horwood, L. John. "Childhood exposure to alcohol and adolescent drinking patterns," *Addiction*, 1994, 89.

children whose parents allow them to drink: See, for example, Esau, Cecelia A. and Hutchinson, Delyse. "Alcohol Use, Abuse, and Dependence," *Adolescent Addiction: Epidemiology, Assessment and Treatment*, Esau, Cecelia A., ed. Burlington, MA, 2008. See also Komro, K. A.; Maldonado-Molina, M. M.; Tobler, A. L.; Bonds, J. R.; and Muller, K. E. "Effects of home access and availability of alcohol on young adolescents' alcohol use," *Addiction*, 2007, 102.

teenagers who don't drink at home: See, for example, Van der Vorst. See also Abar, Caitlin; Abar, Beau; and Turrisi, Rob. "The impact of parental modeling and permissibility on alcohol use and experienced negative drinking consequences in college," *Addictive Behaviors*, Vol. 34, 2009.

much more tolerant of substance abuse: See Luthar, Suniya S. and Goldstein, Adam S. "Substance use and related behaviors among suburban late adolescents: The importance of perceived parent containment," *Development and Psychopathology*, Vol. 20, 2008.

three times more likely to binge drink: See Long Foley, K.; Altman, D.; and Durant, R. H. "Adults' approval and adolescents' alcohol use," *Journal of Adolescent Health*, Vol. 35, 2004.

"the greater number of drinks": The quote is from an interview the study's lead author gave *Science Daily*: "Relaxed Attitudes Toward Alcohol and Youth May Increase Risk Of Binge Drinking in College," *Science Daily*, June 11, 2009. For the study, see Abar.

parents strongly disapprove: See, for example, Walls, Theodore A.; Fairlie, Anne M.; and Wood, Mark D. "Parents do matter: a longitudinal two-part mixed model of early college alcohol participation and intensity," *Journal of Studies on Alcohol and Drugs*, November 1, 2009.

far worse problems: An Ivy League president told Califano that "during his tenure of more than a decade, every case of rape and date rape at his university involved alcohol abuse." See Califano.

Note: The majority of states and hundreds of town councils have passed laws that hold parents civilly and criminally liable when they serve alcohol to minors, or when they know that someone else has served alcohol to minors in their home. See, for example Tilghman, Andrew. "When kids bend elbows, parents break the rules," *The Times Union*, March 24, 2002.

"she believed I had been": Interview.

CHAPTER 8

social psychologist Henri Tajfel: See Tajfel, H.; Billig, M. G.; and Bundy, R. P. "Social categorization and intergroup behavior," *European Journal of Social Psychology*, Vol. 1, no. 2, 1971. See also Baumeister and Leary.

flip of a coin: See Tajfel; see also Bettencourt, B. A.; Dorr, N; Charlton, K.; and Hume, D. L. "Status Differences and In-Group Bias: A Meta-Analytic Examination of the Effects of Status Stability, Status Legitimacy, and Group Permeability," *Psychological Bulletin*, Vol. 127, July 2002, 4; see also LaFontana.

split people into groups by lottery: See Locksley, A.; Ortiz, V.; and Hepburn, C. "Social categorization and discriminatory behavior: Extinguishing the minimal intergroup discrimination effect," *Journal of Personality and Social Psychology*, Vol. 39, 1980.

The need to belong: See, for example, Baumeister and Leary.

survival and reproductive advantages: See, for example, Bukowski, William M. and Sippola, Lorrie K. "Groups, Individuals, and Victimization: A View of the Peer System."

Group membership improves odds: See, for example, Baumeister, et al.

members of social categories: See, for example, Tajfel and Turner. See also Mlicki, Pawel and Ellemers, Naomi. "Being different or being better? National stereotypes and identifications of Polish and Dutch students," *European Journal of Social Psychology*, Vol. 26, 1996.

children intuitively understand: See, for example, Gavin.

children typically have split: See, for example, Xie.

tall, friendly, good at sports: Interview, Dominic Abrams. See also Abrams, Dominic and Rutland, Adam. "The Development of Subjective Group Dynamics," *Intergroup Attitudes and Relations in Childhood Through Adulthood*.

to reach a cookie jar: Interview, Abrams.

By fourth grade: See, for example, Xie.

play favorites with their own group: See Tajfel; See also, for example, Baumeister.

"in-group bias": See Turner, J. C.; Tajfel, H.; and Brown, R. H. "Social comparison and group interest in ingroup favoritism," *European Journal of Social Psychology*, Vol. 9, 1979.

doesn't mean they dislike outsiders: See, for example, Brewer, Marilyn. "Conflict and In-Group Bias," August 2007, San Francisco. An address by Marilyn Brewer, professor of psychology at Ohio State University, to mark the award of Distinguished Scientific Contribution for 2007 by the American Psychological Association.

Note: People expect their own groupmates to behave more positively toward group interests. See, for example, Baumeister.

assign more favorable characteristics: See, for example, Hymel, S.; Wagner, E.; and Butler, L. "Reputational Bias: View from the Peer Group," *Peer Rejection in Childhood*, New York: Cambridge University Press, 1990.

assume that their groupmates': See, for example, Baumeister.

in simplistic ways: See Linville, P. W. and Jones, E. E. "Polarized appraisals of outgroup members," *Journal of Personality and Social Psychology*, Vol. 38, 1980. Cited in Baumeister.

display more group favoritism: See, for example, Bettencourt.

copying high-status groups: See, for example, Hymel. See also, Berger, Jonah; Heath, Chip; and Ho, Ben. "Divergence in cultural practices: Tastes as signals of identity," unpublished manuscript, 2008.

social creativity strategy: See Tajfel, H. *Differentiation Between Social Groups*, London: Academic Press, 1978.

Robbers Cave State Park, Oklahoma: See Sherif, Muzafer; Harvey, O. J.; White, Jack B; Hood, William R.; and Sherif, Carolyn W. *Intergroup Conflict and Cooperation: The Robbers Cave Experiment*, 1954/1961.

José Saramago: Saramago is Portuguese but Danielle assumed the staff wouldn't know that.

give out personalized apparel: Interviews.

On the first day of biology: Interview.

social circles have been established: See, for example, Hymel.

a different part of the brain: See "Interview: Deborah Yurgelun-Todd." *Frontline*, pbs.org. University of Utah psychiatry professor Yurgelun-Todd, the Director of Cognitive Neuroscience at The Brain Institute, is a leading researcher of the adolescent brain. Her findings indicate that teens "are not able to correctly read all the feelings in the adult face. So that would suggest to us that when they're relating to their parents or to their friends' parents or to their teachers, they may be misperceiving or misunderstanding some of the feelings that we have as adults; that is, they see anger when there isn't anger, or sadness when there isn't sadness." Parents could utilize her research by taking care to verbally explain their emotions when they are talking to middle school students.

students frequently reflect: See, for example, Kinney, David A. "From Nerds to Normals: The Recovery of Identity among Adolescents from Middle School to High School," *Sociology of Education*, Vol. 66, No. 1, January 1993.

don't yet have the ability: Children cannot accurately process social information that's beyond their cognitive abilities. See, for example, Cameron, Lindsey and Rutland, Adam. "An Integrative Approach to Changing Children's Intergroup Attitudes," *Intergroup Attitudes*.

peaks from age eleven to thirteen: See, for example, Windle, Michael; Spear, Linda P.; Fuligni, Andrew J.; Angold, Adrian; Brown, Jane D.; Pine, Daniel; Smith, Greg T.; Giedd, Jay and Dahl, Ronald E. "Transitions Into Underage and Problem Drinking: Developmental Processes and Mechanisms Between 10 and 15 Years of Age," *Pediatrics*, 2008, 121.

"Where do I belong?": See, for example, Noam, G. "The Psychology of Belonging: Reformulating Adolescent Development," Esman A. H.; Flaherty, L. T.; Horowitz, H. A., eds., *Annals of the American Society of Adolescent Psychiatry*, Hillsdale, NJ: The Analytic Press, 1999.

"wego" instead of an ego: Ibid.

often don't recognize: Ibid.

to form an identity: See, for example, Bukowski and Sippola.

group as having clear characteristics: Ibid.

"strong, if not totalitarian": Ibid.

skills necessary for group problem-solving: Ibid.

"As this consensus is elusive": Ibid.

Middle schoolers are more likely to: See, for example, Craig, Wendy M.; Pepler, Debra; Connolly, Jennifer; and Henderson, Kathryn. "Developmental Context of Peer Harassment in Early Adolescence," in *Peer Harassment in School* . . .

with puberty comes: See, for example, Horn, Stacey S. "The Multifaceted Nature of Sexual Prejudice: How Adolescents Reason About Sexual Orientation and Sexual Prejudice," in *Intergroup Attitudes* . . .

would call me man chest: Interview.

more antagonistic interactions: See, for example, Gavin.

The rate of cyberbullying: See Rodkin, Philip C. "The Bully-Victim Relationship: Historical Foundations and Peer Supports," Federal Partners in Bullying Prevention Summit, August 11, 2010.

groups most want to separate: See, for example, Gavin.

"Kids in middle school are": See Anderegg.

sensitive to negative evaluations: See, for example, Gavin.

are increasingly advised: See, for example, Bukowski, William; Sippola, Lorrie; and Newcomb, Andrew. "Variations in patterns of attraction of same- and other-sex peers during early adolescence," *Developmental Psychology*, Vol. 36, 2000.

value dominance and aggression: See, for example, LaFontana.

plateaus in the seventh and eighth grades: Ibid.

the social goals: Ibid.

so important to students: See, for example, Shrum, Wesley and Cheek, Neil H., Jr., "Social Structure During the School Years: Onset of the Degrouping Process," *American Sociological Review*, Vol. 52, No. 2, April 1987.

More subcultures: See, for example, Kinney.

group boundaries aren't so strict: See, for example, Gavin.

social understanding has broadened: See, for example, Horn, Stacy S. "Adolescents' Reasoning about Exclusion from Social Groups," *Developmental Psychology*, Vol. 39, No. 1, January, 2003.

discount stereotypes: Ibid.

By the end of high school: See, for example, Gavin.

drop in self-esteem: See, for example, Eder, Donna. "The Cycle of Popularity: Interpersonal Relations Among Female Adolescents," *Sociology of Education*, Vol. 58, No. 3, July 1985.

CHAPTER 9

to his classmates, a musclehead: Interview.

child who was socially awkward: See, for example, Bishop, John H.; Bishop, Matthew; and

Gelbwasser, Lara. "Nerds and Freaks: A Theory of Student Culture and Norms," *Brookings Papers on Education Policy*, 2003.

One's status drops: See, for example, Buhs, Eric S.; Ladd, Gary W.; and Herald, Sarah L. "Peer Exclusion and Victimization: Processes That Mediate the Relation Between Peer Group Rejection and Children's Classroom Engagement and Achievement?," *Journal of Educational Psychology*, Vol. 98, No.1, 2006.

German gym teacher: See, for example, Watson, Goodwin B. "Character Tests and Their Applications through 1930," *Review of Educational Research*, Vol. 2, No. 3, June 1932. See also Bishop, Bill.

first impressions cling: See, for example, Asch, Solomon E. "Forming impressions of personality," *Journal of Abnormal and Social Psychology*, Vol. 41, Issue 3, 1946.

people " 'rent' categories": See Wortham, Stanton. "From Good Student to Outcast: The Emergence of a Classroom Identity," *Ethos*, Vol. 32, Issue 1, 2004.

we expect him to behave: See, for example, Bigler, Rebecca S. and Liben, Lynn S. "A cognitive-developmental approach to racial stereotyping and reconstructive memory in Euro-American children," *Child Development*, Vol. 64, Issue 5, 1993. See also Hymel.

"I feel like I have to act": Interview.

"Students who break away": Interview.

more likely to remember: See, for example, Hymel.

surfaces during elementary school: See, for example, Rogosch, F. and Newcomb, A. F. "Children's perceptions of peer reputations and their social reputations among peers," *Child Development*, Vol. 60, 1989.

Canadian researchers asked experienced judges: See Findlay, Leanne C. and Ste-Marie, Diane M. "A Reputation Bias in Figure Skating Judging," *Journal of Sport & Exercise Psychology*, 2004, 26.

keeps the status quo intact: See, for example, Findlay.

"Popular children acquire": See Hymel.

The halo effect: See Nisbett, Richard E. and Wilson, Timothy DeCamp. "The Halo Effect: Evidence for Unconscious Alteration of Judgments," *Journal of Personality and Social Psychology*, Vol. 35, No. 4, 1977. See also Asch, Solomon E. "Forming Impressions of Personality."

we don't realize when it's kicking in: See Nisbett.

"The dynamics of group life": See Coie, John D. "Toward a theory of peer rejection," in *Peer Rejection in Childhood*, Asher, Steven and Coie, R., eds., New York: Cambridge University Press, 1990.

society needs "deviants": Ibid.

deviant group members are: See, for example, Abrams and Rutland.

A group might assume: Ibid.

"black sheep effect": See Marques, José M.; Yzerbyt, Vincent Y.; and Leyens, Jacques-Leyens. "The 'Black Sheep Effect': Extremity of judgments towards ingroup members

as a function of group identification," *European Journal of Social Psychology*, Vol. 18, 1988.

a deviant member is more of a threat: Ibid.

cliques or "best friends" turned: Interviews.

"Bitching, gossiping, or storytelling": See Owens, Laurence; Slee, Phillip; and Shute, Rosalyn. "Victimization among Teenage Girls: What Can Be Done about Indirect Harassment?" in *Peer Harassment in Schools*.

"Gossip is like word vomit here": Interview.

"experience some relief": See Coie.

series of studies: Interview, Stacey Horn.

Goths, druggies, and dirties: See Horn, Stacey S. "Adolescents' Reasoning About Exclusion from Social Groups," *Developmental Psychology*, Vol, 39, No. 1, 2003.

"a legitimate way of regulating": See Horn, Stacey S. "The Multifaceted Nature of Sexual Prejudices," in Levy, Killen, etc. See also, Horn, Stacey S. "Mean Girls or Cultural Stereotypes?", *Human Development*, 2004, 47, in which Horn states, "They are likely to evaluate exclusion as acceptable in circumstances where an individual doesn't 'fit in' with the overall norms and values of the group or where the individual, by virtue of who they [sic] are, may potentially threaten the functioning or identity of the group."

provided a new detail: Ibid.

"function as social categories": See Horn, Stacey S. "Adolescents' Reasoning About Exclusion from Social Groups."

asked high school freshmen to judge: See Horn, S.; Killen, M.; and Stangor, C. "The influence of group stereotypes on adolescents' moral reasoning," *Journal of Early Adolescence*, Vol. 19, 1999.

excluded from friendship: See Killen, Melanie; McGlothlin, Heidi; and Henning, Alexandra. "Explicit Judgments and Implicit Bias." In *Intergroup Attitudes* . . . Thank you to Melanie Killen for discussing these issues with me.

first, fourth, and seventh graders: See Killen, M; Sinno, S.; and Margie, N. G. "Children's Experiences and Judgments About Group Exclusion and Inclusion," *Advances in Childhood Development and Behavior*, 2007, 35.

teens often rely on stereotypes: See, for example, Horn, Stacey S. "Adolescents' Reasoning . . ."

adolescents become more aware: See, for example, Enesco, Guerrero and Callejas, Solbes. "Intergroup Attitudes and Reasoning About Social Exclusion in Majority and Minority Children in Spain," in *Intergroup Attitudes* . . .

de-prioritize fairness and morality: See, for example, Horn, Stacey S. "Adolescents' Reasoning . . ."

CHAPTER 10
In nine classes: See Bigler, R. S.; Spears, C. B.; and Markell, M. "When groups are not created equal: Effects of group status on the formation of intergroup attitudes in children," *Child Development*, Vol. 72, 2001.

"The honors students use": Interview.

English Language Learner (ELL) students: Interview.

"The veteran teachers and administrators": Interview.

"Teachers may take the social structure": See Hallinan, Maureen T. and Smith, Steven S. "Classroom characteristics and Student Friendship Cliques," *Social Forces*, Vol. 67, No. 4, June 1989.

"the same grade all four years": Interview.

"I think you should write": Interview.

"once a kid is a": Interview.

subjective views: See, for example, Findlay, which cites Murphy, Kevin R.; Balzer, William K.; Lockhart, Maura C.; and Eisenman, Elaine J. "Effects of Previous Performance on Evaluations of Present Performance," *Journal of Applied Psychology*, Vol. 70, Issue 1, February 1985, and Horn, T. S.; Lox, C.; and Labrador, F. "The self-fulfilling prophecy theory: When coaches' expectations become reality," in J. M. Williams, ed., *Applied Sport Psychology: Personal growth to peak performance*, Palo Alto, CA: Mayfield, 1998.

"let the in-crowd get away": Interview.

"not expecting them to follow": Interview.

colleagues joke around more: Interview.

"I see teachers participate": See Katz, Beth Anne. "A Diamond in the Rough, Waiting to be Found," *Intelligencer Journal*, May 16, 2009.

honors and awards: Interviews.

"Administrators favor the families": Interview.

many of the programs that schools implement: Interviews.

"It disgusts me to think": Interview.

"preferential treatment of the athletic program": Interview.

students in the environmental technology shop: Interviews.

the comparative lack: See, for example, "Science project; Scientists can't simply be hired, they must be created, and leaders from President Obama to state CEOs say investing in science and math programs early is key," *Star Tribune*, May 11, 2009; see also, "Obama's Test; Can America Boost Learning in Math and Science?" *Pittsburgh Post-Gazette*, December 22, 2008; See also Alexander, Steve. "Nobel winner: America is neglecting science," *Star Tribune*, October 20, 2008; see also Holt, Rep. Rush (D-NJ). "Oust mediocrity as the standard for achievement," *The Hill*, March 1, 2010.

Trends in International Mathematics: See, for example, Glod, Maria. "Scores on Science Test Causing Concern in U.S.," *The Washington Post*, December 10, 2008.

"I have seen adults treating": Interview.

"the most plastic and adaptable": See Berns.

CHAPTER 11

an excellent student: See, for example, Sanchez, Maria. "Missouri Girl Suspended for Cancer Tribute," *WCSH6 TV*, 2008. Note: Amelia Robbins is not related to the author.

special relationship with her dad: See, for example, Morehouse, Paula. "Mountain Grove School District relents on girl's pink hair," *KY3 News*, August 26, 2008.

brain cancer: See, for example, Robbins, Amelia. "'Distraction' only meant as tribute to father," *Springfield News-Leader*, September 3, 2008.

"the cancer color": See, for example, Saavedra, Marie. "School suspends student over colored hair," *KY3 News*, August 20, 2008.

"You're suspended until": Ibid.

ACLU got involved: See, for example, Morehouse.

"We want it to be equal": See "School suspends student over colored hair," *KY3 News*, August 21, 2008.

fewer than 25 percent of US residents: See Bishop, Bill.

deters minorities from voting: Ibid.

also withdraw from volunteering: Ibid.

"What had happened over three decades": Ibid.

Diana Mutz's findings: See Mutz, Diana C. *Hearing the Other Side: Deliberative versus Participatory Democracy*, New York: Cambridge University Press, 2006. Cited in Bishop, Bill.

"Elementary school taught us": See Katz.

imbued with deep spiritual meaning": See, for example, "Graduation feathers should be held high," *Indian Country Today*, July 27, 2005.

with eagle feathers sewn: Ibid.

An Idaho school: See, for example, Rave, Jodi. "Eagle feathers bring honor to graduation ceremonies," *The Bismarck Tribune*, May 28, 2006.

withheld a Cherokee student's: See *Indian Country Today*.

dress more "manly": See, for example, Stevens, Alexis. "Cobb teen told he can't dress like a female at school," *The Atlanta Journal-Constitution*, October 6, 2009.

"(running at a set speed)": See, for example, Evans, Brent R. "Everyone Wins! Connecting Learners with Success Opportunities," April 2006. Cited in Trowbridge, Steve. "Educational rituals: questioning how we educate our children," *Phi Delta Kappan*, January 1, 2007.

Godin told Psychology Today: See Marano, Hara Estroff. "Maverick Messenger," *Psychology Today*, July/August 2010.

Schools impose a hierarchy: See, for example, Shepherd, Jessica. "Fertile minds need feeding: Are schools stifling creativity?", *The Guardian*, February 10, 2009. See also Jeffrey A. Lackney. "Changing Patterns in Educational Facilities," Summary of REFP workshop presented at the annual meeting of CEFPI, Vancouver, 1998.

two schools in Ireland: See, for example, Ruane, M. "Let's cut to the chase: how much conformity should we demand of our schoolkids?", *Irish Independent*, Feb. 21, 2009.

"values conformity and control": See Contenta, Sandro and Rankin, Jim. "Are schools too quick to suspend?", *Toronto Star*, June 8, 2009.

"capacity for divergent thinking": See Munro, Neil. "Start with yourself, mister," *The Times Educational Supplement*, March 10, 2006. (The report's author also quoted an education seminar participant who said that "trying to introduce change in a university is like trying to move a cemetery: You can expect no help from the people inside.")

schools were extinguishing: See, for example, Shepherd.

"All children start": Ibid.

Creative Partnerships: Ibid. See also www.creative-partnerships.com/about.

"School doesn't encourage": Interview.

"All the girls fake tan": Interview.

"Right now, my forearms": Interview.

boys who are underweight: Interview.

share levels of depression: See Paxton, Susan J.; Schutz, Helena K.; Wertheim, Eleanor H.; and Muir, Sharryn L. "Friendship Clique and Peer Influences on Body Image Concerns, Dietary Restraint, Extreme Weight-Loss Behaviors, and Binge Eating in Adolescent Girls," *Journal of Abnormal Psychology*, Vol. 108, No. 2, 1999.

first study to examine eating disorders: Ibid.

Note: Also, dynamic social impact theory suggests that the more time individuals spend in one another's company, the more alike they will become. See, for example, Berger, Jonah; Heath, Chip; and Ho, Ben. "Divergence in Cultural Practices: Tastes as Signals of Identity," Stanford University, March 2005. See also Poulin, F. and Boivin, M. "The role of proactive and reactive aggression in the formulation and development of boys' friendships," *Developmental Psychology*, Vol. 36, 2000.

"I've struggled with anorexia": Interview.

" 'mess in a dress' ": Interview.

Students in gangs: Interviews.

they had to "act white": Thank you to Amy Kramer and the National Campaign to Prevent Teen and Unplanned Pregnancy for facilitating this group discussion. For an examination of the meanings and the interpretations of "acting white," see, for example, Carter, Prudence L. "Straddling Boundaries: Identity, Culture, and School," *Sociology of Education*, Vol. 79, No. 4, October 2006. Also, Grace Kao includes an interesting discussion of "talking white" versus "talking black" in Kao, Grace, "Group Images and Possible Selves Among Adolescents: Linking Stereotypes to Expectations by Race and Ethnicity," *Sociological Forum*, Vol. 15, No. 3, 2000. More broadly, she states, minority adolescents "face another dimension of social categorization: group images that link ethnicity to innate ability not only directly imply norms of behavior for members of each group, but also specify their distinct areas of expertise in various realms of social and academic life," much like Noah described the assumptions peers made about him because he was Asian.

"In math, someone told": Interview.

"With some of my friends": Interview.

"There's still pressure to act": Interview.

incentive-based voluntary uniform policy: See Jamison, David J. "Idols of the Tribe: Brand Veneration, Group Identity, and the Impact of School Uniform Policies," *Academy of Marketing Studies Journal*, Vol. 10, No. 1, 2006.

"The people who don't care": Interview.

"The young always have the same": See Crisp, Quentin. *The Naked Civil Servant*, First published in Great Britain by Jonathan Cape, 1968. Cited in Berger, Heath, and Ho.

can even overtake the desire: See, for example, Mlicki.

Men are less likely: See, for example, Berger, Jonah and Heath, Chip: "Who Drives Divergence? Identity Signaling, Outgroup Dissimilarity, and the Abandonment of Cultural Tastes," *Journal of Personality and Social Psychology*, Vol. 95, No. 3, 2008.

"People resolve [this tension]": See Berger, Heath, and Ho.

"the narcissism of minor differences": Many thanks to Lakehead University professor Todd Dufresne and University of Miami professor Edward Erwin for discussing this concept with me. Dufresne is also the author of *Tales from the Freudian Crypt: The Death Drive in Text and Context*. Stanford: Stanford University Press, 2000.

distributed yellow Livestrong: See Berger and Heath.

forked-tail effect: See, for example, Freedman, Jonathan L.; Carlsmith, J. Merrill; and Sears, David O. *Social Psychology*, Englewood Cliffs, NJ: Prentice-Hall, 1974. See also Englis, Basil G. and Solomon, Michael R. "To Be and Not to Be: Lifestyle Imagery, Reference Groups, and 'The Clustering of America,'" *Journal of Advertising*, Vol. 24, No. 1, Spring 1995.

"may want to be treated": See Berger, Heath, and Ho.

CHAPTER 12

twelve groups of vervet monkeys: See Raleigh, M. J.; McGuire, M. T.; Brammer, G. L.; Pollack, D. B.; and Yuwiler, A. "Serotonergic mechanisms promote dominance acquisition in adult male vervet monkeys," *Brain Research*, Vol. 559, 1991.

rhesus monkeys with high levels of serotonin: See Mehlman, P. T.; Higley, J. D.; Faucher, I.; Lilly, A. A.; et al. "Correlation of CSF 5-HIAA concentration with sociality and the timing of emigration in free-ranging primates," *American Journal of Psychiatry*, Vol. 152, 1995, and Higley, J. D.; King, S. T., Jr.; Hassert, M. F.; et al. "Stability of interindividual differences in serotonin function and its relationship to severe aggression and competent social behavior in rhesus macque females," *Neuropharmacology*, Vol. 14, 1996. Cited in Knutson, Brian; Wolkowitz, Owen M.; Cole, Steve W.; et al. "Selective Alteration of Personality and Social Behavior by Serotonergic Intervention," *American Journal of Psychiatry*, Vol. 155, 1998: 3.

administered to volunteers a drug: See, for example, Knutson.

"socially affiliative" behaviors: See Tse, Wai S. and Bond, Alyson J. "Serotonergic intervention affects both social dominance and affiliative behavior," *Psychopharmacology*, Vol. 161, 2002.

"can modify social status": Ibid.

a region of a particular gene: See Burt, S. Alexandra. "A Mechanistic Explanation of Popularity: Genes, Rule Breaking, and Evocative Gene-Environment Correlations,"

Journal of Personality and Social Psychology, Vol. 96, No. 4, 2009. Two caveats: First, Burt wrote, "This study is the first to explicitly identify a pathway through which a specific gene influences individuals' social status." When I asked her whether her study referred to likeability or social status, she said, "The operationalization of the ratings was primarily based on likeability (although we'd expect likeability to be correlated with social status)." Second, it's helpful to keep in mind, as Burt noted, that "Because one's genes cannot directly code for other individuals' reactions, it is biologically impossible for this association to be direct. Instead, any legitimate association must be mediated via the individual's attributes or behavior."

"notable risks for development": See Schwartz, David; Nakamoto, Jonathan; Gorman, Andrea Hopmeyer; and McKay, Tara. "Popularity, Social Acceptance, and Aggression in Adolescent Peer Groups: Links with Academic Performance and School Attendance," *Developmental Psychology*, Vol. 42, No. 6, 2006.

Note: *This can apply to the aggressors or victims*: Rachel Simmons, author of *Curse of the Good Girl* explained to me, "Once you're on the inside, you're usually struggling to stay there. To get and stay popular, your status has to be paramount, and that means you'll do pretty much anything, including be a target or an aggressor, to keep your place. At the end of the day, trying to be accepted at the highest level usually causes kids to lose their selves to the race."

less likely to do well: See, for example, Schwartz. See also Kiefer.

If a student's social aim: See Kiefer.

"likely to lead to disruptive": Ibid.

This connection is especially strong: Ibid.

"I wanted to date a 'normal' ": Interview.

"My weight is never good enough": Interview.

"Deep down, I know it's wrong": Interview.

characterized with negative traits: See, for example, Gavin. High-status groups are more biased toward their own cliques than are low-status groups. See Bettencourt.

"involvement in risky behaviors": See Schwartz.

CHAPTER 13
divisions that didn't seem all that different: Interviews.

learned the term "narnian": Interview.

"I'm always single": Interview.

"bottom of the food chain": Interview.

Gamers: Also, scientists have discovered that playing casual video games can vastly improve adults' moods and stress levels. See Russoniello, Carmen V. and Parks, Jennifer M. "A Randomized Controlled Study of the Effects of PopCap Games on Mood and Stress," Psychophysiology Lab and Biofeedback Clinic, East Carolina University. Note: PopCap underwrote the study.

adept at problem solving: See McGonigal, Jane. "Gamers have skills. Let's tap 'em. Video games are training people to solve tough, real-world problems," *Christian Science Monitor*, November 5, 2007.

"collective intelligence": Ibid.

floaters are already skilled: See, for example, Shrum, Wesley and Cheek, Neil H., Jr. "Social Structure During the School Years: Onset of the Degrouping Process," *American Sociological Review*, Vol. 52, No. 2, April 1987.

the number of floaters: Ibid.

"some combination of school success": See Anderegg.

a childlike mindset: See, for example, Janecka, Laura. "Think Like a Kid," *Psychology Today*, July/August 2010.

geek chic: See, for example, Angier, Natalie. "In 'geek chic' and Obama, new hope for lifting women in science," *New York Times*, January 19, 2009.

nerd merch: See, for example, O'Neil, Lauren. "It's hip to be square: Nerd merch brings in the bank," *Toronto Star*, June 17, 2010.

nerdcore hip-hop artists: See, for example, Tocci, Jason. "The Well-Dressed Geek: Media Appropriation and Subcultural Style," paper presented at MiT5, Massachusetts Institute of Technology, April 29, 2007.

"the social pariah outcast aesthetic": Ibid.

massive mainstreaming of spheres: Ibid.

few trickle-down effects: Interviews.

a "cool nerd" subset: Interviews.

Paul Allen, Sergey Brin: These names are cited in many places; this particular list was in Varma, Roli. "Women in Computing: the Role of Geek Culture," *Science as Culture*, Vol. 16, No. 4, December 2007.

Steve Jobs: Jobs, an outsider in school whom classmates viewed as odd, intense, and a loner—and who is now called "arguably the greatest innovator of the digital age"—is also an example of quirk theory. See, for example, Young, Jeffrey S. and Simon, William L. *iCon: Steve Jobs, The Greatest Second Act in the History of Business*. Hoboken, NJ: John Wiley & Sons, 2005.

four twelve-to-fourteen-year-olds won: See, for example, Hutchinson, Bill. "News Readers Hurry to Help the Nerd Herd," *New York Daily News*, March 27, 2009.

"Nerd HERD! (YES!)": See Carlson, Jen. "Christine Zaremba & the Nerd Herd," *Gothamist*, April 15, 2009.

"drama dorks": Interview.

a deviant in one group: See, for example, Abrams and Rutland.

"High school was so unimaginably": Interview.

"The best thing to do": Interview.

"outcasts in a heartbeat": Interview.

the Eagles and the Rattlers were so hostile: See Sherif.

"dramatic" and "striking to all observers": Ibid.

"I just wish people could": Interviews.

"It's hard because sometimes": Interview.

"But you're smart": Interview.

"Adolescents who were unpopular": See Kinney.

Mississippi county school board: See, for example, Joyner, Chris. "Both sides claim win in Mississippi lesbian teen's prom lawsuit," *The Clarion-Ledger*, March 24, 2010.

Committed suicide after being harassed: See, for example, Strauss, Valerie. "How to make schools safer for gay students," *Washingtonpost.com*, Oct. 4, 2010.

"If someone asked why I was counting": Interview.

"I've had to make a new group": Interview.

"Continuously pretending to be": Interview.

line-matching conformity experiment: See Asch.

By extension, Asch's discovery: See, for example, Berns, who makes his point in *Iconoclast*.

Perceived popular kids: See earlier endnotes for each of these separate studies.

"It is essential for children": See Balter, Lawrence. "When Peers Pressure: You can prevent friends from exerting undue influence," *The San Diego Union-Tribune*, March 9, 1996.

effective communicator: For tips on how to talk to teenagers, I like the Passport chapter of *Queen Bees and Wannabes*, which has many suggestions that apply to kids of both genders. See Wiseman, Rosalind. *Queen Bees and Wannabes*, New York: Crown, 2002.

Outcast High: Interview

Lobby for changes: We should not assume that it is easy for even the best intentioned administrators to make these changes. As one researcher phrased it, "Schools . . . have a dual task. They should exert regulation . . . but also become sites of social change and emancipation. These tasks have met new challenges in the globalized world in which neo-liberal restructuring of education emphasizes accountability, choices, and markets, with decreasing consideration of equality and social justice." See Lahelma, Elina. "Tolerance and Understanding? Students and Teachers Reflect on Differences at School," *Educational Research and Evaluation*, Vol. 10, No. 1, 2004.

What Schools Can Do: By improving the well-being of their students, administrators improve the overall success of the school. Many researchers have demonstrated that the "sense of belonging to school is critical to the success of public education." See Ma, Xin. "Sense of Belonging to School: Can Schools Make a Difference?" *The Journal of Educational Research*, Vol. 96, No. 6, July-August 2003. Ma also writes: "Unless students identify well with their schools (i.e., feel welcomed, respected, and valued), their education participation always will be limited. . . . Gang-related problems increase when students do not have a sense of belonging to their school."

western Missouri middle school: Thank you to the students who participated in the discussion and the administrators who organized it for me.

"Some people want to sit": Interview.

"Mix It Up at Lunch Day": Teaching Tolerance is a project of the Southern Poverty Law Center. See www.tolerance.org/mix-it-up/lunch-day.

Teachers who open their rooms: At many schools, teachers do not have their own classrooms. These teachers can help students by helping them to find a safe space in which to spend the lunch hour.

"are generally defiant": Interview.

University of Delaware: See Gaertner, Samuel L.; Dovidio, John F.; Guerra, Rita; Rebelo, Margarida; Monteiro, Maria Benedicto; Riek, Blake M.; and Houlette, Melissa A. "The Common In-Group Identity Model: Applications to Children and Adults," *Intergroup Attitudes* . . .

"The best way to achieve peace": See, for example, Rebecca Tuhus-Dubrow. "Those People," *The Boston Globe*, January 6, 2008.

significantly reduce alcohol: See, for example, Haines, M.; Barker, G.; and Rice, R. "Using Social Norms To Reduce Alcohol And Tobacco Use in Two Midwestern High Schools," *The Social Norms Approach to Preventing School and College Age Substance Abuse: A Handbook for Educators, Counselors, and Clinicians*, H. W. Perkins, ed., San Francisco: Jossey-Bass, 2003. I also consulted FCD materials. See also Neighbors, Clayton; Fossos, Nicole; Woods, Briana A.; Fabiano, Patricia; Sledge, Michael; and Frost, Deborah. "Social Anxiety as a Moderator of the Relationship Between Perceived Norms and Drinking," *Journal of Studies on Alcohol and Drugs*, Vol. 68, No. 91, January, 2007.

"Informational campaigns stress": See Cialdini, Robert B. "Basic Social Influence Is Underestimated," *Psychological Inquiry*, Vol. 16, No. 4, 2005.

the robotics club's success: Interview, Christine Zaremba.

"We're the kings of the nerds": See Peim, Benjamin. "B'klyn 'Nerd Herd' wins NY Lego robot contest, now striving to raise cash for Robotics World Fest," *New York Daily News*, March 26, 2009. The St. Edmund's principal told the press, "This has just been the most amazing day. Kids actually think being a nerd is cool now." See Hutchinson.

"We're teaching our students": Interview, Zaremba.

they would have been lost: Interviews.

"When I moved to Dallas": Interview.

"I'm just as guilty": Interview.

"Sometimes adults get too focused": Interviews.

"I've made efforts": Interview.

"It may not seem like much": Interview.

The British government funneled: See, for example, Shepherd, Jessica. "Fertile minds need feeding: Are schools stifling creativity?", *The Guardian*, February 10, 2009.

United Kingdom able to invest: Ibid.; Interview, Pamela Burnard.

Sachse High School: Interview, Cheryl Beard. Thank you to Diane Wilcox for facilitating the group discussion with teachers and administrators in which I first learned about Sachse's reading program, and to Andrea Bottorff, the teacher who first told me about it.

Improve clique relations—among staff: "In a philosophical examination of issues related to sense of belonging, Edwards (1995) advocated that school administrators ensure that teachers must feel a sense of belonging to school so that they, in turn, can help their students feel a sense of belonging." See Ma, Xin.

"a hostile environment": Interview.

"ask students about them": See, for example, the description of the Generation Y program in Weinberger, Elizabeth and McCombs, Barbara. "Applying the LCPs to High School Education," *Theory Into Practice*, Vol. 42, No. 2, Learner-Centered Principles: A Framework for Teaching, Spring, 2003. See also Rigby, Ken. "Health Consequences of Bullying and its Prevention in Schools," in *Peer Harassment in Schools*.

"special bully meetings": Interview.

"There has to be": See Healy, Rita. "A Long Shadow," *Time Europe*, May 6, 2002.

CHAPTER 14

the jellybean jar game: See Berns. I highly recommend *Iconoclast* for further reading.

"The more diverse the group": Ibid.

Note: Diverse groups do not polarize. See, for example, Fishkin, James S. and Luskin, Robert C. "Experimenting with a Democratic Ideal: Deliberative Polling and Public Opinion," *Acta Politica*, Vol. 40, 2005.

"The more influence a group's members": See Surowiecki, James. *The Wisdom of Crowds*, New York: First Anchor Books, 2005.

Acknowledgments

I am exceptionally lucky to have supportive parents who have always encouraged me to be myself and clearly communicated that they love me not despite my goofy idiosyncrasies, but because those quirks help to make me who I am. A line on an acknowledgments page is not nearly enough to thank them.

I especially want to thank my mom, kind and wise, caring and fun, witty and talented, cheerful and enthusiastic, and an exemplary role model. Her selflessness, thoughtfulness, and generosity in assisting me with both book and non-book matters were a major reason I was able to turn in this manuscript on time. She is the best mother a child could have.

Dave Robbins is a constant source of inspiration, compassion, encouragement, and amusement. Missy Robbins provided invaluable assistance with locating journal articles and commenting astutely from a teacher's perspective. Andrew Robbins, who skillfully handles my Web sites, also kept me laughing from afar. Ira Robbins, my most lovingly, wonderfully meticulous reader, made this book so much better than it was.

The following people have my utmost appreciation for their support, friendship, and frequent reminders that while I love what I do for a living, life outside of work is also a blast: Ryan R., most of all— and Amy L., Nick and Andrea B., Gwen A., Andey K., Kelly L., Ellie A.

(my go-to grammer guru), Vicki and Matt G., Kristy K., and the magnanimous Jake F. Additional heartfelt thanks to Lita G.

I'm so grateful to be paired with Gretchen Young, a smart, insightful editor who constantly demonstrated her passion for and devotion to this book. An author could not ask for a better editor. On top of that, she's one cool chick. (Er, legitimately, sociometrically cool.) Elizabeth Sabo was patient and tireless; I could always count on her for upbeat answers to my (probably too many) questions. My awesome publicist, Christine Ragasa, blew me away with her ideas from our first meeting onward, as did associate publisher Kristin Kiser and super-stupendous marketing guru Bryan Christian, who rounded out the *Geeks* creative team. Many thanks to publisher Ellen Archer and the rest of the gang at Hyperion, which I've been fortunate to call home for nine years.

Paula Balzer, my dear friend and trusted agent of more than a decade, went above and beyond with this book, and I'm not just saying that because she sent me no-reason chocolates. I'm also indebted to Michael Prevett for his steady support and good humor. Sebastian Rupley, the only non-family member I entrusted to serve as a manuscript reader, provided terrific guidance and zeal for this project. Thanks also to Lindzi Scharf, who supplied some Hollywood reporting assistance; Adrian Biffen of Aerohost; and Will Balliett, for his support.

A million thank yous to Danielle, Blue, Regan, Joy, Eli, Noah, and Whitney for the time, effort, and most of all, heart they contributed to this book. I am lucky to know them. Thanks also to all of the students, teachers, and other experts whom I interviewed. Even if their words were not quoted, their insights informed my writing.

And finally, thanks, as always, to my amazing and loyal readers, whose feedback I treasure, whether at my lectures, via email, or on Facebook at Facebook.com/AuthorAlexandraRobbins (and now on Twitter @AlexandraRobbins). Your unflagging encouragement makes me smile.